Designing the Modern City

Designing the Modern City

Urbanism Since 1850

Eric Mumford

Yale University Press
New Haven and London

Designed by Jeff Wincapaw
Set in Akagi Pro type by Julie Allred,
BW&A Books, Inc.
Printed in China by 1010 Printing
International Limited
Cover design by Jena Sher

Library of Congress Control Number:
2017939210
ISBN 978-0-300-20772-9

A catalogue record for this book is
available from the British Library.

This paper meets the requirements
of ANSI/NISO Z39.48-1992 (Permanence
of Paper).

10 9 8 7 6 5 4 3 2 1

Cover illustrations: *(front)* Reinhard
and Hofmeister; Corbett, Harrison, and
MacMurray; and Hood, Godley, and
Fouilhoux, 30 Rockefeller Center, 1931–
39 (detail of fig. 70); *(back)* Eisenmann &
Smith, Cleveland Arcade, 1890 (Library
of Congress Historic American Building
Survey).
Frontispiece: Lower East Side, New
York, 1890 (fig. 35, detail).

Contents

Acknowledgments

Many thanks first to Katherine Boller, my editor at Yale University Press, for her enthusiastic support in seeing this book to completion, and to Michelle Komie, for commissioning it in 2012. Thanks also to the other members of the Yale University Press team for their excellent work in making this book a reality. Research for this book benefited from the support for a 2012 Creative Activity Research grant from Carmon Colangelo, dean of the Sam Fox School of Design and Visual Arts, Washington University. It has also had the strong support of former Washington University Dean of Architecture Bruce Lindsey and Director of Architecture Heather Woofter. My colleagues Margaret Garb, professor of history, Sungho Kim, and Seng Kuan, whose knowledge of East Asian urbanism is unparalleled, have also been particularly helpful. I also thank my many other Washington University faculty colleagues and students, too numerous to list here individually.

Many other scholars have also provided some key insights in the writing of this book, notably Sharif Kahatt, whose invitation to teach at the Pontifical Catholic University of Peru, Lima, in 2013 offered me some important new perspectives on current issues in world urban development. Special thanks also to Mary McLeod at Columbia University; Eve Blau at Harvard Graduate School of Design; Ivan Rupnik at Northeastern University in Boston; John Hoal of H3 Studio and Washington University in St. Louis; and Jennifer Yoos and Vincent James of VJAA in Minneapolis, all of whom have thoughtfully expanded my knowledge of many aspects of this material. I am also intellectually indebted to my many former teachers, fellow scholars, and neighbors over the years who have made the research and writing of this book so intellectually productive. As always, this book could not have been completed without the ongoing encouragement of my wife and two daughters, whose patience during the long process of research and writing has been exceptional.

Introduction

The earliest evidence of cities, often defined as relatively dense and often fortified human settlements with houses and nonagricultural workplaces of some kind, dates to at least 8,500 BC. After the Mesopotamian "urban revolution" in the 3000s BC, in and around what is now Iraq, there emerged many ancient cities featuring temple complexes built around monumental ziggurats, and today offering remnants of early writing systems. By 500 BC, various kinds of cities, typically with populations of less than a few thousand, began to appear in many parts of the world. The ancient Romans, whose imperial capital was the first city of over one million, called the physical pattern of the city the "urbs," which is the source of the English word "urban." In the early twentieth century a field of inquiry and action called "urbanism" began to be identified. In Britain, France, northern Europe, and the eastern United States, questions of urbanization had become pressing by then, as factory jobs and railways were beginning to draw large rural populations into fast-growing cities. At the time of the first traces of cities, the world's human population was probably under 5 million people, and by AD 1700, it had risen to only about 791 million, less than 11 percent of today's world population. By 1900, with industrialization well under way, world population was still under 2 billion, and by 1950, it was only 2.5 billion, much of it in Europe and Asia. Other than Tokyo and Shanghai, the world's largest cities in 1950 were all still in Europe, Russia, or the United States. Today, with the world population around 7.5 billion, the fastest growing parts of the world are in South Asia and Africa. With the exception of New York, all of the world's ten largest metropolitan areas are also now in Asia, with six of them in China and India, the world's most populous countries.

Many technical and social changes since about 1850 have set world population and the size of cities onto this course of massive expansion. These changes have certainly included the growth of world trade, initially facilitated by maritime empires, double-entry bookkeeping, and the use of gunpowder, as well as by the continuing development of more advanced economic systems that encouraged innovation and the search for new markets, which often led to large trading networks and in some cases, colonial empires. These directions greatly advantaged small groups with superior access to military resources and relevant knowledge, which massively expanded their abilities to both control and enslave, and, at times at least, to enrich, ever-growing numbers of people.

This book is an account of how key figures in design over the past century and a half have responded to these changing social, technical, and economic urban circumstances with both realistic proposals and more theoretical concepts that have often had a major impact. It considers built outcomes that in some cases, as in nineteenth-century Paris, Berlin, Vienna, and Barcelona, or in twentieth-century New York, New Delhi, and Tokyo, resulted in urban environments that are still admired, as well as often providing the urban frameworks for many later design interventions. It also traces the various twentieth-century revisions to what began to be called "town planning" or "urbanism" in France around 1910, which extend from Hampstead Garden Suburb in London to Chandigarh and beyond. By focusing on these contending and sometimes mutually antithetical mainstream projects and discourses about how urban designers should approach their work, I describe both how cities were designed, as well as trace ideas about how various designers thought that they should be designed.

This book is not intended to be an encyclopedic history of global urban development since 1850, which would rightly be mainly focused on detailed specific histories of how patrons, builders, designers, workers, and government agents have shaped particular cities. Nor is it intended to be primarily a history of urban technologies and their impacts on the natural world. Instead, it is an account of how key figures in design responded to changing social, technical, and economic circumstances with design proposals and built projects, creating what are now mainstream discourses about how urban environments should be designed, a field that can broadly be called "urbanism." This focus necessarily puts the most weight on the often contending ideas about the design of cities by a diverse range of figures. These include Napoleon III, an elected nineteenth-century French president who declared himself emperor; Ildefons Cerdà, the Barcelona engineer who coined the term "urbanization"; Camillo Sitte, father of the idea of "city building according to artistic principles"; Frederick Law Olmsted, founder of the field of landscape architecture; the Garden City theorist Ebenezer Howard; Patrick Geddes, advocate of regionalism seen in light of "place, work, and folk"; Le Corbusier, a central figure in both modern architecture and modernist urbanism; Josep Lluís Sert, Catalan émigré architect, president of CIAM (International Congresses of Modern Architecture), and institutional patron of the postwar field of modern "urban design"; Henri Lefebvre, radical postwar French theorist of the popular "right to the city" and the "politics of space"; and Aldo Rossi, Milanese champion of the architectural importance of historic cities and their traditional urban forms. It also includes accounts of the urban design concepts of groups such as CIAM and the Congress for the New Urbanism, along with their antecedents, successors, and critics. The first part of the book focuses on what were until recently understood to be mainly European imperial and American urban patterns, and which are now often, in transformed ways, becoming global patterns. The complexity of this transfer, and its still-emerging outcomes in the many new cities and urban environments of Asia, the Middle East, sub-Saharan Africa, and elsewhere, is addressed in the last chapter.

The academic literature on pre-nineteenth-century European developments is extensive, but there is less on urban design within the massive changes that have taken place since 1850. Françoise Choay's *The Modern City: Planning in the 19th Century* (1969) was a pioneering work on nineteenth-century urbanism whose brief summaries and clear drawings are still useful today. The numerous books of Leonardo Benevolo, published between 1963 and 1993, collectively provide clear accounts of the many specific European urban design outcomes just mentioned. More polemical are the many ambitious mid-twentieth-century works of Lewis Mumford (1895–1990, no relation to the author) and the influential writings of the Italian Marxist historian Manfredo Tafuri (1935–1994). Tafuri's successful questioning of modernist overconfidence in the ability of architects and designers to reform industrial societies in the interest of the working class opened the floodgates of critical reinterpretation of such design efforts that still continues to this day. While his rethinking of the role of designers in urban environments was unquestionably necessary, an unfortunate byproduct has been that far fewer textbooks have been published on these topics. There are some important exceptions, like Spiro Kostof, *The City Shaped* (1991) and *The City Assembled* (1992), with their specially commissioned drawings of many key projects, or Peter Hall's *Cities of Tomorrow* (1988), an intellectual history of modern planning. There is also the more encyclopedic text of Stephen Ward, *Planning the Twentieth-Century City* (2002).

There is also usually some mention of modern urbanism in various architectural history survey texts, such as Kenneth Frampton, *Modern Architecture* (2007), Jean-Louis Cohen, *The Future of Architecture Since 1889* (2012), or Kathleen James-Chakraborty, *Architecture Since 1400* (2014). What is still needed, and which this book provides, is an overall account of the major efforts by designers to shape urban form around the world since the nineteenth century, combining social, economic, and political history with a clear focus on specific design ideas and their built outcomes.

CHAPTER ONE

The Emergence of Modern Urbanism

European Cities in the Nineteenth Century

Many of the most admired European cities today, places such as Rome, Florence, Venice, and Paris, have for centuries served as points of inspiration for later efforts to design urban environments. These urban environments, now often overrun with tourists and fraught with social conflicts, were produced in a cultural environment where strictly economic concerns were always subordinate to the agendas of state and religious authorities. Urban space was a projection of state power, which was represented by new and appropriated monumental imagery, as in the Rome of Pope Sixtus V (1585–90), where the design of new straight streets, fountains, and churches was particularly influential on later developments.

In France, Louis XIV, who ruled as an absolute monarch from 1643 to 1715, not only beautified Paris with the new East Front of the palace of the Louvre (1671), then the largest building in Europe since ancient times, but also constructed a vast new royal palace complex, Versailles, on 2,000 acres (800 hectares) nearly twelve miles (20 kilometers) southwest of Paris (fig. 1). The construction of Versailles (1661–1715) was made possible by improved surveying, grading, and drainage techniques, as well as by considerable skill in both architecture and landscape design. Its centerpiece was an immense palace whose corridor organization of separate wings, faced with Renaissance classical stone detailing and large windows, inspired many subsequent governmental complexes. Its gardens and waterways, which paralleled and were to some extent inspired by those of the Muslim world, were rigidly organized along axes that converged at the king's bedroom, which was also his office and reception room. The immense size of Versailles and its finely crafted classical architecture and garden design were intended to demonstrate without any doubt the French monarchy's ability to control territory and to overawe visiting diplomats, as well as to give pause to any potentially insurrectionary nobles and foreign leaders. It was a widely imitated model for other palaces in Europe, particularly in the Rhineland and some other

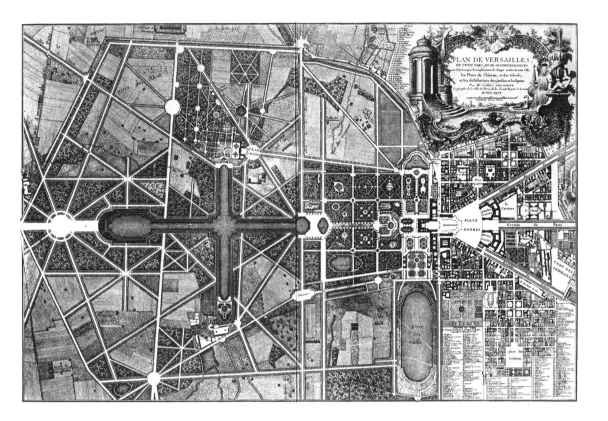

small princely states in what later became Germany, whose many rulers found Versailles to be a compelling model for their own palaces and gardens, as at Karlsruhe and elsewhere.

The controlled architectural and landscape environment exemplified by Versailles was influential for urban design in existing cities as well. European rulers began to manage the appearance of the urban environments under their control to make them appear grander and more "regular" than the untidy and often unsanitary medieval urban environments, which usually included many wooden structures on crowded streets without adequate drainage. They did this by regulating and limiting housing types and organizing buildings along straight streets that were sometimes patterned into geometric shapes. They also on occasion mandated uniform street widths, and they introduced the large-scale planting of street trees, as at Unter den Linden in Berlin (1647). Sometimes these rulers also commissioned designers and artisans to construct plazas adorned with fountains and statuary honoring themselves and their dynasties. By the eighteenth century such practices were widespread, in both Europe and its far-flung colonies, where they were often influenced by indigenous urban design practices.

The growth of cities allowed idealized Renaissance-type plans to be actually built as extensions of medieval centers, notably in Berlin, where much of the medieval city was extended by its Prussian rulers with new

1. Plan of Versailles, with gardens by André Le Nôtre (Abbé Delagrive plan, 1746).

classical streets and plazas. In Paris, though there were some episodes of such urban beautification, such as the Place Royale (now the Place des Vosges), Place des Victoires, Place Vendôme, and the Place Louis XV (now the Place de la Concorde), much of the city remained medieval in form well into the nineteenth century, despite the upheavals of the French Revolution (1789–93). It was nevertheless the extensive and influential discussions there led by such noted architects and theorists as the Abbé Laugier and Pierre Patte, who promoted the advantages of designing cities with a variety of agreeable urban spaces and street layouts, that then prompted many of the real urban transformations of Paris in the nineteenth century.

LONDON AS AN EMERGING GLOBAL METROPOLIS

By 1800, London, the capital of the British Empire, was growing rapidly in both population and metropolitan territory, while Beijing, the capital of the Qing Empire (1644–1912), was still the center of the world's largest economy, and the largest city in the world, as it had been for several centuries. By 1825 London, with a population of 1.3 million, had become the world's largest city, a position it held until the 1920s. It was arguably the first capitalist megacity, a center of world financial, trade, and administrative networks, and it drew vast numbers of immigrants first from the surrounding countryside, then from Ireland, and eventually from around the world. Many of today's world megacities are its successors, either founded or extended during the heyday of European colonialism. These include many of the largest cities in India, which had served as British colonial outposts: Chennai (Madras, 1639), Mumbai (Bombay, 1665), and Kolkata (Calcutta, 1690), the capital of British India until 1912. They also include Singapore (1819), Lagos, Nigeria (1851), Johannesburg, South Africa (1886), and Yangon (founded as Rangoon, Burma, 1852). Though culturally distinct, the Chinese coastal "treaty ports" established by the British and other European powers after the Opium War ended in 1843, which included Canton (now Guangzhou), Shanghai, Tientsin (now Tianjin), Hankow (now part of Wuhan), Hong Kong, and others, also once featured many similar urban elements. And even cities that today exemplify other cultural traditions were strongly influenced at points by the British example in their modern development, notably places like Karachi, developed as an outpost of the Dutch East India Company before coming under British rule in 1839; São Paulo; and Tokyo, known before 1867 as Edo.

Like London, most of these cities were also divided places, where relatively small numbers of wealthy and socially well-connected residents lived in proximity to immense numbers of their servants, tradesmen, laborers, and the unemployed. In British colonial settings, cities were normally also explicitly segregated between native "black towns" and European "white towns," establishing patterns of racial and ethnic division that often still structure urban patterns today. Even more than previous cities, they were also heavily reliant on food grown elsewhere in the countryside. In 1850 they still resembled earlier cities in being mostly hand-built of masonry and wood, and were composed of small, low-rise buildings on narrow streets without indoor plumbing or public water supplies. Electricity, automobiles, and safe passenger elevators did not exist, and indoor plumbing was a rare luxury. Much of the urban life of these colonial cities was structured by walking distances, and, much like those of the ancient world, their built-up areas rarely exceeded a few square miles or kilometers. Such cities were heavily reliant on water and horsepower for long-distance transportation, as passenger railways were introduced in Britain only in the 1820s, and the mass production of auto-mobiles by Henry Ford in the United States would not begin until 1913.

In both colonial and other cities, unprecedented elements began to appear in large nineteenth-century cities as well, and in the many smaller ones within their political, commercial, and cultural areas of influence. These new urban elements included peripheral garden cemeteries and public landscape parks, and residential commuter suburbs of expensive detached villas, served by regularly scheduled urban stagecoach, horse-car, and commuter railway lines. Yet only rarely did most cities include the first large metropolitan sewer systems, such as the ones designed and built in Hamburg in the 1840s and in London beginning in the late 1850s.

London is a metropolitan area where urban technical, social, and design transformations of the nineteenth century can still be seen in a variety of built artifacts and urban environments (fig. 2). Peripheral to the European continent, London by the 1700s was an unusual combination of a royal capital and a Northern European port city, and housed not only a powerful court centered on the monarchy but also a mercantile culture with long-established trading and cultural links across the English Channel. This set of conditions, where national political power and transnational commercial power were highly localized in one place, led to the rapid growth of a commercially driven urban society, "the greatest emporium in the known world." London had two medieval centers, one the merchant-dominated "square mile" of the City of London, which included the "Steelyard" trading complex of the Hanseatic League, and the other the royal capital in the nearby City of Westminster, centered on the Gothic cathedral where the English monarchs are still crowned. By 1700, London had begun to spread well beyond its ancient center on the River Thames, with the nobles and socially rising merchants seeking elegant terrace houses (row houses to Americans) in the new planted squares of the West End, just beyond Buckingham Palace and St James's Park, royal palace grounds that were sometimes opened to the public. This pattern of growth was unlike most other European continental capitals, even those, such as Berlin, that also had in their original formation

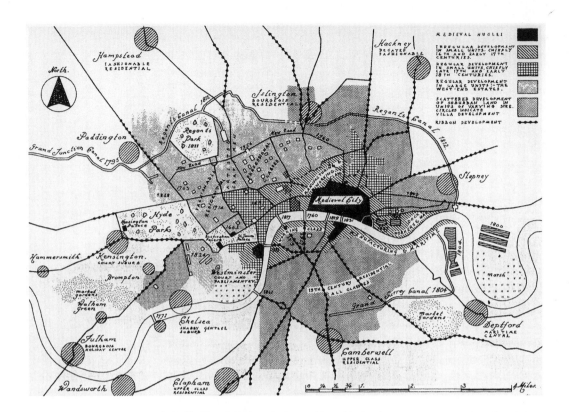

2. Map of London
development to 1830
(drawing by Alison
Shepherd, from John
Summerson, *Georgian
London* [New Haven:
Yale University Press,
2003], 3).

two separate urban settlements that later merged. London also differed from Rome, where the Vatican City, the seat of the popes of the Catholic Church, also functioned as the secular capital of their once-extensive territorial holdings until after the beginnings of the unification of Italy as a nation-state in 1861.

In its rapid territorial expansion in the early nineteenth century, London and other British cities such as Birmingham and Liverpool developed differently from the much more centralized cities of Europe. Those capitals and trading cities, of which Paris, Madrid, and Lisbon were also centers of world empires, had always been tightly controlled, and were usually relatively ethnically and culturally homogenous environments dominated by either a court and aristocracy, or a small circle of intermarried wealthy merchant families, or both. Urban development outside the city walls was for the most part strictly prohibited by law, to preserve valuable agricultural land. Except in Holland, Venice, Ragusa (Dubrovnik), and a few other places, ethnically different groups were rarely welcomed into the urban environment, and if tolerated at all, were often allowed to live only in specified areas. This was, of course, particularly true for European Jews, who in Venice were confined to the area called the "Ghetto," established by law in 1516 and abolished by Napoleon I only in 1797. At the same time, the Renaissance princes, popes, and other urban nobles in Italy during the 1400s, who provided a model for many European rulers for centuries afterward, often emphasized that the city should be an impressive and culturally uplifting environment for both spiritual and secular reasons. Their points of reference were the ancient Roman architect Vitruvius's *Ten Books on Architecture* and the Florentine humanist Leon Battista Alberti's (1404–1472) influential treatise *On the Art of Building* (1452), both written as design guides for powerful rulers.

In London, these Renaissance ideas about urban form were received much more slowly. King Charles I (reigned 1625–49) attempted to introduce a European-type absolute monarchy in England, which included his patronage of the Italian-educated English Renaissance architect Inigo Jones (1573–1652). Charles I approved the building of London's first square, Covent Garden in 1630–37, but his rule ended with the English Revolution and the defeat of his "Cavalier" supporters by radical Protestant "Roundheads," and he was beheaded in 1649. Oliver Cromwell then dictatorially ruled the emerging British Empire until 1661 as a Puritan theocracy. Renaissance urban design, like the former king's collection of continental art, was viewed with deep suspicion. After the Restoration of the monarchy in 1660, more modified Renaissance practices of city building were introduced into England in a politically acceptable way. Unlike his predecessors, the new king, Charles II, depended on retaining the support of Parliament, many of whose members were supported by increasingly wealthy merchants and tradesmen.

After the destructive Great Fire of London of 1666, Parliament passed what is arguably the first comprehensive building legislation in the English-speaking world, the 1667 London Rebuilding Act. It required that in the future, all new houses in London were to be built of brick rather than wood, as a response to the immense destruction of medieval wooden houses in the City of London in the Great Fire. Written in part by the architect Sir Christopher Wren (1632–1723)—who also designed the rebuilt St. Paul's Cathedral in a Renaissance style, completed in 1708—the Rebuilding Act specified four brick row-house types, ranging from four-story, 900-square-foot (84-square-meter) or more "first rate" houses down to very small two-story "fourth rate" houses, with the "rates" referring to the amount of taxes to be imposed on owners. Wren also set out a rule for the heights of urban streets, whereby the height of any building should not be more than half the width of the street it faced. The familiar urban patterns that resulted from these provisions of the 1667 London Rebuilding Act intentionally imposed a brick-fronted, Renaissance-inspired uniformity on the rebuilt City of London, as well as on parts of many cities and towns of the former British Empire, in places ranging from Derry in Northern Ireland (founded in 1622), to Charleston, South Carolina (1670), Philadelphia (1681), Calcutta (now Kolkata), India (1690), Sydney, Australia (1788), and beyond (fig. 3).

This Renaissance-inspired brick terrace or row-house pattern was the basis for the development of eighteenth-century British colonial cities around the empire, and also appeared in climatically modified form with

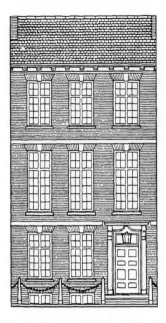
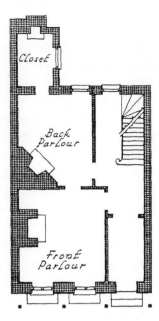

3. Typical street front and plan of a London row house, 1670–1700, as required by the 1667 Rebuilding Act (John Summerson, *Georgian London* [New Haven: Yale University Press, 1988], 51).

Indian-inspired side "verandas" in townhouses in more tropical British colonial cities like Calcutta and Charleston. In 1667 Wren had also hoped to regularize the London street plan and introduce new diagonal boulevards like those built in Rome in the 1580s by Pope Sixtus V, but the difficulty of reassigning urban lots in the new pattern to the owners of fire-destroyed properties made this plan politically impossible. The streets of the City of London were thus rebuilt largely on their previous medieval plan.

As London grew in wealth and international importance, both the elite West End of London and what ultimately became the working-class East End were gradually expanded onto former private agricultural estates. Large landowners typically commissioned the street layouts themselves, and paid for the construction of the new residential streets and squares, which they hoped would be highly profitable. The row houses were leased to builders on ninety-nine-year leases, allowing the owners to retain land titles over centuries as these areas often grew immensely in value. Similar physical patterns, with local variations and different ownership patterns, can be traced in many other English and early North American cities, in areas such as Beacon Hill in Boston or Society Hill in Philadelphia.

London's population was first reliably recorded in 1801 at 900,000 residents, when it was still largely a city of brick row houses on narrow streets, sometimes facing occasional semi-public open squares. As its wealthier citizens, typically merchants or owners of country estates seeking urban residences, flocked to the West End and nearby areas built around the new residential squares, the old commercial center of the City of London became depopulated. New, horse-drawn weekday commuter transport services from these residential areas to the now mostly commercial areas of the central city began to proliferate. At first, these mainly served the better-off workers who paid substantial sums to ride to work in comfortable horse-drawn omnibuses, which ran on regular schedules. Soon, less affluent workers began to take the new horse-drawn trams from working-class districts, mostly located in East London, to central workshops and factories. In the West End, the visionary architect John Nash (1752–1835) convinced the Prince Regent that he should sponsor an architecturally unified new shopping street to mark the eastern edge of the fashionable residences, a street that would lead to a large new semi-public park on a former royal hunting ground called Regent's Park (fig. 4). This ambitious project was anticipated in the extensions of Bath, a fashionable resort town in the mid- to late eighteenth century, and in the construction of the Edinburgh New Town (1767–1850). Both projects put grand stone classical facades over groups of terrace houses, producing the effect of palaces organized around public squares. At Bath, one such plaza was circular, and a large "crescent" of terrace houses (1767–74) was designed by John Wood the Younger to face a park.

Nash also designed a small number of new suburban villas in "Park Villages" adjacent to Regent's Park, some in the Gothic style, whose revival was then a novelty. A few years earlier, Nash had also designed Blaise Hamlet, a group of suburban homes near Bristol, which is sometimes considered to be the first Anglo-American suburb (1811). The building of Regent's Street and Regent's Park, completed by the 1820s, also included the Regent's Canal, which connected through new tunnels to the intercity Grand Junction Canal (1801), a waterway that ran between London and the Midlands, speeding the shipment of coal and timber. These large park, suburb, and infrastructure projects, much admired at the time, established early models for much subsequent world metropolitan development. Their enormous popular and financial success ensured that London would grow very differently from Paris, and would soon cover a vast metropolitan area, different in its territorial spread from all previous cities in human history.

At the same time, in fast-growing English industrial cities such as Liverpool, Manchester, and Birmingham, new patterns of dispersed metropolitan development also appeared, some of it first noted by the German socialist Friedrich Engels (1820–1895) in his *The Condition of the Working Class in England* (1845). He wrote that "with the blossoming out of manufacture . . . the more madly was the work of building carried on, without reference to the health or comfort of the inhabitants, with sole reference to the highest possible profit, on the principle that no hole is so bad but that some poor creature must take it who can pay for nothing better." Engels also observed that the factory owners and the financial and legal professionals who worked for them were increasingly seeking

4. John Nash, Regent's Park, London (1811) and Portland Place, from 1832 map (A. E. J. Morris, *History of Urban Form: Prehistory to the Renaissance* [New York: Wiley, 1972], 203).

suburban residences, commuting to them by horse-drawn omnibus or early passenger rail lines from their central-city offices and exchanges. The immense demand for housing in these early industrial centers— where wage labor, often very harsh, was still often preferable to semi- or actual starvation in rural areas—led to new forms of urban development. Though dense by contemporary North American suburban standards, these cities also expanded rapidly with vast new areas of middle- and working-class row houses, whose form followed municipal "by law" legislation intended to prevent fires, but which often also deprived their residents of sunlight and air circulation, and were usually deficient in waste removal and sanitation as well.

The Emergence of Modern Urbanism

Nineteenth-Century Innovations: Industrial Complexes and Railway Systems

As the outer edges of London and other English cities began to be built up with rows and rows of such new two-story brick houses, with adjacent commercial high streets of small shops suited to the character and means of the area, the horse-drawn commuter conveyances faced new competition from steam engine–powered commuter rail lines. These had first been introduced as an expensive commuter transit option in London in the 1830s. Railroad technology had developed from ancient and medieval uses in mining, using carts pulled by workers or animals on tracks, to become a major way that raw materials were moved to factories in industrial areas by the 1700s. Railway speeds then greatly increased with the invention and use of the steam engine in England in the eighteenth century. By the 1820s, steam-powered rail lines for paying passengers, running on regular schedules, had begun to link some English and North American cities, including lines between Newcastle and Stockton and between London and Birmingham in England, and between cities in the Northeast Corridor in the United States. Early railroad lines were also built in South Carolina, Cuba, and elsewhere.

By the 1850s, such regular ticketed rail services had established the pattern for the many national railway systems that began to be built and operated around the world. These included not only the early French, Belgian, and Swiss national rail systems, but also the extensive privately built rail networks in British India (which also included present-day Pakistan, Bangladesh, Myanmar, Nepal, and Bhutan). These networks were expanded in the 1850s across the Indian subcontinent from the growing port cities of Mumbai and Chennai, and from the British colonial capital, Calcutta, now Kolkata (fig. 5). These railways served other fast-growing centers of industry that emerged during the era of British colonial rule, including Ahmedabad, Hyderabad, Karachi, and Lahore, the latter two now in Pakistan.

Territorial rail networks were also constructed in the mid-nineteenth century in Prussia, beginning in 1837 and centered in Berlin; the Austro-Hungarian Empire, centered in Vienna, whose successor states include Austria, Slovenia, Croatia, Hungary, the Czech Republic, Slovakia, and parts of Poland, Romania, Serbia, and western Ukraine; and the Russian Empire, centered in St. Petersburg, which in the mid-nineteenth century also included much of present-day Poland, the Baltic republics, Finland, Georgia, and Kazakhstan and its neighboring states. In the Ottoman Empire—centered in Istanbul and including present-day Turkey and most of the Middle East between Iran and Tunisia, as well as parts of southeastern Europe—key ports such as Izmir, Beirut, Haifa, Alexandria, and Thessaloniki built their own regional rail networks, while

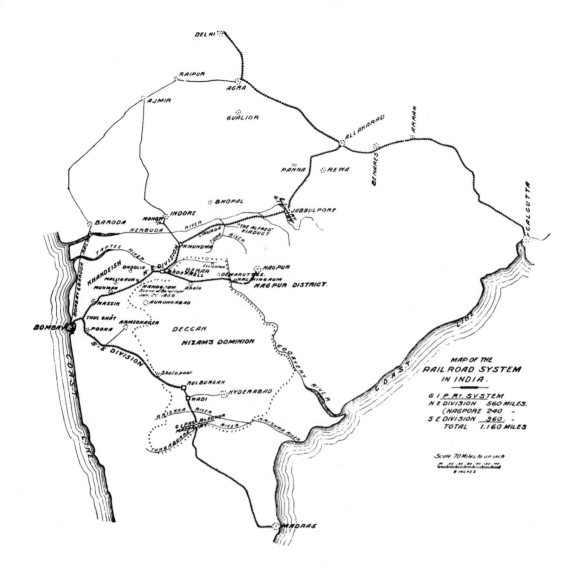

The following text labels appear on the map:

DELHI
RAIPUR
AGRA
AJMIR
GUALIOR
ALLAHABAD
ARAH
PANNA
REWA
BENARES
BHOPAL
INDORE
JUBBULPORE
CALCUTTA
BARODA
MHOW
NERBUDA RIVER
"THE ALFRED"
VIADUCT
KHUNDWA
TAPTEE RIVER
DHOOLIA
N. DIVISION
BERAR
NAGPUR
OOMARUT EE.
BURHANPOOR TRENCH
KHANDEISH
MALLIGAUM
KHOSPELL
NAGPUR DISTRICT.
MUNMAR
Scene of Bagel fight
Jan. 24. 1858
AHOLA
NASSIK
AURUNGABAD
BOMBAY
THUL GHAT
POONA
ARMEDNAGAR
DECCAN
BOMBAY & BARODA TR.
S-E DIVISION
NIZAM'S DOMINION
COORLEY RIVER
Sholapoor
MULBURGAN
HYDERABAD
COAST LINE
WADI
KRISHNA RIVER
RAICHUR
G.I.P.RY. MADRAS
RIVER
TUMBHUDRA
KRISHNA RIVER

MAP OF THE
RAIL ROAD SYSTEM
IN INDIA.

G.I.P.RY. SYSTEM
N E DIVISION   560 MILES.
(NAGPORE 240   "
S E DIVISION   360.   "
TOTAL   1,160 MILES

Scale 70 Miles to an inch
8 INCHES

5. Railway map of India, 1870, showing the trunk lines to Delhi and the major eastern port cities of Madras (now Chennai) and Calcutta (now Kolkata), which was the British colonial capital before 1911.

Istanbul maintained its primacy as the maritime center of the region until 1918 (fig. 6).

Such large, centrally financed and administered rail networks enhanced the importance and greatly increased the populations of the established imperial capitals, as well as those in regional centers such as Turin, Zurich, Copenhagen, and Stockholm. Early national rail systems had also appeared by the 1850s in Cuba, then still a Spanish colony, and in Argentina (1855), centered on Buenos Aires, which had become independent of Spain in 1816. They also soon began to be built elsewhere in Latin America and Asia as well. Yet in China, British imperial efforts to build railways were for a long time fiercely resisted by the Qing dynasty, which accurately saw them as a threat to its control of its national territory, and the first large railway lines there were built only after 1905.

In London the first rail commuter lines appeared shortly after the establishment of intercity lines linking London to Birmingham and the

The Emergence of Modern Urbanism

6. New Karaköy to Tophane road, Istanbul, circa 1900, with the Nusretiye Mosque at right (Library of Congress).

Midland industrial cities, and initially converged at new stations called London Bridge, Fenchurch, and Euston (1837). Their success encouraged many other private railway companies to build their own terminal stations close to the City of London. These eventually included new stations at Paddington (1838), King's Cross (1857), and St. Pancras (1865). Such expansion greatly raised urban land values and stimulated higher-density new development nearby. By 1851, the year of the Great Exhibition, which also produced Joseph Paxton's technically innovative Crystal Palace, there were sixty commuter trains running per day between suburban Greenwich and the London Bridge station. By the 1860s the success of rail transport in London made new bridges over the Thames River necessary, and also led to the building of new railway viaducts through inner-urban areas and the clearance of many working-class residential areas for large railway yards.

The unprecedented speed and scale of rail travel greatly encouraged metropolitan expansion, which occurred as the British Empire was spreading Enlightenment ideas around the world. The outcomes included an emphasis on individual rights and the consequent abolition of slavery (1807) across the Empire, followed by the eventual elimination of the international slave trade by British military efforts. The British Empire also introduced its comprehensive legal system, which is still widely used in many countries today. It set the world stage for the post-1945 era, when the United States for a time attempted to take on a similar world leadership role. Yet Britain and the other European colonial empires imposed strict racial hierarchies at home and abroad, leading to the contradictory social outcomes that are still evident. These hierarchies, thought at the time to be based on scientific research, placed northern Europeans at the top and black sub-Saharan Africans at the bottom of colonial social structures, resulting in the growth of cities such as Shanghai in China and Johannesburg in South Africa as powerful white-minority dominated financial, industrial, and administrative centers.

In the nineteenth century, cities within the Anglo-American cultural sphere tended to grow somewhat randomly along rail routes from existing centers, creating industrial and residential areas in what had been farmland. Such privately financed, investment-driven, and uncoordinated growth was typically conceptualized as potentially unlimited and ideally unconstrained by governmental authority. Few regulations were put in place to control what came to be called "development" of this kind. In London, as eventually in many other places, notably the Northeast and Midwest of the United States, these patterns were minimally regulated by central authorities and were largely the result of the interplay of cultural and commercial forces in relation to both existing natural features and established patterns of land ownership. Such metropolitan growth, occurring as it did within the continuing remaking of the world by human economic and political activities, brought a new way of living into being, one highly dependent on rail transportation, clean water supplies, and the use of new drainage technologies on an unprecedented scale. The surveying, grading, and tunneling technologies that made these innovations possible, along with a larger scale of the organization of labor, had developed gradually before 1850. As British and American interests extended the implementation of these practices, they were often notably indifferent to existing "native" patterns of land use, particularly those involving irrigation systems and traditional forms of collective landholding. This often led to complex and disruptive outcomes, though in many cases, European- and American-built infrastructure systems also established patterns that are still widely used today.

By the early 1800s these techniques of metropolitan development were used and extended in booming English industrial cities, where industrial growth was at first centered on textile manufacturing, which had expanded from the early mechanized mills in South Lancashire after 1760. Cotton picked by slaves on plantations in the Americas and by laborers in India was shipped to Liverpool, which then grew rapidly as a port. By 1820, finished clothing and textiles were being mechanically woven in the mills of nearby Manchester. The growth of these cities set a pattern for much subsequent industrial urban development, creating worldwide networks of ports and factory centers. Their growth was based on the incredible profitability of large factories, which used raw materials to produce salable consumer goods for a world market. This move from agricultural to industrial production went along with increased urbanization, as it still does today.

Between the early 1700s and 1801 (the date of the first English national census), the urban dwellers of England and Wales rose from representing 20 to 25 percent of the population to 33 percent, out of a national population of 9 million. By 1851, 54 percent of the population of England and Wales, around 18 million people, was urbanized. This year was the first time that the divide between rural and urbanized population was statistically identified. By 1901, England was already 80 percent urbanized, close to the 2014 figure of 84 percent for the United States, and well above the 2010 world average of 54 percent urbanized. In England, investment capital flowed into new residential building, most of it brick terrace houses sited at the edges of the built-up areas. The low cost of land produced a high standard of housing relative to the European continent, with lower residential densities, so much so that in 1824, metropolitan London already covered four times the land area of Paris.

Public Health, Environmental Regulation, and Urban Infrastructure

This higher standard of living came with large environmental costs, which were evident as early as the 1830s. The burning of coal for fuel caused the central London region to be perpetually under a thick cloud of black smoke, stimulating migration to the less-developed edges. An even graver danger appeared with the first cholera epidemic of 1831, whose causes at the time were not yet understood. Many noted, however, that while in 1800 the Thames River was still swimmable and full of edible salmon, and still serving as the main source of London's private water supply, by the 1830s it had become extremely polluted by sewage. This was attributable in part to the growing use of new indoor flush toilets, whose waste flowed into sewers that drained directly into the Thames. Edwin Chadwick (1800–1890), secretary of the governmental Poor Law Commission, advocated a system of workhouses for the unemployed indigent, and was also one of the first public health advocates. He oversaw one of the first detailed sociological studies of urban life, published as *The Sanitary Condition of the Labouring Population of Great Britain* (1842). Chadwick's advocacy of a centralized national public health authority to address these conditions made him politically unpopular, but the threat of another cholera epidemic led to the passage of the first Public Health Act of 1848, which created local health boards funded by tax revenues to address a range of public health needs.

These included regulation of polluting industries and the identification of houses unfit for habitation, as well as the provision of new sanitary cemeteries, public parks, and public baths. Concerns about public health also led to the first efforts at detailed public regulation in London of urban building, which in turn led to local building code restrictions on the free use of land. These codes varied slightly from one municipality to another, but were to some extent standardized by the Local Government Board model building regulations of 1875. Their first objective was to ensure the through-ventilation of dwellings, based on the then-current medical theory that diseases were mainly transmitted by vapors from rotting matter. The free movement of air in and around the house was considered essential, and each house was required to face what was then considered a wide street, and have an open space behind it. This seemingly basic requirement was in fact fiercely resisted by developers of working-class housing, who by the 1840s had made the back-to-back house arrangement, in which two rows of houses without indoor plumbing shared the same rear wall, the usual type of workers' housing. Efforts to ban these house types in the 1840s failed, but the 1875 model bylaws successfully forbade their further construction.

For similar public health reasons, the Towns Improvement Clauses Act of 1847 had suggested 30-foot (9.14-meter) widths for all streets used by wheeled traffic, and 20-foot (6-meter) widths for nontraffic streets. By the late 1800s, 36- or 42-foot (11- or 12.8-meter) widths were often legally required for new "bylaw" residential streets, and these were never to be more than 50 feet (15.2 meters) maximum in width. The interaction of these increasingly stringent regulations with the traditional practices of builders by the late 1800s led to standardized English bylaw urban layouts. These consisted of long streets of two-story row houses built at, or slightly set back from, the street line, with a minimum of cross-streets (since these reduced leasable square footage). Each urban house typically had a rear garden, separated by low walls from its neighbors, and was accessed by a rear alley running the length of the entire block. In poorer areas the back houses, which had little natural light, were served by a series of narrow pedestrian passages or tunnels cut through the rows of houses that faced the street.

At the same time, these new regulations, intended to provide for the free circulation of air, proved to be inadequate in themselves to stem the spread of infections, which in many cases began to be traced to polluted drinking water supplies. In 1854 Dr. John Snow (1813–1858) proved that cholera was carried by bacteria in water from one contaminated pump in Broadwick Street in the Soho area of London, and he mapped the local spread of the disease. This led to a new focus on clean urban water supplies and the removal of waste. The pollution of the Thames River and its tributaries in particular led to the formation of the London Metropolitan Board of Works in 1855, which was empowered to create an efficient drainage system for the whole London region, as well as to provide for new highways for horse-drawn vehicles. Sir Joseph Bazalgette (1819–1891) was appointed its Chief Engineer, and he designed and oversaw the construction of many miles of new brick sewers to take the flow of all the streams leading into the Thames downriver, where the water was then pumped up and out into tidal areas closer to the ocean.

The system included three large intercepting sewers north of the river, and two south of it, along with two pumping stations. Though rarely considered an example of urban design, the new Victoria Embankment (1862–70), built as part of the system over the low-level sewer placed on the north bank of the Thames River, and the new Albert Embankment, built on the South Bank of the Thames to prevent flooding, produced major transformations of the London riverfront, creating new value for riverside properties and increasing redevelopment nearby on both sides of the river.

In was also in this same context that the world's first subway system, the London Underground, was begun in 1863, based on ideas for an underground steam locomotive railway that had been put forward since at least the 1830s. It carried 38,000 passengers between Paddington Station and Farringdon Street on opening day, and was soon expanded by various private companies. An underground "Circle Line" linking the major rail stations was completed in 1884, using mostly new "cut and cover" tunnels, whose construction caused considerable disruption. In 1890 the City of London witnessed the opening of the first deep tunnel line, which was also the first to be electrified. By the early twentieth century, London's massive growth caused American investor Charles Tyson Yerkes (1837–1905), who had built most of the Chicago Loop's elevated lines in the 1890s, to buy the London District line, to which he then added three new electrified underground lines. Around this same period, the private companies operating the various competing lines agreed on a joint marketing arrangement, and color-coded maps of the entire system began to be issued, the antecedents of modern subway maps. The London Underground as a public transit system was not created until 1933, around the same time that Harry Beck designed its now-familiar diagrammatic, color-coded route map, which was then widely imitated in other cities.

URBAN MODERNIZATION: PARIS, 1852–70

The modernization of Paris was carried out from 1852 to 1870 under the direction of Emperor Napoleon III and his chief official for the Paris region, Baron Georges-Eugène Haussmann (1809–1891). New wide boulevards, lined with six-story apartment houses with similar stone classical facades, were cut through the existing city, linking the new train stations; and a modern sewer system and utility lines were constructed beneath the streets. Two large new landscape parks, the Bois de Boulogne and the Bois de Vincennes, were also created from former royal estates, and other new parks were built. Most of Paris at the time of the French Revolution (1789–92) had remained a jumble of narrow, unsanitary, and difficult-to-police medieval streets. Commercial cart and passenger carriage traffic took hours to move across town, even after it had passed through the imposing tax collection gates (1784–91) designed for the city authorities by Claude-Nicolas Ledoux (1736–1806) in the *octroi* (customs) wall that ringed the city on all sides. Ledoux had also designed one of the first utopian industrial settlements for the prerevolutionary government saltworks at Chaux, begun in Arc-en-Senans in 1775, but such Enlightenment efforts at urban order had few direct outcomes in Paris at this time.

Efforts to modernize and regulate the fractious capital of the French Empire (still then the world's second-most powerful state, even after its defeats by the British Empire in 1763 and 1815) did occur, but the overall form of Paris remained medieval until the 1850s. Earlier efforts at urban beautification—involving new arcaded streets with shops like the 197-foot-wide (60-meter) rue de Rivoli (1804–48), secular monuments like Napoleon's Arc de Triomphe (completed in 1836), and the regulation of building street setbacks and heights—were carried out in the same environment as the discovery of many technical innovations, developed in part from the teaching and research of the École Polytechnique, which was founded in 1794, just after the French Revolution.

Paris remained the intellectual center for approaches to the design of the built environment, the result of the revolution's goal of preventing the return of "ignorance, superstition, and error." The teaching of the École Polytechnique was also seen by the French Revolutionary state as a central part of its national defense. It was there that the profession of engineering, involving quantifiable measurement and calculation, rather than a knowledge of ancient and Renaissance design precedents, began to be developed as a discipline separate from architecture, which continued to be taught in Paris in the reorganized École des Beaux-Arts. Both schools then became models for the many similar institutions of professional training in architecture and engineering founded elsewhere around the world down to the 1930s.

Even after the defeat of Napoleon I, Paris remained "the capital of the nineteenth century," as it was famously described by Walter Benjamin in the 1930s in his essay "Paris: Capital of the Nineteenth Century" (fig. 7). Benjamin called attention to the numerous new phenomena that appeared in Paris after 1815, including the utopian socialist concepts of Charles Fourier (1772–1837), a traveling salesman who envisioned a future society whose members were organized voluntarily according to the kinds of activities that they liked to do, who would live collectively in palace-like "phalansteries." Fourier penned his ideas at about the same time that the word "socialism" seems to have first been used (1835), and he may have coined the term "feminism" in 1837. Benjamin pointed out that the new glass-roofed, iron-framed Paris shopping arcades that began to appear after 1822, serving as centers of trade in the luxury goods demanded by a rising middle class, manifested "an emphatic striving for disassociation with the outmoded," and they also perhaps hinted at "the dream of a classless society." These structures also, of course, anticipated later shopping malls and the vast expansion of consumer societies in the twentieth century, beginning with Paris department stores in the 1850s and shopping structures like the Milan Galleria (1861–77). Benjamin also called attention to the rise of photography, the beginnings of World Exhibitions, the new importance given to private living space as something antithetical to the workplace, and to the critical poetry of Charles Baudelaire (1821–1867). The latter, who first put forward the idea of urban modernity and of the flâneur, the urban wanderer who moves in the crowd from department store to café, reading the newspapers and decrying the commercialization of the art market, made the modern city a subject of his (sometimes banned) lyric poetry.

All these disparate new urban phenomena culminated in the 1850s, when Paris began to be transformed from a medieval city to a model of urban modernization. Louis Napoleon, the nephew of the first Napoleon, was elected president of France in 1848, and, in the face of political opposition, assumed dictatorial powers and declared himself Emperor Napoleon III in 1852. His modernizing, socially conservative program was to encourage investment and economic growth in Paris while simultaneously upholding the status of the church and aristocracy, in ways that proved to be popular for over a decade. He appointed a capable provincial administrator, Baron Haussmann, as Prefect of the Seine (the Paris region) from 1853 to 1870, to carry out his vision of a rebuilt Paris of

7. Gustave Caillebotte, *Paris Street, Rainy Day,* 1877 (Art Institute of Chicago).

8. Plan of Haussmann's Paris, 1854–1889 (D. H. Burnham and Co., *Plan of Chicago* [Chicago: Commercial Club, 1909], 16).

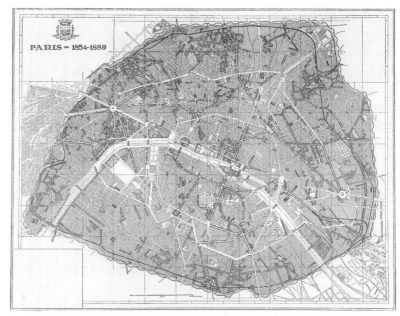

PARIS – 1854-1889

XVII. THE TRANSFORMATION OF PARIS UNDER HAUSSMANN: PLAN SHOWING THE PORTION EXECUTED FROM 1854 TO 1889.
The new boulevards and streets are shown in yellow outlined with red.

grand boulevards, with new classical monuments and impressive cultural facilities. By aggressively attracting investment in real estate, Haussmann was also given the means to modernize the regional water supply and drainage systems, and to provide new traffic routes to the many new railway stations then being built or proposed. France was a world leader in railway engineering, but the construction of the national rail system approved in 1841 had progressed very slowly. For both Napoleon III and Haussmann, the old streets and buildings of medieval Paris, accumulated over many centuries of French imperialism, had little value. For both, their goal was to harness new technologies already in use in London to create a modern city, while at the same time retaining all the impressive classical grandeur of a Renaissance city, which they still saw as an essential element to maintain the aura of imperial authority. The key aspect in their rebuilding of Paris would be a new boulevard-based traffic system to unify its vast consumer market and workshops, creating a network of new routes to speed traffic across the city. At the same time, they sought to create Baroque perspectival effects centered on modern, mostly secular landmarks such as the train stations, the new city hall, and a new opera house (fig. 8).

Haussmann commissioned a planimetric survey, based on the triangulation of the entire city. He then used this survey, along with the kind of topographic maps that French military engineers had perfected in the eighteenth century, to plan the new boulevards. He had the resulting detailed map of Paris engraved at a 5:1000 scale and mounted on a large wheeled screen in his office, where he could monitor the rapid progress of the emperor's urban vision. The visual aspects of the plan were important to both Napoleon III and Haussmann, and the new privately developed luxury apartment buildings that lined the boulevards were all required by law to be six stories (66 feet/20 meters) tall, and to allow for a continuous line of commercial uses at the sidewalk level. This type of apartment building had developed in Paris in the eighteenth century, and versions of similar building regulations had been put in place at that time (fig. 9). These were then codified under Napoleon I in 1807, in a law that empowered towns to draw up street plans and to allocate public land for them. The primary element of Haussmann's efforts was to speed the flow of traffic, then just beginning to be called "circulation," for both commercial and security needs. The wide boulevards and required interior courtyards of the new apartment buildings also assured the good ventilation then thought to be necessary for public health reasons.

Napoleon III's boulevard plan was organized as a double concentric ring of traffic circulation around a "great cross" of two main orthogonal routes, the north-south boulevard Sébastapol-Saint Michel, and the east-west rue de Rivoli. The latter ran past the Louvre, the former royal palace, which had been nationalized after the French Revolution in 1793 to become the first large public art museum, and was an ongoing focus of French government patronage. Other new boulevards served (not always perfectly) the new privately built train stations, which, after the opening of the first international train service between Strasbourg (France) and Basel (Switzerland), also began to link Paris to the rest of France and Europe. "Nodes of relation" were created at the main boulevard intersections, and a hierarchy of planted areas, including parks designed by Haussmann's associate Jean-Charles Adolphe Alphand between 1871 and 1891, such as the Parc des Buttes-Chaumont (1867) and the planted boulevard of the Champs-Elysées, which led northwest from the Louvre.

These transformations of Paris in the 1850s and 1860s assumed an urban population increase of millions, which in fact occurred, as many residents from the countryside and smaller cities in both France and other parts of Europe began to move to the rapidly growing capital. This necessitated the establishment of an outer ring of new boulevard and apartment house districts, annexed in 1860, which were then included into the twenty Paris arrondissements (districts) that were established at that time. The construction of the boulevards and of some 40,000 new buildings required immense demolitions and the displacement of existing urban residents, but this did not slow the politically popular and successful transformation of Paris into a commercial capital and consumer spectacle. Instead, new forms of urban culture and politics emerged, ranging from the "Bohemianism" of poets like Baudelaire, and some of the first turns toward realistic painting of modern urban life by Edouard Manet and others, to new political directions inspired by the sometimes divergent ideas of Comte Henri de Saint-Simon (1760–1825), Auguste Comte, Karl Marx, and Friedrich Engels. The promise of a modern global

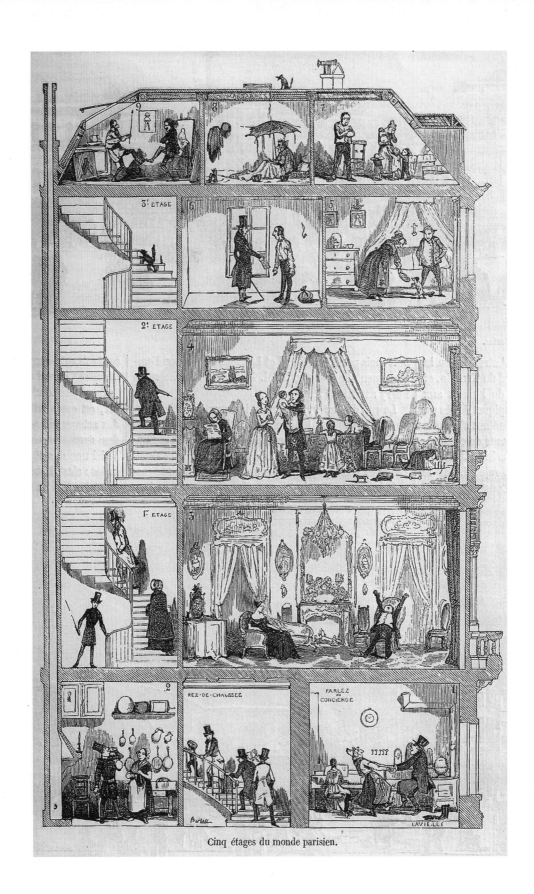

Cinq étages du monde parisien.

world of technology, consumer products, and new art forms suggested by the 1851 Great Exhibition in London, housed in Joseph Paxton's glass greenhouse of the Crystal Palace, was to be fully realized in the transformation of Paris, where much of the central city became a modern consumer spectacle unlike anything previously seen in human history.

At the same time, in France the conservative social reformer Frédéric Le Play (1806–1882) began to do some of the first empirical field research on the family structure and work relationships among workers, which he published under the patronage of Napoleon III in 1855 as *Les ouvriers européens* (European Workers). Le Play was trained in mining technology and had overseen the French government's collection of mining statistics in 1834. He was then appointed a professor at the École des Mines in 1840. His goal in collecting social statistics was to develop a classificatory system of the patriarchal working-class family, based on data that he had collected between 1829 and 1855. He was the first social scientist to distinguish clearly between workers, the non-working poor, and "criminals."

Le Play's focus on direct study and classification of social conditions paralleled the emergence of communism, which was first articulated in the *Communist Manifesto* (1848), written by Karl Marx (1818–1883) and Friedrich Engels, two German philosophers then living in Paris and active in the emerging socialist movement. Marx moved to London in 1849, where he was a major influence on the International Workingmen's Association, and wrote *Das Kapital* (*Capital: A Critique of Political Economy*, 1867–83), his extremely influential analysis of what he saw as the inevitably conflictual relationship between workers and the owners over the industrial "means of production." Discarding previous historical approaches, which tended to emphasize either religious perspectives or the German philosopher G. W. F. Hegel's (1770–1831) innovative concept that there was a Zeitgeist, or "spirit" of each age, Marx and Engels instead interpreted modern European history materialistically. They argued that the victory of the bourgeois (the capital- and property-holding mercantile middle class) in the French Revolution over absolute monarchy and the aristocracy, would be followed by a protracted and violent struggle between the workers and the bourgeoisie over who should benefit most from the labor of the workers. Marx and Engels thought the outcome would inevitably be in favor of the latter, leading many Marxists for a century afterward to think that they had developed a truly scientific theory of history.

Le Play's work was rooted in a similar, and at the time new, concern about the living conditions of the growing number of workers in European industrial cities, but was put forward from an opposite political position. Napoleon III's popular autocratic government was supported by political forces that sought to forestall communist and other revolutionary activities, but was not averse to social reforms in themselves.

9. Edmond Texier, *Tableau de Paris* (Paris: Paulin et le Chevalier, 1852), vol. 1: 65. Section showing the different social class levels of a typical Parisian apartment house.

Instead of violent political revolution, Le Play's work inspired the idea that the design of physical and social settings could have a major impact on social life, one centered on the patriarchal nuclear family. This insight led to various efforts to provide working-class philanthropic housing. Napoleon III put Le Play in charge of the Paris Exhibition of 1867, which was focused on the relationship of art and industry. Its centerpiece was Le Play's "Colisée de Fer" (Iron Colosseum), which organized to present the arts and industries of the various nations exhibiting into seven concentric rings of circulation. These were surrounded by restaurants on the perimeter, and at the center they focused on a garden dedicated to the arts. It was designed so that a visitor could also cut across the rings along paths to compare different products of a single country, and included a long path that graphically explained the history of the world, as seen from the perspective of the French Second Empire.

Napoleon III's reign was relatively brief, and ended after he unwisely attacked Prussia, leading to the French defeat of 1871. Paris was briefly occupied, and the occupation was followed by the socialist Paris Commune, which chaotically tried to rule the city for about a year before giving way to a return of bourgeois order under the French Third Republic. During this time many official sites were damaged or destroyed, notably Napoleon III's new Tuileries palace, adjacent to the Louvre. Yet the urban transformations that Haussmann had set in motion continued, making Paris an extremely influential world urban model. Haussmann's work was carried forward by others, notably Eugene Hénard (1849–1923), an architect for the Paris public works department, who invented the traffic circle, and who also introduced the diagramming of different types of urban traffic patterns. Hénard put a particular emphasis on understanding both underground and vehicular transport in the structuring of cities, and was one of the architects, along with Henri Prost and others, who by 1910 began to suggest that what they called *urbanisme* could extend the realm of design into the larger context of metropolitan development.

In other cities, specific street improvements often used the Haussmannian approach, such as the plan for the Paseo de la Reforma (1855–70s) in Mexico City, begun when Mexico was briefly under French domination, and urban renovation in central Rio de Janeiro in 1903–6, including the Avenida Central. The Viviani Plan for Rome (1873), which proposed the building of the Via Nazionale and the Corso Vittorio Emanuele, also took a Haussmannian approach. In Cairo, the Khedive Ismā'il restructured the city beginning in 1867 on Haussmannian lines for the opening of the Suez Canal, centered on the new district of Ismailiya. Haussmann's Paris also inspired large new districts in Brussels, Budapest, Belgrade, Milan, Stockholm, Buenos Aires, and many other cities. In the English-speaking world, the Haussmann influence was more limited, requiring, as it did, highly autocratic administrative procedures of land acquisition, clearance, and relatively high-density rebuilding, which were then usually alien to existing practices of private land development. Boston provided a partial exception, in its ambitious building of new urban districts in the 1850s on filled-in tidal lands for the Back Bay and South End neighborhoods. These were built out with imposing, sometimes French Second Empire–inspired mansard-roofed brick row houses and, eventually, grand hotels, churches, public buildings, and public statuary. Commonwealth Avenue in the Back Bay, laid out by Arthur Delevan Gilman in the 1850s on filled land beyond the old city of Boston, was a hybrid of French and English influences, with its brick row houses for "Boston Brahmin" families designed in a variety of historic styles. It linked the very old Boston Common, one of the first public spaces in English-settled North America, and the adjacent newly built Public Garden, to fast-growing areas along the urban periphery.

Haussmann's Paris provided an urban model not only in European-oriented cities in the Americas, but also in much of the French and British empires. In Algiers, the Algiers embankment extended the urban model of the Adams Brothers Adelphi Terrace in London, a raised platform for dock storage with classical business buildings above (fig. 10). Many of the French-built new parts of the city in the nineteenth century were also designed along Parisian lines. In India, the British used Haussmannian techniques to cut new boulevards through existing old cities to both improve sanitation and to better facilitate military governance and crowd control.

10. C. F. H. Chassériau, Algiers embankment, Algeria (photo by William Henry Jackson, *Harper's Weekly*, 1895, 229/Library of Congress).

Spain, despite its imperial past, by the later nineteenth century had become an impoverished country after the Napoleonic wars, with the loss of most of its Latin American empire in the 1820s, and with continuing social unrest in what was then still a largely agricultural nation. During the reign of Queen Isabel II (reigned 1833–68), Catalonia began to emerge as an industrial region with a growing industrial working class. Trade with the Americas contributed to the success of its textile manufacturing, some of it based on cotton imported from plantations in Cuba, which remained a Spanish colony until 1898. The population of Barcelona had risen dramatically to 150,000 in 1850, one of the highest urban densities in Europe. A railway line was begun in 1848, and in 1854 the city walls were demolished. The adjacent plain, then still largely under Spanish military control, began to be seen as an area of potential urban expansion. The City Council held a competition for the design of this area, called the *Eixample* in Catalan, or *Ensanche* in Spanish, which was won by Antonio Rovira y Trias. His scheme was a Haussmann-like plan with radiating boulevards, but instead in 1859 a plan by the Catalan engineer Ildefons Cerdà (1815–1876) was chosen by the national Ministry of Public Works (fig. 11). In the previous decade, Cerdá had coined the term *urbanización* to describe the expansion process of modern industrial cities, and in 1854 had

11. Ildefons Cerdà i Sunyer, Map of Barcelona and Its Improvements and Enlargement: (Eixample/ Ensanche), Barcelona, 1859 (Museu d'Historia de la Ciutat, Barcelona).

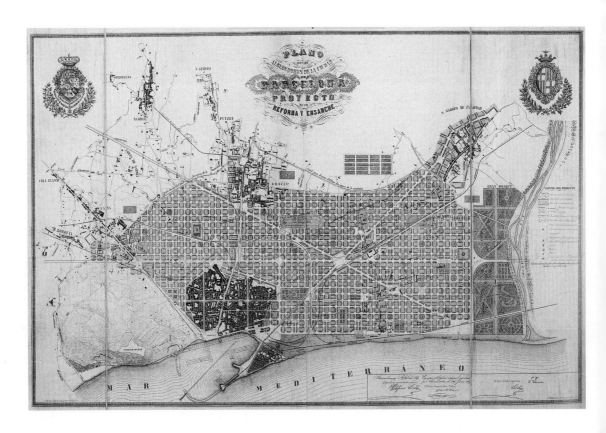

begun work on a topographic plan of the areas around Barcelona's Old City. Inspired by the ideas of Comte Henri de Saint-Simon, the French count and political theorist who had developed the idea that artists and designers should form an "avant-garde" to work with scientists, industrialists, and workers to envision future societies, Cerdá proposed that the extension of the city, now potentially developing at the new scale of the railroad, should be based on principles of public health, and combine the advantages of urban and rural life. He had conducted a "social survey" in 1856, in which he found that the typical working-class resident of Barcelona had only 26 ¼ square feet (8 square meters) of living space, while the wealthy typically had 69 square feet (21 square meters) per person. His extension plan was not fully carried out as designed, but its blocks, each with 450 chamfered corners, facing 66-foot (20-meter) wide streets with 16.4-foot-wide (5-meter) sidewalks, created small urban plazas at every intersection. The plan also included an existing planted avenue, the Passeig de Gràcia (1829), and four large Parisian-type boulevards, structuring the city beyond the medieval Gothic Quarter and giving it a distinct urban character.

Other aspects of the Cerdà plan, which called for building relatively low-rise apartment buildings on two sides of each block, leaving the centers open for planting, were overruled by developers, who then built taller buildings facing on every street front. Eventually warehouses and other low-rise buildings were also built in the rear courtyards. As the first phase of the construction of the Eixample slowed in 1866 with an economic crisis, Cerdá published his *General Theory of Urbanization* (1867). Using his own work as an example, he argued for the integration of environmental and social needs into the physical design of urban as well as rural areas. Cerdá's ideas were also one of the sources for the French area of research called *urbanisme* by 1910, and are related to the English and American concepts of "town planning," established by Ebenezer Howard, Raymond Unwin, and others in the early twentieth century.

These new social and political ideas about "urbanism"—defined as the conscious design of streets, housing, parks, and commercial and social facilities into rational patterns whose design expresses the cultural aspirations and responds to the social needs of particular cities and regions—appeared as human capacities to alter the built environment were beginning to change dramatically. Driving this change were innovations in railway building (including new tunneling and bridging technologies) and the first large-scale uses of repetitive manufactured building components like iron framing elements and standardized glass panes, both initially made possible by the organization of large numbers of working laborers and by coal-fueled, steam-powered machinery. Such developments would lead later polemicists of modern architecture like Sigfried Giedion (1888–1968) to see all these disparate new phenomena as inherently linked and expressing a new, modern spirit. Many scholars have now shown that the improvement of industrial technologies was not always or necessarily tied to social change, and in fact the new world of industrialized living continues to produce a variety of design responses, some very conservative and often hostile to the visual expression of new technologies or revolutionary social ideas.

Not all cities changed in the same ways at the same time in the nineteenth century. In areas still strongly influenced by ancient Mediterranean, Islamic, and east and south Asian cultures, dense, low-rise pedestrian-scaled cities of traditional houses or blocks of multifamily masonry buildings without plumbing continued to be built, and remained typical well into the twentieth century. Yet the combination of social, economic, and technical changes in the nineteenth century permanently altered the relationship of humans to their environment, and set in motion patterns of development that now show no signs of slowing, despite their evident future environmental costs. New means of manufacturing and rail transportation, new ways of removing waste and ensuring at least minimal sanitation, and new ways of acquiring and administering knowledge about the urban environment were the first steps toward the global megacities that are still rapidly growing. In London, Paris, Barcelona, and the many cities culturally influenced by them, these new technologies did not immediately alter earlier urban patterns, but they did make possible the middle- and upper-class commuter areas and suburbs where the wealthy could live in comfortable, sanitary, often relatively pastoral surroundings and still work in urban centers, resulting in new kinds of social and cultural life that are still evolving, even as digital technologies often seem to make the distinctions between urban, suburban, and rural seem ever less relevant.

CITY BUILDING: VIENNA AND GERMANY, 1848–1914

In 1848, Vienna and Budapest were the two capitals of the Austro-Hungarian Empire, a territory that then included much of Eastern Europe and parts of western Ukraine, ruled by the Hapsburg emperor and his German-speaking bureaucracy. Most of the Austro-Hungarian provincial capitals also had German-speaking elites, who closely followed events and trends in Vienna. These capitals included Prague in Bohemia and Brno in Moravia (both now in the Czech Republic); Krakow in Western Galicia (now part of southern Poland); L'viv (then known as Lemberg, in eastern Galicia, now in Ukraine), Chernivtsi (Czernowitz) in Ukraine; and Ljubljiana (Laibach) in Slovenia, an Austrian province then known as Carniola. Cities administered from Budapest, now the capital of Hungary, by the German-speaking imperial bureaucracy included Zagreb in Croatia and Sibiu (then known as Hermannstadt) in Transylvania, now in Romania. In Vienna itself, after an 1848 revolution led by the middle class, the ruling Hapsburg royal family agreed to a constitutional monarchy

The Emergence of Modern Urbanism

and limited self-government for the capital. The monarchy then also embarked on an ambitious effort to extend and modernize the city, inspired in part by the example of Paris. In 1852, Emperor Franz Joseph appointed a committee to make a proposal for Vienna's expansion, in part to address a growing housing shortage. He also ordered the demolition of the old fortifications around the medieval city in 1857, and called for designs for a new ring boulevard to take their place. The general concept of such a "Ringstrasse" had been proposed earlier, but in 1858 a town planning competition was announced for its detailed design.

Eighty-five competition entries were received, which were reviewed by a large jury that included many government bureaucrats as well as two representatives from the city of Vienna, along with a few architects and builders. Three first prizes were awarded at the end of 1858 to entries submitted mostly by architect-professors at the Vienna Academy of Fine Arts, who included Ludwig Förster (1797–1863). A committee that included both the prize members and some of the jury was then appointed to produce the final Grundplan (master plan), which was approved by the emperor in fall 1859. Construction on the Ringstrasse was under way by 1860, and the city received imperial approval to annex the areas just beyond the old fortifications, whose demolition began in 1859. The precise location of the Ringstrasse as constructed was taken from the Förster proposal, but was made wider (187 feet/57 meters), and the parallel "heavy traffic road" that Förster had proposed was built only in the northwest section (fig. 12). Most of the Ringstrasse was completed by 1870, and by 1890 many new public buildings and a new wing to the imperial palace (Neue Hofburg), as well as some 590 new luxury apartment houses, had been built in conjunction with its development. For the court and city business leaders, the Ringstrasse development was a huge economic success, occurring even as the empire's European prestige was slipping in the wake of its defeat by Prussia in 1866. At the same time, high land prices meant that less expensive housing could not be built in central Vienna, ensuring social segregation and, perhaps, a certain tendency toward class conflict.

The success of the Ringstrasse, itself inspired in part by Haussmann's Paris, soon had repercussions across Europe. Germany as a unified nation did not exist until 1871, when the Prussian Empire, by then centered in Berlin, had extended its control over a large territory that after 1871 was called the German Empire (Deutsches Kaiserreich, 1871–1918). Parts of it included areas that were later lost to France (1918) in the west, and to Poland (1946), and Russia (1946) in the east, but the residents in its major cities, which included Hamburg, Frankfurt-am-Main, and Munich (the capital of the previously independent Kingdom of Bavaria), as well as Königsberg (now Kaliningrad, Russia), Danzig (now Gdańsk, Poland), and Breslau (now Wrocław, Poland), after 1871 all began to develop a sense of being part of a unified German nation. This German unity was ensured

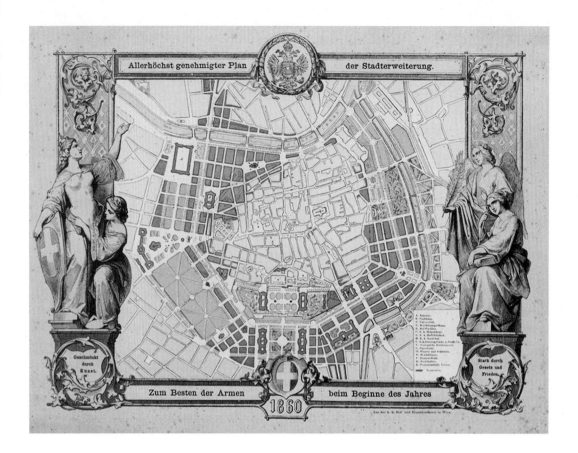

12. Map of the Vienna Ringstrasse development, 1860, with the irregular streets of the medieval city at center (Historisches Museum der Stadt Wien).

by relatively centralized control from Berlin, as well as by an extensive new railway system and other centralized state and economic organizations, such as a customs union. At the same time, local approaches to planning and architecture varied greatly from one city and region to another, and ethnic minority populations were often large.

These German cities in the mid-nineteenth century also struggled with tensions between the well-established tradition of relatively autocratically planned Baroque Residenzstädte like Munich or Karlsruhe—cities that were centered on royal or aristocratic palaces, whose design was inspired by Versailles—and the new, less clearly organized mercantile centers, which were developing in ways parallel to English industrial cities. The princes' efforts to impose stately order on these cities using Renaissance techniques of perspective, requiring that new buildings be classical in design and that they line up along straight street lines, began to come into conflict with the need by investors and entrepreneurs to build rail lines and large factory complexes to accommodate rapid industrial growth, which also brought new residents. Demand for inexpensive housing near the factories and rail stations greatly increased, as workers moved from farms in the countryside to plentiful industrial jobs in and around these then fast-growing cities. Urban tenements, defined as urban working-class apartment blocks, often poorly daylit and lacking indoor plumbing, began to appear with industrialization. Worker housing demand was at first met by subdividing centrally located, once-aristocratic houses into multiple units, but developers soon found it profitable to build tall *Mietkaserne* (literally, rent barracks), whose crowded conditions caused serious public health problems that were a major source of concern, and eventually led to the first forms of legislative control of building development in German cities.

In 1855 the chief of the Prussian royal police, Karl von Hinckeldey, commissioned an expansion plan for Berlin in response to the growing chaos in the dense medieval center of the city. Von Hinckeldey also commissioned a new water system and a Berlin building code (1853), setting a precedent for other cities throughout the German Empire. The Berlin expansion plan (*Bebauungsplan*) was made in 1862 by an inexperienced engineer, James Hobrecht (1825–1902). Hobrecht's plan was an overscaled version of Haussmann's expansion of Paris, with new *viertel* (districts) that extended the dense existing city in all directions along wide new boulevards (fig. 13). It also included some of the Berlin open spaces and boulevards planned by Peter Josef Lenné in the 1840s. Despite much criticism, Hobrecht's Berlin expansion master plan remained legally in force until 1919. The new boulevards, all 82 to 98 feet (25 to 30 meters) wide, in some cases intersected with others that ran in a roughly concentric way around the central areas. Unlike Haussmann's Paris, Hobrecht's Berlin plan lacked a clear overall organization for its major streets, and the new districts were in many cases laid out either on a grid centered on something like London squares, or with diagonal streets radiating from circular baroque plazas.

Aspects of the Hobrecht plan were also inspired by the earlier central Berlin planning of Karl Friedrich Schinkel, but the main concerns behind the Hobrecht plan were not aesthetics or monumentality. Its newly laid out large urban blocks (656 × 984–1,312 feet/200 × 300–400 meters) quickly triggered a boom in land speculation, as loose or nonexistent regulations allowed developers to build huge tenements with many internal courtyards on these large blocks. Their courtyards were allowed to be as small as seventeen Prussian feet (about 22 feet/6.7 meters) square, the dimension required for the turning radius of a Berlin fire department wagon. Hobrecht had envisioned that his plan would allow large gardens to be laid out in the centers of the blocks, but nothing prevented these areas from being built out with more tenements, which also usually lacked sewer connections.

The obvious failings of the Hobrecht plan did not prevent him from becoming a widely sought-after expert on town planning in Germany, but as early as 1870 the plan was being criticized nationally, leading to a movement to give city governments more power to map, acquire, build on, and maintain new streets according to a coherent plan. These led to the passage of the first Prussian town planning act in 1875, which

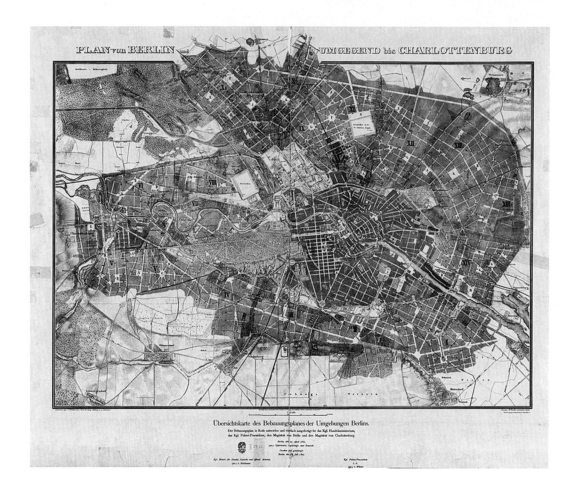

PLAN von BERLIN und UMGEGEND bis CHARLOTTENBURG

Übersichtskarte des Bebauungsplanes der Umgebungen Berlins.

13. James Hobrecht, Berlin Expansion Master Plan, 1862. The plan was much criticized for its large blocks, which led to the speculative building of many *Mietkasernen* (rent barracks) for poor in-migrants from the countryside.

gave cities the legal right to plan urban extensions. It was also the context for the influential treatise of Reinhard Baumeister (1833–1917), an engineer in Karlsruhe, whose study entitled *Stadterweiterungen in technischer, baupolizeilicher und Wirtschaftlicher Beziehung* (Town Extensions: Their Links with Technical and Economic Concerns and with Building Regulations, 1876) established the field of *Städtebau,* or "city building." The 1875 Prussian Planning Act gave municipalities the authority to expropriate land to build new streets, and it legalized the development of new urban areas by public sector authorities, allowing them to determine the routes of railways, urban transit systems, road networks, and water and sewage systems. Baumeister's text was intended to offer a set of patterns for how to organize street patterns and public spaces, and it quickly became a standard reference for German urban designers. Unlike Camillo Sitte's now more well-known book *Der Städtebau* (1889), Baumeister's work was for the most part not particularly concerned with either the aesthetic experience or the cultural significance of urban environments. At the same time, he codified the legal and technical practices of European urbanism that had developed from the Renaissance down to the time of Haussmann's Paris.

In the nineteenth century this kind of urban planning was seen more as a kind of engineering rather than architectural endeavor, continuing the split between the two professions that had appeared after the founding of the École Polytechnique in Paris in 1794. The Polytechnique, the world's first modern engineering school, was the model for the many *Technische Hochschule* and polytechnics that were established in Germany, Scandinavia, Italy, the Americas, and elsewhere in the nineteenth century. Closely linked to military activities since the Napoleonic era, these programs emphasized calculation and the use of scientific procedures to advance engineering expertise useful to business and industry, rather than continuing to focus on the correct architectural uses of the classical tradition, the approach that would continue to be taught in most schools of architecture down through the 1930s.

Published around the same time as the 1875 Prussian Planning Act, Baumeister's *Stadterweiterungen* was written to provide clear, rational methods to guide the urban expansions in Germany that were the result of the construction of railways and of industrial growth after 1850. The process of industrialization in Germany had some parallels to that of England, but cities such as Berlin were developing in a much denser and more centralized way than had English cities. In 1891 the average number of inhabitants per residential building in Berlin was fifty-two, in contrast to eight in London, then still largely a city of individual row houses. At the same time, German municipal authorities usually had more authority than was typical in England to regulate building construction. Berlin's population grew by 4 percent per year between 1843 and 1872, and cities such as Munich, Dresden, Hannover (where Baumeister had studied civil engineering), Frankfurt, and Stuttgart were all growing at a rate of over 2 percent per year around this time. Baumeister's work was an effort to respond to the 1874 urban policy manifesto of the Verband deutscher Architekten und Ingenieurvereine (German Architectural and Engineering Association), which declared that urban planning should primarily be about determining transport lines and street layouts in a free-market context.

Key planning decisions were defined by the association as the setting out of a coherent urban transportation structure, leaving the design of individual buildings to the private sector, but were also to include the regulation of buildings for issues of fire safety, access, health, and structural stability. The 1874 urban policy manifesto also emphasized the importance of shared responsibilities between the authorities and private developers, without challenging the capitalist basis of urban development. In this context, Baumeister's book set out the main tasks of city extension as providing new housing, understood to be privately financed, and expediting traffic circulation. The latter was of particular concern, in that new railway stations and embankments were causing massive traffic bottlenecks and disrupting the orderly expansion of cities onto surrounding agricultural land. In 1876 a second Prussian planning act was passed, allowing cities to set *Fluchtlinien* (building lines along streets) and allowing assessments to adjoining property owners for the costs of new streets and sewers. It was based in part on similar laws already passed in the state of Baden-Wurtemberg in southwest Germany in the 1860s, and is sometimes seen as the beginning of modern urban planning legislation.

A further step toward administrative control of the urban building environment was the *Normale Bauordnung nebst Erläuterungen* (Standard Building Code) published by Baumeister in 1880, which was followed by various local and state building codes, including the Saxon *Allgemeine Baugesetz* (General Building Act) of 1900. These codes had immediate impacts on building projects in Germany, notably on the extension of Cologne in 1881. Inspired by the success of the Vienna Ringstrasse, the city held a competition to plan the area of the old fortifications around the medieval city. Twenty-seven entries were received, and the first prize was awarded to two architects from Aachen, the director of its public works, Josef Stübben (1845–1936), and architect Karl Henrici (1842–1927). Their scheme proposed a new ring street three miles (6 kilometers) long, with linking side streets leading into new areas with ample public open spaces. It also established a new business area to the south and a villa district to the north. Stübben was then hired by the city of Cologne to carry out the plan, whose success led him to become one of the most influential planners in Germany, laying out new streets and districts not only in Cologne but also eventually in Berlin, Dresden, and Munich.

These events in Germany soon prompted a strong counter-response in Vienna. Camillo Sitte (1843–1903) was a Viennese Arts and Crafts high school principal who had studied architecture there in the 1860s. He had also studied the physiology of vision and space perception, and had made several trips to Italy and Germany to study Renaissance art, particularly Piero della Francesca's use of perspective. Like many nineteenth-century Europeans, Sitte also became an enthusiast of the music of Richard Wagner, and seems to have once been commissioned to design stage sets for Wagner's opera *Parsifal*. His work as a design teacher was not particularly focused on urbanism, so it was a surprise when in 1889 he published his *Der Städtebau*, later published in English as *City Building According to Artistic Principles*. Reacting against both the Paris-inspired construction of the Vienna Ringstrasse and Baumeister's technical methods, Sitte argued against the long-standing Renaissance way of building cities with large open squares and long perspectival boulevards. Instead, he proposed that contemporary designers study and imitate the irregular and picturesque urban plazas of medieval Italian and old German towns. Like Richard Wagner, whose wildly successful operas steeped in Germanic history and mythology had proposed a new nationalist cultural synthesis of all the arts into a *Gesamtkunstwerk*, or total work of art, Sitte

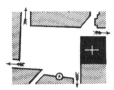

Fig. 22. Ravenna: Piazza
del Duomo

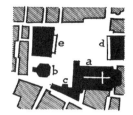

Fig. 23. Pistoia: Piazza del Duomo.—
a. Cathedral.—b. Baptistery.—c. Bish-
op's Palace.—d. Palazzo del Comune.
—e. Palazzo del Podesta. [From Martin]

14. Camillo Sitte, *Der Städtebau nach seinen künstlerischen Grundsätzen* (*City Building According to Artistic Principles* [Vienna, 1889], 172).

saw the possibility of creating new forms of social interaction and collective identity by evoking the enclosed and culturally resonant forms of old European town squares.

Sitte's starting point was the questioning of the classical tradition that had begun in England with critics such as John Ruskin (1819–1900), who saw the impassioned craftwork of medieval craftsmen as far superior to what he viewed as the routine and oppressive classicism of the nineteenth century, carried out by paid construction workers with no emotional identification with their increasingly mechanized work. In his *City Building According to Artistic Principles,* Sitte advocated rejecting the technically oriented urbanism of Haussmann and his German codifiers such as Baumeister and Joseph Stübben. He instead argued for designing enclosed civic plazas inspired, as mentioned earlier, by those of medieval Italian and German cities (fig. 14). Sitte's book struck a popular chord in Germanic lands in the late nineteenth century, and though he was not a trained planner, he was nonetheless then commissioned to design urban extensions throughout the Austro-Hungarian Empire. He designed urban extensions for Ostrava/Mariánské-Hory (then known as Marienberg), Olomouc (Olmütz), and Český Těšín (Teschen), all now in the Czech Republic; Bielsko-Biała (Bielitz), Poland; and Ljubljana, now the capital of Slovenia.

Josef Stübben seems to have seen Sitte's book as a useful revision of Baumeister's strictly engineering-based approach, and in 1890 published his own *Der Städtebau,* which soon became the standard reference work for urban planners in central and Eastern Europe. Stübben's approach set out a clear methodology for planning cities, one based on traffic circulation and land uses, and it took into account the lines of railways and waterways. Stübben's approach advocated a four-step process to organize the overall urban environment, beginning with 1) establishing legal building lines on outer radial streets where construction is just beginning; 2) setting the positions and levels of these outer ring streets; 3) laying out new radial streets back to the center as needed; 4) laying out diagonal boulevards to distribute the traffic of the outer radial streets into various inner-city districts. Within the framework, he followed Sitte in pointing to specific European squares as models for new development, and went beyond Sitte in offering a "dimensional table of European squares," with precise measurements, as a model for specific urban design decisions. Stübben also described the new zone regulations then just beginning to be put in place in German cities like Cologne and Frankfurt. These not only set out legally binding building lines, but also established districts where the number of stories and the maximum heights of buildings were regulated. Stübben's text distinguished between the regulation of individual detached houses (since the 1840s the increasingly difficult-to-achieve goal of German reformers for working-class housing) and multi-unit "block buildings" in cities. For the latter, the major problem was the lack of light and air, which could only be addressed by what today would be described as form-based codes.

These bulk zoning codes developed out of various local attempts in Germany at building regulation after 1880, and by 1901 had resulted in legislative codes like the Cologne zone system. Following Stübben's recommendations, this system set out four types of urban districts: 1) the Old City within the line of the medieval fortifications (coded in blue on zoning maps); 2) "urban suburbs" (coded red); 3) "rural suburbs" (shown with no map color); and 4) villa districts (green). Each had different limits on allowable numbers of stories and building heights, ranging from one to four stories and up to 66 ½ feet (20.3 meters) in the Old City (Zone 1), to one to two stories and 38 feet (11.6 meters) in the rural suburbs (Zone 3). Villa districts were also limited to two stories, but there dwellings were allowed to rise to 52 ½ feet (16 meters). Each zone also had limits on lot coverage, ranging from a maximum of 75 percent coverage in Zones 1 and 2 down to 40 percent maximum allowable coverage in Zone 4. This kind of bulk zoning was the inspiration for the first zoning ordinances in the English-speaking world in the early twentieth century, but in those ordinances (such as that put in place in Los Angeles in 1909) usually only land use, not building bulk, was regulated by zoning, with the New York City bulk zoning ordinance of 1916 being a very important exception.

Taken collectively, the work of Baumeister, Stübben, and Sitte laid the foundations in the late nineteenth century for the Germanic field of Städtebau, which continues in many European countries to the present. It first appeared in fully developed form in Vienna in 1892–93, after the Ringstrasse itself had mostly been completed. A competition was held that year for a city *Generalregulierungsplan* (general regulatory plan), and was won by Otto Wagner (1841–1918), the dynamic Vienna architect and educator. Wagner's book *Moderne Architektur* (1895) was the first to argue that architects had to take on the design of the practical and technical aspects of the urban environment such as transit stations, viaducts, and speculative residential apartment buildings. Wagner's entry for the 1893 Vienna competition proposed a three-dimensional *Bebauungsplan*

15. Otto Wagner, *Die Gross-stadt* (The Metropolis [Vienna, 1911]). A systematic plan for urban expansion based on high density apartment houses organized into walkable districts.

(building mass plan) that organized the city as a three-dimensional system with an architectonic unity, continuing Sitte's preoccupations with urban spaces, but also ordering them within a relatively rigid classical framework. Wagner's work was informed by the aesthetic theories of Adolf von Hildebrand and August Schmarsow, who had begun to emphasize abstract qualities of visual perception detached from any particular systems of signification. Ideas still current in the teaching of art, such as the difference between figure and ground, and the idea that abstract architectural space can be analyzed in itself, began to inform Wagner's work at this point. He further developed this direction in his book *Die Gross-stadt* (The Metropolis, 1911), where he suggested that the large cities of the late nineteenth century could be designed as a set of interrelated gridded residential districts, each with its own civic structure and amenities, and that these could potentially continue to grow over an unlimited area (fig. 15).

By this point, Germanic city building had developed from the Ringstrasse in Vienna and Hobrecht's 1862 Berlin plan, the application of Haussmannian strategies of urban redevelopment, to the Prussian legal codification of planning and building practices in 1875, into the profession of *Städtebau.* Before the early 1900s, this profession had no exact parallel in England and the United States, even as "town planning" projects began to emerge there. *Städtebau* differed from Anglo-American planning in being more precisely focused on the legislative control of both the three-dimensional form of cities, and on the placement and design of transportation routes and other infrastructure within them. Both were understood by city officials, developers, and designers to be essential aspects of urban development. By 1910 *Städtebau* had also begun to be affected by parallel initiatives like the City Beautiful movement in Anglo-American contexts, and much of the subsequent history of urbanism involves the complex interchanges and internal debates among divergent initiatives that have shared common aspirations and methods in various distinct linguistic and cultural spheres.

FURTHER READING

Walter Benjamin, "Paris: Capital of the Nineteenth Century," in *Reflections,* translated by Edmund Jephcott (New York: Schocken, 1978), 146–62.

Barry Bergdoll, *European Architecture, 1750–1890* (New York: Oxford University Press, 2000).

Eve Blau and Monika Platzer, eds., *Shaping the Great City: Modern Architecture in Central Europe, 1890–1937* (Munich: Prestel, 1999).

Joan Busquets, *Barcelona: The Urban Evolution of a Compact City* (Rovereto, Italy: Nicolodi, 2005).

Zeynep Çelik, *The Remaking of Istanbul: Portrait of an Ottoman City in the Nineteenth Century* (Seattle: University of Washington Press, 1986).

Francis D. K. Ching, Mark Jarzombek, and Vikramaditya Prakash, *A Global History of Architecture* (Hoboken, N.J.: Wiley, 2007).

Friedrich Engels, *The Condition of the Working Class in England* (London, 1887).

Robert Home, *Of Planting and Planning: The Making of British Colonial Cities* (London: Spon, 1997).

Stephane Kirkland, *Paris Reborn* (New York: St. Martin's, 2013).

Paul L. Knox, *Palimpsests: Biographies of 50 City Districts* (Basel: Birkhauser, 2012).

A.E.J. Morris, *History of Urban Form: Prehistory to the Renaissance* (New York: Wiley, 1972).

Donald Olsen, *The City as a Work of Art: London, Paris, Vienna* (New Haven: Yale University Press, 1986).

Antoine Picon, *French Architects and Engineers in the Age of the Enlightenment* (Cambridge: Cambridge University Press, 1992).

John Summerson, *Georgian London* (New Haven: Yale University Press, 2003).

Anthony Sutcliffe, *Towards the Planned City* (New York: St. Martin's, 1981).

Emily Talen, "Form-Based Codes vs. Conventional Zoning," in Anastasia Loukaitou-Sideris and Tridib Banerjee, eds., *Urban Design: Roots, Influences, and Trends* (London: Routledge, 2011).

Gwendolyn Wright, *The Politics of Design in French Colonial Urbanism* (Chicago: University of Chicago Press, 1991).

CHAPTER TWO

Cities in the Americas and the International Influence of the City Beautiful Movement

EUROPEAN COLONIAL AND EARLY NATIONAL URBAN PATTERNS

While London and Paris were the centers of large European world empires in the nineteenth century, other cities that were strongly influenced by them, such as Shanghai, Bombay (now Mumbai), Mexico City, Rio de Janeiro, and Buenos Aires, also expanded and changed socially and technologically during that time. In the new nation-states of the United States of America (1776–83) and in what in 1867 became the Dominion of Canada, cities began to develop in ways that were unprecedented in both their height and geographical spread. These transformations took place in a complex geographical situation where European colonial influences intersected with the settlement patterns of both existing indigenous cultures and an immense and productive natural landscape, which held extraordinary commercial prospects for the European colonial powers of Portugal, Spain, France, and England, and, to a much lesser extent, for Holland, Sweden, Denmark, and Russia. Some of the indigenous American cultures were to an extent also already urbanized, notably in Mesoamerica and Peru, and their violent and complex conquest by Spain in the early 1500s led to many hybridized urban outcomes, many still influential today.

Since the Spanish and Portuguese empires had first claimed parts of the New World in the 1490s—the two continents that were both named "America" in 1507 by Martin Waldseemüller, a European mapmaker—Iberian medieval practices of urban settlement had begun to be widely applied throughout the southern continent, as well as the southern parts of the northern one. From Argentina to Mexico and the American Southwest, and from the Caribbean to California, Spanish colonial settlements followed a highly regulated and similar form. This had developed from earlier ancient and medieval continental European practices, such as the

16. The Spanish Royal "Laws of the Indies" (1573), for town layouts, as applied with grid plans in Cuba, Santo Domingo, and Nueva España (New Spain, then Mexico after 1810) (Jaime Lara, *City, Temple, Stage* [Notre Dame: University of Notre Dame Press, 2004], 98; courtesy Pontifica Universidad Javieriana, Bogotá).

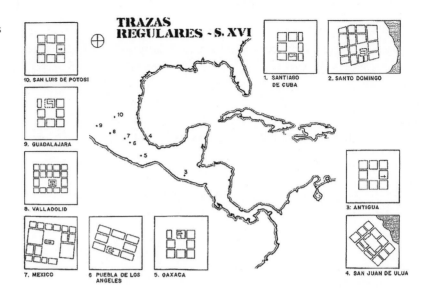

bastide towns in France, or the German *Zahringer* towns in Eastern Europe. Well after many cities in the New World had already been laid out, similar practices were codified by the Spanish monarchy in Madrid in 1573 as the "Laws of the Indies," which set out basic principles for compact colonial urban settlement (fig. 16). These laws, which remained in force for centuries afterward, derived to an extent from earlier ancient classical and European medieval practices. In some cases, they also paralleled the gridded settlement patterns of pre-Columbian cultures such as those of the Aztecs in Mexico and the Incas in Peru.

Following Vitruvius, the Laws of the Indies indicated that it was important for administrators to choose a relatively elevated site for a city, with a good supply of fresh water, surrounded by sufficient farmland to feed the proposed population. The plan was to be determined in advance of settlement, and then surveyed, or "outlined by means of measuring by cord and ruler." Each city was to be centered on a rectangular plaza surrounded by an extendable network of streets, which in Spanish-founded settlements almost always was in the form of a grid, though this was not explicitly specified. The central plaza's length was to be proportioned such that its width was one-and-one-half times its length. It was to be larger than 200 × 300 modern feet (61 × 91 meters) and no larger than 300 × 800 feet (91 × 244 meters). The plaza, and the streets that extended from it, were to be arcaded. Around the plaza were to be sited the main church or cathedral, adjacent to various government and other public buildings such as hospitals, as well as shops and merchants' houses. Sited nearby was to be a common cattle pasture, and beyond the built-up areas were agricultural lands, typically worked by poor peasants, often descended in part from the indigenous people who had been converted to Catholicism after the Spanish conquest, or in some cases by African slaves.

The urban code of the Laws of the Indies was only one aspect of a completely regulated social order, one that transposed the feudal structures of medieval Europe into the many demographically and ecologically very different environments of the Americas. A variety of cultural hybrids developed there between the Spanish and Portuguese colonizers and the different indigenous cultures. These resulted in the numerous complex hierarchical social orders, which often produced urban settlements and the different kinds of architecture, which sometimes continued indigenous practices. Yet only the Europeans were by the 1400s in possession of oceangoing ships, advanced navigational techniques, and firearms, which made possible their conquest of the New World. They remade it, often very brutally, in ways that extended European culture, including its languages, Catholicism, and architectural and urban patterns; these massive efforts had many repercussions back in Europe itself.

In North America, on the other hand, with the exception of Mexico (ruled from Mexico City as the Kingdom of New Spain, 1535–1821) and Cuba (a Spanish colony that became independent of Spain as a quasi-independent protectorate of the United States in 1898), the Spanish had a relatively minor impact. The first permanent Spanish colonial outpost in what is now the United States, St. Augustine, Florida, founded in 1565, was a strategic fortification built to resist French claims on the area. More significant Spanish-founded cities were Santa Fé, New Mexico (1609), and San Antonio de Béxar (1718) in what later became Texas, both then ruled from Mexico City. The plazas and grid plans of these later cities provided a clear demonstration of the continuing use of the Spanish Laws of the Indies almost one hundred and fifty years after they had first been issued. In California, named by the Spanish in 1535, and in most of the rest of the American Southwest, Spanish colonial settlement came later, mostly around mission churches in the late eighteenth century, two centuries after the foundation of Mexico City and of Lima, Peru, the two key administrative cities of Spain's American empire.

Following the economic success of the Spanish in gold and silver mining and of the Portuguese in introducing agricultural plantation systems in northeast Brazil, using enslaved Africans as their main labor force, other European powers also sought to profit from the immense mineral and natural wealth of the Americas. The French colonized the river valleys of the St. Lawrence and the Mississippi, founding the cities of Québec (1608), Montréal (1611/1642), New Orleans (1718), and St. Louis (1764) along these strategic waterways. The French also named and established Detroit (1701), a fort at a site whose name refers to "the straits" that connect Lake St. Clair and Lake Erie. Beyond French Canada (now largely the Canadian province of Québec), and some Caribbean islands and coastal areas, seventeenth-century French imperial commercial interests were mainly focused on the enormously profitable fur trade

17. Plan of Philadelphia, 1700s, founded 1682 by the English Quaker religious leader William Penn.

with various Native American groups in both the Great Lakes and the immense Mississippi-Missouri River watersheds.

English colonial efforts in the New World began in the late 1500s and were less centrally controlled by its monarchy than were the French and Spanish colonization efforts. They included settlement colonies and early efforts by semi-officially sponsored English pirates to prey on Spanish gold and silver shipments on the "Spanish Main," the regular shipping routes from Lima to Panama and from Mexico to Havana, and then directly across the vast expanse of the Atlantic Ocean to the Spanish port of Cádiz. Ultimately the English were able to take control of some Spanish Caribbean islands, notably Jamaica (1655), but by then they had focused their main settlement efforts on agricultural production along the eastern seaboard of North America. The first permanent English settlement was Jamestown, Virginia (founded 1607), the first of what later became the slave-worked plantation societies of the American South. It was followed by the foundation of more mercantile colonial cities in New England by English Protestant religious dissenters, where slavery was also often legal until at least the late eighteenth century. The largest of these was Boston (1630), founded by the Puritans as the chief city of the Massachusetts Bay Colony. To its south was New Amsterdam/New York, founded as an international trading center by the Dutch East India Company in 1624 at the mouth of Hudson River. Along with the entire Dutch colony of New Netherlands, which included parts of present-day eastern New York State and New Jersey, it was then taken over and renamed New York by the English in 1665. In the American South, the absence of towns in colonial Virginia was frequently noted, and fewer important cities emerged in that region during colonial times. Charleston, South Carolina (1670/1680), the main English colonial seaport and African slave market for the South Carolina rice plantations, was joined in 1733 by Savannah, a checkerboard grid-planned settlement founded by James Oglethorpe. It was located in what was then the southernmost English colony, Georgia.

All of these English colonial cities first developed as relatively small, pedestrian-scaled, and usually water-based settlements, often consisting of little more than a few fortified streets. Though parallel in many ways to provincial towns in Europe, and unlike most larger European cities, these English North American cities began to have grid plans somewhat like those of the older Spanish-founded cities of Latin America, despite the profound religious and cultural differences between the empires of England and Spain. The first use of the grid by English Puritan settlers was at New Haven, Connecticut (founded 1636), and grid plans were then used in quite different circumstances in Charleston and in Philadelphia (1681), the primary city of the Quaker-founded colony of Pennsylvania. Philadelphia became the most important city of British colonial America, and was briefly the capital of the United States after the American Revolutionary War (fig. 17). In these cities, British colonial efforts to segregate

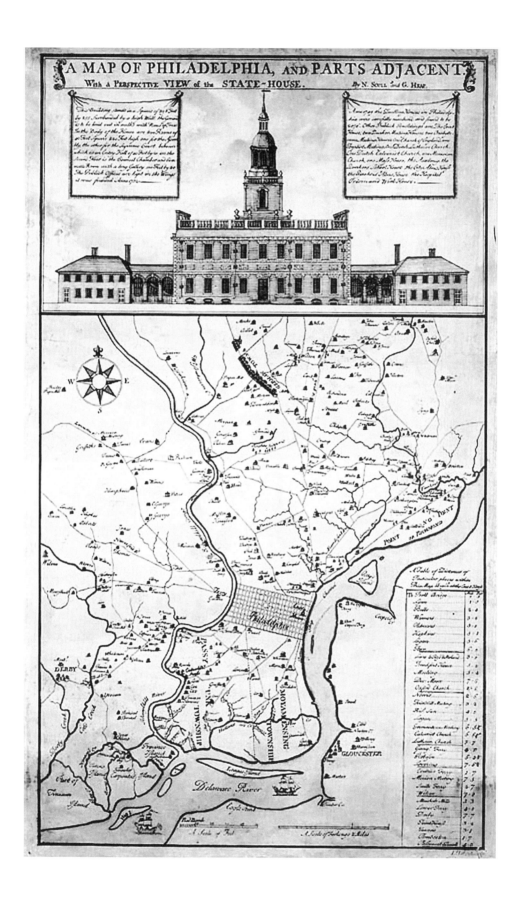

45

European populations from "native" populations broke down, as the enslavement of Africans meant that it was impossible to separate slaves from the households where they lived and worked.

After American independence was won from the British Empire in 1783, often violent American acquisitions of western lands began, which were then inhabited by many different groups of Native Americans. In 1785 the U.S. Congress passed a Land Ordinance to establish a uniform six-square-mile (1,554-hectare) survey grid to guide future American agricultural settlement west of Pennsylvania. From a "point of beginning" near East Liverpool on the Ohio border, this grid extended over a vast territory by the mid-nineteenth century and was the largest area in human history to be centrally planned at one time. The ordinances of 1785 and subsequent ones were the product of Thomas Jefferson's vision of the United States as a republic of free white independent farmers. Jefferson (1743–1826) was one of Virginia's largest plantation owners, a Virginia state legislator, the coauthor of the Declaration of Independence, and third president of the United States. Jefferson saw the America of the future as a country of both modest and wealthy white landowners who would need only to assemble when they had to make decisions together, meeting in somber, classically designed buildings that he thought should be located in small state capitals like Richmond, Virginia, far from the unrest and corruption of large imperial and commercial cities like London or Paris. Each new state was then to be organized into a series of counties, each with its own county seat with a courthouse square. Often unpretentious at the start, these county courthouses were rebuilt in grander ways later in the nineteenth century, often in a lavish Beaux-Arts style that sometimes rivaled that of state capitols.

In 1790, Jefferson's simple grid plans for the new national capital city of Washington in the District of Columbia were considered too modest, and so for the initial layout of the new capital, city officials turned to one by Pierre L'Enfant (1754–1825), a French-born engineer who had fought alongside the future first president, George Washington, in the American Revolutionary War. L'Enfant's 1791 plan for the new capital included large diagonal avenues, open squares, and hilltop sites for key monuments like the U.S. Capitol and the President's House, later the White House. These were organized in a monumental layout reminiscent of Versailles, where L'Enfant's father had worked as a landscape gardener. Yet despite the intended Baroque grandeur of Washington, it was Jefferson's democratic, and at the same time profoundly anti-urban, agrarian outlook that shaped the new nation. The 1785 national orthogonal survey grid established a pattern of rural townships, each divided into thirty-six sections of one square mile (640 acres/259 hectares), which was gradually extended across the continent.

In the vast, newly settled areas of the Midwest, South, and West, this new grid survey method was used instead of the earlier Eastern

Anglo-American irregular survey patterns, rooted in medieval English practices, which had set boundaries by "metes and bounds." The medieval system used natural landmarks such as streams, rocks, and trees to determine lot boundaries. Instead, the 1785 regular grid, inspired by the ancient Roman practice of centuration, organized the newly settled areas in the more regular way that was considered rational at the time, reducing conflict. It also facilitated the sale and development of land in frontier areas by large numbers of investors in and settlers coming from Europe and the U.S. East Coast. The grid was also structured so that funds from land sales of certain sections in each township were set aside to fund public schools. Four sections per township were also set aside to provide future revenues as the land came into productive agricultural use with settlement and rose in value.

Within the new territories of the United States, new states were created, beginning with Ohio in 1803, each with its own, usually centrally located, gridded state capital town like Columbus (founded 1812). Ohio's capital was followed by Indianapolis (1820); Jefferson City, Missouri (1821–25); Jackson, Mississippi (1822); and Lansing, Michigan (1835). Slavery, once legal in all the English and French colonies, was abolished in Pennsylvania in 1781, and that state's southern border, surveyed in colonial times and known after its surveyors as the Mason-Dixon Line, became the northern border of American states where slavery was still legal. This line was then extended roughly westward, following the Ohio River. Eventually tensions between North and South erupted over slavery's further westward expansion, which resulted in the American Civil War (1861–65). Slavery was abolished by President Abraham Lincoln with the Emancipation Proclamation in 1863, and during the mostly disastrous period of northern Reconstruction of the South (1865–77), it became a poorer region, avoided by northern investors. The South remained a predominantly agricultural region until the 1950s, and long-established rural patterns of racial segregation have continued to shape its development to the present.

Farther north, by 1850, two main bands of American pioneer urban settlement developed westward, one related to the Ohio River transportation corridor, which included the cities of Pittsburgh (1758), Cincinnati (1788), Louisville (1778), and St. Louis (1764), a French settlement that, like New Orleans, became an American city in 1803, after President Jefferson's purchase of the large Louisiana Territory from France. These cities developed for the most part along similar lines as did the existing mid-Atlantic cities of Philadelphia, Baltimore (1729), and Washington, reproducing not only their grid plans and brick row-house patterns, but also in many cases their urban governmental structures, local culture, and urban institutions such as fire departments, prisons, and hospitals. As this westward urban expansion took place, the older Eastern cities were themselves rapidly extending their land areas in similar ways.

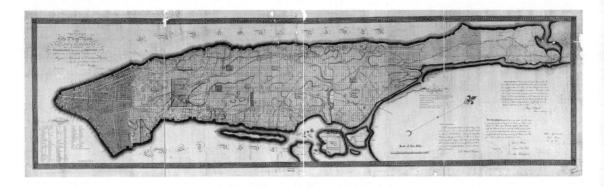

18. Commissioner's Plan of New York City, 1807–11 (Library of Congress, Geography and Map Division). This plan established the numbered streets and avenues north of Houston Street to West 155th Street.

The new urban grids, like those of the Commissioner's Plan of New York City (1807–11), which expanded the nation's largest city northward along numbered streets and avenues north of Houston Street, differed from those of the Spanish Laws of the Indies or earlier European-founded colonial cities. The New York City grid made little provision for either central plazas or the shared common grazing areas often found in earlier colonial settlements (fig. 18). Its street grid was instead conceptualized as a neutral instrument to facilitate real estate sales and development, with the assumption that the city could continue to grow endlessly outward from its point of initial settlement by the Dutch below Wall Street. In most cities, early platting set standard urban lot sizes, which in New York after 1811 measured 25 × 100 feet (7.62 × 30.48 meters), and usually slightly larger in western cities. For reasons of both transportation and defense, the new cities were typically sited on a river or lakeshore. As in New York, in their early years these cities' newly laid out streets were often numbered, and sometimes, as in St. Louis, they also used the tree-street names of central Philadelphia, or the names of early presidents.

In the northern tier of settlement that stretched from New England and New York State through the upper Midwest, the fever of new town-building from the 1810s onward was stimulated by the building of canals and then, by the 1830s, railroads. Canal networks, which had originated in Mesopotamia and had existed in China and some other places for centuries, were a much more efficient means of internal transportation than dirt roads. Their development began in North America in the late eighteenth century, and followed similar patterns as in Britain. The financing and construction of them reached their heyday in the 1820s and 1830s. In 1825 the Erie Canal opened, linking the agricultural areas of the upper Midwest to New York City by way of Buffalo (founded 1801), Albany, and the Hudson River, giving New York City a decisive commercial advantage over the Mississippi River port of New Orleans, which nonetheless remained the fifth-largest city in the country in 1850. In the new northern cities of upstate New York and near the Great Lakes, the physical form of these new cities typically consisted of houses and small commercial buildings built of wood rather than brick.

By the 1830s "balloon framing," still the standard form of American residential construction, had begun to be used in Chicago, though it may either have developed earlier in upstate New York or have derived from Mississippi Valley colonial French wood-construction methods that used vertical timber posts. The introduction of industrial processes of lumber milling, which allowed for the sale and use of standard precut pieces of wood like two-by-fours and other pieces of "dimension lumber," as well as the new availability of inexpensive standard metal nails to connect them into frames, made wood residential construction a cheap and flexible way of building in new fast-growing settlements like Buffalo, Cleveland (founded 1796), Detroit, and Chicago (1830).

By 1850 the government of the United States had claimed its continental national territory, which in various places had borne the imprint of more than two hundred years of European colonization and settlement and overlaid many indigenous cultures. The interactions of European settlers and enslaved and free Africans throughout the Americas had laid the basis for hemispheric demographic patterns that differed profoundly from those of most of the rest of the world. Portuguese, French, Dutch, German, and British urban and architectural patterns had also been introduced, with many local variations, and the social and physical underpinnings were in place for the immense urban growth that was already beginning to occur.

NEW TECHNOLOGIES AND NORTH AMERICAN URBAN CHANGE AFTER 1850

In most North American cities, whether in the mid-Atlantic corridor, which extended along the Ohio River to St. Louis, or in the northern tier of fertile agricultural land and waterways that extended out from Ohio to Minnesota and beyond, street grids, rectangular lots, and standard simple wood or brick construction practices determined most of the visible urban outcomes. "Architecture," as it was then understood, was generally confined to a few monumental structures like fortifications, churches, capitols, courthouses, and prisons, some of which still survive. Urban patterns remained compact as the result of technical limitations, which included the absence of streetcars, indoor plumbing, indoor toilets, and central heating. All of this began to change dramatically in the early to mid-nineteenth century as a series of both technical and social transformations affected urban patterns. The invention of the steamboat in the 1810s reshaped water transport, just before passenger and freight railway networks started to operate by the 1830s. Ambitious plans to link eastern seaport cities by rail to the Midwest began to be carried out, as well as an 1833 railroad linking Charleston and Savannah to Hamburg, now North Augusta, South Carolina.

Within cities, new horse-drawn rail services supplemented stage coaches and ferries, paralleling similar transformations in England, and steam passenger railways started operating in the 1820s. As in England, urban water supply and sewer systems also began to be improved, leading to public works like New York City's Croton Aqueduct (1842), which provided one of the first dependable supplies of clean water for an American city. It consisted of forty-one miles (65 kilometers) of cast-iron pipes set in brick masonry, running from the Croton Dam in Westchester County across the High Bridge aqueduct over the Harlem River, to a new reservoir in what later became Central Park, and then south to a distributing reservoir at 42nd Street, on the site of what is now the New York Public Library.

Additional new technologies also augmented the urban transformations then well under way. These included the wireless telegraph, first used by the U.S. Post Office in 1844 to send a short written message between Washington and Baltimore. Also important was the use of Bessemer steel, produced by a process invented in the 1850s that made iron fireproof at high temperatures. It began to be used for railroad tracks and in the framing of bridges like the Eads Bridge over the Mississippi at St. Louis (1874) and in the production of the steel cables of John Roebling's Brooklyn Bridge (1876), which joined the then-separate cities of New York and Brooklyn. These technologies made faster and more extensive intercity railway networks profitable, like the ones that crossed mountains and immense deserts, linking the eastern cities to California beginning in 1869. The national railroads also led to the introduction of the four standard American time zones by 1883, as well as to establishing the foundations for a national urban industrial and consumer economy that would by 1900 be no longer primarily based on agriculture.

This post–Civil War economy instead became centered on rail transport and large industrial enterprises, which were often administered from the major rail-based cities, where the offices of banking, finance, and insurance companies were also located. These kinds of firms began to require larger office spaces than could be housed in small four- to five-story brick commercial structures. The safety passenger elevator, invented by Elisha Graves Otis in 1853, and displayed at the New York Exhibition in 1854, was first used in John Gaynor's cast-iron-fronted Haughwout Building at Broadway and Broome Street in New York in 1857. With the post–Civil War economic boom, when the rail-based northern industrial cities began to grow rapidly, developers found that higher-floor office space served by luxurious and reliable passenger elevators was actually more popular than office space closer to the street. This reversed traditional hierarchies that had placed the greatest real estate value on the floors that were one or two flights above street level. The use of elevators soon led to the construction of many early skyscrapers (a term introduced at this time) in New York City and then, after 1880, in Chicago, where by the mid-1880s Bessemer steel framing began to be used for their construction.

Skyscrapers began to alter the appearance of these major American cities, creating the new phenomenon of the "skyline," first noted in New York in the 1880s, and further increasing the already rising land values in many downtowns. New York City had nothing taller than church spires and an occasional large warehouse or smokestack until the 1870s, but by the 1880s it was already developing the iconic skyscraper image of lower Manhattan, augmented by the French sculptor Frédéric Auguste Bartholdi's *Statue of Liberty* (1886), sited on an island in New York Harbor. Smaller new skyscraper downtowns also appeared in northeastern and midwestern cities, as well as in San Francisco, so renamed in 1847, just before it became part of the United States at the end of the Mexican War (1845–48). A Spanish mission and the small village of Yerba Buena had been established there in 1776, which had then begun to develop as an international trading center while still under Mexican rule in the 1830s. After the 1848 Gold Rush, San Francisco, which then was "the city" to everyone in business on the West Coast, grew rapidly as the key commercial hub of the West. It was also one of the few American cities to begin hosting a large Chinese immigrant population in the nineteenth century, which faced considerable racial discrimination from the American settlers.

By 1879, gas street lighting, first used in London in 1807, also began to be widely introduced in North American cities. Lighting using electric current was developed over the course of the nineteenth century, and arc lights had been used experimentally to light the National Gallery in London in the 1850s and along the Avenue de l'Opéra in Paris in 1878. Electricity's urban commercial potential was finally tapped by Thomas Edison, a Milan, Ohio-born entrepreneur, inventor, and expert on telegraph technologies. After developing one of the first incandescent light bulbs in 1879, Edison convinced investors to build a central electric generating station at 255–257 Pearl Street in lower Manhattan in 1882. This allowed electric power to be distributed to a one-square-mile (259-hectare) area extending north from Wall Street along the East River to Peck Slip and Spruce Street, beginning the process of electrification that has continued around the world to the present. In the same year, Edison was the instigator of a steam-powered electrical generating station built in London on Holborn Viaduct, and by 1887 there were 121 Edison Electric Company power-generating stations. His inventions also included the first phonograph to record sound, in 1878, and the first movie camera, introduced in 1891. By 1894 there were public screenings of motion pictures in Europe and the United States, and in Mumbai soon after. Electrification also made possible electric streetcar lines, which began experimentally in Berlin in 1879 and which were quickly expanded to form networks in various cities, including one of the first in Richmond, Virginia.

19. Map of Chicago, showing sewers, paved streets, and bridges, 1873 (Homer Hoyt, *100 Years of Land Values in Chicago* [Chicago: University of Chicago Press, 1933], 92).

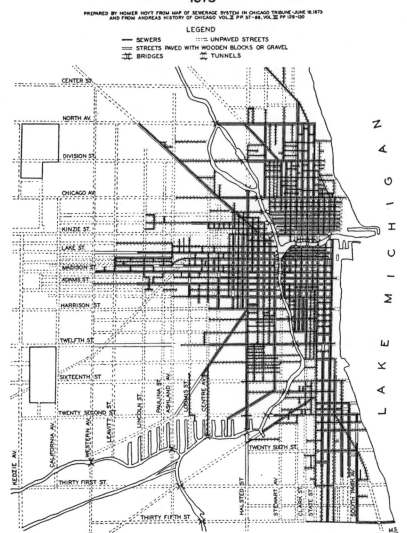

These innovations both intensified the real estate value of central urban areas and led to even more land being developed farther out from urban centers, as commuting times decreased and more modern conveniences like flush toilets became available in new suburban areas. In many cities, notably in Boston and in Chicago, these new streetcar suburbs were typically built up with inexpensive wood-framed houses and small apartment and commercial buildings, constructed a few at a time by many small contractors, who were often recent European immigrants. These areas were accessed by horsecar and eventually streetcar lines laid along the major streets, with water, sewer, and natural gas lines installed beneath. Chicago was first platted with a grid of streets 60 feet (18.3

meters) wide in 1830 along the Chicago River, around the junction of its north and south branches west of State Street (fig. 19). The city grew rapidly in all directions as railway lines from northeastern coastal cities made it their western terminus, where trains were unloaded and then reloaded at some of its many railway stations if continuing on farther west.

New rail lines were then extended westward from Chicago to Salt Lake City (founded 1847), Omaha (1854), Kansas City (1853), Denver (1858), and in 1869 to Sacramento (1850) and San Francisco. Many other railway cities were also platted along similar lines beginning in the 1830s, including Atlanta (1837), Houston (1836), and Dallas (1841), which all grew modestly after the Civil War with the expansion of the national railroad networks but remained minor regional centers until after World War II. Like Chicago, these cities were both important distribution centers for agricultural products drawn from large surrounding areas and were also centers of manufacturing, which drew in immigrants from elsewhere.

The many employment opportunities in these fast-growing cities drew both in-migrants from the American countryside and European immigrants, many of them initially from Ireland and German-speaking countries. Chicago grew the most rapidly, rising from 30,000 people in 1850 to almost 300,000 by 1870, when it overtook St. Louis in population and displaced it as the main city of the American West. In 1871 a huge fire destroyed many of Chicago's wooden buildings, but the city was rapidly rebuilt in more substantial materials. By the 1880s steel framing allowed for the construction of downtown business buildings much taller than anything previously built by humans (except for a small number of cathedral spires and the like) and some now-demolished and largely forgotten skyscrapers in lower Manhattan built in the previous decade (fig. 20).

These new business establishments were also where the telegraph, which could transmit text wirelessly only, began to be supplemented by the voice-transmitting telephone, first exhibited at the Philadelphia

20. Some of the first skyscrapers in the world (left to right, from New York City Hall, 1802–12): George B. Post, World (Pulitzer) Building, 1889–90, demolished; R. M. Hunt, New York Tribune Building, 1873, demolished.

Centennial exhibition in 1876, along with the typewriter, early electric lights, Heinz ketchup, and kudzu, an invasive vine then valued for its erosion-controlling properties. This exhibition was also notable for its re-creation of an early American colonial kitchen, which started the fashion of reviving American eighteenth-century English colonial architecture and decoration, seemingly taking the opposite direction culturally from the unprecedented technological developments also on display at the exhibition.

North American railroad cities were also beginning to differ in many social and political aspects from cities of the past. They rapidly assimilated large numbers of mostly European immigrants, creating new urban cultures centered not on traditional religious and craft activities, but on business and recreation. Mass sports like baseball developed in these cities, and the urban elites enthusiastically imported the European Enlightenment ideas of the art museum, the public library, and the research university, the latter mostly based on German models. More traditional popular institutions also greatly expanded as well, ranging from taverns to churches, clubs, and trade schools. These cities offered unprecedented economic opportunities for millions, but also generated new forms of social conflict and often had extremely overcrowded and unsanitary living conditions. They consumed vast amounts of fossil fuels, notably coal, which, as in London and other British cities, generated permanently smoky environments that made noon look like nighttime, and at the same time provided unprecedented levels of bodily comfort for those residents able to pay their rent, taxes, and utility bills.

By the end of the nineteenth century, a long list of technical improvements had transformed American urban life. These included clean water supplies and municipal sewer systems; communication technologies such as the telegraph, telephone, photography, and film; as well as safe passenger elevators, steel framing, gas lighting, and electricity. These were centrally important to the emergence of both new building types like the skyscraper, and to new ways of living in bucolic suburban environments that were increasingly the aspiration of a large and rising middle class.

THE AMERICAN PARKS MOVEMENT

By the 1880s in Chicago, speculative builders like S. E. Gross were able to build entire outlying urban districts of wooden cottages, served by streetcars and rail lines and with sewer, water, and gas connections to eager working-class buyers. These districts—which included parts of the Lakeview neighborhood within the Chicago city limits (which were then extended by incorporation to include much of Chicago's present area in 1889) as well as new inner suburbs like Brookfield—were the beginnings of the larger-scale mass suburban developments that characterized many American cities by the twentieth century. The many social and public health problems in their older central areas were often identified as stemming largely from overcrowding and a lack of access to nature. These were seen as root causes of urban social problems, including crime, disease outbreaks, and family breakdown, and the solution for many seemed to be clearly to reduce residential densities and to increase open space and greenery within urban environments.

In the earlier decades of the nineteenth century, models for how to do this had typically followed pioneering European examples such as Regent's Park in London (founded 1819) and Père Lachaise cemetery in Paris (1804), the first garden cemetery. To reduce the spread of epidemics, sanitary experts advocated that garden cemeteries should be created at the urban periphery, as at the first one in the United States, Mount Auburn Cemetery (1836) near Boston. The design of the garden cemeteries was based on that of the grounds of eighteenth-century European estates, called "parks," a term that originally referred to a forested hunting area. These were often created in the 1700s by evicting peasants from their small and inefficient plots, a process called "enclosure." These developments remained well outside of cities proper until the mid-nineteenth century, but this "pastoral ideal" exerted a strong cultural influence as cities were rapidly growing along denser and more traditional lines. By the 1850s the wealthy and socially prominent began to move to rail-accessible suburban enclaves designed like English pastoral estates. There were several such suburbs begun even before 1860. Llewellyn Park, developed by Llewellyn S. Haskell some twelve miles (19.3 kilometers) west of Manhattan in Orange, New Jersey, in 1853, and designed by Alexander Jackson Davis (1803–1892), was an early and influential example of an elite suburb laid out in a parklike way in relation to natural features. It included a fifty-acre (20.2-hectare) central area known as the "Ramble." Like the garden cemeteries, its naturalistic design was inspired by eighteenth-century English country estates, which sought to appear simply as unbuilt natural enclaves, rather than the highly designed and expensively constructed environments that they in fact were.

A key proponent of these new pastoral directions in the United States was Andrew Jackson Downing (1815–1852), a landscape gardener and horticulturalist. Downing's publications were American versions of the writings of English authors such as J. C. Loudon, and were put forth at the same time as the ecstatic visions of the Hudson River School painters and the philosophy of Transcendentalism articulated by Ralph Waldo Emerson and his associates. In the 1840s Downing published popular treatises and pattern books like his widely read *Architecture of Country Houses,* which advised that middle-class homeowners surround their family life with lawns, trees, flowers, and views of nature. Downing hired the young English architect Calvert Vaux (1824–1895) as a design associate in 1850 for his growing practice designing the landscaped grounds of large Hudson

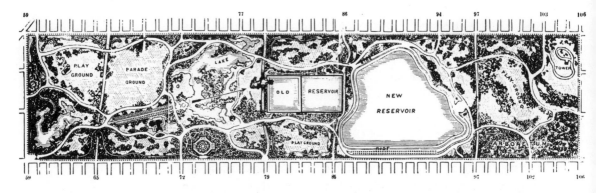

21. Frederick Law Olmsted and Calvert Vaux, "Greensward" plan for Central Park, New York, 1858 (Library of Congress, Geography and Map Division).

River estates. Downing was then commissioned by President Millard Fillmore to redesign the area between the White House and the U.S. Capitol as a picturesque pastoral landscape. In 1851 Downing also advocated that New York City (which then included only Manhattan and part of the South Bronx) acquire a large tract of land at the edge of its built-up area for a public park. This idea was strongly supported by advocates of public health, as well as by some urban real estate developers. Urban public parks were then rare, mostly found only in a few German and English cities. The model Downing may have had in mind was Joseph Paxton's Birkenhead Park (founded 1845), located in a suburb of Liverpool.

Downing was killed in a steamboat accident in 1852, but his involvement with park design in New York City was continued by Vaux. In 1853 the New York State legislature passed an act approving the city's acquisition of the land for the new park, then mostly still a rough landscape unsuitable for either agriculture or urban development, and inhabited in part by the residents of a racially mixed illegal informal settlement. The city then purchased almost 800 acres (324 hectares) for the proposed Central Park, and Vaux convinced the city to hold a competition for its design. He also approached Frederick Law Olmsted (1822–1903), a former journalist and sometime gentleman farmer then working as the superintendent of the site-clearing crews for the proposed park. In 1858 Olmsted and Vaux submitted a design they called "Greensward," which was then selected and became the basis for one of the most successful landscape designs in history (fig. 21). Olmsted was familiar with Downing's work and ideas, and as a journalist had visited gardens in Europe in the 1850s, including Regent's Park in London and Birkenhead Park. In his 1858 report on Central Park, Olmsted set out the sequence of its construction, beginning with drainage and heavy grading and then continuing through soil enrichment to the building of roads and walks, including many bridges designed by Vaux. This was followed by the planting of 240,000 new trees and shrubs, and the construction of picturesque park structures, many of which survive to this day.

Olmsted and Vaux's design for the 843 acres (341 hectares) of Central Park used patterns from earlier English park design, but also introduced the idea of organizing park circulation by allowing for different speeds

Cities in the Americas and the International Influence of the City Beautiful Movement

of traffic. These ranged from the high-speed open cut routes directly across the park for business traffic; to the park drives, intended for carriages; to the many winding pedestrian paths that bridged over or tunneled under the park drives to avoid accidents. Olmsted, who coined the term "landscape architecture" early in the Central Park design process, also designed many different kinds of environments in the one-half mile by two-and-a-half mile (0.8 × 4 kilometer) rectangular park, from the rugged naturalistic terrain of the Ramble to the French formality of the Mall, which terminated in a classical fountain, the Bethesda Terrace. Large areas like the Sheep Meadow were also set aside for what Olmsted envisioned would be walks and for the contemplation of natural beauty as an antidote to the noise and relentless commercial competition of the dense, dirty, and economically growing city. All of this required extensive excavation and site grading, creating an artificial landscape that nonetheless seemed to be a product of nature.

After the success of their Central Park design, the Olmsted and Vaux partnership designed some fifty urban parks, parkways, and residential suburb projects that set a pattern for American metropolitan development that in some ways continues to the present. In 1860 they were commissioned to lay out new streets in northern Manhattan, above West

22. Frederick Law Olmsted, Riverside, Illinois, 1869. The left half of the plan was not built, but was later developed by S. E. Gross on a grid plan as part of Grossdale, incorporated in 1893, and renamed Brookfield in 1905.

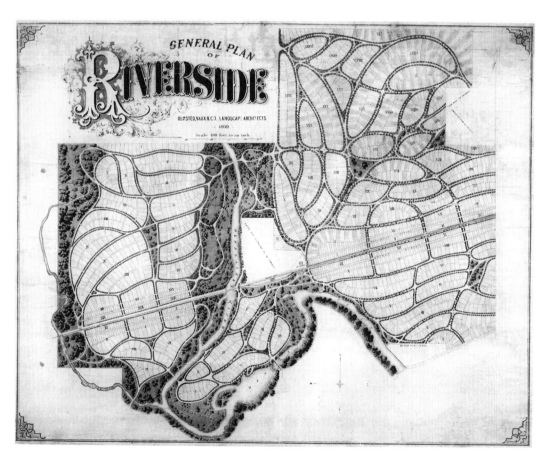

155th Street, where the 1807–11 grid plan had ended. Olmsted began to articulate the importance of transportation routes in shaping future development, and around the same time he was commissioned to plan a neighborhood near the new College of California in Berkeley. There he first argued that regional climate as well as site topography should guide landscape design, and he suggested linking the new East Bay development to Oakland and the ferry landings to San Francisco with a landscaped parkway. In 1865 Olmsted and Vaux were commissioned to design Prospect Park in Brooklyn, then a large separate city, producing another canonical American park design. They also proposed a series of boulevards adjacent to it in the Eastern Parkway district (1868), which linked the new park to areas of outlying development to the east, extending the park's natural qualities throughout the city. The state law that created the Eastern Parkway district prohibited business uses in residential areas and required that all construction be set back to at least 30 feet (9.2 meters) from the street line. Olmsted also advocated that there be at least 50 to 100 feet (15.25 to 30.5 meters) between the houses. Both measures anticipated the American suburban zoning laws that began to be passed after 1909. These projects were also in part the result of Olmsted's trip to Paris in 1859, where he had met with Haussmann's associate Jean-Charles Alphand and admired the new avenue Foch (then called the avenue de l'Impératrice), which led to the Arc de Triomphe in the Place d'Étoile. Tree-lined, this new Parisian boulevard was 459 feet (140 meters) wide and had main and secondary roadways for different speeds of traffic, and was faced with imposing urban mansions.

Olmsted's work anticipated the continuing enlargement of American "metropolitan towns." He saw clearly that new parks and parkways increased property values at the urban periphery. In 1867 the city of Buffalo commissioned Olmsted and Vaux to design not only several new parks, including Delaware Park, but also a new tree-lined parkway system to link them through new neighborhoods of houses, sited with required setbacks from the street. The following year Olmsted, by then increasingly working on his own, was commissioned to design an influential parklike commuter suburb near Chicago, to be called Riverside. The site was a 1,600-acre (648-hectare) tract along the Des Plaines River some eleven miles (18 kilometers) west of the center of Chicago, then not yet called the Loop. On his first site visit, Olmsted was taken aback by the flatness of the Chicago area but recognized that the mix of elms and oaks along the rugged banks of the river could become a public ground, with carriage drives and walkways creating an organizing structure for an attractive commuter suburb a short train ride from Chicago (fig. 22). He argued that this new environment would combine the advantages of urban and rural life. Olmsted's partnership with Vaux ended in 1872, but his firm, which he moved to the Boston suburb of Brookline in 1883, received some 550 commissions before his death in 1903.

In 1878 Olmsted was commissioned to extend Commonwealth Avenue in Boston into the Muddy River area, a tidal flat. He designed the new Fenway as a parkway linking what would become one of Boston's cultural centers to the new 520-acre (210-hectare) Franklin Park (built in 1885), near where Olmsted had in 1872 laid out the grounds of the Arnold Arboretum. Many other cities commissioned the Olmsted firm as well, with widely admired projects that ranged from the original Stanford University campus in Palo Alto (1891) and some preliminary planning for Golden Gate Park in San Francisco, to Riverside Park in New York and Mount Royal Park in Montreal, which was then the center of English-speaking business activity in Canada. Other Olmsted landscape designs include preliminary sketches for Belle Isle in Detroit, and new parks and parkways on the Buffalo and Boston Fenway model in Chicago, Milwaukee, Louisville, and Rochester.

A former apprentice of Olmsted, Charles Eliot (1859–1897), opened his own office in Boston in 1886, where he became a vigorous champion of the preservation of unbuilt areas in fast-growing American metropolitan areas. His ideas led to the passage of Massachusetts state legislation allowing for the creation of the Trustees of Public Reservations in 1891, the first organization to acquire natural and historic places and administer them for public access. This effort, which also inspired the National Trust in Britain, led to the creation of the Boston Metropolitan Park system in 1893. Eliot joined the Olmsted firm as a partner that same year, and soon took a leading role, doing extensive work for the Boston Metropolitan Commission using an early "natural systems" approach to landscape design and management before his untimely death in 1897. The firm was then continued by Olmsted's son Frederick Law Olmsted, Jr. (1870–1957), and his nephew John Charles Olmsted (1852–1920).

In the decades after Olmsted and Vaux's design for Central Park was selected, the American parks movement transformed the American metropolitan environment. Olmsted's park, parkway, and residential suburban planning set design patterns that to some extent still have worldwide influence today. The work of Charles Eliot and the Olmsted descendants was also centrally important for efforts to protect large tracts of land in expanding metropolitan areas from development, and led directly to the establishment of the first professional degree program in landscape architecture at Harvard University in 1900, founded by Frederick Law Olmsted, Jr.

THE CITY BEAUTIFUL MOVEMENT, 1893–1940

The rapid technical and social changes of the nineteenth century, many of them occurring in just a few decades before and after the Civil War, created congested, chaotic, and unsanitary central cities unlike anything ever seen before. These conditions led to demands from business and

23. Dankmar Adler and Louis Sullivan, Wainwright Building steel frame under construction, St. Louis, 1891 (*Engineering Magazine*, 1892). One of the first tall office buildings whose exterior design was intended to celebrate its height.

cultural elites by the 1890s for more orderly, and perhaps more acceptably traditional, urban forms. Despite the influential pioneering innovations in steel-framed skyscraper design of Louis Sullivan (1856–1924) and his Chicago contemporaries (fig. 23), other architects stepped forward to instead adapt classical models of urbanism to the new urban world of technology, social transformation, and mass entertainment and consumerism. The 1893 World's Columbian Exposition in Chicago, usually known as the Chicago Fair, was overseen by Chicago architect Daniel H. Burnham (1846–1921) and included the New York architects McKim, Mead, and White. It crystallized a way of designing highly controlled urban environments as popular spectacles, sited in a parklike setting well away from both smoky factories and downtown congestion (fig. 24). Its central court was lined with monumental classical buildings housing exhibitions of various agricultural and industrial products, centered on a triumphal arch and a giant statue of the goddess *The Republic* by Daniel Chester French.

After 1900 the Fair's success gave rise to a planning movement known as the City Beautiful movement. The Fair's chief coordinating architects, Burnham and Charles Follen McKim, along with landscape architect Frederick Law Olmsted, Jr., went on to oversee a new plan for Washington, D.C., in 1901–2 as members of the Senate Park Commission to replan the symbolic center of the nation (fig. 25). Their McMillan Plan,

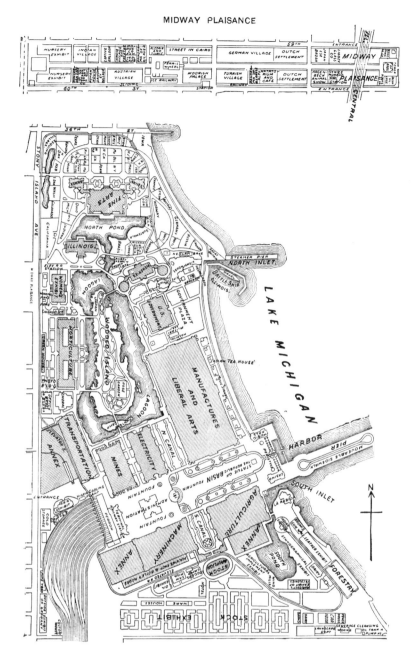

24. D. H. Burnham et al., Plan of the World's Columbian Exhibition, Chicago, 1893 (*Shepp's World's Fair Illustrated* [Chicago: Globe Bible, 1893], 17).

advocated by Senator James McMillan of Michigan, a railroad president and banker, was intended to extend and improve Pierre L'Enfant's 1791 Plan. The National Mall had been partially landscaped by A. J. Downing in 1850, but since then it had also filled in with random storage and agricultural uses, including an elevated railway line in front of the Capitol. To prepare their plan, the designers visited Paris, Rome, Venice, Vienna, Budapest, Frankfurt, Berlin, and London. On their return, Burnham convinced the president of the Pennsylvania Railroad to fund putting the elevated line in front of the Capitol into a tunnel (now Interstate

395), allowing for the redesign of the Mall in a way similar to how it still appears today. Other parts of the plan called for two new monuments on the recently reclaimed 100 acres (40.4 hectares) of land west of the Washington Monument (1848–84).

One, "a Pantheon to illustrious men of the nation," was to be similar to McKim, Mead & White's Hall of Fame terrace at New York University's Bronx campus (1894, now Bronx Community College). It was to be sited on an axis south of the White House, where the Jefferson Memorial was later built (1935–43). The other was to be a Lincoln Memorial (1914–22), with a reflecting pool in front and a new memorial bridge across the Potomac River to Arlington National Cemetery beyond. New museums and government buildings were to line the Mall, and new executive office buildings were called for around Lafayette Square, north of the White House. The plan also included a new park network proposed by Olmsted, Jr., to follow existing waterways, like Rock Creek Park, as well as new boulevards and a new Union Station linked by a new Senate Park to the Capitol. This station was designed by Burnham's firm, and was a new gateway to the city for most visitors in this still mostly pre-automobile era.

Most of the McMillan Plan of Washington was completed by 1940. In the early 1900s it inspired many clients to commission D. H. Burnham and Company and the firm of McKim, Mead & White, as well as others, for similar City Beautiful projects. Burnham prepared the Group Plan for Cleveland in 1903, much of it carried out by other architects in the following years, and designed a master plan for San Francisco in 1905. The latter could have been implemented after the massively destructive earthquake and fire of 1906, but there was no mechanism to replat the existing streets and property lines according to the new plan in a generally agreed-upon

Cities in the Americas and the International Influence of the City Beautiful Movement

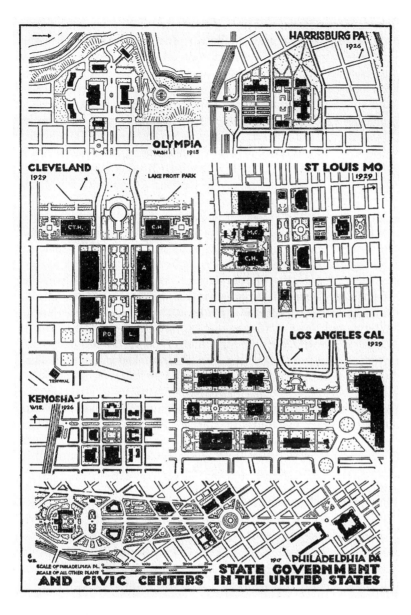

26. American City Beautiful Civic Centers (Thomas Adams, *Outline of Town and City Planning* [New York: Russell Sage Foundation, 1935], 235).

way. Only the Civic Center complex, designed by other architects, and the circular drive and stepped terraces of Telegraph Hill resulted from Burnham's proposals. Many other American cities, such as St. Louis, Kansas City, Indianapolis, Denver, Los Angeles, and Philadelphia, then also commissioned and built projects by others for elaborate classical civic centers, museums, libraries, boulevards, and public schools (fig. 26).

The City Beautiful Movement was less successful in reorganizing the dense grid-patterned urbanism of Manhattan, where high land values made it almost impossible to create the grand new boulevards and public spaces that were being built in other cities at the time. Nonetheless, impressive new museums, libraries, public schools, parks, and train stations

EXPRESS CONCOURSE
MAIN WAITING ROOM
RESTAURANT
TO ALL SUBWAYS
TO 42ND STREET
EXPRESS TRAIN ROOM
CAB DRIVE
SUBURBAN CONCOURSE
SUBURBAN RAMP
INTERBORO SUBWAY
RAMP FROM SUBURBAN TRAINS
TO INCOMING STATION AND STREET
HUDSON & MANHATTAN TUNNEL
SUBURBAN TRAIN ROOM
BELMONT TUNNEL

27. Reed & Stem; Warren & Wetmore, Grand Central Terminal, New York, 1903–14 (Avery Architectural and Fine Arts Library, Columbia University).

were constructed across the five boroughs in this era, many of them the products of the philanthropy of the immense new wealth of the "robber barons," industrialists and financial speculators who had profited enormously from the industrial growth of the country since 1865. A notable and still-functioning train station from this era is Grand Central Terminal (1903–14), designed by a joint venture of the Minneapolis firm Reed and Stem and the New York society architects Warren and Wetmore (fig. 27).

After Washington, D.C., the culmination of the City Beautiful movement was the 1909 *Plan of Chicago* by Burnham and Edward H. Bennett (1874–1954), commissioned by the Commercial Club of Chicago. This group included some of the leaders of the largest businesses in the city, including Charles Dyer Norton (1871–1922), an insurance executive; Frederic A. Delano (1863–1953), then president of the Wabash Railroad, who was concerned about rail congestion in the Chicago area; and merchant Charles A. Wacker. Burnham's plan was unprecedented in examining and making planning proposals for the network of rail routes, highways, and potential parkways and forest preserves in the area fifty to sixty miles (81–97 kilometers) from the Loop, then about a two-hour drive for those few who owned automobiles. Along with its more well-known monumental civic center and lakefront aspects, the plan also proposed the creation of a central clearing and warehouse storage yard in the southwestern part of the city, linked by new rail lines to improved harbor facilities along Lake Michigan. The plan also included a proposal for new parklands to the west, extending the 1904 proposal of Dwight Perkins to set aside from development what would become the Chicago Forest Preserves, designed by landscape architect Jens Jensen (1860–1951).

Cities in the Americas and the International Influence of the City Beautiful Movement

With their Plan of Chicago, Burnham and his associates set out in more detail the schematic regional proposals made for new parkways in the 1907 Plan of St. Louis, and produced the first full regional plan for an American city. Unlike many later such plans, many of Burnham's proposals were actually carried out, some by his associate Edward H. Bennett, who designed most of the bridges and embankments of the Chicago River (1913–27), as well as the extension of North Michigan Avenue from the Loop (fig. 28). The plan's proposals also led to the construction of Navy Pier, Grant and Burnham Parks, new cultural institutions such as the Museum of Natural History and Shedd Aquarium, and the construction of Northerly Island, envisioned in the plan as one of a chain of islands to be built in Lake Michigan. Its general vision also prompted the eventual decking in the 1930s over the Illinois Central Railroad tracks along the lakefront to create the platform for what is now known as Millennium Park (2000).

At the same time, aspects of Chicago's later development differed radically from the Plan of Chicago. The monumental civic center that Burnham proposed at Halsted and Congress Streets was not built, and instead became the site of the "Chicago Circle" interstate interchange between Interstates 94 and 290. The many high-rises built since 1909 do not give the city the Paris-like appearance of uniform facades that Burnham had intended. Nevertheless, in the 1980s and 1990s, the 1909 Plan of Chicago was revived as a reference point for New Urbanism in Chicago, and the neo-Beaux-Arts design of the Harold Washington Library (Hammond, Beeby, Babka, 1988–91) and many urban residential developments reflect its continuing influence.

City Beautiful neoclassical planning strategies and new American building technologies also began to be exported internationally after the American victory over Spain in the Spanish-American War of 1898. Manila, the capital of the Philippines, a Spanish colony since the 1500s, was then controlled by the United States from 1898 to 1942, and a plan for it was made by Burnham in 1904. He was also commissioned to do a plan for the Philippine summer capital of Baguio, where he proposed a new street plan and made recommendations for siting new parks, railway lines, and public buildings in ways that were similar to some of his American plans. As in several other of his plans, including the one for Chicago from 1909, Burnham recommended tree-lined, diagonal Paris-like boulevards radiating from the civic core and cutting across the street grid. This would not only allow for the construction (ideally, at least) of many impressive new street-fronted buildings, but would also speed traffic circulation across the city.

Burnham also recommended that the old Spanish-style houses of Manila should be "taken as examples of future structures" to be built there, and suggested that abundant foliage be planted and that fountains be installed. Like Olmsted, he advocated that the waterfront areas

D.H.BURNHAM & E.H.BENNETT -Consultants- 1908

28. D. H. Burnham and Co., *Plan of Chicago* (Chicago: Commercial Club, 1909).

be developed as public parks, and he proposed new parks at the outskirts of the city, as well as moderate-size playing fields in denser urban areas. For the old Spanish city he recommended that the sixteenth-century walls be retained, but that the adjacent moat be filled in to create circular parks. He also recommended that the existing urban canal system (*los esteros*) be renovated and used as a transportation system. Burnham himself did not stay long in the Philippines, but turned the detailed design work over to the Beaux-Arts educated Yale graduate William E. Parsons (1872–1939), who designed many buildings in Manila in the following decades.

Burnham's work also anticipated many other early-twentieth-century urban design practices, though it did not immediately lead to the creation of American professional training programs in planning or urban design. His example of exporting City Beautiful ideas and American building technologies into the Philippines had immediate outcomes elsewhere, notably in Puerto Rico, another former Spanish colony, which became part of the United States after 1898, and in Cuba, which, though it became a nominally independent republic, was politically under U.S. influence until 1959. In Havana, Colonel George Waring, Jr. (1833–1898), an American sanitary engineer who had designed the municipal sewer systems in Memphis and New Orleans, was commissioned not only to design a new sewer system but also to plan a new electric grid, as well as design new tram and telephone services. As part of this effort, American engineers designed the Havana Malecón, a new oceanfront boulevard and park; and American architects like Bertrand Grosvesnor Goodhue and the firm of McKim, Mead & White, as well as other prominent New York firms, designed many new buildings there. By 1925, when Jean Claude Forestier (1861–1930) was commissioned by the president of Cuba to prepare his celebrated master plan for Havana, the French architect's work combined Beaux-Arts design with American technical innovations and with the park and parkway planning practices of the Olmsteds.

URBANISME IN FRANCE, 1901–39

Despite the urban sites of most Beaux-Arts projects, the École des Beaux-Arts itself did not have any formal training programs in urban design before 1917. Julien Guadet (1834–1908), professor of architectural theory at the school, who wrote all the annual student design competition programs from 1894 to 1908, rejected the idea that cities could be conceptualized as overall objects of design. Instead of urbanism, he favored an "architecture of public ways," which would be sited within urban environments that had grown gradually over time by "chance and circumstance." Guadet had little interest in the social or historical aspects of architecture, and saw new materials such as iron as only appropriate for utilitarian structures. Instead, he continued the Beaux-Arts practice of emphasizing the importance of traditional cut stone as the most suitable architectural material, which he thought should still be correctly used following canonical classical principles. By 1910 all of these attitudes began to be challenged from urbanistic, social, and technical directions. For *urbanisme*, Sitte's work was a key starting point, but it was then developed in various social and technical directions by a group of stellar graduates of the École around 1900.

These included Léon Jaussely (1875–1932), the winner of the 1903 Rome Prize competition, the highest level competition at the École. The competition program that year called for "a public square," and Jaussely designed his monumental classical composition, sited next to a river, to be a stage set for metropolitan life, filled with both *flâneurs* and new technologies such as racing cars. In the previous year, Jaussely had won a lesser competition for a design for a "Peoples' Square in the metropolis of a great democratic state," which he sited near the Bastille in Paris. His proposal called for a traffic-free square for public gatherings, as well as a "Peoples' University" with adjacent "Grandes Ateliers des Productions Nouvelles" (large new production workshops) and a "Great Popular Theater." The design also set out areas for popular entertainment, gyms, a swimming pool, and a place for exhibiting the "art of the people." Jaussely's goal was to achieve "liberation of the spirit through social education," which should be expressed in new forms. Yet despite its radical challenge to the aristocratic social order that underlay the Beaux-Arts model of architectural education, Jaussely's design remained firmly in the classical tradition, as would his later work, which included his new master plan for Barcelona in 1903.

Some of Jaussely's near-contemporaries at the École who won the Rome Prize in these same years shared his social and technical concerns. They developed related ideas in ways that laid the groundwork for the French field of *urbanisme,* a term that began to be used by this group around 1910. They included Henri Prost (1874–1959), the 1902 winner of the Rome Prize with a design for a "national printing office." In 1910 Prost won an important competition to extend the city of Antwerp, Belgium, where he demonstrated his concept that urbanism was the "art of building cities," synthesizing the achievements of Haussmann and his Germanic successors with the ideas of Sitte, and at the same time responding to the new social and infrastructural demands of the early twentieth century. Prost consulted with a wider range of experts and ordinary people than was typical for an architect at the time to better understand both the technical challenges and popular wishes in extending the city beyond the line of its demolished fortifications. Yet Prost's project remained entirely within the social norms of the time in separating different classes by "quarters," within which there would be a range of housing types for different income and status levels. His plan was based on analyzing the traffic patterns of the region, retaining the old canals, and proposing new elements that ranged from a new artificial lake surrounded by luxury hotels to a worker's garden city on the outskirts, with social services and its own park. With both its positive and negative aspects, Prost's project was an exceptionally forward-looking scheme, suggesting the zoning of separate residential, commercial, and industrial areas, proposing a new cultural infrastructure, and including hospitals and even a hotel for people traveling by air, a form of mass transportation that was being introduced with the use of airships in Germany.

Prost then went on to work in Morocco, where the French had established a major military presence in 1910. He was commissioned by the Resident-General Hubert Lyautey (1854–1934) to extend Moroccan cities from their traditional Arabic casbahs (old cities) with new quarters for European businesses and immigrant workers. Lyautey had also issued a series of urban regulations, inspired by the French philanthropic efforts of the Musée Social, a group of industrialists, influential citizens, and professional experts founded in 1894 and devoted to the reform of French society, to address the multiple challenges of fast-growing industrial areas. These had resulted in the 1902 French law that required all large towns to create and enforce public health regulations, inspired by similar laws first passed in England in 1848. In 1907 Le Playist Musée Social had established its Section d'Hygiène Urbaine et Rurale (Urban and Rural

Hygiene Department), inspired by the example of German urban zoning, American settlement houses, and the English Garden City movement.

Part of the Musée Social's efforts included attempts to replan the site of the former fortifications that had ringed Paris, replacing them with a long-range program of housing, new traffic streets, parks, parkways, and new public buildings. One of the architects involved was Eugène Hénard (1849–1923), a Beaux-Arts trained architect who had overseen the 1889 Paris Exposition and then worked for Travaux de Paris, the city public works department. In 1903 Hénard had issued a series of innovative proposals to address the city's multiple challenges, including multilevel streets, which helped to ease traffic congestion. This proposal paralleled the better-known multilevel Manhattan visions published by Moses King in the same decade, which then inspired New York architects like Harvey Wiley Corbett to propose similar ideas in the 1920s. Hénard also proposed traffic circles with a two-way flow of vehicles as a solution to urban congestion, the first presentation of a simple traffic flow solution that was first applied in the United States at Columbus Circle in New York City in 1905. A related concept, using one-way traffic in the circle, was used by Parker and Unwin at Letchworth Garden City in England in 1907 and was later widely used in Europe and worldwide; these circles were often known as "rotaries." Hénard also popularized the diagrammatic representation of urban circulation networks using same-scale maps, a concept that had been pioneered by Cerdà in the 1850s (fig. 29). Hénard's work and his inventorlike approach to urbanism would be influential for Le Corbusier by the early 1920s.

The most well known of these École-educated *urbanistes*, as they came to be called after the foundation of Société Française des Urbanistes (SFU) by Hénard, Prost, and others in 1911, was without question Tony Garnier (1869–1948), who had won the Rome Prize in 1899 with a project for "the main branch of a central bank." A fellowship student from Lyon who began studies at the École in 1889, Garnier was strongly drawn to socialist politics in France and to the writings of Émile Zola, notably *Travail: Labor; A Novel*. Unlike many École professors and students, he also took seriously the theories of Eugène-Emmanuel Viollet-le-Duc (1814–1879), who since the 1860s had placed a strong emphasis on the visible appearance of construction techniques as essential to architecture. Garnier shocked the Beaux-Arts education establishment with his proposal for an ideal socialist industrial city to be built entirely out of reinforced concrete. In his ideal "Cité Industrielle" all the buildings would be built out of this material using a system perfected in the 1890s by the French engineer François Hennebique (1842–1921). It combined traditional cement, known since ancient times, with steel reinforcing bars. Unlike Auguste Perret (1874–1954), a Paris architect and contractor who was at the same time successfully adapting concrete to the proportional systems of the classical tradition, Garnier was proposing, with the Cité

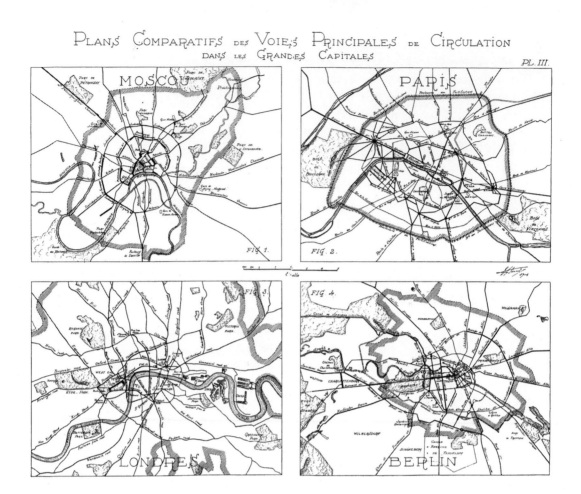

PLANS COMPARATIFS DES VOIES PRINCIPALES DE CIRCULATION
DANS LES GRANDES CAPITALES

PL. III.

MOSCOU FIG. 1.

PARIS FIG. 2.

FIG. 3. LONDRES

FIG. 4. BERLIN

29. Eugene Hénard, same-scale diagrammatic maps of urban street systems, 1903 (Eugene Hénard, *Études sur l'architecture et les transformations de Paris* [Paris: Éditions de la Villette, 2012], 162–63).

Industrielle, new concrete forms at the scale of the city. Both architects, along with Hénard, would soon profoundly shape the work of Le Corbusier and the future of architecture.

The Cité Industrielle was produced during Garnier's three years of study as a Beaux-Arts Rome Prize winner, paid for by the French government, during which Garnier did the required documentation of classical monuments. First sketched in 1901 and not published until 1917, the project synthesized many of the new social and technical directions of the time in a compelling series of architectural drawings (fig. 30). Its plan was to be a flexible checkerboard of streets, like an American industrial town, but instead of rigid social hierarchies, it was premised on the abolition of private property and the idea that all the land would be a continuous parklike green space, available to all. The basic housing unit would be concrete single-family houses open to this public green space on all sides. Police, courts, jails, and military bases would disappear, as Garnier was convinced that they would no longer be necessary in a city run by and for the working class. Industry would be given its own district, well away from housing, and schools would be the focal point of the residential quarters, each with ample space for student recreation.

30. Tony Garnier, Cité Industrielle (industrial settlement), project for an ideal socialist city near Lyon, France, 1904, published in 1917.

There would be no universities, as Garnier believed that their patronage by wealthy capitalists would not allow the people attending them to consider fundamental social change. In their place, technical education would be provided for free. Health facilities would be sited in the best areas, with ample sunlight and green space for good hygiene. The center of the Cité Industrielle was reserved for a mix of administrative and public functions, including meeting halls, offices, museums, municipal libraries and archives, and a generous provision for sports and entertainment facilities.

While Garnier's project and the proposals by Hénard and the Musée Social remained largely unbuilt in Paris, related ideas were implemented on an extensive scale after 1910 in French-controlled Moroccan cities. After his success in the Antwerp competition, Henri Prost was commissioned to design and implement major urban master plans for cities such as Rabat and Casablanca in the 1910s (fig. 31). He then eventually returned to France in the 1920s to apply these ideas to Paris, where he developed the Plan d'Aménagement de la Région Parisienne (1934), the result of a long process that began when the decision was finally made to demolish the city's 1840 fortification wall in 1919. In 1938, Prost was commissioned by the Ataturk government of Turkey to develop a masterplan for Istanbul, much of which was then carried out.

Most of the key figures of French *urbanisme* (Jaussely, Prost, Hénard, Hébrard, Bouvard, Agache, Forestier, and Garnier) are often forgotten

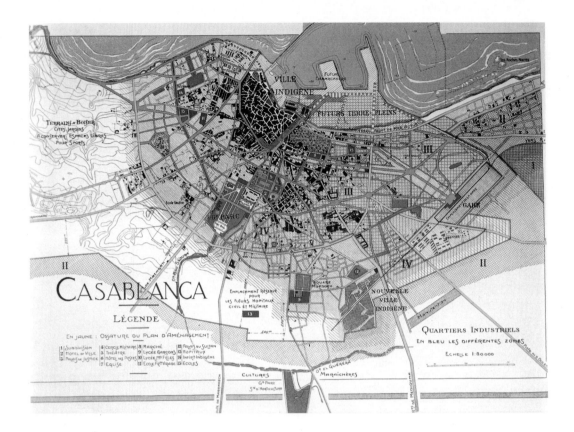

31. Henri Prost, Development and Extension of Casablanca, Morocco, 1917 (*France-Maroc*, 1917, from Jean-Louis Cohen and Monique Eleb, *Casablanca: Colonial Myths and Architectural Ventures* [New York: Monacelli, 2002], 77). A model for French urbanism worldwide to the late 1940s.

today, yet their work shaped sectors of many cities globally, and their professional practice and teaching laid the basis for later urbanistic approaches, even though the classical architectural aspects of this direction were almost completely rejected after 1950.

IMPACT OF THE CITY BEAUTIFUL MOVEMENT AROUND 1910

In London, where in 1900 national pride tended to favor medieval styles and suburban villas, the influences of the American City Beautiful movement and French *urbanisme* were more limited. The Metropolitan Board of Works, established in 1855, was replaced in 1889 by the London County Council, whose main focus was transportation improvements and efforts to address the housing shortage, without undertaking massive efforts to reorganize the structure and appearance of the entire city. Continuing the pattern set by the Houses of Parliament (1837), new government buildings tended to be in neo-medieval styles, such as G. E. Street's New Law Courts (1867–82). An exception was the Kingsway-Aldwych improvement (1899–1905), a busy roadway lined with uniform classical facades that was seen by King Edward VII as a beautification of the British imperial capital.

Around the same time, in 1905, Bombay (now Mumbai) was being transformed with new Paris-type boulevards intended to speed traffic and improve sanitation. In most British colonial cities, however, planning still tended to be piecemeal, as in London. Old divisions that can be traced back to the 1600s between the original native "black town" and the newer, usually more suburban European imperial "white town" persisted. Nonetheless, some cities had begun to grow into large industrial and governmental centers by 1900, including Karachi, Lahore (both now in Pakistan), and Rangoon, Burma (now Yangon in Myanmar).

A partial exception to these patterns was the new capital for the Union of South Africa, created in 1910 by combining four separate colonies. The British imperial authorities, victorious over the rebellious Boers (Afrikaans-speakers of Dutch ancestry whose revolts against British rule were put down in 1881 and 1902), decided to build an imposing new capital complex that would symbolize the union of the two "white races" whom it was thought were destined to rule over the large indigenous majority. Named after nineteenth-century Afrikaaner leader Andries Pretorius (1798–1853), it was the executive capital of the newly formed Union. Its architect was Sir Herbert Baker (1862–1946), who had been sent by British colonial administrator Cecil Rhodes to visit ancient classical sites in the Mediterranean so his designs would better symbolize imperial authority in Africa, which were to be explicitly modeled on those of the Roman Empire. His capitol complex for Pretoria included both a Roman dome, symbolizing unity, as well as two towers based on those at Sir Christopher Wren's Greenwich Hospital (1692).

The popular success of Pretoria's architecture occurred as King George V unexpectedly made the announcement at the end of 1911 that he was ordering the capital of India to be moved from Calcutta, the long-established British seat of power in India, to Delhi. British power and influence in the region had increased since 1858, and a new capital had been discussed since 1867. Delhi had been the capital of the Mughal Empire, and the British presented themselves as their imperial successors, building both a cantonment, or military base, and a civil station, or European enclave, there. By the 1880s eight railway lines converged on the city, at what had become the center of the Indian railway network, which allowed European imported goods to be widely distributed, and raw materials to be easily exported. In Bengal, political unrest was becoming a problem, and the move to Delhi would also bring the capital closer to the British summer capital, Simla.

After the king's announcement, a Delhi Town Planning Council was established (an early official use of the term "town planning" for such a project), which included the eminent English architect Sir Edwin Landseer Lutyens (1869–1944). The site selected in 1912 was just south of old Delhi, and was eventually named "New Delhi" in 1926. Lutyens produced an initial layout, but some members of the council objected to its partly gridded streets, and briefly brought in Henry Vaughn Lanchester (1863–1953), another English architect, whose curving street plan was also soon rejected. Lutyens then recommended that Sir Herbert Baker be appointed executive architect, and the final plan was approved in 1913, with many of the buildings then designed by both. In 1916 Lutyens and Baker disagreed sharply over the angle of the incline of the main processional road, but the final design was nonetheless immensely popular in its melding of classical and Indian elements, and New Delhi has remained the capital of India after independence from the British Empire in 1947 (fig. 32).

Though similar in some ways to the 1902 extension of central Washington, D.C., New Delhi's plan was innovative in several ways. It included both large classical planted boulevards, including diagonal boulevards organized into hexagonal patterns, and imposing governmental buildings that effectively combined Western and Indian elements. The geometry of the plan, centered on Raisina Hill, was generated by views of historic monuments, with one major axis leading from the Government House to a historic Hindu fortress, and another at a 30-degree angle leading to the historic Jamma Masjid in Old Delhi (1644–56). Like the Washington plan, it also called for a large new rail station facing a new urban square, an interface between the capitol complex and the existing city. Lutyens's Government House was the centerpiece of the plan, sited at the crossing of the two main axes, the east-west one 440 feet (134 meters) wide and the north-south one 330 feet (101 meters) wide. As with the other official buildings, it took as its starting point the English classicism of Wren, but combined it with an eclectic mix of South Asian elements such as the *chujja* (the projecting stone cornice) and *chattris* (small roof pavilions), as well as a dome inspired by the form of a traditional Hindu stupa. The large fountain bowls on the roof symbolized the ingenuity of English engineers in building water and sewer systems in the subcontinent. Indian arches were also used, and Lutyens invented new column capital designs, where abstracted Indian stone bells replaced Ionic volutes. The large formal gardens were a version of a Mughal garden, emphasizing the historic succession of empires.

Just to the south of the Government House, across a large courtyard, Baker designed two Secretariat buildings housing the various colonial administrative ministries. As at Pretoria, he again used the cupolas of Wren's Greenwich Hospital, adding loggias on the ground floor to provide views, and including more chattris as well as *jaalis* (South Asian stone window grills). Adjacent to the Secretariats, after administrative reforms in 1919, a Council house for limited representative government was built, with a dome symbolizing a united India. Other buildings by various architects filled out the plan, and the east-west axis led on to an Anglican cathedral, intended as a counterpart to the historic mosque. Surrounding this government district were areas of bungalows, sited in greenery, for officials, who were organized into sixty-one civil service categories. Europeans and Indians were strictly segregated by race, and housed according to class hierarchies, which were reflected in the varying lot sizes that ranged from smallest for servants to largest for highest officials. New Delhi, officially

DELHI

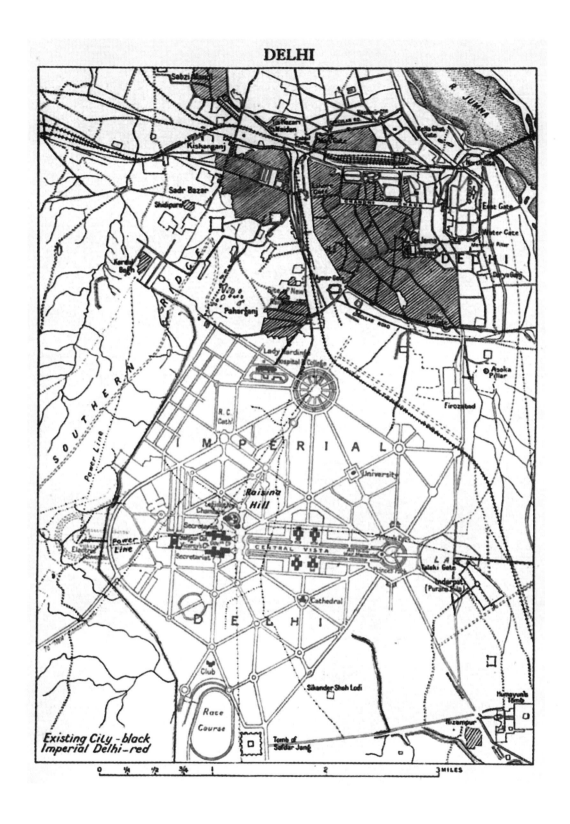

32. Sir Herbert Baker and Sir Edwin Lutyens, New Delhi, India, 1913–31.

opened in 1931, was important not only for its successful urban design, but also for its role in introducing new technologies such as telephones, radio, cinemas, and an airport to South Asia.

A related, though somewhat different impact of the City Beautiful Movement was also evident in the 1912 competition for Canberra, a new capital for Australia. The previously separate seven British colonies of Australia were combined into one Commonwealth in 1901, but a site for a capital was not agreed upon until 1908. Seeking to create a national capital "to rival London in population, Paris in beauty, Athens in culture, and Chicago in enterprise," an international competition for Canberra's design was announced in 1910. The short deadline and lack of an announced jury, as well as the small amount of prize money, led the Royal Institute of British Architects to boycott it. Nonetheless, 138 entries were received from around the world, but the jury of two engineers and one architect could not agree on the finalists, who included Walter Burley Griffin (1876–1937) and Marion Mahony Griffin (1871–1961), former Chicago associates of Frank Lloyd Wright, as well as the Finnish architect Eliel Saarinen (1873–1950) and the French urbanist Alfred Agache (1875–1959). Ultimately a government commission was appointed to combine the best features of the six finalist designs, which then strongly resembled the plan submitted by some of the Australian entrants. The resulting "Board Plan" was rejected entirely by a newly elected government, which in 1913 instead supported the first prize choice of Griffin and Mahony Griffin by two of the members of the jury.

Their city plan sought to symbolize democratic government in its organization of the capitol, with the executive building on top of a hill, the legislature below, and both supported at the base by the judiciary building, a concept that the Griffins illustrated with sectional diagrams. This expression of functions departed to some extent from the Beaux-Arts patterns of the City Beautiful movement. According to the plan, the city was to be organized as a series of polygonal, radioconcentric figures linked by large axial parkways located with views of nearby mountains and bridging across a lake (fig. 33). Centered on the capitol, these parkways would lead to civic center and market center areas, as well as to residential suburbs nearby. Continuing opposition to the Griffin project led to many disputes prior to the definitive plan of 1918, and finally Griffin resigned as Canberra's designer in 1920. Other than some of the parkways and the street geometry of the capitol and civic center areas, most of Canberra as built did not follow the Griffin and Mahony Griffin design.

In some ways urbanism was more developed in practice in the United States and in continental Europe, but the first professional training program in "Civic Design" was established at Liverpool University in 1909. Its faculty included several classical architects then actively practicing in the British Empire, including Sir Patrick Abercrombie (1879–1957), who taught there from 1915 to 1935, and Stanley Adshead, who then went on to

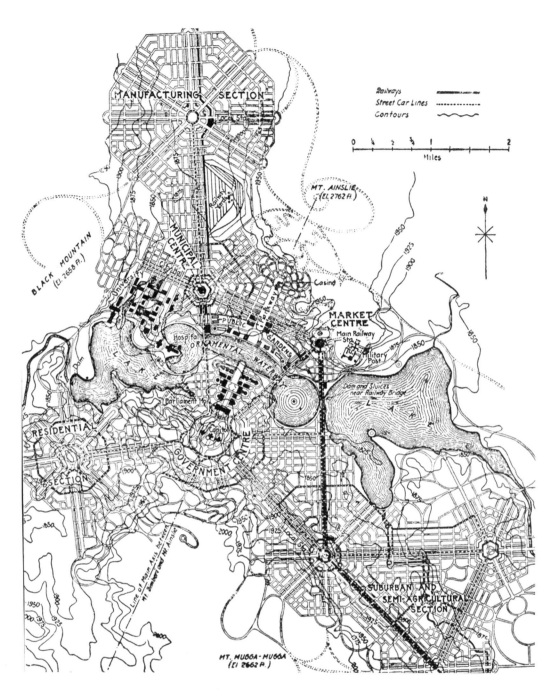

Railways
Street Car Lines
Contours

0 ¼ ½ ¾ 1   2
            Miles

N

MANUFACTURING SECTION

MT. AINSLIE
(El. 2762 Ft.)

BLACK MOUNTAIN
(El. 2658 Ft.)

MUNICIPAL CENTRE

City Hall

Casino

University

MARKET CENTRE
Main Railway Sta.

PUBLIC GARDENS

Hospital

ORNAMENTAL WATER

Military Post

Dam and Sluices near Railway Bridge

Parliament Ho.

Capitol

GOVERNMENT CENTRE

RESIDENTIAL SECTION

Dam

Line of Major Axis between Mt. Bimberi and Mt. Ainslie

Local Sta.

SUBURBAN AND SEMI-AGRICULTURAL SECTION

MT. MUGGA-MUGGA
(El. 2662 Ft.)

found the Town Planning program at University College London in 1914. Like Prost, Eugène Hébrard, and other French urbanists, these architects sought to adapt City Beautiful–like classicism to both new technologies and widely varying local cultural situations. They worked with the idea, shared by their official clients, that a well-organized society expresses its existence in a well-directed and well-planned way. This was the basis of Civic Design studio teaching at Liverpool, which also included lecture courses in landscape art, engineering, and the practical aspects of town

33. Walter Burley Griffin and Marion Mahony, Canberra, new capital of Australia, 1913.

planning. Adshead and Abercrombie also taught a course in "social civics," which attempted to relate urban design with the emerging social sciences.

Many of their Liverpool Civic Design program students received important imperial commissions, including Clifford Holliday (1897–1960) in Malta and in British Mandate Palestine (present-day Israel and Palestinian territories); William Holford (1907–1975) in South Africa and postwar England; and Linton Bogle in Lucknow, India. Many graduates were also active in Australia. Five or six students per year came to the Liverpool program from many parts of the British Empire, including British India, Hong Kong, Canada, Ceylon (present-day Sri Lanka), Iraq, Egypt, and present-day Malaysia and Singapore, as well as Thailand, an independent kingdom. The program's influence was greatest in the 1920s. Later, similar programs were established in Alexandria (1942) and Cairo (1950), spreading the early-twentieth-century combination of British Town Planning with the American City Beautiful movement across much of the world.

Today this classical "town planning" direction is still strongly associated with British colonialism, and it remains a complex topic to understand historically. Capitals like Pretoria and New Delhi still sometimes function similarly to how they were designed, despite political independence and the immense social changes that have taken place since then. Much additional research could be done on the ways that this direction sometimes set underlying patterns for other cities in South Asia and Africa that have grown enormously, often in less planned ways, over the past half-century.

FURTHER READING

Hilary Ballon, *The Greatest Grid: The Master Plan of Manhattan, 1811–2011* (New York: Museum of the City of New York/Columbia University Press, 2011).

Daniel H. Burnham and Edward H. Bennett, *The Plan of Chicago* (Chicago: Commercial Club, 1909).

Jean-Louis Cohen and Monqiue Eleb, *Casablanca: Colonial Myths and Architectural Ventures* (New York: Monacelli, 2002).

Mark Crinson, *Modern Architecture and the End of Empire* (Aldershot, England: Ashgate, 2003).

William Cronon, *Nature's Metropolis: Chicago and the Great West* (New York: Norton, 1991).

Albert Fein, *Landscape into Cityscape: Frederick Law Olmsted's Plans for Greater New York City* (New York: Van Nostrand Reinhold, 1981).

Thomas Hines, *Burnham of Chicago* (London: Oxford University Press, 1974).

Paul Knox, *Palimpsests: Biographies of 50 City Districts* (Basel: Birkhäuser, 2012).

Richard Plunz, *The History of Housing in New York City* (New York: Columbia University Press, 1990).

John Reps, *The Making of Urban America* (Princeton: Princeton University Press, 1965).

Wolfgang Sonne, *Representing the State: Capital City Planning in the Early Twentieth Century* (Munich: Prestel, 2003).

Lawrence Vale, *Architecture, Power, and National Identity* (London: Routledge, 2008).

Matthew Wells, *Engineers: A History of Engineering and Structural Design* (New York: Routledge, 2010).

CHAPTER THREE

From Tenement Reform to Regional Planning, 1840–1932

LONDON AND NEW YORK

By the mid-nineteenth century, the poor health and social conditions in English industrial cities had become a major source of concern. Edwin Chadwick's *Report on the Sanitary Condition of the Labouring Population of Great Britain* (1842) is often cited as a turning point in changing public attitudes about the need for government action to address these conditions. It was commissioned by a government commission appointed to determine the causes of a cholera epidemic in Whitechapel, a working-class area in the East End of London. By this time, the term "slum" was beginning to be applied to such dense, crowded areas of London, a term that perhaps derived from the German word *Schlamm*, meaning mud or mire.

In 1841 the Metropolitan Association for Improving the Dwellings of the Industrious Classes was founded in London, followed in 1844 by the founding of the Society for the Improvement of the Condition of the Labouring Classes. Model housing by these private groups in the 1840s was built both in the form of terrace houses, with larger windows and rear yards than were typical, and as five-story apartment blocks with open-access galleries. Though cold in winter, these galleries were used to get more light into the apartments, and to provide the cross-ventilation then thought to be essential to prevent the spread of infectious diseases, instead of using internal, enclosed double-loaded corridors (fig. 34). The Metropolitan Association opened its first model tenement in 1846, and by 1870 it was yielding the association an annual profit of 5.25 percent on invested capital, far less than the profits then available in operating more conventional slum housing.

Around the same time, the continuing growth of industrial cities and the spread of infectious diseases in urban areas led to passage of the first Public Health Act by the British Parliament in 1848. This was followed in 1851 by specific legislation mandating the sanitary inspection

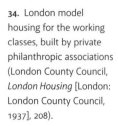

34. London model housing for the working classes, built by private philanthropic associations (London County Council, *London Housing* [London: London County Council, 1937], 208).

DWELLINGS ERECTED IN 1846 BY THE METROPOLITAN ASSOCIATION

DWELLINGS ERECTED IN 1844 BY THE SOCIETY FOR IMPROVING THE CONDITIONS OF THE LABOURING CLASSES

of "Common and Labouring Classes' Lodging Houses." That was also the year of the Great Exhibition, when model dwellings were put on display by the Society for the Condition of the Labouring Classes, sponsored by the Prince Consort Albert, the husband of Queen Victoria. One of these was the multistory courtyard building called the Model Housing for Families, or Parnell House, designed by Henry Roberts in Streatham Street, Bloombury (1850). Parnell House, by using an elongated U-shaped plan, provided eight well-ventilated and sunlit units per floor, accessed by open galleries that allowed light on both sides of each unit. It was intended to demonstrate an improvement over a typical slum building, showing that the same or an even greater number of families could be comfortably housed on a central London site as in a typical slum building.

Parnell House was also intended to provide an alternative to the then-widespread English urban pattern of narrow two-story row houses, whose lack of light and open space the provisions of the Public Health Act did not radically improve. These terrace or row houses typically had four small rooms, two on each floor, with privies and sometimes a single water tap located in a rear courtyard. By contrast, in the multi-story Parnell House apartments each apartment unit had three separate bedrooms. These units demonstrated that better housing could improve health and social outcomes for what was beginning to be conceptualized as a normative working-class family, with a father working and a mother remaining at home. Other model houses, notably the Model Cottages designed by Roberts and sponsored by the Society, were put on display for visitors interested in housing questions at the Great Exhibition in 1851. It was suggested that the construction and renting of such dwellings could produce a 7 percent annual rate of return, less than slum housing developments but still potentially acceptable to investors of the time.

The belief that poor housing conditions in industrial working-class areas of cities might trigger social unrest was a central concern for elites at this time. The issue had been raised by, among others, the German journalist and socialist activist Friedrich Engels in his *The Condition of the Working Class in England* (first published in German in 1845), one of the first detailed examinations of the various social and urban outcomes of the industrial revolution. Engels was pessimistic about reform housing and in 1848 published in London with Karl Marx the "Manifesto of the Communist Party" on behalf of the Communist League, later the Communist International. The manifesto called for the revolutionary overthrow of capitalist societies by industrial workers everywhere, to produce generally better conditions for the working class, rather than giving Communist approval to piecemeal philanthropic housing reform efforts like Parnell House. But in mainstream British political life, such philanthropic efforts soon acquired significant support. Several private philanthropic associations dedicated to building model tenements were active in London by the 1860s, and another Housing Act was passed in 1868.

In 1859–69, philanthropist Angela Burdett-Coutts (1814–1906) commissioned architect Henry Darbyshire to design the Columbia Square housing complex, a five-story Gothic Revival housing block with courtyards that also included an elaborate market building. In 1869 the Improved Industrial Dwellings Company built the Bethnal Green estate in the East End of London, a six-story apartment complex with uniform street frontages and internal courtyards. In 1871 architect and historian Sir Banister Fletcher (1866–1953) designed a project for "Model Houses for the Industrial Classes" in London. Its apartment layouts, with living rooms facing the street and with common gardens in the rear, anticipated many later apartment floor plans in the twentieth century. In this context, earlier efforts to legislate better housing were seen as inadequate, and in 1875 and 1879 additional Housing Acts (called the Cross Acts) were passed by Parliament, empowering local authorities to clear and reconstruct "unhealthy areas."

The Metropolitan Board of Works, established in London in 1855 to build sewers and other infrastructure, used the 1875 Housing Act, along with the 1875 Public Health Act (described by planner Thomas Adams in 1932 as a "charter of sanitation") as the legal basis for sixteen London slum clearance projects, covering a total area of 42 acres (17 hectares). After displacing 22,872 people, 27,730 were recorded as being "provided for" through these efforts. Several other projects on sites cleared by the Metropolitan Board of Works were built by the Peabody Trust in more elite areas of Westminster (Great Peter Street) and Holborn (Little Coram Street). Something very similar to later slum-clearance model housing made its first appearance at Sir Charles Barry's Beaconsfield Buildings (1879), sponsored by the Victoria Dwellings Association, a group of five-story tenements set in parallel rows spaced apart from each other, housing 1,100 people. These London philanthropic housing projects, though rarely known to modern architects, were the first large-scale urban slum-clearance efforts.

In 1889 the London Metropolitan Board of Works was replaced by the regional London County Council (LCC), the world's first effort at metropolitan government for a large urban region. Yet another Housing Act was passed in 1890, which allowed the LCC to undertake projects for "improvement" and "reconstruction"—early uses of terms that would become standard in modern planning. The LCC then went on to carry out thirteen such slum-clearance efforts between 1890 and 1912. By then, Charles Booth (1840–1916) had begun his *Life and Labour of the People* (1889–1903), a foundational work of urban sociology that, when published, included "maps descriptive of London poverty" showing the living areas of seven classes, from the wealthy to the poorest. The LCC's improvement plans cleared some of these poorest areas, as at the five-story Boundary Street estate, Bethnal Green (1893–1900). There, the LCC rebuilt nearly fifteen acres (6 hectares) of a slum area, and provided housing for 5,700 residents in Queen Anne–style brick apartment blocks, with ample green space and public amenities. The LCC also built new housing, like the seven-story Millbank Estate (1897–1902), and other housing for London residents displaced by street widenings and the construction of new Thames River bridges and tunnels, as well as three lodging houses for single working-class men. By 1899 it began to turn its development activities to suburban apartment housing, which included Totterdown Fields, housing 20,000 residents in the suburban area of Tooting, and developments in Tottenham, Croydon, and Hammersmith, areas then at the edge of the metropolitan region.

By the 1850s, such British efforts at private philanthropic housing had inspired efforts elsewhere, particularly in France and Germany. In Paris, the Cité Napoleon (1851) was a model housing block built near a new railway station, the Gare du Nord. It was soon paralleled by the Cité Ouvrière (Workers' Settlement) in Mulhouse, a French city near Basel, Switzerland, sponsored by local industrialists and housing reformers. A rare example of a Fourierist phalanstery was also built in Guise by André Godin in 1859, but was not widely imitated. In Germany, Roberts's Model Dwelling cottages were favored by housing reformers there, and were understood to be a prototype for working-class housing, instead of the large Mietkasernen (rent barracks) courtyard tenements then being built extensively in Berlin.

In New York City, the New York Association for Improving the Condition of the Poor, founded in 1845, commissioned a model tenement, inspired by Parnell House, in the Five Points slum in what is now Chinatown. The Workingmen's Home, designed in 1855 by John W. Ritch, was intended to house working-class African Americans. It imposed a strict hygienic and moral code on its residents, including mandatory Protestant religious services. After its sale in 1867 to less high-minded owners it apparently became a notorious slum for European immigrants and was later demolished. Nonetheless, numerous other philanthropic housing projects were constructed in Manhattan and Brooklyn (a separate city until 1898) before World War I. Notable among these were the projects by Alfred Treadway White (1846–1921) in Brooklyn that included the Tower Buildings (1879), a set of six-story walk-up buildings with gallery-access corridors and indoor plumbing that covered only 52 percent of its total site, in contrast to the 80 percent coverage then typical of tenement buildings. Yet the success of such projects was limited, as they offered little competition to privately built tenement housing, much of it constructed and operated by recently arrived immigrants.

The Tower Buildings were built around the same time as the first American efforts to legislate a minimum amount of light and air in tenements. By the 1860s in New York, "tenement" was understood to refer to a four- to six-story working-class walk-up apartment building that covered nearly all of a typical 25 × 100 foot (7.62 × 30.5 meter) Manhattan lot. The buildings normally lacked central heating or indoor plumbing and provided multifamily privies in the rear courtyards. They had many small, windowless interior rooms, each typically inhabited by an entire immigrant family. The spread of disease in areas like the Lower East Side, where tenements predominated, had become a concern to all classes after numerous cholera epidemics. There was also a very real danger of major fires, such as those in New York in 1832, 1849, and 1866.

These conditions led to the first American official efforts to regulate tenement fire safety, ventilation, and light. Passed a year after the New York state legislature first set minimum building-construction standards, the New York Tenement House Act of 1867 required only exterior fire escapes. A competition to design a model tenement held by the *Plumber and Sanitary Engineer* magazine in 1878 was won by architect James E. Ware (1846–1918), a designer of fireproof warehouses, whose design called for two water closets (for toilets) per floor and for small light shafts on either side of the main access stairs. This design led the New York state legislature to pass the Tenement House Act of 1879, which required three-foot setbacks in the middle of the lot from the side property lines, creating six-foot (1.83-meter) light shafts when one five-story

35. Lower East Side tenements and row houses on "The Bend," Mulberry Street, New York, 1890 (Jacob Riis, *How the Other Half Lives* [New York: Charles Scribner's Sons, 1890], 48).

tenement was built adjacent to another. Around 60,000 such "Old Law" tenements were built in New York between 1880 and 1901, an immense and still sometimes highly visible built outcome of one of the first efforts in the United States to regulate urban building form through legislation.

Housing reformers were highly critical of the minimal improvements to tenement light and ventilation provided by the Old Law, and in 1884 the law was expanded to eliminate exterior privies and to require a water supply on all floors, as well as requiring electric street lighting in all tenement districts. Nonetheless, concerns about tenements continued, and calls for extensive reforms increased after the Danish American journalist Jacob Riis (1849–1914) published an article, "How the Other Half Lives" in *Scribner's Magazine* (1889), followed by a book of that title in 1890, illustrated with many of his photographs of tenement conditions (fig. 35). This prompted greater public outrage, and further reform efforts led to the passage by the New York state legislature in 1901 of the "New Law," which set national standards for multifamily housing. It mandated that such multifamily buildings not cover more than 70 percent of their sites, and required that interior airshafts be at least 24 × 24 feet (7.32 × 7.32 meters), or 12 × 24 feet (3.66 × 7.32 meters), if at the lot line. Every room had to have an exterior window of set minimum dimensions, and for the first time detailed interior fire exit requirements were legally specified. The provisions of this 1901 New York City ordinance codified the form of New Law tenements as well as of standard middle-class urban apartment buildings in New York City built before 1930. Its provisions were then copied in many other American cities, determining by legislation the plan form of much multifamily housing there before the 1930s.

Most North American cities did not have the severely crowded conditions of New York, where in 1890 two-thirds of the inhabitants lived in tenements. By 1920, most poor Americans elsewhere lived in detached, single-family houses surrounded by open space, though these typically still lacked indoor plumbing or electricity. These were rarely the focus of housing reform efforts.

THE GARDEN CITY MOVEMENT IN ENGLAND
AND INTERNATIONALLY

Decentralized models of urban housing reform had been of interest to some factory owners and inventors since the early nineteenth century. The industrialist Robert Owen (1771–1858) first proposed model communities for his workers in the textile mills of New Lanark, Scotland, as early as 1810. Owen then attempted to create a utopian community of scientists and other Enlightenment experts in the unlikely location of New Harmony, Indiana, in the 1820s. Neither effort was completely successful, though the U.S. Geological Survey owes its origins to Owen's efforts at New Harmony, and much of the historic village, mostly built just prior to Owen's efforts by the Rappites, a German Protestant sect, has been preserved. Nonetheless, Owen's interest in the housing of workers and the need in the industrial era to organize community life had a long-lasting impact. In New England, Boston mill owners built industrial towns such as Lowell, Massachusetts (1822), and Manchester, New Hampshire (1810; extended 1838), which included industrial canals and housing of various kinds for workers, sited near five- to seven-story brick mill complexes often arranged in quadrangles. Beyond their original planned cores, which sometimes included strictly organized communal housing for young female millworkers from nearby farms, these mill towns soon included peripheral slums for Irish, French Canadian, and other immigrants.

Other British and American investors, industrialists, and settlers built or proposed many model communities in the nineteenth century. These included Hygeia, a model town named after the Roman goddess of health, intended for a site across the river from Cincinnati in 1827, and Adelaide, Australia (1837), a gridded new town surrounded by a greenbelt that became a model for many other new cities in Australia and New Zealand. Salt Lake City, founded in 1847 by the Mormons, a Christian sect, as the capital of the new state of Deseret (later Utah), was in this same tradition, with its grid plan centered on a symbolic central square surrounded by major religious structures. In England, James Silk Buckingham's ideal town of Victoria (1849) was another unbuilt example of an ideal industrial community, from around the same time as Saltaire, a model industrial town built in the Aire Valley of Yorkshire in 1852 by the industrialist Sir Titus Salt. Another such proposal by Benjamin Richardson, also called *Hygeia: A City of Health* (1876), advocated a new city of wide, tree-shaded avenues where public health would be the governing principle.

These ideas were also being implemented in the many commuter suburbs of London and other large nineteenth-century cities. One well-known example is Bedford Park (1875–78), a half-hour rail commute from central London. Its developer carefully planned a new residential development of semi-detached houses (two otherwise detached houses that shared a wall between them, then a common English urban building type) on an eighteenth-century estate, laying out the streets to save trees that had been planted by a curator of the Royal Horticultural Society. This layout resulted in long, narrow blocks, where the elegant double houses on 50 × 75 foot (15.24 × 23 meter) lots were set back 15 to 20 feet (4.57–6.1 meters) from the street lines. The architects E. W. Godwin and his successor, Richard Norman Shaw (1831–1912), designed most of the houses in picturesque historical revival styles that set a pattern for much later suburban development worldwide.

The model town of Pullman, Illinois, designed by S. S. Beman in 1880 just south of Chicago by George Pullman, then the leading American manufacturer of railroad sleeping cars (fig. 36), combined earlier utopian settlements with elements of an elite commuter railway suburb. At a time when it often took an overnight railway trip to conduct business between one American city and another, Pullman palace sleeping cars were an essential aspect of long-distance transportation. Pullman found it difficult to keep craftsmen with the woodworking skills necessary to fabricate the cars' elaborate fittings from moving to other companies, and he decided that a model worker's town, sited a short railway journey south of the Chicago Loop, would be a way to retain his company's

36. Map of Pullman, Illinois, 1885, with east at the top. A model company town built to retain skilled craftsmen by George Pullman, a large Chicago manufacturer of railway sleeping cars.

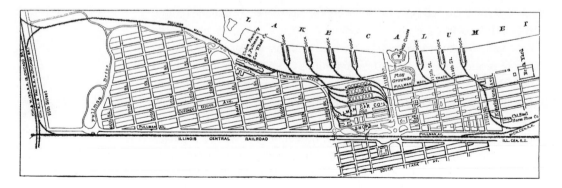

skilled labor. The town of Pullman as built included a range of rental housing types ranging from middle-class mansions down to model tenement-type apartments, corresponding to the various job levels in the factory. These were all a short walk from the Pullman factory complex. Pullman also included many amenities such as a produce market, an early shopping arcade, and a landscaped park, as well as access to a nearby boating lake. It was a much-studied company town model in the late nineteenth century, and it inspired similar efforts in England, notably Port Sunlight (1888), built by the Lever Brothers soap company, and Bournville (1893), built by the Cadbury chocolate company. These model industrial towns combined the earlier factory-town organization, where a full range of services was provided by a paternalistic employer, with the patterns of the residential commuter development, at a time when housing sited in landscaping and outdoor recreation areas was becoming fashionable.

This emerging movement was given a clear theoretical basis by the English stenographer and utopian theorist Ebenezer Howard (1850–1928) in his *To-morrow: A Peaceful Path to Real Reform* (1898), republished as *Garden Cities of Tomorrow* (1902). It appeared at the same time as Adna Ferrin Weber's *The Growth of Cities in the Nineteenth Century* (1899), which called attention to the rapid, recent world urbanization that was then occurring. Howard's efforts led to the formation of the Garden City Association in England in 1901, whose goal was to relocate workers from overcrowded, unsanitary, and often dangerous urban areas to newly built Garden Cities sited amid agricultural fields at the metropolitan periphery. There, both industrial and other jobs, as well as a full range of cultural and recreational activities, would be available to the residents (fig. 37). Howard had spent several years in the United States in the 1870s, and after a stint in 1873 as a would-be farmer in Howard County, Nebraska, he relocated to Chicago. In the fast-growing midwestern city he had been impressed by the proximity of industry and housing to agricultural areas and forests in developing outlying areas. Howard returned to London in 1878 and by the 1890s began to advocate his Garden City idea, based on the concept that massive industrial cities like London should be reorganized into compact smaller tracts of 6,000 acres (2,428 hectares), each housing not more than 32,000 people. Each Garden City would be linked to others by municipal railway and would be surrounded by a greenbelt of parks and farms to feed the residents. The built areas of each Garden City would be on a relatively compact 1,000 acres (405 hectares), and these would contain a full range of employment, cultural, entertainment, and housing options, providing all the advantages of the city as well as those of the countryside, without the negative aspects of either.

The English economist Alfred Marshall (1842–1924) had in 1884 put forward the idea that the decentralization of industry and workers along rail lines to less expensive land outside of the metropolitan areas should

37. Ebenezer Howard, diagram of a "group of slumless smokeless cities," 1898 (Ebenezer Howard, *To-morrow: A Peaceful Path to Real Reform* [London, 1898]).

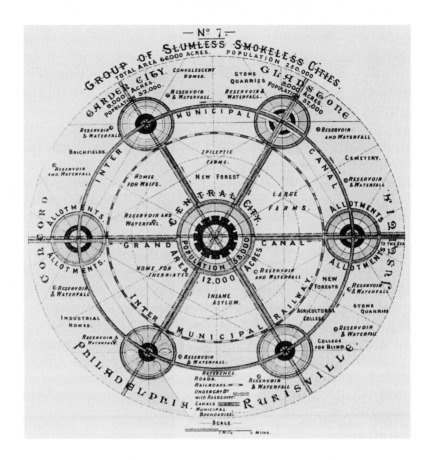

be centrally coordinated, and Howard's Garden City proposal provided a diagrammatic design model for how this could be done. Howard also advocated that the financing for the necessary new infrastructure come from the sale of bonds at 4 to 5 percent interest, with the new residents then paying rent into a common fund to pay off the bondholders, and thus eventually obtaining joint ownership of their Garden City.

Theorized by Howard, but supported financially and politically by philanthropically inclined English industrialists at a time when 80 percent of the rural land of England and Wales was still owned by fewer than seven thousand mostly aristocratic landholders, the Garden City movement was immensely influential both in England and internationally. It launched the profession of town planning in the English-speaking world and encouraged planned urban decentralization as the solution to a range of social and environmental problems. Howard's ideal Garden City of thirty-two thousand was to have six wards of five thousand to six thousand people, each designed to be like a small town in itself, and would be constructed ward by ward, with gardens available to all. Most lots would be 20 × 130 feet (6.1 × 40 meters). The wards would be organized near large boulevards 120 feet (37 meters) wide leading to a 145-acre (59-hectare) central park and civic center, which would include a glass Crystal Palace shopping arcade as well as a town hall, a library, a museum, and concert and lecture halls.

Howard had proposed the Garden City Association in 1899 to advance his ideas, and Ralph Neville, a London lawyer to large industrialists, became its chairman in 1901. Neville and his clients were more concerned about the potential for urban class violence than was Howard, and they saw the "decadence" and "increase of emotionalism" in town dwellers as a problem that could be solved by decentralization. They also feared that urban living was physically weakening working-class young men, potentially undermining the British Empire's world military preeminence. The higher quality of life in Garden Cities would also, it was thought, satisfy working-class demands for higher wages. Other industrialists, notably George Cadbury and W. H. Lever, also supported the Garden City Association. Under the direction of its first secretary, Thomas Adams (1871–1940), a widely publicized inaugural conference was held in Bournville in September 1901, attended by 1,500 British municipal officials. This was followed a few months later by the start of land acquisition for the first Garden City, Letchworth, on a 3,800-acre (1,538-hectare) site 34 miles (55 kilometers) northeast of London in Hertfordshire.

Letchworth marked the point where the utopian socialism that had inspired Howard began to shift toward the reformist, business-centered goals of industrialists who were active in the Garden City Association. The architects who won the 1903 competition for its design, Barry Parker (1867–1947) and Raymond Unwin (1863–1940), already had extensive experience designing model housing groups for English coal companies and other large concerns. The socially well-connected Barry Parker had joined with Unwin, a distant relative who was an Oxford University–educated engineer with strong socialist convictions, in founding the firm of Parker and Unwin in 1896. Unwin was also influenced by the ideas of John Ruskin and William Morris, and had been the secretary of the Manchester Socialist League in 1886. At the founding conference of the Garden City Association at Bournville in 1901, Unwin had advocated that cities buy up land on their edges and hold it for future Garden City–type development. This was a modification of Howard's idea of cities surrounded by greenbelts, and was being carried out in German cities like Frankfurt-am-Main in the 1890s.

Previously, in 1902, Parker and Unwin had been commissioned by the owner of a large cocoa-processing company, Joseph Rowntree, who had also attended the Bournville conference, to design a new model working-class housing settlement on land he owned outside York. The result was New Earswick (1902), located on 130 acres (53 hectares) on the Rowntree estate. Its 28-acre (10.12-hectare) site comprised 150 houses organized into rows of two, four, and six units, all facing a central green, and used a medieval revival design inspired by the ideas of Ruskin and Morris. Following them, Unwin argued that medieval villages had an organic unity

38. Barry Parker and Raymond Unwin, Letchworth Garden City, 1903 (C. R. Ashbee, *Where the Great City Stands* [London: Essex House, 1917], 45), the first Garden City to be built.

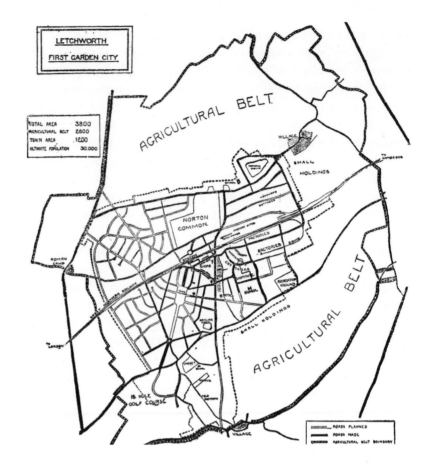

that reflected their clear social hierarchies, which gave them a "crystalline structure" that was manifested in their visually comprehensible physical form. At the same time, at New Earswick, Parker and Unwin produced an innovative site plan where every house faced toward the sun, requiring the adjustment of standard gridded street layouts. Each house also had its own interior bathroom on the second floor, and an outside lean-to storage shed.

Parker and Unwin's design for Letchworth (1903) was in fact less innovative than the one for New Earswick, reflecting their relative inexperience with large-scale urban design (fig. 38). Its street plan was a relatively conventional Beaux-Arts layout, strongly axial in plan and centered on a prominent central site for a "labour church," which remained unbuilt for many years, due to lack of funds. The more innovative aspects of Parker and Unwin's work were evident in the design of Homesgarth, a cooperative housing quadrangle for twenty-four families, designed on the model of Oxford colleges. One side of the quadrangle was for a common dining room, a recreation room, and a nursery, with the costs of dining and maid service to be shared jointly by the residents. Yet despite the intentions of Howard and Letchworth's architects, who envisioned a future society based on the cooperative Garden City model, ultimately

From Tenement Reform to Regional Planning, 1840–1932

most of the residents of Letchworth were well-off "free-thinkers" rather than industrial workers. Many of them were also skilled artisans, but the town was quickly caricatured in the national press as a center of theosophy, vegetarianism, and other then-unconventional social directions. Its industrial park was quite successful, and the printer J. W. Dent, publisher of the Everyman's Library, and other firms moved to Letchworth from London for more available space. Its commercial success and location then beyond the outer edges of the London metropolitan area made it too expensive for the unskilled laborers whose housing conditions were what the Garden City movement had been founded to address.

This was also largely true at the other well-known outcome of the early Garden City movement, Parker and Unwin's Hampstead Garden Suburb (1907). It was developed near Hampstead Heath, a tract of land near London that had been preserved in the nineteenth century as open space. The land was owned by the Reverend Samuel Augustus Barnett (1844–1913) and his wife, Dame Henrietta Barnett (1851–1936), who were Anglican philanthropists living in the working-class East End of London. In 1896 it was announced that Charles Tyson Yerkes (1837–1905), the American financier and builder of many of the Chicago elevated lines, was going to extend the London Underground rail line into the area, with a new station to be built at Golders Green. Dame Barnett was able to buy up and preserve 80 acres (32 hectares) of a former college property nearby as an extension of Hampstead Heath. She then turned to developing the adjoining 243 acres (98 hectares) as a "garden suburb for the working classes," commissioning Parker and Unwin for the design, which began construction just before the new Underground station opened. Hampstead Garden Suburb was intended to be an alternative to then-typical outlying London development, which still usually took the form of row houses on narrow streets, with little greenery, whose popularity often soon produced severe traffic congestion. At Hampstead, Parker and Unwin sorted out the different speeds of traffic, limiting the through traffic to the edges of what would later be described as "superblocks," and using cul-de-sacs and required 10-foot (3-meter) front setbacks to create a bucolic atmosphere that anticipated many later suburban developments.

These design innovations required an Act of Parliament (1906) to allow an exception to the standard bylaws based on conventional row-house street patterns. Architecturally, Hampstead Garden Suburb was not radical, but it did include a range of housing types, from mansions to multifamily units, which were designed in brick and stucco in a variety of simplified revival styles, evoking both northern English vernacular styles and the work of Sir Christopher Wren. As at Letchworth, some cooperative housing quadrangles such as The Orchard (1909) were included, but the overall density was kept very low for the time, at eight houses per acre (0.4 hectare). Efforts were also made to sharply distinguish between

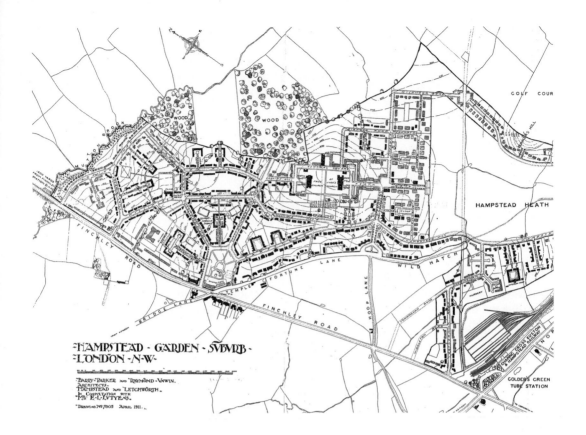

39. Barry Parker and Raymond Unwin, Hampstead Garden Suburb, London, 1907 (Raymond Unwin, *Town Planning in Practice* [London: Unwin, 1909], fold map VI).

the built and unbuilt areas, notably with the 787-foot (240-meter) brick Great Wall that marked the edge of the Heath extension. A classical Central Place was also provided, faced by Sir Edwin Lutyens's two churches (1908), also inspired by the work of Wren. Lutyens's designs were not entirely in line with Unwin's medievalizing and more picturesque Garden City vision. Unwin was fascinated by the urban design ideas of Sitte, and somewhat improbably combined some of Sitte's ideas with his decentralist Garden City approach. Hampstead Garden Suburb was an immense success, with over five thousand residents by 1912, and it quickly became a worldwide model of Garden City design (fig. 39).

Hampstead Garden Suburb's relatively dense suburban design also reflected the almost simultaneous introduction into England of two directions that converged with the Garden City movement around this time. One was a new awareness of German urban planning, introduced into England by the philanthropist Thomas Coglan Horsfall (1841–1932) in his *The Improvement of Dwellings and Surroundings of the People: The Example of Germany* (1905), written for the citizen's council of Salford, a suburb of Manchester. Horsfall described the legal basis of the three-dimensional control of urban development in German cities, and advocated that similar powers be conveyed to English municipalities. He emphasized the importance placed in Germany on state aid to build affordable housing in cities "where good houses cannot be bought at reasonable prices."

Horsfall also emphasized the German focus on efficient traffic circulation patterns, particularly for "the transit of workpeople and school children to and from the outskirts of the town." His emphasis on municipal action to improve housing conditions and to prevent the negative outcomes of overly dense speculative housing found a wide audience in England, where urban areas were viewed with alarm by many at the time.

The French Garden City Association was founded in 1903 in France, where it was the cooperative social reform aspects of Howard's vision that attracted the most interest. The group's secretary, the lawyer Georges Benoît-Levy (1880–1971), was also associated with the Musée Social, and attended the first International Garden City Congress in 1904. He visited Letchworth, and lived for six months in Bournville and Port Sunlight. He also published *La cité jardin* (The Garden City) in 1904 and *Les cités jardins d'amérique* (American Garden Cities) in 1905, the latter expanding the concept to include urban parks. In France, the Garden City concept often met with resistance, as it seemed to be another anti-urban manifestation of the Anglo-American suburban ideal.

Benoît-Levy also complicated the reception of the movement in France in two ways, first by choosing the term *cité*, which does not accurately translate as "city" in English, but was instead usually used as a term for workers' housing projects. Benoît-Levy also combined Howard's concentric diagram with the Ciudad Lineal (linear city) concept of Arturo Soria y Mata (1844–1920), a version of which was eventually built along a rail line east of Madrid (fig. 40).

The Musée Social began to advocate the Garden City concept in France after 1907, though few actual French Garden cities were built before World War I. It was the immense destruction of that war, which destroyed 625 French towns and over 450,000 buildings, that gave Garden City planning a new relevance in the northern French areas requiring reconstruction. The movement also had some influence in the Paris banlieues (the outlying municipal areas beyond the central city limits), notably at Suresnes (1921–39), planned by Alexandre Maistrasse on 59 acres (24 hectares) some 6 miles (10 kilometers) west of Paris. It was

40. Arturo Soria y Mata, Linear City project, Madrid, 1882 (Arturo Hernandez, *The Problem of the Land in Spain* [Madrid, 1926]).

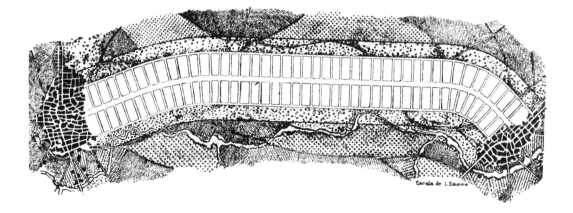

commissioned by Mayor Henri Sellier, who was inspired by the work of Parker and Unwin. At Suresnes, the initial English-type model cottages soon gave way to more typical five-story apartment buildings, resulting in a much higher density of forty-two units per acre (0.4 hectare) than the twelve units per acre advocated by Unwin and other members of the Garden City Association. Like some other similar French projects from this time, Suresnes included more green space, including communal gardens, than typical continental urban development, and also had curving streets with views of a picturesque church and school. Its higher-density pattern of 2,500 units made it a model for New York apartment house complexes in the 1920s and 1930s, resulting in odd and still understudied hybrids of the bucolic aspirations of the Garden City movement and French suburban apartment-house design.

In Germany, the Deutsche Gartenstadtgesellschaft (German Garden City Association) was founded in 1902, five years before a coalition of German industrialists and designers founded the German Werkbund (1907). A key figure in both was Hermann Muthesius (1861–1927), who had studied and reported on English domestic architecture as a cultural attaché at the German embassy in London from 1896 to 1903. His book, *Das Englische Haus* (The English House), presented the then-new suburban combination of historic revival styles with the latest domestic technologies to a German audience, citizens of a recently created empire that was just then emerging as a potential competitor to British, French, and American economic and cultural hegemony. The Werkbund was intended to improve the quality of German products for export, bringing manufacturers, designers, and government authorities together around shared standards. Garden City reformist ideas about rehousing industrial workers in greener, healthier, and more decentralized settlements were quickly subsumed into a German imperial nationalistic agenda, which also took in a variety of design approaches, often including the ideas of Sitte.

The Krupp family, manufacturers of the munitions that were central to Germany's growing military strength, had been building model housing "colonies" for its workers in various German cities since 1863. In 1909 they commissioned a Darmstadt architect and member of the Werkbund, Georg Metzendorf (1874–1934), to design their Garden City of Margaretenhöhe (fig. 41). Its picturesque site was on a plateau surrounded by wooded ravines southwest of the industrial city of Essen, and was laid out as a Sittesque neo-medieval village, surrounded by 124 acres (50 hectares) of forest. The settlement was reached by a 580-foot (177-meter) sandstone bridge that led directly through an archway under apartments to the main market square. Metzendorf's assistants at Margaretenhöhe included Hannes Meyer (1889–1954), a communist Swiss architect who later directed the Bauhaus from 1928 to 1930, and Richard Kaufmann (1887–1958), who became a Zionist emigrant to what was then British Mandate Palestine in 1920.

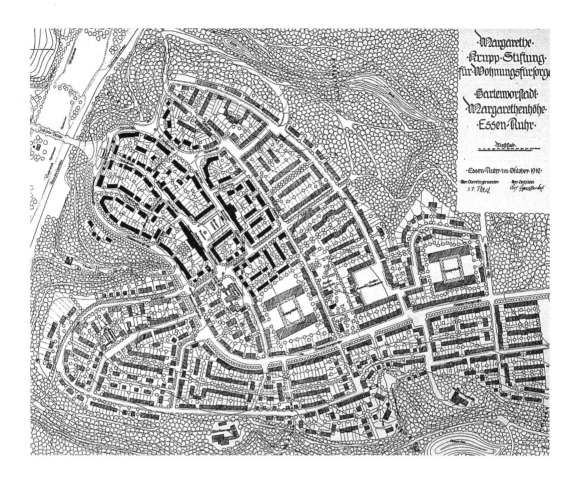

Garden City reform directions also led to the design of many other medieval-style Garden Cities in German-speaking countries, much of it inspired by the work and teaching of Theodor Fischer (1862–1938) in Munich. Examples include the Garden City of Hellerau (founded 1906), near Dresden, by Richard Riemerschmid and Heinrich Tessenow (1876–1950), and the early work of architects like the future Expressionist Bruno Taut (1880–1938), who at his Garden City of Falkenberg (1913–14), near Berlin, specified that the eighty traditionally styled houses be painted in bright colors. Other figures now better known as modern urbanists also began their careers with Garden City settlements, like Hannes Meyer, who designed Siedlung Freidorf (1919) near Basel, and Ernst May, who created Siedlung Goldschnieden (1919–20) in Wrocław-Złotnicki. The city-planning work of the Hamburg city architect and urbanist Fritz Schumacher (1869–1938) also began around this time.

Many of the outcomes of the Garden City movement in Germany took the form of suburban developments, rather than self-sufficient towns surrounded by greenbelts, as at Taut's Siedlung Reform (1912–15), near Madgeburg, and in the many other extensions of major German cities. A German project close to Howard's original social reform goals was Siedlung Hof Hammer in Kiel (1920), designed by the landscape architect

41. Georg Metzendorf, Margaretenhöhe, workers' garden city built by Krupp Munitions near Essen, Germany, 1909, surrounded by a small forest.

Leberecht Migge (1881–1935) and the architect Willy Hahn. In addition to fifty two-story, traditionally styled houses for suburban commuters, this project provided large plots for subsistence gardening for one hundred unemployed shipyard workers. It set aside land for two "compost parks" and used dry toilets for collecting human waste as fertilizer. It also included birch-lined paths, a public park, and a school, nursery, and playground.

By the early 1920s, Garden City approaches had become a major aspect of Germanic town planning, and the more well-known modernist housing settlements of Weimar Germany, discussed in the next chapter, continued many of these same directions. In other countries, related ideas appeared around this same time.

A parallel synthesis of earlier city building and Howard's ideas also strongly influenced the Finnish architecture and planning of Eliel Saarinen (1873–1950). In his plan for Greater Helsinki in 1917–18 in newly independent Finland, Saarinen brilliantly combined the strategies of Haussmann's Paris with these new approaches, suggesting that the city could be tied together with wide boulevards linking compact, walkable districts bounded by greenery, each with its own Sittesque enclosed public square. Due to its high cost, little of the Saarinen plan was carried out as designed, but some of its general principles have in many cases shaped planning in the Finnish capital and elsewhere since then.

SIR PATRICK GEDDES, RAYMOND UNWIN, AND THE BEGINNINGS OF TOWN PLANNING

Horsfall's account of German planning made its appearance at around the same time that the ideas of Sir Patrick Geddes (1854–1932) began to have a wide influence. Geddes was a Scottish biologist, an early urban sociologist, and pioneering theorist of regionalism. In the 1870s he had dropped his early studies at the Royal College of Mines in London to study zoology in France, where he became familiar with the radical geography of Elisée Reclus (1830–1905), an anarchist member of the Paris Commune in 1871. After the end of the Commune, Reclus had been expelled by the French government to a remote corner of southwest France, where he developed his idea that human societies and their economic bases could be understood with reference to their natural conditions of existence, ideas that he then published between 1875 and 1894 as *La géographie universelle* (Universal Geography). Geddes was also familiar with the work of Reclus's French contemporary Paul Vidal de la Blanche (1845–1918), later a more well-known advocate of related ideas such as environmental *milieu* and *genres de vie* (lifeways).

During a research trip to Mexico in 1879–80, Geddes also became aware of the French social theories of Frédéric Le Play, particularly Le Play's emphasis on the triad of "place-work-family" as central to stable working-class life. Geddes translated this concept as "place-work-folk," shifting the Second Empire reformer's emphasis from the family unit as the basic element in a then still largely Catholic French society to a more abstract idea of regionally based organic human communities. After returning to Scotland to teach zoology at Edinburgh University from 1880 to 1888, Geddes came into contact during a visit to London with the Fellowship of New Life, a group focused on understanding Indian philosophy. His work and teaching in the natural sciences had also made him aware of the work of Herbert Spencer, who argued that concepts drawn from biological evolution could also be applied to the evolution of human societies. This complex mix of ideas led Geddes to question the specialization by academic field that is still the basis of modern research universities and that first developed in Germany in the nineteenth century. Instead, he advocated direct action to impact in a positive way his immediate social and physical surroundings in Old Town Edinburgh. In 1880 Geddes had married Anna Morton, a wealthy heiress and Liverpool social worker who strongly admired Octavia Hill's efforts in the 1860s, financially supported by John Ruskin, to improve London tenement conditions. Patrick and Anna Geddes founded the Edinburgh Environment Society and bought several Old Town slum tenements, which they renovated between 1886 and 1896, eventually also receiving some public funding from the town council in 1892 for their efforts. During this period, Patrick Geddes also supported the early feminist movement, advocating that university student dormitories for women be administered by the women students themselves.

At the same time, Patrick Geddes's political views were less radical than those of many others in late nineteenth-century European cities. In 1888 he published *Cooperation versus Socialism,* indicating his distance from the Labour socialism then becoming politically powerful in Britain. He also began conducting a summer school in Edinburgh 1891, and in 1892 opened the Outlook Tower, his first civic exhibition space, inspired by Ruskin's museum for working men in Sheffield. The Outlook Tower was a series of public displays with a panoramic view of the city and its regional and continental surroundings (fig. 42). Geddes saw urban life as both based on available natural resources (place and folk) and organized not into classes, as in socialism, but instead organized by vocation, or occupational groups (work), whose activities he saw as related to place-based geographical and social possibilities. He saw the conflicts among these groups as more significant to human social life than the abstract dialectical historical movements identified by Marx and Engels. Geddes argued that Western urban life had to be understood historically, emerging at first from the ancient Greek polis and its ideals of democracy, and then historically becoming the less democratic, but more organized, Roman *civitas,* which included both the town *municipum* and its food-producing agricultural *pagus,* or countryside. Because of transportation

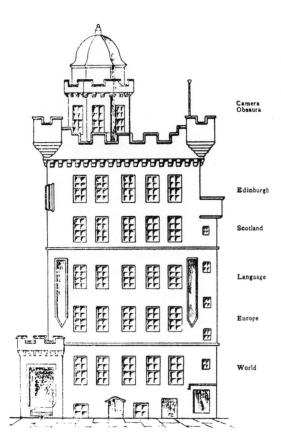

Camera
Obscura

Edinburgh

Scotland

Language

Europe

World

42. Sir Patrick Geddes, Outlook Tower, Edinburgh, diagrammatic elevation (Sir Patrick Geddes, *Cities in Evolution* [London: Williams and Norgate, 1915], 324).

limitations, the polis and its successors could never grow beyond their natural agricultural limits.

Geddes was among the first to see clearly that in the emerging modern world of industry, railways, and massive worldwide urban growth, these geographically limiting conditions were no longer completely determinative. Instead, he advocated a new kind of planning on a regional scale, which would be based on a civic survey to understand all the human and natural conditions of the new large industrial urban "conurbations" that he was among the first to identify. Such a survey would also require an understanding of the "morphology" of the city, a term he borrowed from biology to describe the systematic study of urban patterns. He had also read Peter Kropotkin, *Farms, Fields, and Factories* (1898), an influential book by a Russian émigré that argued for an "anarchist communism" as the basis of society, where free, property-owning individuals would live cooperatively. Kropotkin (1842–1921) was among the first to argue that new, decentralized sources of hydropower could render the large coal-based industrial cities obsolete, and that as a result, new small-scale industry could be scattered across the countryside. By 1900, Geddes was using the term "neotechnic" to describe this emergent condition, which he contrasted with the earlier "paleotechnic" urban conurbations.

Geddes also made two lecture trips to the United States in 1899–1900, where he met the philosopher and educational reformer John Dewey (1859–1952), then just beginning his extremely influential experiments in public education in Chicago, and Jane Addams (1860–1935), who in 1889 had founded Hull House, the Chicago settlement house based on London's Toynbee Hall that laid the groundwork for much subsequent American social work. Geddes was also impressed by Swami Vivekananda (1863–1902), one of the most well-known exponents of Indian philosophy abroad, who had introduced Hinduism to the United States in a speech at the 1893 Chicago World Exhibition. In 1900, Geddes organized a summer school at the Paris Exposition, where he then met the philosopher Henri Bergson (1859–1941), whose ideas of "creative evolution" would soon impact French urbanism, and Paul Otlet (1868–1944), who was beginning his efforts to create a world city of culture, communication, and documentation that would be called the Mundaneum. In 1903, Geddes was commissioned by Dunfermline, a city of 25,000 in Scotland, to redesign a park in a more socially and environmentally engaged way. This was funded by a gift from the town's most famous scion, the American steel industrialist Andrew Carnegie (1835–1919). Geddes's report on this effort, which set out his methods, soon began to circulate widely.

Geddes's methods began with the idea of a regional survey, similar to those conducted by botanists of trees and other vegetation. He argued it should seek to identify the human equivalent of "social species" of plants, which tend to thrive and then exclude other species. The results could then be mapped, which would assist with detailed field observations. Then, social interventions could be cautiously proposed to improve existing social and environmental conditions. These might follow the model of Geddes's "conservative surgery" in Old Town Edinburgh, where his renovations of old buildings and efforts to create small amounts of new open space by spot clearances were eventually combined with building new student residence halls and the public museum at the Outlook Tower. Geddes was also an early advocate of the use of photography in civic surveys, relating the photos of conditions he and his students observed to their precise locations on maps. He suggested that the city of Dunfermline make a list of its historic buildings, a Ruskin-inspired idea that appeared well before the rise of most legally oriented municipal historic preservation efforts. Geddes also proposed an early version of an "adventure playground" for children in Dunfermline.

In 1904 Geddes was invited to present his ideas at the London Sociological Society, where he delivered his paper "Civics as Applied Sociology." For Geddes, the shaping of the new urban environments could no longer be done only by architects and landscape architects, but required a deep understanding of the natural and social conditions of the buildings and their inhabitants, which he saw as "a drama in time." This involved not only historical research but also extensive research into

43. Sir Patrick Geddes, Valley Plan and Valley Section, 1917 (Volker Welter, *Biopolis: Patrick Geddes and the City of Life* [Cambridge, Mass.: MIT Press, 2002], 104).

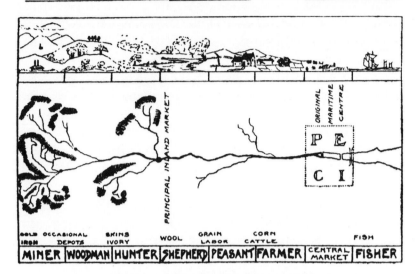

THE ASSOCIATION·OF·THE VALLEY·PLAN WITH THE VALLEY SECTION

RURAL·OCCUPATION·&·MARKET·TOWN·

contemporary sociological and geographical conditions. In 1909, Geddes published his concept of the "Valley Section" as a way of spreading a better understanding of the relationship between place, work, and folk (fig. 43). He proposed that what would now be called a "transect" running along a river valley, from its source in the mountains to its mouth at the ocean, could be analyzed in light of the occupations of the inhabitants and the built forms these produced along its course. Geddes emphasized that large cities typically originated as ports, and he was in fact quite hostile to purely administrative capitals, built without regard to their natural surroundings. The Valley Section then abstracted various forms of settlement in relation to both natural surroundings such as agricultural plains and mining areas. His focus was on the ways that the inhabitants of each geographical area made their livelihoods within it. Geddes adapted the botanical categorization methods of the French biologist Charles Flahault (1852–1935) to try to better understand human adaptation to various environments. Eventually he began to link the concept of the Valley Section with his efforts to abstract categories of various human types, "people, chiefs, intellectuals, and emotionals," which he thought persisted throughout history in different societies, ideas that he then presented in his many exhibitions.

Geddes's emphasis on regionalism and the importance of natural systems in relation to human settlements quickly merged with the ideals of the Garden City movement, and then eventually radically overturned Beaux-Arts ideas of urban composition. European classical approaches to urban design that had developed over centuries were primarily concerned with the visually effective organization of street patterns, monuments, and facades, and their proponents had relatively little interest in organizing the everyday social uses of space by the majority of the population. By the early 1900s, Britain had become 80 percent urbanized, but strongly anti-urban feelings had developed, with many people at all social levels blaming British elites for their grim, dark, and smoky industrial surroundings. The Garden City movement appealed to both workers and industrialists as a solution to these problems, by decentralizing industry and allowing the workers to both live closer to nature and to have shorter commutes. Geddes's focus on regionalism and the importance of natural conditions for economic life, and his interest in entire metropolitan areas, converged with the approaches advocated by Howard and by Parker and Unwin, establishing a set of planning goals and practices that in some cases have continued to the present.

Aspects of this new approach were put in print by Raymond Unwin in his *Town Planning in Practice* (1909), a book whose publication coincided with the founding of the Liverpool University School of Civic Design, the first professional planning program offered at the university level in the English-speaking world. Unwin, like Geddes, was strongly influenced by Ruskin, but also by Sitte, asserting in his first chapter that "Civic Art" was the "expression of civic life." At the same time, Unwin praised Howard, and noted the example of Letchworth, which he and Barry Parker had designed, and called attention to Horsfall's *The Improvement of the Dwellings and Surroundings of the People: The Example of Germany*. Unwin suggested, a little inaccurately, that there "the same problem of rapid increase of towns had been dealt with on lines much akin to those advocated by Mr. Howard." Like earlier English housing reformers, Unwin attacked the monotonous "bylaw" row-house streets of inner London, whose density was forty houses per acre (0.4 hectare). He instead presented a variety of examples of the "individuality of towns" that ranged from the *Marktplatz* of medieval Karlsruhe across a variety of ancient and modern examples. In his fourth chapter, "Of the City Survey," Unwin summarized Geddes's approach, introducing the idea of "survey before plan" into planning practice. He linked it to early traffic surveys of London, as well as to wind intensity diagrams issued by the British Meteorological Office. Unwin also illustrated examples of the decentralization of industry in Letchworth, while at the same time continuing to advocate the importance of central squares for public buildings. The remainder of *Town Planning in Practice* successfully brought Germanic town-planning practices then already in wide use in Germany into the British Empire and the Americas, laying the groundwork for the Garden City–oriented town planning profession that persisted at least to the 1970s.

In 1909 the Town Planning Act, the first legislation allowing local authorities to propose large-scale town-planning projects, was passed by the British Houses of Parliament. This act was a direct outcome of efforts by the Garden City Association, which was renamed the Garden Cities and Town Planning Association in 1909. It pertained to "any land which is in course of development or appears likely to be used for building purposes." Its political support drew from the concern about the rapid, mostly unplanned urbanization of agricultural lands, and the increasingly unequal distribution of land in England. Existing streets determined by the bylaws of the 1875 Public Act were typically 36 to 50 feet (11–15.24 meters) wide, and existing legislation allowed dense patterns of very small row houses, which often lacked plumbing and indoor bathrooms, to be built in close proximity to industrial and commercial properties. The Garden City movement had a complete approach to urban development ready as an alternative, one whose built outcomes were already being demonstrated at Hampstead Garden Suburb. In the five years after the Town Planning Act's approval by Parliament, 105 town planning projects were proposed under its provisions, with the first completed one in Birmingham. The 1909 Town Planning Act's approval was accompanied by the founding of the first professional program in planning, the School of Civic Design at the University of Liverpool, endowed by W. H. Lever (later Lord Leverhulme) and directed by Professor Stanley Adshead (1868–1946). The Royal Institute of British Architects (RIBA) also hosted a Town Planning conference in London in 1910, inviting experts from Europe and the United States, who included Geddes, who presented his "Cities and Town Planning Exhibition," begun in Edinburgh in the 1890s.

It was also at this point that Raymond Unwin's *Town Planning in Practice* was published as a guide to the practices of the new profession. Thomas Adams, then-secretary of the Garden Cities and Town Planning Association, later noted that Unwin's book had moved the discussion of town planning beyond the previous political debates about unconstrained private property rights versus a focus on how governments could protect property values through legislation. The Town Planning Institute, a new professional group, was then organized to promote town planning education. It soon had five hundred members, including architects, engineers, surveyors, and lawyers. It began publishing the *Journal of the Town Planning Institute*, which focused on specific land-use planning problems from a technical perspective. Within a few years, planning in Britain began to expand its focus on the design of new Garden City–type housing estates, like those being built extensively by the LCC, to include the layout of arterial roads. An Arterial Road Conference was held in 1913, and a draft road plan proposed for the 1,000-square-mile (2,590-square-kilometer) London region was endorsed by representatives of 115 local authorities. Thomas Adams, who in the 1920s would become a key figure in the Regional Plan of New York and Environs, later described this as "in effect the first regional plan in England."

The impact of the 1909 Town Planning Act also had immense effects worldwide, particularly since much of the world was then under some kind of British rule or commercial influence. Australia passed a similar Town Planning Act in 1920, which created a Ministry of Town Planning, and New Zealand passed such a law in 1926. In South Africa, the Cape and Transvaal provinces also passed planning legislation introducing Garden City ideas into the racially segregated, pre-apartheid republic. In Canada, where North American–type agricultural and urban grids had been introduced by the British authorities in the nineteenth century, the influence of English Town Planning law varied by province, with Nova Scotia, New Brunswick, and Alberta passing laws in 1915 that were similar to the 1909 English Town Planning Act. In Western Canada, City Beautiful–type planning was carried out by English planner Thomas Mawson (1861–1933) in his unbuilt plans for Calgary and Regina in 1912–15. In Ontario, the outcomes at this time were more parallel to the American acceptance of residential zoning, except in Ottawa, the industrial town founded in the 1820s that was chosen as the capital of Canada in 1857. There, a set of government buildings, including a Gothic-style Parliament, had been built as the result of an 1859 competition. After the 1893 Chicago fair, a series of proposals were made to give Ottawa a suitably imposing design for a national capital, culminating in the Federal Plan Commission's City Beautiful proposal of 1915. Unlike similar plans for Washington, D.C., in 1902, these plans were for the most part not carried out.

Elsewhere in the British Empire the model of the 1909 Town Planning Act led to the enactment of similar legislation in Singapore and the Malay States (now Malaysia) in 1927. The impact of the 1909 Act was not as large in British India, where the urban issues were of a different kind. The design of the new imperial capital of New Delhi, discussed in chapter 2, was a relatively unusual effort by the British, one strongly influenced by the American example of the City Beautiful movement. Instead, the focus of earlier British legislation in India had been on "insanitary and over-crowded areas," which had led to the formation of Improvement Trusts to clear and rebuild slums by the imperial authorities. The model for these was the Bombay Improvement Trust, founded in 1898. Its mission was to control and develop new areas with traffic streets, and to open up especially crowded parts of towns and cities. Typically this involved laying out a new urban quarter with a grid of streets replacing the existing, often irregular street pattern. Multistory model tenements, called *chawls*, were then constructed by the Improvement Trusts (fig. 44). These usually had a series of one-room apartments with 10 × 10 foot (3 × 3 meter) rooms to house entire families, and sometimes included a bath or toilet for every six to eight buildings. Similar Improvement Trusts were established in Hyderabad and Kolkata in 1914, and then in some other cities of British India.

Another aspect of the impact of modern Western planning in India was the sojourn there of Sir Patrick Geddes, who was invited by the

British authorities to bring his "Cities and Town Planning Exhibition" to Chennai (then Madras) in 1914. Geddes was already interested in Indian philosophy and indigenous architecture before his arrival, and he expressed enthusiasm for traditional Indian temple cities in his inaugural lecture in Madras (fig. 45). He had read *The Web of Indian Life* (1904), by Sister Nivedita—a Western disciple of Swami Vivekananda whom the great teacher had convinced to come to India to help improve the lives of women—and Geddes initially had hopes of transposing his own ideas about the importance of women to social life there as well. Critical of the tendency of elites of all kinds in India to move away from the old urban centers to more modern outlying bungalow districts, Geddes sought to apply sociobiological strategies to save indigenous patterns of urban culture and form, without becoming involved in political questions. He was aware of the work of D. A. Turner, who in his *Sanitation in India* (1914) had pointed out that the water-borne disposal of human sewage was expensive, and he instead endorsed the traditional practice of using it for agricultural fertilizer. After his arrival, Geddes also became impressed with the nationalist activities of the Mahātmā Mohandas Gandhi (1869–1948), sending him a copy of his Indore planning report (1917) and suggesting that they work together on Civic Reconstruction in India.

44. Bombay Improvement Trust chawl (minimum multifamily housing), Mandvi district, Mumbai, 1908 (Norma Evenson, *The Indian Metropolis* [New Haven: Yale University Press, 1989], 141).

From Tenement Reform to Regional Planning, 1840–1932

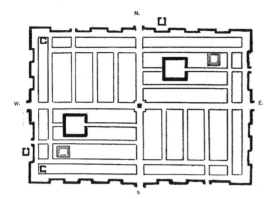

45. Plan of a traditional south Indian town, with temple sites and public water tanks (Henry Vaughn Lanchester, *The Art of Town Planning* [London: Chapman and Hall, 1925], 210).

Geddes was among the first Western planners to note that in India, urban slums were at the periphery of cities, usually built on land normally considered unfit for normal habitation. Unlike the edges of English cities, these areas were dense, but often had unpaved streets and no drainage or clean water supply. He was sharply critical of the efforts of the British urban Improvement Trusts to clear such areas, which he saw as mainly serving the interests of urban property owners and speculators. Geddes thought such philanthropic efforts largely raised central urban land values, making working-class housing there more expensive. He also found the Improvement Trust–built chawls to be prisonlike, mechanistic, and lacking access to nature. Instead of establishing an Improvement Trust for Madras, Geddes advised that the municipality instead appoint a "town planning officer." Geddes then took on this role himself in 1915, and went on to advise many other urban authorities in the subcontinent, writing some sixty planning reports in India from 1915 to 1922.

His first reports were for the city of Madras and some twelve adjacent towns and a nearby suburb, commissioned by the Madras Presidency colonial government. Hired then as a planning consultant by Indian hereditary rulers, such as Maharajas and Durbars, as well as by Municipal Councils, Geddes produced his reports, sometimes assisted by the English architect H. V. Lanchester, who soon after planned suburbs in Yangon and Zanzibar. Geddes made specific recommendations for the city of Dacca (now Dhaka, Bangladesh, 1916); Baroda (1916); Lucknow (1916); Balrampur (1917); Kapurthala (1917); Lahore (1917) Nagpur (1917); Indore (1917); the Barabazaar district of Calcutta (1919); Colombo (now the capital of Sri Lanka, 1921); and Patiala (1922). Geddes also made reports of various kinds on many other cities, including parts of Ahmedabad, Amritsar, Benares, and a historic town near New Delhi. In many of his reports, Geddes continued to emphasize the importance of "survey before plan," advocating the extensive use of mapping and topographical models, as well as the collection of data about many aspects of the social and physical conditions of the cities under study. He also oversaw the production of a large topographical model of the Bengal river system, which includes the Ganges, similar to a model made of the Merseyside watershed in Liverpool in 1896.

In all of his projects, Geddes encouraged mapping and observation of existing environments, rejecting what he called the "mechanocentric" treatment of nature and placing himself on the side of the "gardener, peasant, and citizen" rather than that of the engineers of the colonial Improvement Trusts. Rather than pursue their usual slum clearance plans, Geddes instead advocated what he termed "conservative surgery" to improve urban conditions. Instead of the extensive demolitions typical of the British colonial urban interventions in "slums" at this time, his approach involved minimizing the destruction of existing buildings. His model was based on his and Anna Geddes's activities in the Old Town of Edinburgh, and he had advised that a similar approach be taken in Dublin in 1913. Geddesian "conservative surgery" took into account the fact that former slum dwellers often could not afford the new model tenement housing of the chawls. Instead of relocation, he advocated small-scale, focused urban improvements. In his report, *Town Planning in Balrampur* (1917), Geddes suggested modestly widening narrow streets and opening a sequence of small, tree-lined squares, demolishing as few houses as possible. In many of his Indian planning recommendations, existing temples and their large open water "tanks," which traditionally served as places for bathing and religious activities, became the focus of the modified street layouts. He emphasized that his approach was much less expensive than clearance and reconstruction, with little social disruption, as he noted in his Lahore report (1917). The entire traditional built fabric embodied for Geddes the genius loci, the spirit of the place, linking family to religion, caste, and occupation within a collective pattern. His ideas were taken up in some cities, notably in Lucknow, the capital of the Oudh region, where a declining population and flooding issues made interventions of some kind appear necessary. Working with Lanchester, Geddes made changes in the usual practices of the Lucknow Improvement Trust, which then took on a Geddesian approach to urban planning in the 1920s.

Geddes's ideas found a wide audience in India, where by 1916 he began to be seen as a source of spiritual wisdom, or guru. In 1918, G. S. Ghurye (1893–1983), an Indian sociologist, arranged for Geddes to take an academic appointment in sociology at the University of Bombay (now Mumbai University), with an opportunity to pursue practical field work related to town planning activities in Lucknow, Indore, and other cities. This coincided with the development of a model Garden City settlement, Jamshedpur, by Jamsjetji Tata of the Tata Steel Company. Initially laid out by the engineering firm of Julian, Kennedy and Sahlin, the new city was given a standard street grid, which was then expanded over the next several decades. In the late 1930s the German-Jewish émigré architect Otto Königsberger (1908–1999) extended it with a series of curvilinear boulevards and new residential districts. But Geddes was reluctant to commit to spending most of his time in Mumbai, and eventually left his sociology position altogether in 1924.

In 1919, Geddes had been commissioned by the Zionist Committee in London to plan a Hebrew University in Jerusalem, conceptualized as a center of research and of a revived Hebrew-language culture in the fast-developing Jewish settlements in what is now Israel and the Palestinian territories. The center of historic Jewish civilization in ancient times, this area had a large Arab population and had been ruled by the Ottoman Empire since the 1510s as part of the province of Southern Syria. In 1917, as the Ottomans, then allied with the German and Austrian empires, were being defeated in World War I, the British agreed to the idea of a "Jewish National Home" there. European Jews had already been moving to this region, historically sacred to Judaism, Christianity, and Islam, in large numbers since the 1890s, when the new Zionist Organization, founded in Vienna in response to growing anti-Semitism in Europe, had called for such a national home to be established in 1897. Various European Jewish architects, including Richard Kauffmann, began to design collective settlements after 1900. Like Bruno Taut, Kauffmann had been a student of Theodor Fischer at the Technical University in Munich, and he designed several influential Garden City projects including Nahalal (1921), a cooperative agricultural settlement twenty miles (32 kilometers) southeast of Haifa sponsored by the Jewish National Fund. Its concentric circular plan superficially resembled Howard's Garden City diagram, but was designed to provide eighty agricultural parcels, each measuring 25 acres (10 hectares), with communal facilities in the center surrounded by houses.

Kauffmann also designed three other Garden City–type settlements in what would in 1948 become Israel, including Talpiot (1921), Rehavia (1922), and Beit Hakerem (1922). The British support for the idea of a Jewish National Home, expressed in the Balfour Declaration of 1917, took place after the British, French, and Russian empires had agreed in 1916 to maintain separate "spheres of influence" in former Ottoman territories. The Sykes-Picot treaty of 1916 set some of the boundaries of these territories that would later become Syria and Lebanon (under French mandates until 1943), and the British-controlled kingdoms of Iraq and Transjordan. Jerusalem—a city sacred to Jews, Christians, and Muslims—and nearby parts of present-day Israel were placed under international control, adjacent to areas under British imperial rule, as part of Mandate Palestine. Geddes traveled to Jerusalem with Chaim Weizmann (1874–1952), the president of the Zionist Organization and later the first president of the State of Israel (1949–52), to study sites for the proposed campus, and suggested the one ultimately selected on Mount Scopus. While there, Geddes also proposed the study of traditional Arab villages as models for the new settlements. On his second visit, in 1920, he visited Jewish settlements throughout the region. In 1924, after leaving India, Geddes was commissioned by the head of the town council to develop a plan for Tel Aviv, founded in 1908 as a garden suburb for Zionist settlers near the traditionally Arab city of Jaffa. Wilhelm Stiassny, a Vienna architect, laid out an irregular grid plan for Tel Aviv in 1909, and it was given its present name, meaning "Hill of Spring" in 1910, the title of the Hebrew translation of Theodor Herzl's utopian novel about a future Jewish homeland in Palestine, *Altneuland* (Old-New Land, 1902). On the 1,648-acre (667-hectare) site, Geddes proposed a new rectilinear grid of large "superblocks," which were intended to have no more than twelve houses per acre (0.4 hectare), in keeping with ideas advocated by Unwin in his *Town Planning in Practice*. Tel Aviv grew rapidly thereafter, reaching a population of 150,000 by 1937, and the plan was built out more densely using multistory apartment buildings, many designed by Bauhaus-influenced German-Jewish émigré architects who arrived after the Nazis came to power in Germany in 1933.

In the interwar years, related Garden City and Geddesian ideas were applied throughout areas around the world that were controlled or strongly influenced by British rule. These were often linked to efforts to categorize or racially segregate different populations, often continuing earlier practices of establishing different spatially distinct districts for different groups. Such planning sometimes improved mass living standards to some extent, and at times reflected the idea first put forward in the eighteenth century by the Anglo-Irish statesman Edmund Burke that colonialism implied a trust for the colonial powers to protect native societies from the disruptive effects of modernization. After 1834 the British Parliament had instructed the Colonial Office to regulate legal and territorial relations between settlers and "natives," such as the Aborigines of Australia, or the many indigenous groups in British colonial Africa. These approaches were extended in the early twentieth century by colonial administrators such as Lord Frederick Lugard (1858–1945), the British governor of what became Nigeria from 1900 to 1919, who also served as governor of Hong Kong from 1907 to 1912. Lugard defined the British imperial "mandate" as a "sacred trust of civilization." In terms of city planning, this led to the application by the British authorities of the idea of the "dual city," which was to be segregated between the modern European section and the "traditional" native quarters. This approach was similar to that used by Henri Prost and other French colonial planners at the same time, and in both cases European superiority was assumed as a scientifically established fact. Lord Lugard's *Dual Mandate for Tropical Africa* (1922) set out a clear framework for this racial and spatial segregation, which was then often used in planning for other parts of the empire as well.

URBANISM AND MODERNIZATION IN JAPAN AND CHINA
BEFORE 1930

In Tokyo, Western-influenced modernization had begun after the American opening of Japan to the outside world in 1853. The Japanese government had cut off most contact with Europe in 1614, when it officially banned Portuguese and Spanish religious conversion efforts, which had begun in 1549. After the Meiji dynasty restoration in 1868, the Japanese Empire began to emulate Western models in government, engineering, and urban planning. In 1869 Edo was renamed Tokyo, which means "eastern capital." Railway construction there began in 1872, and the Irish-born Thomas Waters oversaw the reconstruction of central Tokyo's Ginza business district in brick after a massive fire that year. In 1886 two German architects were invited to plan central Tokyo and design major government buildings, and a Tokyo City Improvement Ordinance was passed in 1888.

In this context, Tokyo began to import London apartment housing models as early as the 1890s, and during the Taishō period (1912–26), an urban middle class began to develop. It combined elements of Japanese and Western culture, and offered greater freedom for women within a still very patriarchal society. Western-influenced Japanese models of urban development could already be found throughout the expanding Japanese Empire, which began with the acquisition of Taiwan (1895) and continued with the annexation of Korea, renamed Chōsun after its formal incorporation into Imperial Japan in 1910. It also included an expanded Japanese role in southern Manchuria, now part of China, where the Japanese began to build a railroad after their defeat of Russia in 1905. In this context, City Beautiful formal planning was applied by the Japanese in the main port of Manchuria, Port Arthur, named after an English nineteenth-century navigator, and later renamed Lüshun (now part of Dalian, China). Japanese influence had grown in the region even before the 1932 creation by Japan of Manchukuo, a puppet state nominally ruled by the last Chinese Qing emperor until the Japanese defeat in 1945.

In 1916, Japan's Home Minister Gotō Shimpei (1857–1929), an urban reformer who had been president of the South Manchurian Railway (1906–8) and head of Civil Affairs in the Japanese colony of Taiwan (1898–1906), established the Metropolitan Research Association in Tokyo. It then successfully advanced national legislation in 1919 that addressed city planning, building regulations, and, in 1921, the establishment of cooperative Housing Associations. These efforts were informed by similar legislation in Germany, Britain, and the United States, and continued the same LePlayist focus on the nuclear family (*katei*) and its dwelling as the basic social unit of modern society. Traditional Japanese building culture was disdained by the reformers to some extent at this point, particularly for its use of timber construction, which was seen as unsafe. Commercial

46. Gotō Shimpei, Tokyo master plan, 1923 (Henry Vaughn Lanchester, *The Art of Town Planning* [London: Chapman and Hall, 1925], 218).

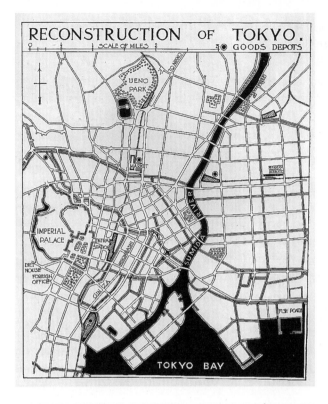

construction also was regulated by the 1919 code, and steel-frame building technology, with passenger elevators, which had been first used extensively at Uchida Yoshizō's Marine Insurance Company building in Tokyo (1918), became part of standard practice across the imperial Japanese domains, which then included Seoul (renamed Keijō by the Japanese from 1910 to 1945), Taipei, and some other Asian cities.

In 1921 the Japanese Housing Association law set up a system of government subsidized low-interest (4.8% over twenty years) loans for members of housing cooperative societies to fund new affordable housing. In 1923 the Great Kantō earthquake destroyed much of Tokyo, and Gotō Shimpei, by then its mayor, encouraged the preparation of a new master plan for the city, which included a new sewer system (fig. 46). In 1924 the Dōjunkai (Mutual Benefit Society), was established for the immediate relief of those displaced. Its founders included Uchida Yoshizō, then chief of the Dōjunkai architecture section, who by this point had become an important early twentieth century Japanese urbanist. The Dōjunkai built some 9,000 apartments from 1924–42. Many were low-rise, reinforced concrete structures of about one hundred to seven hundred units with modern utility connections, and in some cases these buildings included clinics and childcare facilities. One project, the Ōtsuka Women's apartments, had communal dining facilities and restricted male access to a public reception room. These housing experiments, which paralleled those of Holland and Weimar Germany, occurred as the Garden City movement also appeared in Japan, in the form of the Denen-Chōfu set-tlement (1921–32), which was constructed on a rail line some 4.35 miles (7 kilometers) southwest of the Tokyo-Shibuya station. Its large lots and relatively expensive land made it more like a nineteenth-century com-muter suburb than Ebenezer Howard's vision, but it was a step toward the higher-density suburban expansion of Tokyo and other Japanese cit-ies along commuter rail lines in the 1930s. It was around this time that privately owned Japanese railway companies began to build shopping nodes with department stores at Tokyo's major commuter rail stations, setting a pattern still widely found in many East Asian cities.

In China, twentieth-century urban development took place more slowly. Foreign influences greatly increased after 1905, when the Qing Dowager Empress dropped her opposition to foreign railroad build-ing. Since 1843, British, French, and eventually German, Japanese, and American and other Western commercial influences had been growing in China, and foreign "spheres of influence" were agreed upon among them. In addition to Hong Kong, a British colony since 1841, and nearby Macao, part of the Portuguese Empire since the 1500s, these included the "French Concession" part of Shanghai, a key port city that also in-cluded the British and American business areas of the "International Settlement." Both sections of Shanghai were administered as colonial cities and were occupied by Western elites (called "Shanghailanders") and a large population of Chinese workers. British authorities oversaw the building there of the Bund in the 1920s, a riverfront boulevard of imposing high-rise business buildings and hotels, and elsewhere numer-ous other European-inspired developments appeared. The Yangtze River Valley and the province of Shaanxi, with its historic city of Xi'an, was in the British sphere, while the Germans had commercial rights from 1897 to 1918 in the Shandong Peninsula and in its major city, Qingdao, where they built a waterfront promenade. Italian architects and other Western architects were active in Tianjin and elsewhere. In Manchuria, the Japa-nese controlled the southern area, including the city of Shenyang (then known as Mukden), while Northern Manchuria remained under Russian influence. This complex quasi-colonial situation persisted to an extent after the Chinese Revolution of 1911, which replaced the empire with a strife-torn republic led at various points by its founder, Sun Yat-Sen (1886–1925).

The Republic of China signed a peace treaty with Japan in 1914 and entered World War I on the Allied side, which then allowed Japan to ac-quire the former German trading rights in the Shandong Peninsula in 1919. The outraged Chinese student protests in response to this outcome initiated the "May 4th Movement." Elements of this movement, together with the inspiration some Chinese intellectuals found in the Russian Oc-tober Revolution of 1917, led to the founding of the Communist Party of China (CPC) in 1921. By 1923, Sun Yat-Sen's Kuomintang (KMT) party had begun garnering support from the Soviet Union, and introduced the Leninist concept of "democratic centralism" in the context of Soviet military assistance. In 1925, after Sun Yat-Sen's death, KMT military leader Chiang Kai-shek broke with this direction, marginalizing the CPC and quickly taking over much of China. He moved the national capital to Nanjing (Nanking) in 1928, and Beijing (then usually transliterated as Peking) temporarily ceased being the capital and was renamed Beiping. As the new capital, Nanjing was expanded, and an ambitious effort was made by the Nationalist government to combine American City Beautiful planning principles with traditional Chinese architectural forms there. This was in part a response to the growing role of the United States in China. From 1928 to 1937, Chiang Kai-shek's KMT Nanking government, often advised by American experts, began to modernize China, building railways and roads and combining Confucian precepts with KMT ideology. At the same time, the highly stratified traditional Chinese social structure was left largely intact, with many poor peasants working in the countryside.

In European-dominated Shanghai, a new mass housing type, the *li-long*, had emerged by the 1850s. It combined elements of English urban terrace houses and tenements with small courtyards, producing a dense fabric of two- to three-story brick buildings on gated narrow lanes. Often lacking much natural light, li-longs nonetheless served a wide range of income levels, and became the normative building stock of interwar Shanghai. In this same context, professional architectural education began to emerge. The first architect in China to be educated overseas was Zhuang Jin, who graduated from the University of Illinois in 1914, and in 1928 a department of architecture was established at Northeastern University in Mukden (Shenyang). This was headed by Liang Sicheng (1901–1972), a former student of leading Beaux-Arts educator Paul Cret (1876–1945) at the University of Pennsylvania. Liang then brought other Penn-educated Chinese students to the faculty at Mukden, setting a model in Chinese design education for hybridizing the Beaux-Arts with traditional Chinese architecture, which Liang enthusiastically studied and documented.

A TURNING POINT: AMERICAN PLANNING AND URBANISM IN THE 1910S AND 1920S

The American City Beautiful movement was a comprehensive response to the social and infrastructural problems of industrial cities that extended Beaux-Arts design methods into an effort to redesign whole sections of cities. It led to many publications like Werner Hegemann and Elbert Peets, *The American Vitruvius: An Architect's Handbook of Civic Art* (1922), an influential sourcebook of measured drawings of historic European plazas and recent designs.

Though the movement's focus on monumental buildings was already being questioned by the 1920s, the City Beautiful era encompassed the years when many municipal regulatory regimes that still underpin the development of American metropolitan areas were established, notably in the area of land-use regulation through zoning. By 1918 many American cities had adopted zoning ordinances, and by 1929 over 650 American municipalities had planning commissions with varying powers to regulate urban land uses. This outcome was in part the result of the efforts of planners to develop common approaches with influential support from large business and real estate interests, who often looked to Burnham's Plan of Chicago as a model.

Another voice in favor of regulating urban development at this time was the landscape architect Frederick Law Olmsted, Jr. (1870–1957), who with architect Grosvenor Atterbury had designed an American version of an English Garden City at Forest Hills Gardens (1909) on 142 acres (57.4 hectares) in Queens, a short train ride east of Manhattan (fig. 47). Forest Hills Gardens was sponsored by a private philanthropic group, the Russell Sage Foundation, interested in offering new models of urban development for a range of incomes, and the new development was centered on a "station square" that included a hotel and shops. Nearby were

47. Grosvenor Atterbury, architect, and Frederick Law Olmsted, Jr., landscape architect, Forest Hills Gardens, Queens, New York, 1909 (National Park Service).

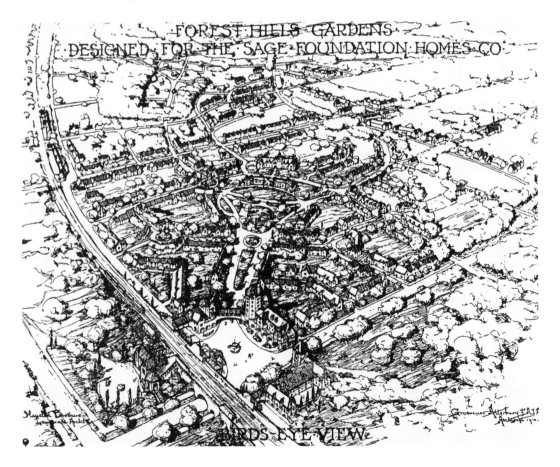

low-rise apartment buildings along a planted boulevard, which extended into areas of attached two-family housing and single-family homes. Atterbury developed a prefabricated concrete construction system for its range of housing types, which were then clad in traditional Arts and Crafts styles evocative of English rural villages. A more Germanic note was struck by the pedestrian-scaled Station Square, a Sittesque enclosed plaza. The housing density was highest in the several-story apartment buildings around and near the square, and then decreased down to more typical suburban densities of single-family homes. Several neighborhood parks were also included. Forest Hills Gardens was intended to be a national model for suburban design, but its reliance on rail transport soon made it seem obsolete, even as its desirable design led to real estate success that eventually only made it affordable for the affluent.

At the first National City Planning Conference, held in Washington, D.C., in 1909, Olmsted, Jr., gave an overview of town planning in the Germanic countries, noting that planning there not only included new street layouts but also addressed elements like building regulations, health ordinances, police rules, and land taxation systems. At the same time, he argued against simply importing such systems into the United States, and instead advocated land-use zoning as a way of controlling future development. There was certainly support for this idea at the popular level throughout the United States, given that citizens' groups since the 1880s—if not earlier—had led local campaigns to protect property values by forbidding saloons, billboards, Chinese laundries, and, sometimes, the construction of multifamily dwellings.

Olmsted, Jr., was also no doubt aware that in 1909, the city of Los Angeles had passed the first American zoning ordinance, strongly supported by the Los Angeles Realty Board. Real estate developers there were eager to separate industrial from residential uses and were openly concerned about the effects of ethnic and racial mixing on residential property values. California had a history of passing ordinances specifically designed to restrict businesses associated with certain ethnic groups, notably the anti-Chinese laundry laws of the 1880s in San Francisco and some other cities. By 1886 the California Supreme Court had recognized the utility of zoning in stabilizing and enhancing real estate values, and had ruled that Chinese laundries could be legally excluded simply because they depreciated the value of the surrounding properties. The 1909 Los Angeles zoning ordinance designated most parts of the city, much of it then just developing along streetcar lines, as Residence Districts, with exceptions made for downtown and local commercial uses, typically along the boulevards. It also set out seven Industrial Districts, mostly along the Los Angeles River and along the numerous freight railway lines that crossed the urban area, many of them running south to San Pedro and Long Beach or east to Ontario and San Bernardino. The California Supreme Court upheld the legality of the Los Angeles zoning ordinance three times between 1911 and 1913, leading the way to the state and then national acceptance of this kind of land-use zoning.

This wider acceptance of legally enforceable controls on private land use occurred just as automobile ownership was starting to become a middle-class phenomenon in the United States. Detroit industrialist Henry Ford (1863–1947) had greatly reduced the costs of auto production in 1913 by introducing the moving assembly line, making it possible for his workers, many of them recent European immigrants, to actually buy the Model Ts that he was manufacturing. Ford, who had grown up on a farm in rural Michigan, was virulently anti-Semitic as well as hostile to East Coast financial elites, ideas he put forward in the *Dearborn Independent* newspaper. He encouraged his workers to leave cities and live in detached houses and drive to work, policies that had a profound effect on Detroit and other American metropolitan areas. At the same time, he was a pioneer in hiring African American workers in his Ford plants, many of whom were eventually able to buy homes in Detroit and in the nearby suburb of Inkster. Just before the United States entered World War I, Ford was contracted by the federal government to build submarines, and he began to construct a new kind of factory to build them in Dearborn, just outside the Detroit city limits. He immediately switched the factory to auto production after 1918. The resulting River Rouge plant set the pattern for the modern, low-rise factory, with motor trucks as well as rail and water transportation bringing in the necessary raw materials as cheaply as possible. Ford then quickly began to build new auto, truck, and other plants elsewhere, spurring the decentralized development of cities like Los Angeles, Dallas, Fort Worth, and many other cities.

Such low-rise, decentralized factory complexes, located near detached, auto-based suburban developments, were an innovation of the 1910s that has had immense and still ongoing effects on worldwide urbanization patterns. The number of registered vehicles in the United States rose from 1.3 million in 1913 to 10 million in 1920, and has continued to increase since then. This widespread use of cars also spurred many responses that intensified the decentralizing trends already under way with streetcar development. The American Automobile Association (AAA) was founded in Chicago in 1902 as a coalition of nine private auto clubs, and a federal Bureau of Public Roads was created in 1905. In 1914, Massachusetts and New Jersey were the first American states to establish state highway departments to regulate traffic, the same year in which the American Association of State Highway Officials (AASHO) was founded. In response to their lobbying, along with pressure from the AAA, in 1916 the federal government began to provide funds to states for highway projects, a direction enthusiastically supported by President Woodrow Wilson, a motoring enthusiast.

Most American roads were gravel or dirt at the time, and it was only with the advent of automobiles and government funding in the 1910s that roads began to be paved and traffic signs installed. New York State and New Jersey began to mandate uniform state road signs by the 1920s, and in 1924 AASHO proposed a system of uniform national numbered routes, which was approved in 1925. Existing national automobile "trails" like the Lincoln Highway, which ran from Jersey City to Chicago to San Francisco, and originally developed in 1913 and paved by a private group, became Route US-30. Various other long-distance two-lane national routes were designated and marked at this time, including Route 66 from Chicago to Los Angeles. By 1930 there were over 234,000 miles (376,587 kilometers) of paved highways in the United States, many of them long-distance routes.

New auto-oriented building types also emerged with the rise of car ownership. Standardized "filling stations" providing motorists with gasoline—a petroleum product originally discovered in the 1850s as a byproduct left over from the processing of kerosene for lamp fuel— began to be widely built by the Standard Oil Company of Ohio in 1907. By the 1920s there were over 100,000 filling stations in the United States. Municipal "auto camps" for passing motorists were also built, and in 1925 what may be the first "mo-tel," the Milestone in San Luis Obispo, California, was built on US-101. Car washes and drive-in markets began to appear in Los Angeles and other cities in the 1920s, and the familiar American commercial strip began to emerge, which then often still had streetcar lines as well as new parking spaces for cars. Downtown department stores began to open branches in auto-accessible locations outside of downtown, as in Wellesley near Boston (1923); in Westchester County north of New York City; in the Chicago suburbs of Evanston, Lake Forest, and Oak Park; and most famously, Bullocks-Wilshire, at 3050 Wilshire Boulevard in Los Angeles (1929). Though still accessible by streetcar from the then-elite and segregated nearby Mid-Wilshire district, Bullocks-Wilshire also provided a large auto parking lot at the rear, the beginning of a trend that has continued unabated ever since.

Chain stores also grew immensely in the auto era, with some 70,000 stores being operated by 1,500 different chains in 1930, such as the Chicago-based Walgreen's drugstores and the New York–based Woolworth's. Suburban retail locations and ample free parking for many of these stores went along with the introduction of self-service retailing, whereby customers themselves brought the goods to be purchased to a check-out counter, a practice that may have been first introduced at the Piggly Wiggly chain in the 1910s, creating a new and now worldwide consumer experience.

The commercial potential of these trends was evident by the 1920s. In an outlying part of southwestern Kansas City, Missouri, residential developer Jesse Clyde Nichols (1880–1950), a Harvard graduate and an early member of the American City Planning Institute, recognized the commercial potential of accommodating automobile access for new development at the edge of the metropolitan area. He began buying up land near what was already called the Country Club District in 1906, eventually acquiring ten square miles (25.9 square kilometers) and building housing for sixty thousand people. This area was at the edge of the new Kansas City parkway system designed by city park board landscape architect George Kessler (1862–1923), a German immigrant who had established his practice in Kansas City with the support of Frederick Law Olmsted in the 1880s. In 1910 Nichols had an existing trolley line extended and commissioned Kessler to plan a new subdivision, Sunset Hills, which had large lots, with unprecedented 200-foot (61-meter) widths. The widespread use of automobiles then made further expansion on this scale possible, and in 1913–14 Nichols also built the elite suburb of Mission Hills, across the state line in Kansas, which had five-acre (2-hectare) parcels. It was arguably the first suburb designed for automobile-only access, less than a twenty-minute drive to downtown Kansas City along Ward Parkway, another Kessler-designed parkway.

Between these new areas and existing older areas, Nichols then developed the multi-block, mixed-use Country Club District shopping area in 1923, which provided large, free auto-parking accommodations for a mix of shops, restaurants, and some high-rise hotels and numerous apartment buildings, all adjacent to a new auto parkway along Brush Creek. In Nichols's nearby residential developments, single-family houses with garages and driveways became typical, and helped to set the national standards for residential development advanced by the National Association of Real Estate Boards (NAREB), founded in 1908 in Chicago and so named in 1916. Like nearly all middle- and upper-income residential developments in the United States at this time, these areas were "protected" with restrictive covenants. These were "deed riders" (legal language added to the property deeds that confirmed legal ownership of a given lot), which excluded certain kinds of people from buying the property. Restrictive covenants typically forbade African Americans from buying into most urban and all new suburban areas, and sometimes Chinese, Jews, Armenians, and other groups whose presence in a given area might have been considered detrimental to future property values were excluded as well.

This kind of residential segregation was the norm in American cities before 1948, in the era when racial segregation was legal, in keeping with the 1896 *Plessy v. Ferguson* case, whereby the Supreme Court had ruled in favor of segregation, as long as "separate but equal" public accommodations were provided to "both races." During the administration (1913–21) of President Woodrow Wilson, a former president of Princeton University who had been raised in various states in the American South, the federal civil service was racially segregated as well, excluding African Americans from all but menial positions.

Only in 1948, with the *Shelley v. Kramer* decision, did the Supreme Court rule that racially restrictive covenants were unenforceable, the first

48. The Mill Creek Valley area of St. Louis was a center of African American life between 1910 and 1959, when it was cleared for urban renewal. View of the southeast corner of Jefferson Avenue and Lawton Street (Missouri Historical Society, St. Louis).

step toward undoing legal racial segregation in housing. Although the segregation ordinances approved by voters in Baltimore in 1910, and in Louisville and St. Louis in 1916, which would have determined the areas where African Americans would be allowed to live, had been ruled unconstitutional on property rights grounds in 1917, in St. Louis its provisions largely determined the racial segregation patterns there (fig. 48). In 1930 the St. Louis Real Estate Exchange provided the U.S. Census Bureau with maps overseen by planner Harland Bartholomew that showed these areas of "Negro Residence," located in older central areas of the city. As in many other cities, these areas were formalized simply through residential sales practices, rather than being implemented by law.

In northern industrial cities like New York, Chicago, Detroit, Philadelphia, and Cleveland, the African American Great Migration caused black populations to grow rapidly, as many individuals and families began to move from Jim Crow segregation and rural poverty in the Deep South in search of what were then plentiful low-wage jobs. These new arrivals were typically much resented by the well-established majority white urban populations, many of them European immigrants. In 1917 a massive race riot took place in East St. Louis, an industrial city just across the Mississippi River from St. Louis, which was at the time the sixth-largest city in the United States. White industrial workers objected to the influx of African Americans, who were being used as strikebreakers, and hundreds of African Americans were violently attacked because of their race, leading to their partial outmigration to other parts of the region, such as Kinloch, Missouri. Two years later, in 1919, on the Near South Side of Chicago, white and black youths clashed on segregated Lake Michigan beaches, leading to a five-day riot that ended in thirty-eight deaths, many injuries, and mass homelessness. The state governor appointed a biracial Chicago Commission on Race Relations to make recommendations, which called attention to the intense competition for residential and recreational space in the city, to discriminatory economic practices in hiring, and to state-sponsored segregation, particularly by police, who in some cases had joined the rioters. It concluded that the mostly newly formed black civic organizations should take a slow, gradualist approach to racial change and not try to raise "race consciousness" among blacks, and to instead encourage interracial cooperation in an era of officially sanctioned racial segregation.

As racial conflict became especially violent in northern industrial cities in the 1910s, racial discrimination remained the norm in suburban residential development nationally. This was explicit in Southern California, where the rapid pace of development, much of it increasingly auto-based, was making Los Angeles a larger city than San Francisco, which since 1850 had been one of the few major urban centers in the American West. In this new situation, one in which racial conflict was increasingly being mediated by spatial separation, zoning controls began to be widely implemented nationally. In 1917 professional planners (defined then as anyone with at least two years of city planning experience), led by Frederick Law Olmsted, Jr., established the American City Planning Institute (later the American Institute of Planners), which advocated land-use zoning ordinances as instruments to implement regional master planning. Yet popular interest in zoning had more to do with recognizing its utility as a legally segregationist way to "protect" property values rather than indicating support for city planning in general. Between 1906 and 1915, efforts to comprehensively plan at the metropolitan level had been proposed and had failed in the San Francisco Bay Area, in St. Louis, and in Philadelphia, largely because of the opposition of some urban and rural interests, as well as the concerns of some suburban towns about losing their autonomy.

At the same time, a different, unanticipated application of "zoning without planning" occurred in New York City, in the effort to regulate central city office-building bulk and the locations of factories. In 1907 the Fifth Avenue Association of merchants had sought to exclude garment factories and their massive numbers of immigrant workers from "invading" the sidewalks of the department store areas along Fifth Avenue north of 23rd Street. In 1911 a mayoral committee had recommended that some sort of city zoning ordinance be passed, and in 1913, planning attorney Edward M. Bassett (1863–1948) recommended that the entire city be zoned. The state then passed the enabling legislation in 1914. The pressing zoning issues in Manhattan had little to do with preserving property values in single-family residential areas, as most of these were rapidly being replaced by high-rise commercial and apartment buildings. Instead, the issue was the height of office buildings like the Equitable Building (built

1915) in lower Manhattan, which blocked most of the daylight to adjacent structures. In July 1916 the City Board of Estimate adopted a zoning resolution for New York City that innovatively sought to control not only land uses, but also building bulk. In this it was inspired by the German zoning codes favored (before 1914) by English and American planners, such as those in use in Frankfurt by the 1890s, but allowing immensely taller buildings. In central business areas like those near Wall Street in lower Manhattan and the emerging Grand Central district at East 42nd Street, the new ordinance allowed one-quarter of the building lot to be towers of any height, and then regulated the built bulk of the remainder of the lot. It did this by establishing a "zoning envelope," which required the street fronts of buildings to slope back from the street at a set point above street level with "angle of light" planes (later called "sky exposure planes"). Building construction technologies in use at the time, based on steel or reinforced concrete frame construction, dictated that this setback be accomplished by a kind of terraced stepping of the building, resulting in a characteristic ziggurat form. This outcome of what would now be called a form-based code was then rendered in drawings by Hugh Ferriss (1889–1962), and, when widely published, became an iconic image of contemporary skyscraper architecture in the 1920s (fig. 49).

The 1916 New York ordinance, which also made an unprecedented use of detailed zoning maps to indicate different land-use districts, regulated uses across the entire city. In some sense this zoning then "froze" existing land uses and prevailing building heights at the point where the new zoning districts were established. At the same time, its allowance for extremely large buildings in many areas, an inevitable acknowledgment of economic reality, was much deplored by planning and zoning advocates at the time, who urged that New York's "unduly liberal provisions in the way of height and size" should not be used for zoning other American cities. The New York ordinance was also relatively unusual in not initially including an industrial land-use category, leaving industry to "unrestricted" areas, and in carrying over provisions of earlier tenement legislation in regulating the size of yards and dense apartment house courtyards.

In other cities, zoning did occasionally function as the means of implementing a master plan, as planners had advocated. In St. Louis, still the fourth-largest city in the United States in 1910, city engineer Harland Bartholomew (1889–1989), appointed in 1916, advocated zoning in the context of his successful implementation of a practical form of planning focused on street widenings to improve auto circulation and the clearance of "blighted" dense central areas. Some of his efforts in St. Louis followed a 1912 proposal by a prominent citizens' group for a "Central Traffic-Parkway," to be designed by George Kessler. This would have extended Market Street west as a grand boulevard from the City Beautiful civic center, which was called for in the 1907 St. Louis plan and was

Figure 1.

Figure 2.

Figure 3.

Figure 4.

49. Hugh Ferriss, renderings of the effects of New York Zoning Ordinance of 1916 (Harvey Wiley Corbett, "Zoning and the Envelope of the Building," *Pencil Points* 4, no. 4 [April 1923], 16).

then actually built. In addition to moving commuters more quickly from downtown from the elite new residential areas of the West End, the Central Traffic-Parkway would have cleared a nineteenth-century row-house and industrial area between 20th Street and Grand Boulevard known as the Mill Creek Valley. By 1912 property values in the area were said to be declining, as African Americans were beginning to move in. The changing racial dynamics there, and in the North Side neighborhood known as the Ville, then a more established center of African American life, led to the proposal for the segregation ordinance in 1916.

The question of urban "blight" was a preoccupation of planners nationally, such as J. Randolph Coolidge of Boston, who influentially defined a "blighted district" at the Fourth National City Planning Conference in

1912 as an area of formerly rising property values where real estate prices had become "stationary or falling." Coolidge insisted that his definition applied only to economic outcomes, rather than social factors. Racial demographics as a planning issue were rarely mentioned by planners directly in their published work before 1948. Yet the vagueness of planners' definitions of blight as involving areas of a "squalid and wretched character" that were a "social liability," requiring more public resources than such areas provided in tax revenues, indicated that the issue did not simply involve the physical organization of certain parts of the city. At the same time, most of the solutions to the problems of "blight" involved some kind of physical rebuilding, typically related to the decentralization of industry and the creation of better traffic circulation and more green spaces in central areas.

Such issues were becoming urgent as different, more decentralized, and ultimately auto-dependent forms of planning began to supplant the City Beautiful approach in the 1910s. Sometimes called the "City Efficient," these were less directly linked to the Beaux-Arts architectural tradition, and were for the most part the further development of nineteenth-century data-driven efforts to address problematic urban conditions, particularly those involving traffic, sewers, and storm water management, usually through physical design interventions based on the collection of statistics and the use of new technologies such as steel and reinforced concrete. Street widenings, new bridges, concrete river channels, and new or improved port facilities were the outcomes of these approaches in many cities.

In Detroit in the 1890s, architect Albert Kahn's brother Julius Kahn (1864–1942) had developed a reinforced concrete construction system similar to the French Hennebique system, which was then used extensively in the construction of factories for automobile manufacturing. Steel-frame skyscrapers, like those built in New York by the Milliken Brothers, who had been the steel-frame contractors for Adler and Sullivan's Wainwright Building in St. Louis (1890–91), began to appear by 1910 in Buenos Aires, Johannesburg, and Sydney. Other American firms were soon building elevator high-rises of ten stories or more in Shanghai, Rio de Janeiro, and elsewhere. In 1904 the United States acquired a strip of land in the Republic of Panama, a former province of Colombia whose independence President Theodore Roosevelt had facilitated in 1903, to build a canal linking the Atlantic and Pacific Oceans. The engineering model for its American engineers was the Suez Canal, designed by French engineers and opened in 1869. In the American Panama Canal Zone (1903–79) the U.S. Army Corps of Engineers and others developed and applied a variety of building techniques for using reinforced concrete, notably in building the system of locks. The canal was begun in 1909 and opened to shipping in 1914, and the techniques involved in its construction were then widely applied in a variety of circumstances.

50. Waddell and Harrington,
Colorado Street Bridge,
Pasadena, California, 1913.

Even before its transition to the world's premier auto-based metropolis in the 1920s, the Los Angeles area was one where reinforced concrete began to be used for a variety of purposes on a grand scale (fig. 50). A new artificial port was constructed at San Pedro, prompting the city to annex a long "shoestring addition" linking it to downtown. Far to the north, an immense aqueduct was constructed under the direction of engineer William Mulholland to the Owens Valley, allowing the annexation and eventual suburban development of the San Fernando Valley.

The entire New York region was also being remade in the 1920s with new highways and parkways, and many industrial workers were beginning to seek housing at the metropolitan periphery, often by following established commuting routes. Parkways, originally conceptualized as carriage drives by Olmsted in his plan for Central Park in 1858, began to be a significant transportation element by the 1920s. Some of the first auto parkways in the world were in the New York City region: the Long Island Motor Parkway (1906–11) and the Bronx River Parkway (1906–23). The Bronx River Parkway was built roughly on the 1844 route of the Harlem Division line of the New York Central Railroad, and was initially planned as a drive in a linear park that also conserved the river valley. As designed by chief engineer Jay Downer and landscape architect Herman W. Merkel, the new four-lane highway was 40 feet (12.19 meters) wide, and linked the new Kensico Dam and Reservoir to New York City, providing direct access to new residential subdivisions in Scarsdale and adjacent areas. The roadway, designed for speeds of up to 25 mph (40 kph), was asphalt paved and without lane markings. The overall width of the Bronx River Parkway median park strip varied, but was typically around

200 feet (61 meters). Some wealthy families in the area donated land for the route, notably in Scarsdale, preserving a substantial tract of forest.

The success of the first section of the Bronx River Parkway led to the creation by the New York State legislature of the Westchester County Parks Commission in 1922, which was charged with creating a system of regional parks, parkways, and outdoor recreation spaces with an associated "scheme of pleasant automobile transportation." Downer was appointed chief engineer to the commission, along with landscape architect Gilmore D. Clarke (1892–1982), who had been the Bronx River Parkway superintendent of construction, and who had commissioned several leading New York architects to design bridges for it. The Westchester County Parkway plan was issued in 1923, and included the Saw Mill (1926–54) and Hutchinson River Parkways (1928), along with the Bronx River Parkway, which opened in 1923. It was envisioned that these parkways would be eventually extended northward to the Taconic State Parkway (1931–32) and to the Bear Mountain Parkway on the west side of the Hudson River. A Cross-County Parkway (1932) was also begun, providing the first section of an intended "metropolitan highway loop" around New York City. By 1926 the rise in suburban land values as a result of the parkways led the commission to recommend that some sections of the proposed routes be abandoned because of the "extortionate prices asked by some of the land owners" to acquire the necessary routes. When the first phase of the Westchester County parkway system was mostly complete in 1932, it included seventy-four bridges, with spans from 19 to 99 feet (5.8–30.2 meters), many of them constructed of reinforced concrete, and four service stations, designed in traditional styles by the architect Penrose Stout.

In 1924 Yale-educated municipal reformer Robert Moses (1888–1981) was appointed to the newly created Long Island State Park Commission by Governor Alfred E. Smith, whose administration was reshaping the state with public initiatives. Moses oversaw the construction of 9,700 acres (3,926 hectares) of new parks on Long Island by 1930, including Jones Beach, a public beach resort accessible only by vehicles, and the Northern and Southern State Parkways. By then, new parkways were beginning to be built in and near other cities. Planner Edward N. Bassett introduced the term "freeway" in 1928, and Benton MacKaye (1879–1975), a member of the Regional Planning Association of America (RPAA), suggested the idea of the "townless highway," a limited-access long-distance route that would encourage "building real communities at definite and favorable points off the road." The concept was included as an element in Henry Wright's New York State plan (1925), which also suggested setting aside large parts of the state, such as the Adirondack Mountains, as nature preserves. It was further elaborated on by MacKaye in 1930, who also established the Appalachian Trail for hikers from Maine to Georgia.

REGIONALISM AND ALTERNATIVE SUBURBAN PLANNING
IN THE UNITED STATES IN THE 1920S

In 1922, Herbert Hoover (1874–1964), then the Secretary of Commerce under President Warren G. Harding, began to advocate model zoning and building codes that could be adopted by municipalities nationally. Hoover was a Stanford University–trained engineer who had worked as a mining engineer in gold mines in Western Australia from 1897 to 1899, and then lived briefly in China before settling in London and making a large fortune. After his involvement in European relief efforts in World War I, which included sending Ford tractors to Russia, he was appointed by President Wilson to the U.S. Food Administration. Later, as Secretary of Commerce, Hoover advocated greater centralization of national economic management by the federal government, and promoted long-term mortgages to middle-class borrowers to encourage mass home ownership. Hoover's *Zoning Primer* (1922) spread the message that zoning was not only legal but was a necessary step for maintaining community health. Hoover suggested standardizing lot sizes, house types, and building materials. He also issued a national model building code in 1922, which set standards for new technologies in house construction for electrical wiring, plumbing for new appliances, as well as for flooring and roofing. In this context, many cities enacted zoning ordinances, whose constitutionality was upheld after some challenges in the *Euclid v. Ambler* Supreme Court decision in 1926. The use of zoning ordinances in many ways simply codified existing American practices of land subdivision, whose outcomes are still evident in many towns dating back to the eighteenth century, but it also typically resulted not only in quasi-legalizing racially segregated residential patterns but also in promoting a smaller range of housing types, in neighborhoods where corner markets and small business establishments were often no longer legal as well.

During this same decade, the Garden City movement had become well known to North American architects and planners. Many earlier industrial workers' towns and garden suburbs had already been built in the United States by then, including places like Garden City, New York, on Long Island (1869), one of many examples of new suburban commuter towns built near open countryside without much overall planning. Their lack of public community facilities led Clarence Perry (1872–1944), a resident of Forest Hills Gardens and author of *Wider Use of the School Plant* (1912), a book that had influentially advocated the use of public school buildings for community afterhours activities, to suggest in 1929 that Forest Hill Gardens could be a model example of the "neighborhood unit."

The term "neighborhood unit" itself had been introduced by Chicago architect and former Frank Lloyd Wright associate William Drummond (1876–1948) in 1913, in his entry to a Chicago competition sponsored by the City Residential Land Development Corporation. Perhaps inspired by European activity at the time in planning new outlying areas, the competition had asked for low-density residential designs for a 160-acre (65-hectare) gridded site on streetcar lines, some eight miles (13 kilometers) southwest of the Loop, approximately in the Brighton Park area. Of the forty proposals submitted, which included a "noncompetitive" entry by Frank Lloyd Wright, the jury of Jens Jensen (1860–1951), a Chicago landscape architect, the architect George Maher, and several others, chose a winning plan by former Wright associate Wilhelm Bernhard that resembled the Forest Hills Gardens plan. Drummond's project was not among the winning entries, but his accompanying text includes the first use of the term "neighborhood unit" to describe such a project. Frank Lloyd Wright's plan was also significant, in that its low-density organization of housing with many communal amenities anticipated his later Broadacre City proposal of the 1930s.

In 1917, as the United States entered World War I, Frederick Ackerman (1878–1950), a New York architect, was sent to England by the American Institute of Architects (A.I.A.) to study defense workers' housing there. On his return he began to advocate similar approaches in the United States. Around the same time, planners led by Olmsted, Jr., began to suggest that city-planning principles be used to design housing for workers in war industries, as well as for "troop cantonments." Olmsted, Jr., designed a prototype plan for such settlements, accompanied by a design manual. Around the same time, Ackerman was able to make the case for a comprehensive approach to the design of new settlements after he had begun working for the U.S. Emergency Fleet Corporation (EFC), a component of the U.S. Shipping Board, which was established during the war. In 1917–18, sixty-seven such projects were planned for sites in forty-seven cities, of which sixty were under contact when the war ended in May 1918. The built results included such new housing settlements as Yorkship Village (1918), in the industrial town of Camden, New Jersey, designed by New York architect Electus Litchfield (1872–1952) on 225 acres (91 hectares) across the Delaware River from Philadelphia. Like many of the other EFC projects, Yorkship Village consisted of small, traditionally styled brick row houses with yards, in this case arranged along diagonal boulevards that led to a central square.

Henry Wright (1878–1936) was a University of Pennsylvania–educated architect from Kansas City who had worked with George Kessler on the landscape design of the 1904 St. Louis Louisiana Purchase Exposition and had practiced in St. Louis between 1904 and 1917. He then worked with Ackerman and New York architect Robert D. Kohn (1870–1953) for the EFC to select architects and planners for the many new workers' "villages." Henry Wright was also directly involved with the design of some of projects, including Colonial Terraces in Newburgh, New York, with the Boston firm of Peabody and Stearns. Many other EFC projects were built, including numerous ones by various architects on multiple sites in Bridgeport, Connecticut, some by the Boston architect R. Clipston Sturgis (1860–1951) and Arthur A. Shurtleff (1870–1957), a landscape architect, planner, and pioneer of playground design. The success of these projects led to the formation of the short-lived United States Housing Corporation within the Department of Labor in 1918, whose chief of town planning was Olmsted, Jr. Though by congressional order all of these projects were quickly privatized by mid-1918, the EFC projects suggested to architects and to some clients the possibility of large-scale urban design for postwar housing settlements.

Clarence Stein (1882–1975) was a Beaux-Arts–educated New York architect who had worked for Bertrand Grosvenor Goodhue from 1911 to 1917, and designed the industrial town of Tyrone, New Mexico (1914–18, demolished in 1969), for a mining company. He joined with Henry Wright and Alexander Bing, a developer of Manhattan apartment houses, to propose a Garden City development similar to the EFC projects for a newly developing outlying part of Queens in 1923. Instead of the standard grid of streets built out with repetitive two-story wood-frame houses, they proposed a range of housing types from garden apartments to single-family houses, with a large central park and "summer colony" along the Atlantic Ocean. Around the same time, Stein, Wright, and Bing began to meet with Lewis Mumford (1895–1990) and others to found the Regional Planning Association of America (RPAA) in New York in 1922. Mumford was a largely self-educated New York author, artist, and cultural critic who had been raised by a single mother in impoverished circumstances. He had first encountered Patrick Geddes's work as a student in a course at the City University of New York in 1917, and then became one of Geddes's many worldwide correspondents, writing with such clarity that Geddes named him his official biographer in his will, a task Mumford was unwilling to take on after Geddes's death in 1932. He nonetheless became an enthusiastic champion of Geddes's ideas in the United States, introducing Americans to Geddesian ideas of regionalism, and the emerging possibilities of planned decentralization using automobiles and hydroelectric power. Mumford also brought Geddes's genealogical approach to the history of urbanism and culture to a popular American audience, questioning the then-triumphant neoclassicism of the City Beautiful movement and reevaluating the importance of American architects like H. H. Richardson, Louis Sullivan, and Frank Lloyd Wright in his *Sticks and Stones: A Study of American Architecture and Civilization* (1924).

Lewis Mumford's enthusiasms at this point extended beyond art and architectural history and criticism, and he became a vigorous champion of the work and ideas of the RPAA. In 1919, during the terms of New York Governor Al Smith (1919–20, 1923–28), who had grown up in a European immigrant environment on Manhattan's Lower East Side, a

Reconstruction Commission was appointed to examine the state's future development. Stein volunteered to chair the Housing Committee of the Reconstruction Commission, which issued its report in 1920. It emphasized that it was currently economically unprofitable "to provide a large part of the population of this State with decent homes according to American standards of living."

The housing shortage in and around New York City was becoming acute, with even Old Law tenements being renovated, with indoor plumbing installed to meet more recent building code requirements. Instead of the prewar focus on "slums" and urban model tenements, Stein's Housing Committee report focused on how to increase the supply of affordable housing along Garden City lines. It recommended the establishment of a central state housing agency and local housing boards to allow cities to acquire land and engage in "housing operations." Following the model of some German cities, notably Frankfurt-am-Main, Stein's report advocated municipal ownership of land to discourage real estate speculation, and suggested that a state-enabling act be passed to authorize cities to acquire land and then build municipally owned housing on it. It also objected to then-standardized street platting, typically laid out in an urban grid, and favored large-scale building of housing districts, rather than the piecemeal construction of houses and apartment buildings by small builders on individual lots. In addition to these suggestions, basically a version of German practices, the Housing Committee report also advocated industrial decentralization and the implementation of Garden City planning that would limit the size of cities to preserve the land around them for agricultural and recreational purposes.

These recommendations were far too radical for the New York State legislature, which instead in 1920 passed a rent control law for apartments and granted a large tax exemption for home builders. All newly built dwellings were tax exempt up to $5,000 ($68,360 in 2016), or $1,000 ($13,672 in 2016) per room for apartments, if construction was started before April 1922 and completed by 1924. Only New York City enacted the necessary legislation to make this state legislation effective, triggering a building boom in the outer boroughs of Brooklyn and Queens. Since the rent controls did not apply to new rentals, the residential building revival that followed did not benefit lower-income groups, though it did ensure that many partially vacant Old Law tenements without indoor plumbing or electricity were renovated, rather than demolished. In the outer boroughs on the recently built subway lines away from Manhattan, Stein complained of "feverish construction" of "rows of ugly, badly built wooden structures." His fellow RPAA member Lewis Mumford likewise criticized the new semi-detached houses of Flatbush, where "surrounding open spaces are covered by a multitude of auto drives and garages," as well as the "dormitory slums" of multistory apartment buildings in "Boston, Chicago, and the Bronx."

Despite some parallel intentions, neither the earlier Forest Hills Gardens development, nor the 1913 Chicago City Residential Land Development Corporation competition, were given much weight by the RPAA. Instead, the group focused its initial efforts on developing a model housing settlement in Queens, which it called Sunnyside Gardens (1923). Unlike Forest Hills Gardens, which was intended for the middle class but soon became a relatively elite enclave, Sunnyside Gardens was planned to house the working class. It was a 16-block, 77-acre (31-hectare) project of 1,200 units, located on a newly opened elevated line (now the number 7 line), a fifteen-minute rail journey from Grand Central Station in Midtown Manhattan. Alexander Bing financially supported the project, creating the City Housing Corporation to act as the developer, which was expected to receive a projected 6 percent return on its invested capital.

The RPAA's goal was to provide an alternative to the gridded single-family house developments then being rapidly built in outlying parts of New York City. At Sunnyside Gardens, Stein and Wright hoped to modify the already-platted street grid, but were unable to do so, resulting in a final project not that much different from earlier two-story row-house patterns. Its main innovations were the communal green spaces within the blocks, intended to provide a range of recreational activities, and Stein's compact unit designs. Like many of the World War I EFC projects, these provided small, sunlit units for families, and also included the new plumbing and electrical provisions that were becoming standard in middle-class housing at this time. Stein's simple, brick pitched-roof exteriors at Sunnyside Gardens continued the design approaches of the EFC projects, but also added amenities like covered parking at the edge of the project, an early model for what would become a standardized pattern in American multifamily residential developments.

The RPAA wanted to offer more collective alternative models of new suburban development, much of it based on English Garden City examples, and these ideas were also advocated by the AIA's Committee on Community Planning, chaired by Stein during 1921–25. It extended this agenda beyond existing metropolitan areas into a Geddes-inspired agenda for "planning whole regions," which would be organized with new highways and decentralized industry to house the less affluent in modern surroundings closer to nature, the kinds of living conditions that had previously been available only to the wealthy. Many of the site-plan and housing-unit strategies of the RPAA were drawn from the experience of the EFC, which were themselves Americanized versions of the kinds of suburban housing estates the LCC had been building since the passage of the 1909 Town Planning Act and the publication of Raymond Unwin's *Town Planning in Practice*.

In addition to Clarence Stein, Henry Wright, and Lewis Mumford, the RPAA also included architects Frederick J. Ackerman and Robert D. Kohn, along with Benton MacKaye. Eventually its membership also included

Tracy Augur (1896–1974), a Harvard-educated planner; Clarence Perry, the advocate of the neighborhood unit; and Catherine Bauer (1905–1964), daughter of the New Jersey state highway commissioner and eventually a key figure in the development of public housing in the United States under the New Deal.

Sunnyside Gardens was followed in 1928 by another experimental RPAA settlement, Radburn, some twenty-one miles (34 kilometers) north-west of Manhattan near Paterson, New Jersey, and described as a "town for the motor age." The site was again developed by Bing's City Housing Corporation, which examined some fifty possible sites before choosing two square miles (518 hectares) on a relatively flat area that, like much of northern New Jersey, had been farmed since colonial times. The construction of the George Washington Bridge (1927–31) over the Hudson River from Fort Lee to Manhattan had already triggered a suburban building boom in the area, and the RPAA intended to demonstrate that alternative patterns of suburban development could also be financially successful. As with other new developments in the area, the RPAA assumed that most of the residents who moved to Radburn would commute back to Man-hattan, as Paterson was then experiencing a decline as a manufacturing center. Stein and Wright were the town planners at Radburn, along with New York architects Ackerman and Andrew J. Thomas (1875–1965), the latter a New York multifamily housing expert who had built many large elevator apartment projects in Queens. Stein later emphasized that Rad-burn was "not a Garden City," as it lacked space for a greenbelt. It was instead more of a Garden Suburb for office workers in Manhattan than a place of its own with employment opportunities.

Radburn's most important design innovation was the use of resi-dential superblocks to allow for pedestrian circulation from the houses to the elementary school, so that no child had to walk more than one-half mile (0.8 kilometer) to school. This concept was both part of earlier Garden City movement efforts to situate housing in relation to natural areas, as in Parker and Unwin's Hampstead Garden Suburb, and a re-sponse to the flood of automobiles in American cities in the 1920s, which were causing many pedestrian deaths, particularly of children. Stein de-scribed the superblock design that separated auto routes from pedes-trian green areas as a response to the question of "how to live in spite of" the car. It required "a radical revision of the relation of houses, paths, gardens, parks, blocks, and local neighborhoods." Traffic was organized by speed, with boulevard-like main roads leading to secondary collector roads around the residential superblocks. Within this layout, cul-de-sacs provided auto access to the houses and their individual garages while preventing through traffic. Pedestrian and vehicular traffic were entirely separated, with pathways running through the large interior parklike areas behind the houses. These ran under or over the auto streets where the two crossed, usually under stone-faced bridges similar to those

Olmsted and Vaux had designed for Central Park. The houses were de-signed to face the interior green spaces, reversing the usual relationship of house to street, with the idea that the street side of the houses would become more the service side, where the designers envisioned that the male residents could work on their cars and garbage could be picked up, eliminating the need for alleys (fig. 51).

The organizing planning element for Radburn was Clarence Perry's "neighborhood unit," based on the population that could live in sub-urban conditions within the one-half-mile (0.8-kilometer) radius of an elementary school. These units were projected to house 7,500 to 10,000 people, each unit with its own shopping center. In the one neighbor-hood unit actually built at Radburn, which was planned to house about 2,800 people, there were 469 single-family homes, 48 townhouses, and 30 two-family houses, all designed by Stein and Wright, and one 93-unit apartment complex designed by Thomas. There was also one of the first drive-in shopping centers, the Plaza Building, designed by Ackerman in a Colonial Williamsburg style. The Depression ended the construction of Radburn as this part of the project was being completed, but its planning innovations almost immediately became influential on suburban design. *American City* magazine ran four articles on Radburn in 1928 and 1929,

51. Stein & Wright, with Frederick Ackerman and Andrew J. Thomas, Radburn, New Jersey, 1928.

and it was prominently featured in the discussions of planning organizations at this time.

Radburn's development coincided with the continuing publication of the *Regional Plan of New York and Environs,* a privately funded effort led by Charles Dyer Norton, one of the key supporters of Burnham's Plan of Chicago. Norton had moved to New York City in 1911 and began to agitate for a similar effort for the tri-state region within fifty miles (80.5 kilometers) of Manhattan. At the Eleventh National Conference on City Planning, held in Buffalo in 1919, Thomas Adams, former secretary of the Garden Cities and Town Planning Association in England and by then a Toronto-based planner, had presented a paper titled "Regional Survey as the Basis for the Regional Plan." Here he linked Geddes's regionalist approach, where "artificial boundaries of cities are becoming more and more meaningless" to the goals of the American city-planning profession. Those goals were defined in 1917 by St. Louis planner Harland Bartholomew as a focus on major street plans, the planning of transportation infrastructure, the systematic provision of recreational facilities across the metropolitan area, and districting for different uses, which would be legally enforced by zoning codes, along with a focus on "urban appearance" and public building groups. In 1921 the Russell Sage Foundation, as a result of Norton's efforts, began to fund preliminary studies about the "basic facts" relevant to planning the New York region.

Frederic A. Delano, by then director of several railway lines and a vice-governor of the Federal Reserve Board, who had also been involved with the Plan of Chicago 1909, began to assemble data on the New York region's harbors and railway terminals, and other planners were soon drawn into various aspects of this nascent regional planning effort. Some aspects of it were paralleled in the Philadelphia region around the same time. This initial survey work was presented to the public by such speakers as Secretary of Commerce Herbert Hoover, Norton, and various New York philanthropists concerned with housing conditions and the built environment. Adams, by then a partner in his London-based firm of Adams and Thompson and a planning consultant to the Canadian government, as well as a visiting lecturer at MIT, was appointed in 1923 by the newly formed Regional Plan Association as "general director of plans and surveys." Adams later described the goal of this effort as primarily to indicate "areas best suited for business and residential use, as well as industrial use and open spaces," for a region that then had a population of about 11.5 million. The plan's survey area included four hundred municipalities in three states, and attempted to plan for the next thirty-five years, to 1958. The multiple volumes of the first *Regional Plan of New York and Its Environs* (RPNY) contain many specific planning proposals, some drawn from the City Beautiful movement, but its most lasting legacy was its effort to organize transportation, port terminals, and industry over the complex topography of the coastal port region.

52. Existing and proposed regional express highway routes, 1929 (*Regional Plan of New York and Its Environs* [New York, 1929], 1: 219).

A major aspect of this organization involved determining the routes for new highways and bridges, and the plan set out an ambitious agenda to create a regional transportation "loop" around Manhattan that would eventually include the George Washington Bridge and the Lincoln Tunnel, both of which supplemented the Holland Tunnel-Pulaski Skyway) auto route (begun in 1919, and later renamed Routes 1 and 9) into Manhattan from New Jersey (fig. 52). The RPNY also recommended that large natural areas be set aside for recreational purposes, and proposed moving most of Manhattan's industrial harbor facilities to Port Newark. Many of these suggestions were later carried out, but the plan's proposal for a suburban ring railway to link the many commuter rail lines that converged on Manhattan was never built, ensuring the centrality and intense congestion of the city's main railway stations thereafter.

The direct impacts of both Radburn and the RPNY were immediately visible in the seven-volume report of the *President's Conference on Home Building and Home Ownership,* convened in December 1931 by President Herbert Hoover. He had been elected in 1928 with the campaign slogan, "a chicken in every pot and a car in every garage." By then it was clear the stock market crash of October 1929 had ushered in an unprecedented

Great Depression, with 25 percent unemployment and eventually half of all American residential mortgages in default, seemingly making a mockery of Hoover's "own your own home" campaign. Hoover was opposed to public housing and government subsidies for the construction of new towns, as advocated by the RPAA, but instead identified the main problem in American housing as the inability of many prospective homebuyers to afford more than 10–20 percent of the purchase price of a new home. The President's Conference organizing committee included Delano, Adams, Bartholomew, and others, who oversaw committees that included some 3,700 experts on various aspects of urban development, including home finance and taxation as well as planning. Its *Planning for Residential Districts* (volume one of the report) strongly advocated the neighborhood unit as the best way to plan new residential areas, suggesting that each one should cover about 150–300 acres (61–121.4 hectares) and have a population ranging from three thousand to six thousand within a half-mile (0.8-kilometer) radius of an elementary school.

In volume three of the President's Conference proceedings, *Slums, Blighted Areas, and Decentralization*, the decentralization of industry and the clearance of areas of "blight" were also advocated, along with the construction of low-income housing at the edges of urban areas. "Blight" was defined as affecting "areas of once high grade residences" that had shifted to a "lower type of use such as boarding or lodging houses, or possibly to mixed business and residential use." These areas might be seen as "analogous to a part of the body suffering from a local infection," and were characterized by land overcrowding, "obsolete" arrangement of lots and buildings, and the invasion of "hostile uses," such as the "objectionable influences of neighboring industries." Race was not mentioned explicitly as a condition leading to "blight." The proposed solution was better zoning and city planning to "stabilize" land uses and "protect" residential neighborhoods for longer periods "to obtain a higher standard of decency and cleanliness than obtains in unzoned neighborhoods." These same motivations were also behind Hoover's Standard City Planning Enabling Act, which he had issued as secretary of commerce in 1928.

A map prepared by Bartholomew showing "principles of land subdivision" was also included in the President's Conference *Planning for Residential Districts* volume, which showed a neighborhood unit of curvilinear streets for new single-family homes, centered on a school in a park. Some distance away was a commercial center with parking, adjacent to some two-story apartments. The *President's Conference on Home Building and Home Ownership* emphasized the importance of restrictive covenants in such areas to preserve property values. A small circular neighborhood-unit diagram, later republished in the British *Town Planning Review* (June 1935), showing a "school and playpark" at the center, was also included, and was later cited by CIAM (International Congresses of Modern Architecture) President Josep Lluís Sert. Where new street patterns were not possible, the *Planning for Residential Districts* volume also included several examples of subdivision layouts on neighborhood-unit principles that could be used instead of a then-more-conventional grid of streets. These planning ideas were all already present in American planning by 1931, but the President's Conference on Home Building and Home Ownership proceedings influentially combined the innovations of the Kansas City Country Club district, Bartholomew's planning practices, and neighborhood unit concepts that had been used at Forest Hills Gardens and Radburn, and put them forward as a complete package for orderly, quasi-state-sanctioned planning guidelines.

Nothing was said directly about racial segregation in the *Planning for Residential Districts* volume of the President's Conference on Home Building and Home Ownership proceedings, but the issue was plainly of concern. In a separate volume, *Negro Housing*, edited by Charles Spurgeon Johnson (1893–1956), an eminent black sociologist and later president of Fisk University, the introduction noted "the problem of escaping bad housing conditions due to segregation," though it added that this was "not the result of any willful inhumanity on the part of our society." Instead, it was somewhat confusingly described as part of the general problem of providing enough housing of "acceptable standards for low-income groups." For them, the Radburn-type neighborhood-unit pattern was not an option, according to the President's Conference on Home Building and Home Ownership organizers, and a different housing model, an updated version of model tenement housing, was offered instead. Key projects were Andrew J. Thomas's Dunbar Apartments (1926), on Adam Clayton Powell Boulevard at West 149th Street in Harlem, a full-block complex of six-story apartments similar to those Thomas had been designing since 1919. Thomas, a self-taught architect with a background in Manhattan apartment building management, had also worked for the EFC during World War I, and had then begun designing such large full-block apartment-house complexes for white tenants for the Queensboro Corporation in Jackson Heights, a fast-growing part of the previously mostly agricultural outer borough. These six-story full-block segregated apartment complexes near rail lines, with central common green spaces, were further developments of the design strategies of earlier model tenement projects, but now also included self-operated passenger elevators, parking, and sometimes swimming pools and other amenities. In 1924 Thomas completed a large housing project for the Metropolitan Life Insurance Company in the Long Island City area of Queens, an early effort at large-scale housing by the same insurance company that would later build Stuyvesant Town. Like the Dunbar Apartments and some parallel experiments at this time, it organized an entire block with U-shaped buildings that provided each unit with light and air, as well as access to the relatively limited public open spaces inside the block. The Queens complexes were, like most new middle-class housing of the time, off-limits to African Americans and sometimes other groups. The sponsoring of the Dunbar apartments by John D. Rockefeller, Jr.'s philanthropic efforts was the result of the Urban League's push to convince housing philanthropists to provide better urban housing for African Americans unable to rent elsewhere.

The President's Conference's effort to offer new models of urban development was powerfully reinforced by President Hoover's creation in 1932 of the Reconstruction Finance Corporation (RFC), an effort to support bank-lending for large projects likely to increase employment. Its projects included both Boulder Dam (now Hoover Dam, 1931–36) in Nevada as well as one of the first large slum clearance projects, Knickerbocker Village on the Lower East Side. Developed by Fred. F. French, who had successfully built the large Tudor City apartment complex (1925–32) for office workers in east Midtown Manhattan designed by H. Douglas Ives, Knickerbocker Village was designed by Frederick Ackerman (of the firm of Van Wart and Ackerman), and opened in 1934. Its three-acre (1.2-hectare) site was cleared of mostly Old Law tenements and earlier structures, and was replaced with a massive 1,600-unit high-rise courtyard apartment building. Like Clarence Stein and Ackerman's row houses at Sunnyside Gardens, the brick exterior facades at Knickerbocker Village were left mostly unornamented. Ackerman was a devoted disciple of Thorstein Veblen, whose popular *Theory of the Leisure Class* (1899) had denounced the lavish consumption and elaborate architectural tastes of the newly rich. Most of the design attention was given to efficient layouts of the apartments and their relationship to the elevator and service cores of the building.

The historical trajectory from nineteenth-century tenement reform to regional planning in the early 1930s was a complex one, with many differences from one country to another. The appeal of the Garden City movement to industrialists and housing reformers in Britain around 1900 as a solution to a variety of urban ills led to the creation of the planning profession there, which also soon included the regionalist and biotechnical ideas of Patrick Geddes. Before the 1930s, these directions had a more limited impact in Japan and its colonies in East Asia, where rail-based urban modernization often took a more high-density form, though in some cases efforts were also made to provide the light, air, and sanitation provisions in housing then being demanded by Western reformers.

In the United States, on the other hand, existing traditions of low-density residential development meant that its hyper-dense immigrant central cities, such as New York, Chicago, and San Francisco, developed in a radically different way than the elite-planned suburbs of Kansas City based on the Country Club District, or much of the Los Angeles metropolitan area. In those environments, Garden City ideas intersected with the decentralist direction advocated by auto manufacturer Henry Ford, producing new environments where the pedestrian and communitarian aspects of the Garden City movement (which had also been present in most previous forms of human settlement) were largely absent, but where land uses were nonetheless strictly zoned to preserve property values. In the 1920s, the RPAA attempted to address those shortcomings in its model designs for communities like Radburn, which then set the basis for government-supported subdivision planning by the early 1930s. These did not challenge the racially segregated and increasingly auto-based nature of American suburban development, and as a result were widely influential.

FURTHER READING

Margaret Crawford, *Building the Workingman's Paradise* (London: Verso, 1995).
James Ford and John M. Gries, eds., *Planning for Residential Districts* (Washington, D.C.: President's Conference, 1932).
Peter Hall, *Cities of Tomorrow* (London: Blackwell, 1988).
James Heitzman, *The City in South Asia* (New York: Routledge, 2008).
Alison Isenberg, *Downtown America* (Chicago: University of Chicago Press, 2005).
Paul Knox, *Palimpsests: Biographies of 50 City Districts* (Basel: Birkhäuser, 2012).
Roy Lubove, *Community Planning in the 1920s: The Contribution of the Regional Planning Association of America* (Pittsburgh: University of Pittsburgh Press, 1964).
Helen Meller, *Patrick Geddes* (London: Routledge, 1990).
Richard Plunz, *The History of Housing in New York City* (New York: Columbia University Press, 1990).
Clarence Stein, *Toward New Towns for America* (Cambridge, Mass.: MIT Press, 1957).
Robert A. M. Stern, David Fishman, and Jacob Tilove, *Paradise Planned: The Garden Suburb and the Modern City* (New York: Monacelli, 2013).

CHAPTER FOUR

The Emergence of Avant-Garde Urbanism in the 1920s and 1930s

SOCIAL CHANGE AND MODERN URBANISM IN EUROPE IN THE 1910S AND 1920S

The ideas of Ebenezer Howard and the Garden City movement led to many complex outcomes in Europe around 1910. These included the early writings on urbanism of Charles-Edouard Jeanneret (1887–1965), the young French Swiss watch-case engraver and outsider architect, who would in 1920 take up the more well-known pseudonym of "Le Corbusier." It was also at this time that the term *urbanisme* was introduced, perhaps first by the Beaux-Arts trained, Rome Prize–winning architect Henri Prost. The term was coined just before Prost also founded the Société Française des Urbanistes (French Urbanist Society) in 1911. Its members included graduates of the École des Beaux-Arts then involved in designing master plans for many growing industrial cities around the world. These included Tony Garnier (1869–1948), whose all–reinforced concrete socialist worker's city, the Cité Industrielle (Industrial Settlement), was a major inspiration for Le Corbusier's later urbanism. The extensive urban design activities of the *urbanistes* took place along with the global expansion of the Paris-based Hennebique engineering firm, a specialist in reinforced concrete that by 1897 had patented its now nearly universal system of using steel reinforcing bars to strengthen poured-in-place concrete. By 1899 the Hennebique firm had twenty-six offices around the world, with 2,700 concrete construction projects that included bridges, housing, and industrial buildings, literally laying the foundations of the later growth of cities like Mexico City and many others.

The effects and outcomes of these new directions were different in Europe than in North America. World War I had largely destroyed the old social order abroad, and in the wake of the unprecedented carnage—much of it the result of both sides using new military technologies such as tanks, airplanes, poison gas, and bombs—radical new visions of peaceful, internationalist future societies appeared. These included the

Expressionist urban visions of the German-Jewish architect Bruno Taut, who published his *Die Stadtkrone* (The City Crown, 1919), a utopian vision of a future society centered on symbolically charged central communal-religious structures like Gothic cathedrals, the temple complex of Angkor Wat, mosques, pagodas, and Hindu temples. Taut, Walter Gropius (1883–1969), and others formed the "Glass Chain," a group of mostly German artists and architects, some of whom had served in the German imperial army. They envisioned a pacifist, socialist future where national borders would disappear. New, organically designed Garden City settlements organized along cooperative socialist principles would reject all previous architectures and create a new world of transparent glass and expressively used steel and concrete.

Expressionism (as it was later called) soon began to find common linkages with other avant-garde directions, including the Italian Futurists' rejection of the architectures of the past and its militarist celebration of speed and new technologies and infrastructures, as shown in the 1914 *La Città Nuova* (The New City) drawings of Antonio Sant'Elia (1888–1916) in Milan. From radically different directions, Adolf Loos (1870–1933) in Vienna rejected the Vienna Secessionists' efforts to create new ornamental systems, while the Dutch De Stijl movement in art, led by Theo van Doesburg (1883–1931), sought a universal visual language of primary colors and simple rectilinear shapes inspired by the paintings of Piet Mondrian. Though emerging in different circumstances, all these avant-garde directions shared a sense that entirely new architectural and urban forms were a necessary component of a new social as well as artistic order. In holding this conviction, they differed from the proponents of the Garden City movement, which had typically used medieval or other preindustrial forms even as they sought to transform industrial urban life to bring more people in closer contact with the natural world in their daily lives in industrial cities.

Though not linked to Expressionism in Germany, an intermediate urban design direction between German Expressionism and earlier medieval revivalism appeared in Amsterdam during the first two decades of the twentieth century. It started with the work and example of H. P. Berlage (1856–1934), a Dutch architect who had won a competition in 1897 to design a new Stock Exchange building in the center of Amsterdam, opposite the central train station. Berlage had also published a Dutch summary of Sitte's *Der Städebau* in 1892, translating "city building" into Dutch as *stedebouw*. In 1902 a Dutch town planning law (*Woningwet*) was passed, supported by a coalition of reform-minded property owners and the recently founded Dutch Social Democratic Workers' Party (SDAP). The law required that each municipality establish a local building code, and, in cities over 10,000 people, issue a plan for future expansion. The Woningwet did not mandate that cities should build new housing themselves, but rather that the municipality would regulate housing construction and encourage local worker-owned housing societies to build model tenements for their members. The Dutch town planning law was passed in the context of other efforts by the SDAP to advance "municipal socialism." Between 1896 and 1900, the city of Amsterdam took over ownership of its water supply, a natural gas factory, and the street-car system. In 1900 Berlage won a competition to replan an area of urban expansion directly adjacent to the old city called Amsterdam South. His plan was approved in 1904, with municipal land acquisition beginning in 1911. In 1908 he began to teach a course in stedebouw in Amsterdam, well before the first Dutch professional program in the subject was established at the TU Delft in 1924.

In 1914 Berlage was asked to substantially revise his Amsterdam South scheme, and the result skillfully combined the boulevards of Haussmann's Paris with ample parks and parkways as the urban framework for new low-rise mass housing to be built by the new workers' housing cooperatives (fig. 53). These had been founded starting in 1906 by various groups, and included housing societies for socialists, Roman Catholics, Protestant Calvinists, a secular workers' consumer cooperative with many Jewish members (De Dageraad, or "Dawn"), and others. Also involved were workers' building societies such as Onze Woning (Our Dwelling) and Eigen Haard (Own Hearth). Unlike Haussmann's Paris, the new housing in Amsterdam South and adjacent newly planned areas was not intended to be primarily a focal point for the display of urban wealth, but instead a place where the workers' cooperative building societies would construct centrally located, affordable housing complexes for their members.

A group of younger architects known as the "Amsterdam School," which included Michel de Klerk (1884–1923), formed around Berlage and the journal *Wendingen* (Turnings). They designed many of the new housing complexes with social services in central Amsterdam, beginning with

53. H. P. Berlage, Amsterdam South master plan, 1915–22.

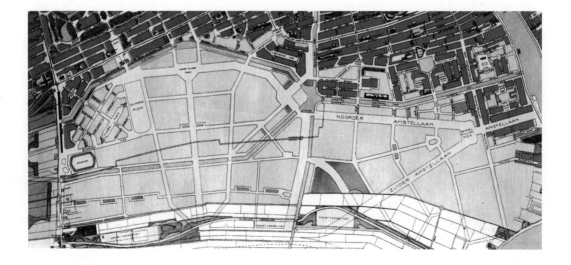

The Emergence of Avant-Garde Urbanism in the 1920s and 1930s

De Klerk's Spaarndammerplantsoen complex (1913–20). They designed a varied brick, low-rise architecture for these new sections of the city, which also included new parks, parkways, bike paths, and urban squares, served by new tram and train lines. The housing forms evoked both medieval rural Dutch architecture as well as more recent housing reform efforts to ensure adequate light and air in model tenements. In Rotterdam, where J. J. P. Oud (1890–1963) was appointed city architect in 1918, less artistically exuberant but nevertheless socially conscious housing directions emerged. These efforts included early projects by Oud himself, which later caused the historian Sigfried Giedion to incorrectly claim that Oud had invented the perimeter block housing type. They also included the work of Michiel Brinkmann (1873–1925), whose Spangen housing (1919–21), a four-story perimeter block complex of attached two-story "houses," was accessed on the upper floor by a pedestrian "street in the air" and was later admired by Alison Smithson, a founding member of the postwar Team 10 group of architects. The Amsterdam School's formal inventiveness and departure from earlier classical forms also inspired the Berlin German-Jewish architect Erich Mendelsohn (1887–1953), whose wartime drawings and radical 1920s architecture became influential worldwide. The work of Berlage and the Amsterdam School, as well as parallel efforts made in other Dutch cities, also indicated that an urbanism conceptualized as primarily about serving the needs of urban workers could also be a source of innovative architecture, simultaneously symbolizing and producing a new set of urban social relations.

In the 1920s these directions also included what came to be called Red Vienna. No longer the capital of a large international empire, as a result of the war, Vienna and its surroundings, with a population of about 2 million, in 1919 became a state within the new small country of Austria. Its elected municipal government was a Social Democratic one, strongly influenced by the Austro-Marxist concept of a "third way" between Western capitalism and the emerging USSR. Unlike Lenin, Austro-Marxist theorists did not call for the violent overthrow of capitalism but instead sought to create a new *Wohnkultur* (culture of living) that would increase working-class solidarity in the urban environment and at the same time better provide for basic needs. To that end the city oversaw the construction of some 400 courtyard apartment buildings, with access to communal services, designed by over 190 architects. Construction costs were financed by high taxes on the wealthy so that rents could be set at no more than a small percentage of the typical income of a semi-skilled worker. Each complex was conceptualized as a *Gemeindebauten*, a "commune" covering a least one, and often several, city blocks, organized around public inner courtyards with play areas, kindergartens, clinics, libraries, laundry facilities, and theaters. It was intended that these communes would eventually replace the highly socially stratified bourgeois city, and gradually literally build the concrete reality of a new

54. Karl Ehn, Karl Marx Hof, Vienna, 1927–30.

socialist urban society. Among the many Red Vienna housing projects, Karl Ehn's Karl Marx Hof (1927–30) is the best known (fig. 54). Though it aimed to radically transform urban life, the architecture of Red Vienna was relatively conservative, with most of it designed by students of Otto Wagner, continuing his skilled prewar melding of historic Viennese urban forms with new programs and technologies. The Vienna experiment attracted considerable interest internationally, including that of the London County Council in the 1930s, which began to use some related strategies in its housing there, and from housing cooperatives in the Bronx. It also drew the attention of Edgar Kaufmann, the Pittsburgh department store owner and later patron of Frank Lloyd Wright, and from a philanthropic housing association in St. Louis, which then built the Neighborhood Gardens perimeter block housing complex (1934) there. Despite this wide interest, the stylistic conservatism of Red Vienna marginalized it within the mainstream of the new modern architectural directions, and it only began to be seriously studied by historians in the 1980s.

The conceptual basis of the housing of Red Vienna had begun to be articulated before the end of the Austro-Hungarian Empire in the work of Otto Wagner and others. Historian and critic Walter Curt Behrendt had published a book in 1911 arguing that the new scale of urban boulevards and large open spaces in cities required the use of large unified blocks, like those of the Vienna Ringstrasse. But for Austrian design theorists of the 1920s like Otto Neurath (1882–1945), it would be the "organized proletariat," rather than monopoly capitalists, who would create this new urban structure. Neurath suggested that the centralization characteristic of proletarian socialism could be combined "architectonically" with democracy and self-government, as the proletariat "has no use for empty appearances." The new city would be shaped by the global industrial organization of business, with railway stations, warehouses, factories, "bold vibrating elevated railway lines," and skyscrapers appearing at particular points. For some theorists, the historic core of the city could also be maintained as the administrative and business center of the metropolis, though for some this seemed to require its complete rebuilding.

Only tangentially linked to each other, if at all, the various new political and artistic directions around the time of World War I—the Amsterdam School, De Stijl, Futurism, Expressionism, and experiments in municipal and regional socialism—all began to converge in the early 1920s, laying the basis for many later approaches to urbanism, architecture, and the arts.

URBANISM AND REVOLUTION, 1917–28

The new urban directions of the Amsterdam School and the work of Berlage in the Netherlands, which remained neutral during World War I, occurred at the same time as the Russian Revolution, another major impetus to the development of modern architecture and urbanism internationally. During World War I, the Russian Empire was overthrown by a democratic revolution in 1917. Within a few months, a second revolution, led by Bolshevik revolutionary leader V. I. Lenin (1870–1924), an opponent of Russia's involvement in the war, and whose return to St. Petersburg had been facilitated by the German Empire, established a dictatorial Soviet communist regime that would last until 1991. Lenin immediately withdrew Russia from the war, and after several years of civil war, Lenin's forces controlled most of the former Russian Empire, which in 1922 they renamed the Union of Soviet Socialist Republics (USSR). As a prewar revolutionary leader, Lenin had influentially revised the communist theory of Marx and Engels. His main focus was not to build worker solidarity through mass labor organizations nor to achieve immediate, practical goals like municipal socialism. Lenin instead emphasized the necessity for the revolutionary leadership of a vanguard party to lead the working class to violently and effectively destroy the power of the bourgeoisie in every economic and political sphere, by any means necessary. He saw such extreme steps as the only way to bring a real socialist society into being, one in which private property would disappear. The new order would theoretically create a fully egalitarian social order ruled by the workers, the "proletariat," who would be organized into self-governing worker councils called "soviets," whose many activities would be directed from above by the Communist Party Central Committee.

In 1918, Moscow replaced St. Petersburg (which was renamed Leningrad in 1924) as the capital of the new state. Lenin and his fellow Bolsheviks' real success in transforming the technically backward and socially conservative Russian Empire into the Soviet Union was possible only through ongoing, extremely violent internal and external struggles across its vast territories. The Bolshevik "Reds" were ultimately successful in defeating the Czarist "Whites," who were supported to some extent by the French and British empires, and Soviet rule necessitated its own highly centralized, bureaucratically organized state apparatus. The Communist Party leadership, which included Red Army founder Leon Trotsky (1879–1940) and the Georgian born Josef Stalin (1878–1953), trained as an Eastern Orthodox priest and having served as the editor of the party newspaper, *Pravda,* successfully introduced mass electrification and the further development of heavy industry. The Soviet regime also invented the "gulag" system of labor camps for dissidents and unleashed the "Red Terror" against urban property owners and wealthy peasants known as "kulaks," as well as persecuting the clergy and other religious leaders. After Lenin's death in 1924, a power struggle occurred between Central Committee members, ultimately leading to a battle between Trotsky, who saw the Bolshevik revolution as the first step toward inspiring communist revolutions everywhere, and Stalin, who advocated "socialism in one country." Stalin had more mass support and eventually won out, and then successfully sought foreign investment to modernize the country, announcing in 1928 the First Soviet Five Year Plan.

The many mass atrocities committed by the Bolshevik regime after 1917, including immense deliberately induced famines in the Ukraine, were not well known in the West until at least the late 1930s. Between 1918 and the mid-1930s, many Western workers and intellectuals welcomed the USSR as a model for a future industrial society without social class distinctions, one in which aristocratic institutions (and their favored classical art forms) would disappear. They hoped these forms and institutions would be replaced by a new art and culture directly serving the masses. Both in the Soviet Union and elsewhere, Western avant-garde movements such as Cubism, Futurism, and Expressionism were combined with politically inspired Soviet art movements, as seen in such architectural works as Vladimir Tatlin's Monument to the Third International (Communist Party Congress) of 1918. This was to be a 1,312-foot (400-meter) steel tower like the Eiffel Tower, with suspended legislative chambers for the new Soviet government. Each chamber would be a different primary shape (cube, sphere, cylinder) and would rotate on different cycles, based on how often they were to be used. For many, Tatlin's tower was seen as the embodiment of the slogan "Steel, glass, revolution."

To fulfill the new social aims, radical educational models were put in place. One of these was VKhutemas, the Higher Artistic and Technical Studios in Moscow, which in 1920 replaced the Beaux-Arts academies in Russia. It did away with the previous Renaissance-based art and architectural training in painting, sculpture, and architecture and instead offered instruction in four areas: graphics, color, volume, and space. Various complex debates emerged among its faculty, including the division between a group called the "Rationalists," led by Nikolai Ladovsky (1881–1941), who then became one of the founders of the ASNOVA group,

55. El Lissitzky, Wolkenbugel (horizontal skyscraper) project, 1923–25 (from ASNOVA 1, 1926).

and the "Constructivists," who included the architect Alexander Vesnin (1883–1959) and the artist Alexander Rodchenko (1891–1956), who taught graphics, photography, and metal construction at VKhutemas. The ASNOVA group for a time also included graphic designer El Lissitzky (1890–1941), who had studied with the Russian abstract painter Kasimir Malevich (1878–1935) and who around 1920 pioneered many of the graphic techniques now standard in "modern" design, some of them already anticipated slightly earlier by the British Vorticist group around Wyndham Lewis (1882–1957). Many of these artists and architects also began to propose visionary future urban environments like Lissitzky's Wolkenbugel (horizontal skyscraper) project of 1924 (fig. 55), or the even more radical visions of Ivan Leonidov (1902–1959).

By the early 1920s these divergent Soviet avant-garde directions also began to be represented at the Bauhaus, a new design school founded by Walter Gropius (1883–1969) in Weimar, Germany, in 1919. After an initial Expressionist period, in 1923 Gropius hired radical Hungarian émigré artist László Moholy Nagy (1895–1946) to teach the Bauhaus "base course." Moholy Nagy brought elements of the Soviet avant-garde's approaches into the new curriculum. These did away with the classical emphasis on the three "fine art" fields of architecture, painting, and sculpture, whose models were to be found in the "canon" (originally a Greek term for a measuring stick) of the best ancient classical and Renaissance examples. Instead of this approach, which had been used by the Catholic church and official regimes of various kinds over many centuries to communicate key ideas to their communicants, constituencies, and citizens, Bauhaus teaching emphasized student learning about the properties of light, color, and the various properties of materials to design industrially produced products that were intended to solve the various practical problems of daily living for the working class.

Bauhaus's teaching rejected traditional ideas of "art" and instead sought to link the new artistic directions represented by painters such as Wassily Kandinsky, Paul Klee, and others with new mass-production and advertising techniques. Moholy Nagy also began to emphasize the ways that photography and film were transforming human perception, requiring new design methods. The Bauhaus at this time developed a present-oriented approach with a strong socialist political orientation, and was largely hostile to historical studies, and certainly to the replication of any historical forms in new design work. At the same time, Moholy Nagy was fascinated by the way that plant forms were related to functional patterns of growth, development, and adaptation, and used the short book *The Plants as Inventors* (1920) by Raoul Heinrich Francé (1874–1943), a Viennese pioneer of organic farming, as a sourcebook of Bauhaus design methods.

The Bauhaus began operating as the former German Empire was undergoing massive social and economic dislocation. Germany between 1919 and 1933 was for the first time in its short history a unified nation governed by an elected democratic government, the Weimar Republic. The internationalist, social democratic orientation of Weimar was vehemently rejected at the time by many on the left, including many workers, artists, and intellectuals who instead sought a violent "November Revolution" to make Germany into a communist state like the USSR. To prevent that from happening, the Weimar government relied heavily on militaristic elements of the right, many of whom then coalesced into the National Socialist (Nazi) party, led by Adolf Hitler (1889–1945) after 1920. The idea became widespread in Germany that the nation's unexpected wartime defeat and subsequent economic crisis (much of it arguably the result of unreasonable French demands for war reparations) was the result of internal subversion and an international conspiracy that linked the Bolsheviks in Moscow and the financiers of London and New York, in what became known as "Judeobolshevism." This was often, though not always, thought to be linked to the emerging Weimar artistic avant-gardes in Berlin and other major cities. By the late 1920s such suspicions helped fuel the rise of Hitler, an Austrian-born war veteran from Bavaria, and his popular, violently anticommunist and anti-Semitic Nazi party, which stressed the innate biological superiority of the Nordic or Aryan "race" and the need to rid the national territory of Jews, Gypsies, and other "racially degenerate" peoples.

The Weimar period was also the context of an emerging international interest in radically new forms of architecture and urbanism. In Paris, in

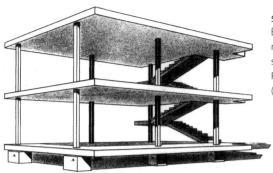

56. Le Corbusier (Charles-Édouard Jeanneret), Domino reinforced concrete structural system, 1914. © F.L.C./ADAGP, Paris/Artists Rights Society (ARS), New York 2016.

1920, Le Corbusier (the name that the former C.-E. Jeanneret took up based on an ancestor's last name, Lecorbésier), founded an avant-garde journal, *L'espirit nouveau* (The New Spirit) with artist Amédée Ozenfant (1886–1966). Its goal was to publicize a Paris modern art movement that they called Purism, a further development of Pablo Picasso and George Braque's Cubism, and to, at the same time, introduce their readers to a variety of new artistic, social, and technical directions. The first issue published articles on Picasso and on De Stijl, and reprinted Loos's influential essay "Ornament and Crime" (1908). Later issues included the first publication of many of Le Corbusier's innovative architectural and urbanistic proposals (fig. 56). These mostly involved the use of prefabricated reinforced concrete standardized housing units, a direction pioneered by Peter Behrens in Berlin around 1910 and strongly endorsed by Gropius, one of Behrens's associates at the time. In making these proposals at the neighborhood and then the urban scale, Le Corbusier drew inspiration eclectically from various sources, ranging from Sitte to Garnier, Parker and Unwin, and Loos. He had also worked for the Paris reinforced concrete architect Auguste Perret (1874–1954), designer of an early and influential reinforced concrete–frame apartment building on the Rue Franklin in Paris (1903), who by the 1920s was also unsuccessfully seeking to change Beaux-Arts teaching methods.

Le Corbusier supported his many artistic and architectural activities at this time by also producing and selling concrete blocks, which he advocated as a means to reconstruct northern French and Belgian cities destroyed during the war. In 1922 he published a series of drawings in *L'espirit nouveau* for a visionary future city, which he called the Ville Contemporaine (Contemporary City). It was inspired both by the actual urban planning work of French urbanists like Henri Prost, as well as the visionary architectural drawings of the Italian Futurists. It remains one of the most influential projects of modern urbanism. Le Corbusier's intention was to offer a reformed version of the immense skyscraper cities of global capitalism that had begun to appear in New York and Chicago by the 1880s. Paris, like most European cities, had a strictly enforced six-story height limit. After World War I there was a real possibility that with international (then mostly British and American) investment and the new technologies of steel and concrete construction, Paris might begin to develop a high-rise skyline like that of Lower Manhattan. Le Corbusier's proposal was intended to be a counter-model of the "chaos" of the typical American downtown, where extremely tall business buildings were built very close to each other, limiting light and air in many offices and creating massive traffic congestion every day at rush hour (fig. 57). In contrast to the close spacing of such buildings in cities like New York and Chicago, Le Corbusier's "Contemporary City for Three Million" was an attempt to create orderly, high-density work environments that would reduce "friction" in the movement of crowds and various forms of traffic.

The Ville Contemporaine would be an orderly model of tall glass skyscrapers spaced 2,225 feet (800 meters) apart, all set on a raised platform and served by new high-speed highways, a central train station, and an airport. The cross-plan office towers would be steel-frame buildings that would be entirely glazed to allow maximum light into every office. Within walking distance of this new kind of downtown, whose regular overall form was inspired in part by the medieval Cambodian temple site of Angkor Wat, new residential districts would be built with linear

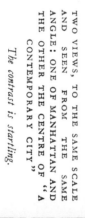

57. Le Corbusier, Contemporary City for Three Million, 1922, contrasted with lower Manhattan (*The City of Tomorrow* [New York: Payson and Clarke, 1929], 173). © F.L.C./ADAGP, Paris/ Artists Rights Society (ARS), New York 2016.

TWO VIEWS, TO THE SAME SCALE AND SEEN FROM THE SAME ANGLE: ONE OF MANHATTAN AND THE OTHER THE CENTRE OF "A CONTEMPORARY CITY"

The contrast is startling.

The Emergence of Avant-Garde Urbanism in the 1920s and 1930s

eight-story apartment blocks set in park-like green areas similar to those of Olmsted and Vaux's Central Park. In addition to streetcars and underground rail lines, which at the time were becoming common in modern cities, Le Corbusier also proposed limited-access high-speed highways (the only one in Europe at that time was the short AVUS expressway in Berlin) and an airport, a building type also just coming into being.

Though not designed for a specific client in mind, and not at all a realistic proposal for Paris in 1922, the Ville Contemporaine immediately captured the imagination of a generation of young architects around the world. In 1923 Le Corbusier published *Vers une architecture*, published in English in 1927 under the title *Towards a New Architecture,* which brought together some of his articles from *L'espirit nouveau* on the need for a new approach to architecture in light of recent new technologies and social changes. In those texts he defended the classical ideal of "Architecture" as rooted in ancient examples like the Parthenon in Athens, while at the same time arguing that architects must begin to approach building design by using the model of industrial and product design, continually adapting forms to uses and changing technologies, instead of simply copying historical patterns. The message of *Vers une architecture* was powerfully paralleled in the teachings of Gropius and Moholy-Nagy at the Bauhaus, and the book was soon translated into German, Czech, English, Japanese, Spanish, Russian, and other languages, leading to Le Corbusier's ascendance as an international celebrity and prophet of a new architecture in the 1920s. He then published the Ville Contemporaine project in 1925 in a book he titled *Urbanisme* (inaccurately translated as *The City of Tomorrow and Its Planning,* 1927). Le Corbusier deliberately appropriated the by-then widely used French term that had previously referred not to modernist urbanism but instead to the more socially conscious versions of Haussmann's Paris that the members of the Société Française des Urbanistes were then designing for cities like Casablanca (Henri Prost, 1914); Havana (J.N.C. Forestier, 1925); Barcelona (Léon Jausselly, 1903 and 1928); Buenos Aires (Joseph Bouvard proposal for the Avenida 9 de Julio, 1912); Rio de Janeiro (Alfred Agache, 1927); and Hanoi, Dalat, and Saigon in French colonial Vietnam (Ernest Hébrard, 1924, 1925).

Despite the many built examples of the work of these earlier French urbanists, much of it still widely admired today for its sophisticated organizations of urban life and its photogenic Beaux-Arts architecture, Le Corbusier's urbanism was of far more interest to many younger architects in the 1920s. In Berlin, Ludwig Hilberseimer (1885–1967) published drawings of an "improved" version of Le Corbusier's vision, where he suggested that the new *Gross-stadt* (metropolis) should be organized vertically. Tall, widely spaced housing slabs would be built above elevated pedestrian walkways, with office buildings at ground level and limited-access highways and rail lines below (fig. 58). He argued that this pattern solved the inevitable traffic congestion problems of Le Corbusier's proposal.

Hilberseimer was one many radical architects in Europe responding to Le Corbusier's urban visions, and many others such as Farkas Molnár (1897–1945) in Budapest (KURI City, 1924) and Richard Neutra (1892–1970) in Los Angeles (Rush City Reformed, 1929) made related futuristic proposals for the total reorganization of urban life. Many of these visions sought to use new technologies of high-rise construction to reduce commuting times while providing every worker with the basic necessary require- ments of sunlight, air circulation, and access to open space. Instead of the extended metropolitan regions that resulted from the application of Garden City ideas, these visions attempted to offer a different kind of centralized city than the Haussmannian model. In the USSR, many archi- tects, planners, and others speculated about the future possibilities for architecture within the modern city along related lines.

All these designers were part of what was termed the "Modern Movement" in architecture by Erich Mendelsohn in 1931. Architects like Oud in Holland and Bruno Taut in Berlin began to combine earlier ur- banistic approaches with both Garden Cities and Bauhaus ideas in the design of large new housing settlements for workers. Oud's Kiefhoek project in Rotterdam, a set of minimal two-story worker's houses with ample light and air (1925–30), and Taut's Hufeisensiedlung (1925–31) in Berlin, comprising 1,027 units in two- to three-story apartment buildings in the outlying district of Britz, and commissioned by city architect Mar- tin Wagner and the Berlin GEHAG public housing authority, both quickly became icons of the movement (fig. 59). These were not the massive, fu- turistic skyscraper cities of Le Corbusier or Hilberseimer's drawings, but were flat-roofed, low-rise settlements of workers' housing with indoor

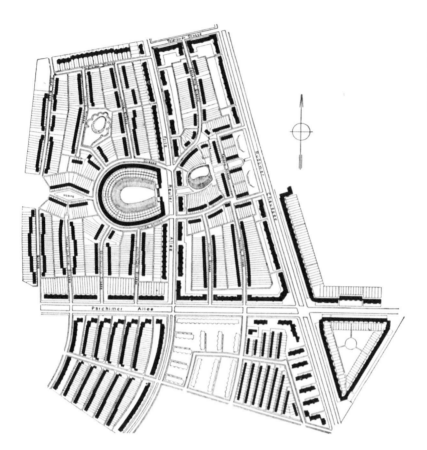

59. Bruno Taut, Hufeisensiedlung, Berlin-Britz, 1925–31 (Henry Wright, *Rehousing Urban America* [New York: Columbia University Press, 1935], 91).

plumbing and central heating, surrounded by green space and sited near transit lines in outlying parts of cities, often close to industrial plants.

Units at Britz were intended for families and ranged from 850 square feet (79 square meters) to 957 square feet (89 square meters). Like Le Corbusier and Hilberseimer, Taut and his associates also sought to create total environments there for better living, with the low-rise housing blocks sited amid trees and grass and provided with plentiful recreational facilities. Sponsored by trade union housing associations or built directly by municipal governments, and funded in some German cities by a new tax on apartment rents, as well as by the postwar American loans of the Dawes Plan of 1925, these *Siedlungen* (settlements) soon became strongly identified as symbolic of leftwing, international socialist political directions. Two projects by Otto Haesler (1880–1962) in Celle, near Hannover, in 1923 were the first modern *Zeilenbau* (row building) settlements to be built, but they were rapidly followed by many others. With their standardized plans and widely spaced housing blocks arranged in parallel rows, these Weimar projects were also in some ways a Bauhaus-inflected version of the large, traditional-style Alte Heide Siedlung designed by Theodor Fischer near Munich in 1918. They also had some antecedents in nineteenth-century barracks and model tenements. They differed in their architectural expression, with painted stucco surfaces replacing brick, and in having flat roofs, considered emblematic of modernity and internationalism in Europe in the 1920s.

In Germany the new direction was countered politically on the right by programmatically similar low-rise housing projects that had pitched roofs and traditional brick details, leading to fierce debates over the political uses of pitched versus flat roofs, and of brick versus white stucco exterior surfaces. The more traditional directions had grown out of the prewar German Garden City movement's advocacy of the *Heimatstil* (Style of the Homeland), an eclectic, romantic return to earlier Germanic cultural periods that emphasized deeply rooted regional dwelling and the particularities of local places and cultures. By contrast, the modern direction in the 1920s rejected such ideas. Instead, the new architecture was to be a scientifically determined set of solutions to the problems of living in modern industrial cities, potentially usable by any human society anywhere. Its advocates had no patience for the elaborate efforts of fellow architects to evoke the forms of the past in new buildings, and they were also mostly hostile to the existing, street-oriented forms of capitalist cities.

A more moderate kind of urban modern architecture also developed in Weimar Germany, Holland, Belgium, Czechoslovakia, Yugoslavia, and some other places in Europe in the 1920s. This was modern architecture in the service of business, exemplified by the department store and other retail buildings and commercial complexes designed by Mendelsohn in many German cities, including two in what is now Wrocław, Poland. The architecture of Mendelsohn's buildings for various commercial clients was developed directly from his Expressionist drawings of the 1910s, where the forms of buildings resembled objects in motion, and resulted in his creation of a new architectural vocabulary that would inspire the "streamlined moderne"of the mid-twentieth century (fig. 60).

At the same time, not all modern architects advocated either "cubic" social architecture or Expressionism. Hugo Häring (1882–1958), who became closely involved in the 1920s with the Berlin "Ring" group of architects, advocated a nongeometric *Neues Bauen,* or "New building," whose built forms would be determined only by functional and site factors. In his 1925 essay, "Wege zur Form" (Approaches to Form), Häring, though drawn to organicist ideas of deeply rooted Aryan racial identity, at the same time rejected orthogonal geometry as an oppressive tool of political control. These views caused him to be as critical of both the Bauhaus and Le Corbusier as he was of the classical tradition. Häring instead argued in favor of an organic approach to design based on use, solar orientation, and material fabrication that would allow the continually evolving inner purpose of each building function to generate its proper form. In 1928 Hans Scharoun (1893–1972), a follower of Häring, and then a young architect who had taught in Breslau (now Wrocław, Poland) and had just moved to Berlin, won a competition for the site

60. Erich Mendelsohn, Schocken department store, Chemnitz, Germany, 1928–29.

plan for Siemensstadt—one of the many new housing and social reform efforts by multiple architects in Berlin in the 1920s and overseen by the Berlin city architect Martin Wagner (1885–1957)—which included mass housing by Gropius, Häring, and others.

In general it was the more "cubic," flat-roofed, Bauhaus direction, termed "International Architecture" in 1925 by Gropius, that began to be recognized as a new architectural direction. In the USSR, a new professional group called OSA (Union of Contemporary Architects) was founded in 1925, chaired by the Constructivist Alexander Vesnin and largely guided by the architect Moisei Ginzburg (1892–1946), who in 1924 had published *Style and Epoch,* an influential introduction of Le Corbusier's ideas into the Soviet context. By this point the Soviet regime had begun to sponsor new forms of building intended to perform as "social condensers," a term introduced by the Constructivists. These included the five multifunctional workers' clubs in Moscow designed by Konstantin Melnikov (1890–1974) in 1927–29, who had also introduced the Soviet avant-garde to the West in his USSR Pavilion at the 1925 Paris Exposition. In these new, often glass-enclosed urban social spaces, it was theorized that the masses would encounter each other outside of their workplaces and begin to voluntarily interact to build a new egalitarian society.

An even more radical effort to restructure social life in the USSR, the "Communal House" concept, proved to be less popular. It was based on the nineteenth-century concept of the phalanstery, proposed by Charles Fourier, where individual rooms would be reduced to a minimum and most of the residential building would be given over to collective dining, daycare, and recreational spaces, much like an ocean liner or a contemporary cruise ship. A government agency in 1928 used this concept to build the Narkomfin apartments, designed by Ginszburg and Ignati Milinis, for its workers in Moscow, in a manner strongly influenced by Le Corbusier. In this same context, the Stroikom (State Building Commission of the Russian Republic) began to conduct studies on how to reduce residential room sizes to a minimum and better integrate collective services along the lines of American urban apartment hotels.

Le Corbusier himself and his team of designers, who included his cousin Pierre Jeanneret (1896–1967) and his interior design associate Charlotte Perriand (1903–1999), arrived in Moscow in 1926 after winning the competition for the Centrosoyuz, the headquarters of the Soviet State Housing Cooperatives association. The building was among the first of the Modern Movement to have a large glass curtain wall, and was designed to be sealed against impure outside air. Designed with what Le Corbusier called "respiration exacte" (exact breathing), the Centrosoyuz was an early example of a forced air heating and cooling system. It was completed in 1935, well before residential air conditioning came into wide use after 1945. Though this system never functioned well, it prefigured post–World War II ubiquitous glass-walled corporate buildings that followed the pattern set by the U.N. Headquarters in New York (1947–52), which was based to some extent on Le Corbusier's ideas.

While in Moscow, Le Corbusier also became directly involved in debates about the form that socialist cities should take. In 1929 this had become the focus of a debate between the so-called "urbanists" and "disurbanists." The former were led by Leonid M. Sabsovich, a member of Gosplan, the Soviet committee for a General Plan; Sabsovich advocated the dissolution of existing cities and their replacement by new collectivized settlements with common facilities, organized into large residential districts. These would not follow the model of the emerging auto-based suburbs of the United States, where by the 1920s each middle-class house increasingly included electricity, indoor plumbing, gas and electrical appliances, and a garage, but would instead have common kitchens, bath houses, and bakeries, all organized into towns of 40,000–60,000 people. As the national electric grid expanded, five new towns near Stalingrad (now Volgograd) were built on this basis, and until 1931 this "urbanist" model was considered to be the official doctrine of Soviet urbanization. The urbanist stance was countered by the more visionary "disurbanist" position taken by the sociologist Mikhail Okhitovich (1896–1937), who argued that since energy sources and means of transportation would soon be provided collectively, society should be "de-stationized" and each individual should be given his own individual dwelling cell. This could produce a fluid, open-ended living environment organized along linear transportation routes, and perhaps eventually some kind of individual private transportation, a decentralist vision that anticipated some of the radical architectural ideas of the late 1960s and later. In the 1920s, these Soviet avant-garde ideas began to converge with the design concepts of Le Corbusier and the Bauhaus, establishing many of the key directions of modern urbanism that in some cases are still operative today.

PREWAR CIAM (INTERNATIONAL CONGRESSES FOR MODERN ARCHITECTURE), 1928–39

In the midst of these new architectural and urban directions, the International Congresses for Modern Architecture, or CIAM, was founded in La Sarraz, Switzerland, in June 1928. Its founding was in part an outcome of the Weissenhofsiedlung housing exhibition in Stuttgart the previous year. A coalition of avant-garde groups from across Europe, including several recent European architect immigrants to the United States, CIAM met regularly in various European countries until September 1939, and again from 1947 until 1956. Its meetings provided a venue where the basic elements of a new approach to architecture and urbanism were debated and formulated. An extension of the philanthropic housing and Garden City town planning directions that extended back to the 1840s, CIAM was focused on the idea that the redesign and future development of industrial metropolises should be based on the biological, psychological, and social needs of the working masses. To facilitate this reorganization, which CIAM members expected would be carried out by reformist or radical authorities of varying political kinds, they offered strategies of diagrammatic urban analysis and reorganization. These included innovation in building typologies, prefabrication, and the integration of landscape elements with built ones. From its founding, CIAM was divided between German-speaking and Bauhaus-centered radical architects active in Germany, Switzerland, Holland, and Eastern Europe, and the more Paris-oriented, French-speaking adherents of Le Corbusier. Its initial impetus came from both Weimar-era socialist internationalism and from Le Corbusier's attempts to overturn the 1927 rejection of his entry in the League of Nations competition, in which officials favored a Beaux-Arts design, which was then built.

The first CIAM meeting, sponsored by the French-Swiss noblewoman Hélène de Mandrot (1867–1948) at her ancestral Swiss chateau near Lausanne, resulted in the issuing of the La Sarraz Declaration in 1928, signed by twenty-four European architects. It demanded that architecture should be taken away from the classically oriented Beaux-Arts schools of architecture and linked to the general economic system. Its signers invoked ideas drawn from the American industrial process theorist and management consultant Frederick Winslow Taylor (1856–1915), who argued for the need to design for minimum working effort through the rationalization and standardization of building components as a way to minimize construction time and costs. Taylor's ideas had been taken up by European socialists, who advocated that these approaches be used not only to increase profits but also to raise living standards for all. CIAM also stressed that architects should seek to influence public opinion in favor of the new architectural approaches.

In these early years of CIAM, Ernst May (1886–1970), who had been appointed the city architect of Frankfurt-am-Main in 1925, Le Corbusier, and other CIAM members developed an approach that would become the basis of much later urbanism on a metropolitan scale. Like the architects of Red Vienna, CIAM architects were motivated by the idea that modern industrial cities should be designed to improve the living conditions of the majority of the population, to increase economic efficiency through transportation improvements, and to protect the natural environment for mass recreation. For CIAM, the basic element of this approach was the design of the individual dwelling and the rejection of the nineteenth-century tenement city, as well as of recent efforts to reform it, such as Berlage's Amsterdam.

The design of the minimal modern dwelling unit was the focus of the CIAM 2, held in Frankfurt-am-Main in October 1929 under the title *Die Wohnung für das Existenzminimum,* which can be translated as "Minimum Housing" or "Housing for the Minimum Wage-Earner." May's work as city architect in charge of the design of twenty-four large working-class peripheral housing settlements sponsored by Frankfurt municipal authorities had grown out of the German Garden City movement. He had worked with Parker and Unwin at Hampstead Garden Suburb near London in 1910–12. After World War I, as a member of the Heimatschutz, he worked for a nonprofit rural resettlement organization in Silesia (an area then part of Germany, and now in southwestern Poland), designing new Garden City–type settlements for Germans displaced by the creation of modern Poland in 1921. May's and Herbert Boehm's competition entry for the extension of Breslau (now Wrocław) proposed a series of new compact garden suburb developments surrounded by open countryside at the edge of the city. This project would not only inform much of May's subsequent work in Frankfurt and briefly in the USSR, but would also be the starting point for many other modern urban directions of the 1930s, which sought to reorganize entire metropolitan regions by alternating green spaces with areas of denser settlement.

While May, like many other Weimar architects, soon rejected the medieval vernacular revivalism of the Garden City movement and the Heimatschutz, he nonetheless continued the Garden City movement's emphasis on providing a range of housing types set in greenery for those of modest income. In site planning, May also continued the earlier Garden City focus on public access to nature and the provision of recreational and communal gathering opportunities nearby. His approaches began to be architecturally influenced by the Bauhaus by 1925, and then became an essential part of CIAM methods. These began to extend from

the design of the minimum housing unit to the design of housing settlements, like those of Mart Stam (1899–1986) and other members of May's design and construction teams in Frankfurt.

Eventually this focus on ideal workers' housing settlements led to efforts to reconceptualize the form of industrial cities in general. For CIAM, this ambitious leap to the urban scale came mainly from the initiative of Le Corbusier, whose efforts in this direction extended back to the early 1920s. It was also Le Corbusier who provided the first direct links for CIAM to Moscow, when he suggested in 1930 that CIAM needed a "doctrine of urbanism" so that it could direct the vast urbanization process then beginning in the USSR under the first Five Year Plan in 1928. In contrast to the "disurbanism" of Ginzburg and Ohkitovitch, who argued for decentralizing Soviet cities along new transportation routes, Le Corbusier continued to insist on the importance of high-density urban living on cleared sites near the center of the city. Soviet officials, however, criticized his approach as capitalist and continuing the economic stranglehold of "gigantomanic" cities of administration over the working masses.

61. Ernst May, Siedlung Römerstadt, Frankfurt-am-Main, 1928.

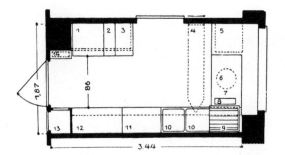

62. Margarete Schütte Lihotzky, Frankfurt kitchen plan, 1926, designed under the direction of Frankfurt-am-Main City Architect Ernst May.

At about the point where his ideas began to be rejected by the Soviets as inappropriate for a communist society, Le Corbusier developed them for presentation at CIAM 3 in 1930 and published them as *La Ville Radieuse* (The Radiant City), in 1935.

Le Corbusier's urbanism also differed from what May had been building in Frankfurt during 1925–31, where he had used housing design approaches developed in the work of Bruno Taut and others under the direction of Martin Wagner in Berlin. They sought to synthesize new technologies in domestic equipment and construction with a new design approach that emphasized closeness to nature, an approach evident in both the allotment gardens for many units, and in the overall site planning, which included parks and parkways along natural features such as river valleys. May brought in a team of architects and others in Frankfurt, which included a former Vienna associate of Adolf Loos, Margarete Schütte Lihotzky (1897–2000), and the radical landscape architect Leberecht Migge (1881–1935), an advocate of allotment gardens for new settlements, who had worked with May in Silesia and who would later be drawn to Nazism. Both Schütte Lihotzky, who went to Moscow with May and other members of the Frankfurt team in 1930, and Migge worked on the May-designed settlements in the Nidda River valley, which offered a new model for metropolitan living based on individual decentralized, low-rise housing settlements with a range of communal facilities (fig. 61). These included the 764-unit Praunheim (1926–29) and the 1,500-unit Römerstadt (initially called Hedderheim, 1927–28). In 1925, Schütte Lihotzky designed the approximately 69.25-square-foot (6.43-square-meter) Frankfurt kitchen for the units in the Römerstadt settlement (fig. 62). This extremely influential design was intended to reduce women's domestic labor, liberating them from their traditionally expected place by the kitchen fireside, surrounded by their children. The Frankfurt kitchen became a standard element in the new settlements, allowing for more compact floor plans that would produce mass housing that made possible what the Swiss art historian and CIAM Secretary-General Siegfried Giedion (1888–1968) would describe in a 1929 pamphlet as "liberated living."

At CIAM 2, May arranged tours of these new projects for the CIAM delegates, who came from fourteen European countries and the United

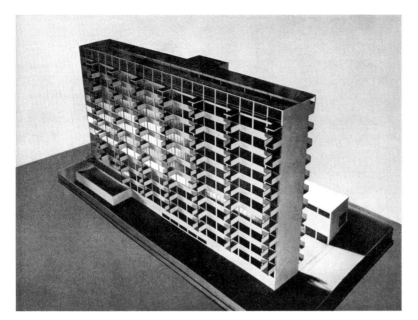

63. Walter Gropius, eleven-story collective housing block competition proposal for Berlin, 1931, view of model (Sigfried Giedion, *Walter Gropius* [New York: Reinhold, 1954], 201). © 2016 Artists Rights Society (ARS), New York/VG Bild-Kunst, Bonn.

States. He also articulated the concept of the *Existenzminimum*, which would become a central idea for much subsequent modernist housing design. At CIAM 2, May's ideas were to some extent shared by those of Gropius, the first director (1919–28) of the Bauhaus in Germany, and by 1930 one of the most influential German modern housing settlement architects. Gropius was also a key figure in the Reichsforschunggesellschaft (RfG), the new national German building research institute established by the Weimar Republic.

In his 1929 lecture at CIAM 2 on "The Sociological Foundations of the Minimum Dwelling," Gropius argued that the entry of women into the workforce required "centralized master households" where each individual would be given a basic Existenzminimum dwelling within a larger structure of communal dining, daycare, and recreational facilities. Unlike May, who was opposed to high-rise housing on economic grounds, Gropius thought that these communal dwellings should probably be multistory apartment buildings sited in extensive areas of greenery, such as the eleven-story high-rise slab for 4,000 units of housing on 100 acres (40.46 hectares) that he and his associates had proposed near the Wannsee lake in the Spandau district of Berlin in 1928 (fig. 63). The individual slabs there were similar to what Marcel Breuer had first proposed as a student in a Bauhaus housing studio in 1924.

Gropius's high-rise housing schemes were not built, but they established a clear model for high-rise mass housing development that would begin to be applied worldwide after 1945, beginning in England. In 1929 Gropius also published a series of sectional diagrams showing parallel buildings from one-story row houses up to ten-story slab blocks, illustrating that the taller buildings allowed for more open green space between them (fig. 64). These appeared around the same time as a set of CIAM plan diagrams "from the block to the housing bar" that showed the "evolution" of the urban block from densely built urban tenements to Zeilenbau housing, with the perimeter block type of Amsterdam or Red Vienna indicated as an unsatisfactory intermediate stage.

CIAM 2 also included the opening of Mart Stam's 207-panel exhibition of same-scale plans of minimal housing units by architects from across Europe. The majority of the plans came from housing projects in German cities, with about half from May's Frankfurt projects. Many of the others were from Brussels, Vienna, Budapest, Paris, and Milan. These were then published by CIAM in 1930 as the book *Die Wohnung für das Existenzminimum,* which also included texts in German and French based on the lectures, emphasizing the linkage between the new architecture and the techniques of modern industrial engineering put into the service of the urban working class.

After CIAM 2, Le Corbusier began to criticize CIAM for focusing on the minimum dwelling without also examining the overall provision of communal services in housing, as was then being done in the Soviet Union by OSA and Ginzburg, who had also been invited to join CIAM on Le Corbusier's recommendation, but who was not allowed to leave the USSR. Le Corbusier, who by this point had made two trips to Moscow for his Centrosoyuz project, contrasted the "piecemeal" communal efforts of May in Frankfurt with the more comprehensive Soviet strategies then being debated during the first Five Year Plan in 1928. This plan called for the construction of two hundred new industrial cities and a thousand agricultural settlements, and Le Corbusier proposed that a future CIAM Congress be held in Moscow. At this key point, various factions of CIAM held different views on the question of whether cities should be decentralized, as in the Garden City movement, or rebuilt at high densities with more greenery and open space at the center of the city. Ernst May advocated the first approach, decentralized settlements at the urban periphery, while Le Corbusier advocated the second, more centralizing urban direction.

Instead of the outlying settlements of Ernst May's Frankfurt, Le Corbusier instead insisted that "modern urbanism can bring a reduction in the overall area of cities so that the distances are shorter. . . . But one must have a categorical separation between traffic and habitation." Further developed and presented at CIAM 3 in Brussels in 1930, this became Le Corbusier's Radiant City ideal of urban design. It would provide a CIAM alternative to modern cities that were "too extended" (*étendu*) and scattered, and at the same time treeless, with dense urban streets and courtyards full of filthy air, noise, and constant and dangerous traffic congestion. Both Le Corbusier and May and other CIAM members agreed that dwelling was a "biological phenomenon," and they also called for "the standardization, industrialization, and Taylorization" of housing production, to be established according to a biological order at the "human

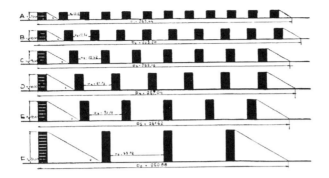

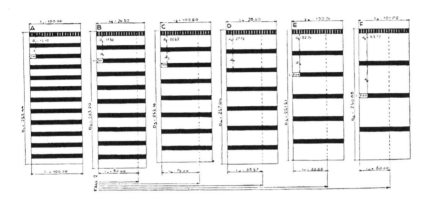

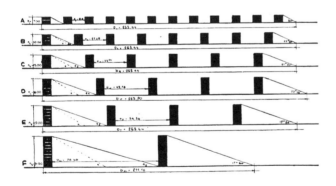

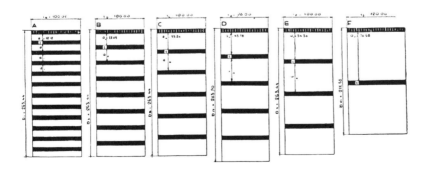

64. Walter Gropius, diagrams illustrating the development of a site with parallel rows of housing of different heights, from one to ten stories, Berlin, 1929 (Sigfried Giedion, *Walter Gropius* [New York: Reinhold, 1954], 204).
© 2016 Artists Rights Society (ARS), New York/VG Bild-Kunst, Bonn.

scale." Gropius's and Le Corbusier's urban proposals were not built at this time, but they set a pattern for a generation of CIAM architects, and along with the work of other CIAM architects like May, had a major impact on Soviet housing and eventually the mass housing of other postwar communist regimes in Eastern Europe, China, and Vietnam, as well as on public housing in the United States and elsewhere from the 1930s to the 1960s.

At CIAM 3, held in Brussels in November 1930 under the title "Rationelle Bebauungsweisen" (Rational Building-Mass Site Planning), CIAM broadened its comparative studies from the design of individual minimum units to the design of "functional" housing settlements, such as those being built by municipal governments in Holland, Germany, and elsewhere. Much of the debate at CIAM 3 centered on the question of high-rise versus low-rise housing, with Le Corbusier and Gropius advocating the former, contrary to the views of May and some of the other CIAM members. It was also at this time that the leading architects of the radical German-speaking wing of CIAM accepted the offer of the Soviet government to design some of the new industrial cities called for in the first Soviet Five Year Plan. May and Hannes Meyer (director of the Bauhaus 1928–30) left Germany in October 1930 to direct teams of architects in Moscow, with varying outcomes. Meyer began to teach in Moscow with his "Rotfront brigade" of former Bauhaus students, some of whom were also former members of the Czech Leva Fronta. Meyer's team also entered the 1932 competition for the reconstruction of Moscow, and designed the industrial city of Nishni-Kurinsk and a settlement in the Soviet "Jewish autonomous region" of Birobidzhan. Meyer soon joined VOPRA (All-Union Society of Proletarian Architects), the Stalinist architectural group that eventually began to dominate the profession in the Soviet Union. VOPRA eventually accepted the shift to neoclassical Socialist Realism, signaled by the winning entry chosen for the 1932 Palace of the Soviets competition, and Meyer left the USSR in 1936, briefly returning to Switzerland before eventually settling in Mexico in 1938.

The appointment of May and other CIAM members to plan extensively in the USSR came at a key moment. In the early 1920s, Lenin's Soviet government had begun to advocate the centrally planned rapid industrialization of the agrarian and aristocratic former Russian Empire. It bought tractors from the Ford Motor Company, and Lenin's Bolshevik successors in the Central Committee, who included Stalin, announced the first Five Year Plan in 1928 to rapidly industrialize the nation. In 1929, Henry Ford was convinced to supply engines for cars and trucks to the USSR, as part of an initiative overseen by Stalin in leading the Avtostroi, a new state bureau for building automotive factories. This agency then commissioned the Austin Company, a Cleveland, Ohio–based industrial building contractor that had recently built the state-of-the-art General Motors' Pontiac Six plant in Detroit, to build a Soviet auto factory in Nizhny

Novgorod that would be twice as large. Soviet specialists were sent to the Ford headquarters in Dearborn to study American automobile production methods, and on their return to the USSR they began working to design an entire industrial city centered on the new auto plant.

At this same point, Detroit industrial architect Albert Kahn (1869–1942) was commissioned to design a new tractor plant in Stalingrad, which by 1930 led to contracts for his firm for hundreds of other auto and truck plants across the USSR. These new plants required extensive housing and other facilities for their workers, and the "correct" socialist design of these housing settlements was a subject of fierce debate among Soviet authorities and architects. The Austin Company's initial housing proposal for the Nizhny Novgorod plant, which called for standard private attached houses with garages, was rejected by the Soviet authorities, and the company was required instead to produce plans for "housing combines" that included communal dormitories, a workers' club, and common nurseries, with 97 square feet (9 square meters) allocated per sleeping room. Under chaotic construction conditions, eventually 12,000 such housing combines were built, before the Austin Company left the project at the end of 1931.

It was arguably at this point that the "neighborhood unit" concept described by Clarence Perry in the first Regional Plan of New York began to be used systematically as a way of designing a large metropolis. May does not seem to have used the term itself, but one of his associates, Eugen Carl Kaufmann, who worked for May in designing new industrial cities in the Donets basin in Ukraine in 1931, later wrote that the May team plan of Magnitogorsk was based on similar principles. Its basic design unit consisted of six apartments with a common wash house, kindergarten, and daycare center. Twenty-two of these basic units were organized into what Kaufmann translated as a "series" of 132 units, and four series made up a "city" of 528 units. Other designers indicated that the maximum Soviet "community unit" of the 1930s was 10,000 residents, on a maximum of 100 acres (40.46 hectares). Further research is necessary to clarify how these urban design directions at this time became the basis for much later Soviet and then communist Chinese urbanism after 1935. The work of May and his associates appears to have been a catalyst for the use of the neighborhood unit as a key element of what then became the standard planning form of what is now usually considered "Soviet urbanism" down to the 1980s.

At Magnitogorsk and elsewhere, May's team combined these neighborhood unit principles for proposed linear cities designed with the principles set forth by Nikolai Miliutin in his *Sotsgorod* (Socialist City), which was briefly (until June 1931) the official doctrine of Soviet urban development. *Sotsgorod* itself was based on the proposals first put forward in 1882 by Arturo Soria y Mata to extend Madrid along transit lines, to produce social outcomes similar to those advocated by Ebenezer Howard.

Miliutin proposed a variant of the Soviet "disurbanist" approach that was also being advocated by Ginzburg, which called for carrying out Marx and Engel's effort to eliminate the economic and social distinctions between city and countryside by decentralizing existing cities along transportation lines. This was not to be random "sprawl," but carefully organized and separated linear zones of production, warehousing, and housing sited along rail lines and close to agricultural areas. The goal was to reorganize both agriculture and industry "biologically," so that labor and transportation costs would be minimized, with organic waste products returned to the soil as fertilizer.

While still employed by the Soviet government, May returned to Germany in June 1931 to lecture at the Berlin CIAM "Special Congress" on this work in the USSR. This event also included the issuing of a detailed set of directives for CIAM 4, planned to be held in Moscow in 1932 on the theme "The Functional City," with the idea that CIAM would now focus on the kind of large-scale urban design activity being done there. After much debate, the directing group of CIAM, led by Le Corbusier, Gropius, and Giedion, rejected the position of the German CIAM member Arthur Korn (1891–1978), later an important design teacher at the Architectural Association in London, and implicitly that of Hannes Meyer, who was not mentioned, that such large-scale urban design should be explicitly oriented toward creating new communist ways of urban living. Instead, they argued that reorganizing cities according to the CIAM "four functions" of "dwelling, work, transportation, and recreation" would improve living conditions and cultural opportunities for everyone, and were applicable in any industrialized urban situation, regardless of political ideology.

This new apolitical direction reflected the reality that their Western clients and some of the other architects then active in CIAM, including Ludwig Mies van der Rohe (1886–1969), director of the Bauhaus from 1930–33, Alvar Aalto (1898–1976) in Finland, and Neutra, who had settled in Los Angeles in 1925, were not working in the USSR. Gropius had already found a middle way between their views, which were the result of their working in Western capitalist societies, and the then-dominant Soviet-oriented wing of CIAM by nominating Amsterdam planner and Dutch avant-garde architect Cornelis van Eesteren (1897–1988) as the president of CIAM in 1930, replacing Swiss architect Karl Moser (1860–1936).

The immediate source of the "four functions" concept for CIAM was the Amsterdam planning work of van Eesteren and his associates, but many of the same ideas were also paralleled in Soviet planning theory at this time. In August 1932, the Soviet All-Russia Central Executive Committee had issued the directive "On the Arrangement of Population Centers," which also called for zoning cities by function, but also insisted on the need to preserve their existing urban aesthetic qualities as well. Like their counterparts in the Garden City and CIAM movements, Soviet planners at this time placed a high value on hygienic, sunlit dwelling

65. Le Corbusier, "We must kill the street!" drawing, 1925 (*Precisions* [Paris, 1930]). © F.L.C./ADAGP, Paris/Artists Rights Society (ARS), New York 2016.

units sited in relation to greenery and recreational opportunities, which they thought could best be achieved by designing large superblock complexes of several buildings of up to six stories tall, usually sited on more outlying sites where land was available and industrial jobs nearby. Both CIAM and Soviet planners shared a focus on equalizing living conditions between the sexes, following ideas already well-established in both European socialism and American feminism at this time about the need to reduce women's traditional domestic chores and childcare activities to allow them to enter the nondomestic workforce.

For most CIAM members at the time, the existing city was a "dead body" that had to be removed, and Le Corbusier had already declared in 1925 that "we must kill the street!" (fig. 65). Instead of reusing the existing city, CIAM attempted to formulate a coherent design approach based first on the analysis of existing urban social, topographical, and climatic conditions and then on a systematic approach to the design of urban elements based on the "four functions." The theme of the planned Moscow CIAM 4 congress in 1932, "The Functional City," would remain central to CIAM for much of its later history. It would provide the basis for much postwar planning, originating in this early 1930s encounter between the ideas of Le Corbusier, Soviet urbanism before Stalinist Socialist Realism, and the work of van Eesteren and his Amsterdam CIAM group, De 8 (The Eight). Though similar in some ways to Le Corbusier's urbanism, Dutch CIAM, which included both De 8 and the Rotterdam CIAM group Opbouw, was not primarily focused on the use of high-rise buildings. Instead, it used detailed statistical information to generate what were thought to be better urban patterns. Van Eesteren had been an associate of De Stijl member Theo van Doesburg, and after studying urbanism in Paris, he had taught town planning in Germany from 1927–29. In a Berlin lecture in January 1928 titled "One-Hour City Building," van Eesteren had dismissed the classical city as mainly a "cardboard city" of superfluous facades, and he instead proposed an urbanism based on the rational distribution of the functional elements of the city. These "units of the metropolis" included industrial buildings, parking lots, garages, sports fields, and skyscrapers, as well as more traditional building types such as train stations and religious buildings. With the necessary statistical information, van Eesteren argued that the urban designer could quickly arrive at the correct urban form, an idea he published in 1928 in an article for the internationalist Dutch journal *i10* titled "Städtebau." Visually this new city would be a "counter-image" of the existing city, based on a De Stijl–derived "plastic equilibrium" of the urban components.

Unlike his Berlin contemporary Hilberseimer, who began teaching at the Bauhaus at Hannes Meyer's invitation around this time, van Eesteren was given the opportunity to implement this approach after being appointed urban designer for the Amsterdam Public Works department in May 1929. Along with his associates, including Theodoor Karel van Lohuizen, who had developed statistical methods in Rotterdam to calculate future urban development based on employment locations, van Eesteren oversaw the production of the Amsterdam Extension Plan for newly annexed areas west and south of the city. It was in some ways a complete rejection of Berlage and the Amsterdam School's approach, replacing Sitte's ideas with those of Weimar Zeilenbau housing and settlement production. This plan, published in 1935, became the basis for the eventual urban structure of mid-twentieth-century Amsterdam, with various elements including new housing districts and parks such as the large Amsterdamse Bos designed by Dutch CIAM members. While developing the plan, van Eesteren's team displayed the results of their statistical studies using same-scale maps, coded in three colors to show areas allocated for workplaces, housing, and recreation, as well as indicating major transportation routes on a separate map.

At the CIAM Berlin "Special Congress" in June 1931, van Eesteren presented these graphic display methods to the delegates, with the idea that they would be the basis for the presentations at the CIAM Moscow Congress planned for 1932. Delegates from eighteen CIAM chapters around the world then prepared similar same-scale maps for thirty-four industrial cities, and the conclusions drawn from them were to provide the basis for the design of the many new industrial cities then being built in the Soviet Union. Many of the CIAM delegates at the 1931 Berlin meeting, who included Aalto of Finland, accepted this model, with even Gropius noting in his remarks that Ernst May had indicated his agreement with its main points.

Ultimately CIAM 4 was not held in Moscow in 1932, as the expected Soviet invitation was not forthcoming. In June 1931, at a "special plenum of the central committee of the All-Union Communist Party," Stalin and his deputy in charge of the Moscow region, Lazar Kaganovich, had announced that the Communist Party had renounced all "foreign theories" of both urbanism and disurbanism, including those of Le Corbusier and Frank Lloyd Wright. Instead, the new focus would be on Moscow as a model of the urban "socialization of everyday activities," with Kaganovich in charge of its development. A competition was held for a new Moscow plan, won by Vladimir Semenov (1874–1960), who had

66. General Plan for the Reconstruction of Moscow poster, with portraits of Josef Stalin (left) and Lazar Kaganovich, the Communist Party leader for Moscow in the 1930s (Koos Bosma and Helma Hellinga, eds., *Mastering the City II* [Rotterdam: NAi Uitgevers, 1997], 194).

studied and worked in the West before World War I and was an advocate of more traditional approaches to urbanism. Semonov's winning design for Moscow was similar in principle to the abortive 1918–24 General Plan for New Moscow, overseen by the architect Alexi Shchusev, which had been stopped as Moscow's population began rapidly increasing in the 1920s.

By the early 1930s, Semenov had been appointed head of the Moscow Municipal Department of Architecture and Urban Planning. His plan was based on the idea that the city's population would be capped at five million in ten years. Its main features were new radial and concentric ring boulevards organized in relation to the Kremlin and the proposed new Palace of the Soviets, with a design by the Rome-educated Boris Iofan (1891–1976) of a stepped classical skyscraper topped with a large statue of Lenin. This design had been chosen by Stalin himself over the designs of Le Corbusier, Mendelsohn, Perret, and other modern architects in a 1932 competition. The choice of this winning design unambiguously signaled to the world the rejection of the avant-garde in the USSR. Le Corbusier's innovative proposal included a structurally expressive parabolic arch, which, though never built, became inspirational for many architects thereafter, including Eero Saarinen. The Moscow plan also attempted "for the first time in history" to limit the spread of a modern city, creating a new, relatively dense socialist living environment within a ten-mile (16-kilometer) radius, with a six-mile (10-kilometer) surrounding greenbelt located at the edge of the city (fig. 66). Future expansion was projected to occur to the southwest, toward the Lenin Hills, to be linked with a grand new boulevard to the Kremlin.

Other aspects of the Moscow plan, officially approved in 1935, included required designs for standard classical facades for the new six- to seven-story socialist housing blocks, which in theory were also to contain a range of collective facilities, including schools, recreation, and day-care centers. These housing blocks were organized into districts (*rayony*), with densities not to exceed two hundred people per acre (0.4 hectare), a reduction from the almost five hundred people per acre then found in parts of Moscow. Each district was to be separated from the next by a green park strip, an idea already present in Eliel Saarinen's Helsinki Plan of 1918. The new Moscow metro system went into construction in 1933, with its first line completed in 1935. Its grand neoclassical stations, modeled on the salons of Versailles and the "best examples of the classic and new architecture," were to be a clear manifestation of the importance placed by the regime on the mass transportation system and everyday worker experience. The banks of the city's two rivers were beautified, and a new central city park, Gorky Park, went into construction. An elaborate canal system linking the city to most of Russia's rivers was also put in place, allowing shipping to arrive there from all the surrounding oceans.

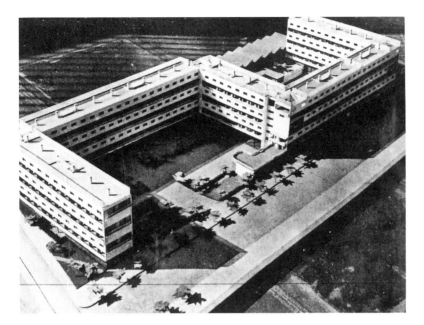

As the 1935 Moscow plan and the new Socialist Realist Soviet directions in urbanism took shape, CIAM decided to meet in 1932 in Barcelona, the Catalan political center of the new Spanish Republic that had been proclaimed in April 1931. The resulting March 1932 meeting was the first time CIAM had met outside of German- and French-speaking Europe, and was hosted by the Barcelona CIAM group, GATCPAC, led by Josep Lluís Sert (1902–83) and Josep Torres Clavé (1906–1939), who had begun to publish a magazine, *AC* (*Actividades Contemporanea/Contemporary Activities*), in Spanish in March 1931. Le Corbusier began to work with this Catalan CIAM group on the Macià Plan for Barcelona (1931–35), the first application of CIAM planning based on the "four functions" to an actual city. Only small portions of the plan were actually carried out, notably Sert, Torres Clavé, and Joan Subirana's Casa Bloc (1933), a gallery access housing project, but parts of the plan were published in various issues of *AC* (fig. 67). The GATCPAC Macià Plan focused popular attention on the fact that Barcelona was predominantly a city of industrial workers, and they suggested the use of CIAM functional categories to reorganize it. Much of their design focus was on working-class recreational facilities along the coast, along with comprehensive planning for new transportation facilities, including highways and airports, projects that were supported by elements of the city's industrial elite, including Sert himself, the son of a textile manufacturer who had been made a count for his services to the Spanish monarchy.

The CIAM focus on the Soviet Union continued with a meeting in Moscow in December 1932 to make another attempt to plan CIAM 4, but by this time it was becoming evident that CIAM's optimism about the future of urbanism in the USSR was not well founded. In an article published in 1932 in *Die Neue Stadt,* the successor publication to May's *Das Neue Frankfurt,* Swiss CIAM member Hans Schmidt (1893–1972) outlined the Stalinist Soviet objections to modern architecture. These were basically that its ideas were simply an outgrowth of the rationalized technology of contemporary capitalism; that its renunciation of monumentality and symbolic expression were symptomatic of the decline of bourgeois culture; that both the "idealistic-utopian" direction associated with Le Corbusier and the ideas of "left utopians" in politics were counter-revolutionary attempts to "bypass the natural stages leading toward socialism"; and that in contrast to "disintegrating contemporary capitalism," Soviet socialism wanted to preserve the cultural values of the past.

Eclipsed in the Soviet Union by this direction, Le Corbusier then began to develop a long series of unbuilt urban proposals in the 1930s that nonetheless had a deep impact on how modern designers conceptualized their urban design work. One strand began with his 1929 lecture tour of South America, where he lectured in French to enthusiastic elite audiences in Buenos Aires, Montevideo, Rio de Janeiro, and São Paulo. He illustrated his lectures with sketches of his visionary "airplane view" urban proposals for these cities. In São Paulo, Le Corbusier invited the Russian émigré modern architect Gregori Warchavchik (1896–1975) to become the first Brazilian member of CIAM, and the first from Latin America. CIAM concepts of housing and urbanism were then closely linked to mostly theoretical developments in design in the Soviet Union from the late 1920s and early 1930s, but Le Corbusier was not himself a communist. He saw progressive industrialists as the most likely patrons for his and CIAM's work in urbanism, which was intended to create a new architectural system capable of reforming urban societies. He then developed the linear megastructure of the Rio proposal as a plan for Algiers (1930), suggesting that a new elevated coastal express highway could be infilled with housing below, leading to a new business center in a pair of towers adjacent to the old Arab casbah, which would be preserved. On the slopes above the old city would be tall, interconnected curving housing slabs set in green areas, with commanding views of the Mediterranean (fig. 68).

In 1933 the further postponement of CIAM 4 by the planned hosts, the Soviet Centrosoyuz, along with the Nazi closing of the Bauhaus in Germany, led to the decision to hold CIAM 4 on a cruise ship sailing from Marseille and in Athens. The Greek CIAM group, represented by Stamo Papadaki (1895–1988), arranged sponsorship by the Technical Chamber of Greece. Around one hundred CIAM delegates, invited guests, and spouses participated in this legendary event. Most of the German group was unable to attend, but the recently founded MARS (Modern Architecture Research) group from Britain was represented for the first time in CIAM, headed by Wells Coates (1895–1958). Groups from Spain, led by Sert and Torres and including Antoni Bonet i Castellana (1913–1989), and from Poland, led by Syzmon (1893–1964) and Helena Syrkus (1900–1982), were

At the opening of CIAM 4, President van Eesteren praised Alvar and Aino Aalto's Paimio Sanitarium (fig. 69), and Giedion noted with regret

68. Le Corbusier, Algiers Plan, 1930 (Le Corbusier and Pierre Jeanneret, *Oeuvre complète, 1929–34* [Zurich: Éditions H. Girsberger, 1935], 140–43). © F.L.C./ADAGP, Paris/Artists Rights Society (ARS), New York 2016.

also present, as were groups from Canada, Italy, and ten other European countries, speaking some eleven different languages. In addition to architects, CIAM 4 also included Moholy-Nagy, who made a film of the proceedings, *Architect's Congress;* painter Fernand Léger (1881–1955); Charlotte Perriand; the graphic designer Otto Neurath (1882–1945); and others.

At the opening of CIAM 4, President van Eesteren praised Alvar and Aino Aalto's Paimio Sanitarium (fig. 69), and Giedion noted with regret that May's documentation of Soviet urbanism from the Berlin meeting had not had much result for CIAM. On the next day, surrounded by the same-scale plans of thirty-three industrial cities, Le Corbusier gave a concise statement of his position on the idea of the Functional City, asserting that the plans prepared for the Congress represented a "biology of the world." To determine how they should be analyzed, he argued that between the "two contradictory and hostile fates" of the individual and the collective, a point of equilibrium can be found. The goal of preparing the same-scale plans with their "conventional signs" was to establish urbanistic rules to prescribe to authorities. He insisted that the fundamental principle was that urbanism is a three-dimensional science, and that height is an important one of those dimensions. These three dimensions imply the notion of time, in that human lives are regulated by the "solar regime" of 24 hours and the year. Within this reality, the urbanist must choose between two tendencies, to extend or to contract the city. If the latter course is chosen, concrete and steel must be used to transmit the

69. Alvar and Aino Aalto,
Paimio Sanitarium, Finland,
1931–33.

"essential joys: the sky, trees, and light." Le Corbusier emphasized that
the base of CIAM's judgments must be "dwelling," the first of a hierarchy
of the four functions (others are work, transportation, and recreation).
He continued by asserting that the natural environment must be saved
from the "leprous suburbs" of existing cities. While the Garden City pattern satisfies the individual, he argued that it loses the advantages of
collective organization. For Le Corbusier, the concentrated city, favored
with access to modern technology, assures the liberty of the individual
within the housing fabric and organizes the collective life in relation to
recreation. He described how the automobile and railway have created
a new scale, and how at the same time the urbanist struggles against a
"great obstacle" to urban reconfiguration: private property. In this talk,
Le Corbusier insisted that the land of cities and countries must be "mo-
bilized" for collective work, but stopped short of calling for a communist
or Fascist expropriation of land in private ownership.

The remainder of the CIAM 4 was then occupied with the presentations of the same-scale plans, which were exhibited in Athens during
the Congress, prior to the return voyage to Marseille. The presentations of each city used the three same-scale maps for each city, and
typically included information about the historical, geographical, and
housing conditions of each. This was followed by a discussion of their
urban issues and problems. The Italian delegate, Gino Pollini (1903–1991),
stated "In the historic guts [*ventre* in the published French transcription]
of Rome, the greater part of the population lives in old houses, with a
density varying between 819 and 230 people per hectare [2.47 acres],"
and similar dense and unsanitary conditions were identified in many of
the other cities analyzed. Problems of long commuting times and traffic

congestion were noted in large cities such as Berlin, London, and Paris. At the same time, some of the first criticisms of urban "sprawl" were articulated at this event, as when Wells Coates noted that because of the standard nature of the free-standing single-family house in London, the population must extend over an immense area. The Canadian delegate Hazen Sise (1906–1974) presented Neutra's West Coast CIAM study of Los Angeles, describing it as an "extended city," and van Eesteren summed up Knud Lonberg Holm's presentation of Detroit with this description: "Private houses of one or two stories of light construction. Result: great consumption of land." Syrkus also noted a tendency in the Warsaw region toward dispersed small individual houses, and so on.

Van Eesteren and Sert were at this time involved in developing plans for Amsterdam and Barcelona, respectively, but these were not ready to be presented at CIAM 4. Le Corbusier also did not present a specific project, but in his discussion of Paris, Le Corbusier articulated the goal of the event by saying, "We must organize a network to carry the life of this organism." To sustain intellectual life, a city must also ensure for the human body the "biological elements" of "air, sunlight, and space." To create space for recreation, a part of the existing city must be demolished, though at the same time, "old things must be respected."

Several versions of the proceedings of CIAM 4 were published soon after, but these were contested by some of the delegates. Complicated debates had occurred at the end of the event over the issue of how land should be acquired to carry out the sweeping urban reforms envisaged by CIAM, with some insisting on direct governmental expropriation of land for urban redevelopment. After this point, reflecting the changing situation for CIAM, Giedion suggested to Le Corbusier that CIAM begin to define itself as an apolitical organization of "technicians," rather than as "politicians" who saw the Soviet Union as a model for urbanism. This decision was formally approved at the London CIRPAC (CIAM Council) meeting in 1934, where CIAM announced that in the future "no political declarations would be made" in its name.

Efforts continued within the USSR up through 1935 to have a CIAM congress there, with the idea that the group would endorse the new official Socialist Realist direction, but this did not occur. After the fourth congress, CIAM met frequently in Europe until the outbreak of World War II, and it had some success in advancing its ideas in some cities in Holland, Belgium, Czechoslovakia, Switzerland, Sweden, and the former Yugoslavia, but the group was unable to win over the majority of official clients to its new urbanistic doctrines.

In Spain, one of the few places where those in power strongly supported CIAM ideas, the Catalan GATCPAC group published a detailed illustrated manifesto showing the new urban planning methods and their application to Barcelona. In his presentation at CIAM 5 in Paris in 1937, Sert, who by this time had been appointed a vice president of CIAM along with Gropius and Victor Bourgeois of Belgium, emphasized that the "chaos" of modern industrial cities was a menace to the moral and physical health of their working-class inhabitants. Like Le Corbusier, whose writings on urbanism in the 1930s had been published as *La ville radieuse* by this time, Sert insisted that cities must be understood as part of an economic, social, and political whole, bound up with the complexity of the biological activities of what he also called the "individual and the collectivity." Like Lewis Mumford and also following Patrick Geddes, whose ideas had become widely influential in Europe in the 1920s and 1930s, Sert argued that the "urbanist" must take into account geographical and topographical circumstances, as well as a particular economic and political situation, to create plans for future development that should be "precise, but not rigid." Sert insisted that producing such plans should be CIAM's goal, so that they could serve as a guide for all the problems of what he called the "reorganization" of modern cities. This would include "precise schematic study of the natural givens of the region," including the climate, topography, natural and agricultural factors, and the location of industrial and residential zones.

To spread its ideas in the complicated and rapidly changing international political environments of the 1930s, CIAM envisaged two international publications resulting from CIAM 4, one to be a popular book with many illustrations and the other a more "scientific" text with all the material related to the thirty-three urban plans presented at CIAM 4. At the London CIRPAC meeting in 1934, Sert was appointed to head a commission to publish the popular volume, and Mart Stam, who was unable to attend this meeting as he had been detained by British officials on his arrival from the USSR, was to oversee the publication of the larger volume, which was to have detailed studies of Berlin and other cities. The manuscript of this more detailed CIAM 4 volume appears to have disappeared. Eventually Sert published a greatly altered version of the planned popular CIAM volume in the United States in 1942 as *Can Our Cities Survive?* Le Corbusier published his own version of the much-debated results of CIAM 4 as *La Charte d'Athènes (The Athens Charter)* in Paris in 1943, during the Vichy period of Nazi occupation. In 1944 Le Corbusier was able to convince the victorious Allies that he had in fact supported the French Resistance to the occupation all along. Like many in France, he had at first been positive about the Vichy government, seeing both it and earlier Soviet communism as possible patrons for his urbanistic ideas, but by 1943 he had gone into hiding. After the war, *The Athens Charter* and *Can Our Cities Survive?* became some of the most widely read documents explaining the CIAM Functional City approach after 1945.

Before World War II, relatively few large CIAM-inspired housing projects had been built in Europe. The first high-rise slab housing to be built there was Willem Van Tijen (1894–1974) and others' Bergpolder flats in Rotterdam (1932–34): this nine-story, seventy-two-unit building, with a

The Emergence of Avant-Garde Urbanism in the 1920s and 1930s

steel frame, a skip-stop elevator serving single-loaded corridors, a nursery, and a communal garden, towered over its low-rise brick neighbors.
There was also a larger experimental urban high-rise project in Drancy,
near Paris—the now-demolished prefabricated concrete towers of la Cité
de la Muette (1934) by Beaudouin and Lods. Most of Le Corbusier's urban
visions remained unbuilt before 1940, though much admired and discussed by architects when published. Louis I. Kahn would later recall that
as a semi-employed, Beaux-Arts trained architect in Philadelphia in the
1930s, "I came to live in a city called Le Corbusier."

CIAM's complex first decade from 1928–39 was pivotal in formalizing an approach to the design of city-regions based on statistically
grounded, industrially produced housing norms, which nonetheless included consideration of communal and natural elements in urbanism. It
was also where many modern architects from different countries began
to work in parallel ways, internationally reshaping the culture of architecture away from the Beaux-Arts model toward modern urbanism, and
creating the intellectual framework for the massive changes in design
education that would characterize the postwar era.

URBANISM AND MODERNIZATION IN THE 1930S:
THE UNITED STATES

In 1932 the young American architectural historians Henry-Russell Hitchcock (1903–1987) and Philip Johnson (1906–2005) presented an architectural exhibition at the recently founded Museum of Modern Art in New
York, which they titled, "The International Style: Architecture Since 1922."
It introduced European and some American modern architecture to the
North American public. Their approach was deliberately apolitical, emphasizing the formal similarities of the new architecture across countries, notably in the work of "Gropius in Germany, Oud in Holland, and
Le Corbusier in France." They chose not to emphasize the leftist political
and urbanistic aspects of the new direction, instead presenting the International Style's links to the earlier works and ideas of Louis Sullivan and
Frank Lloyd Wright in North America. In doing so, Hitchcock and Johnson
made modern architecture more acceptable to mainstream American
clients and audiences, but also minimized its close linkages to CIAM and
its socialist architectural approaches to urbanism. In 1933 Johnson rejected Giedion's suggestion that the Museum of Modern Art in New York
hold a CIAM exhibition, saying that the museum was for "fine art," and did
not take political positions.

Despite the later importance of this "International Style" direction,
the mainstream of American architectural and urban design in the 1930s
still remained within a modernized version of the classical tradition. In
1922 the *Chicago Tribune* had held a large international competition
for the design of its new headquarters tower, prominently sited on the

northward extension of Michigan Avenue that had been called for in the Burnham *Plan of Chicago*. The winning proposal by Hood and Howells was a relatively conventional neo-Gothic skyscraper, but it was the second prize entry by Finnish architect Eliel Saarinen that drew the most praise, notably from Louis Sullivan, who died shortly afterward. Its distinctive setback ziggurat shape met developers' concerns about rentability, even as its form suggested a new era of American skyscraper modernity. Many similar towers were then built in downtowns around the world, by architects such as Ralph Walker (1889–1973) in New York, Albert Kahn in Detroit, and Ladislav Hudec (1893–1958) in Shanghai in a manner that would be termed "Art Deco" in the late 1960s.

In 1929, oil company heir and philanthropist John D. Rockefeller, Jr. (1874–1960), had begun planning to revitalize a six-block area of Midtown Manhattan as a high-end office district with a new opera house facing a plaza. The financial constraints of the Great Depression changed the project into an almost entirely commercial complex, but one in which a substantial amount of pedestrian public space was still included. Rockefeller Center's large architectural team included several firms, including the office-space planning experts Reinhard and Hofmeister; Corbett, Harrison, and MacMurray; and Hood, Godley, and Fouilhoux. The latter firm included Raymond Hood (1881–1934), one of the winning architects in the 1922 *Chicago Tribune* competition. The rebuilt site, previously occupied by tenements and theaters, and owned by Columbia University, was reorganized to link an underground shopping concourse connecting to the new IND subway line then being built under Sixth Avenue. It also included a two-level public pedestrian plaza, an immense gift to the public in real estate terms on such a valuable Midtown Manhattan office site. Rockefeller Plaza was surrounded by high-rises such as the iconic 30 Rockefeller Center, originally the RCA Building, for the new radio network that was then changing American politics and entertainment (fig. 70). The complex also included Radio City Music Hall, roof gardens, and the Rainbow Room restaurant atop the RCA building. Its architecture was conservative relative to the work of Le Corbusier or Bauhaus-trained architects, and included many representational murals and classical sculptures, but it was nonetheless highly praised by Le Corbusier on his 1935 American visit to New York, who saw in it a step toward the realization of his urbanistic concepts.

Le Corbusier's work had also had a major influence on Frank Lloyd Wright, who responded to the Contemporary City for Three Million with his own urban proposal, called "Broadacre City" in 1932 (fig. 71). Wright had initially been positive about Le Corbusier's work, seeing it as an extension of his own and Sullivan's early work, but by the early 1930s he had become critical of the mechanistic aspects of Le Corbusier's urbanism, which relegated "the human individual to a pigeon hole." By this point, dissatisfaction with existing rail and pedestrian-based urban

70. Reinhard and Hofmeister; Corbett, Harrison, and MacMurray; and Hood, Godley, and Fouilhoux, 30 Rockefeller Center, 1931–39. The central tower of a mixed-use development with extensive public spaces and transit links, built in Midtown Manhattan during the Great Depression.

patterns had reached an intense level in the United States, for reasons that still do not seem entirely rational. Frank Lloyd Wright responded to this dark national mood in a 1932 book, *The Disappearing City,* accompanied by an article in the magazine section of the *New York Times* on March 20, 1932. Wright argued against both further centralized city development and the suburban Garden City directions then becoming the inspiration for planners and President Herbert Hoover, and instead advocated the total decentralization of modern cities. Their size, he thought, in line with both the RPPA and many American agrarian reformers going back to Jefferson, was simply the result of economic concentration, and it would be better if future development took place in more agricultural settings, where each family could grow their own food and, to some extent, construct their own housing. He suggested that the functions of the federal government be reduced simply to defense and diplomacy, and

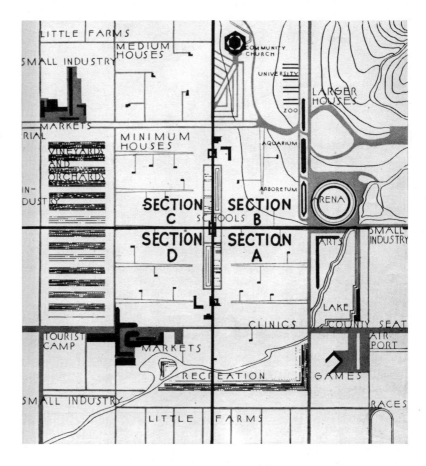

71. Frank Lloyd Wright, Broadacre City, 1932 (Frank Lloyd Wright, *When Democracy Builds* [Chicago: University of Chicago Press, 1945], 54). © 2016 Frank Lloyd Wright Foundation, Scottsdale, AZ/Artists Rights Society (ARS), New York.

that all government take place on the county level, with state and city governments being abolished. In their place, a new national federation for "Usonia" would emerge with three regional capitals, Washington, D.C., for the Northeast, Atlanta for "Usonia South," and Denver for Usonia itself.

Wright's proposal for Broadacre City was intended to offer general guidelines for how this new form of urbanization would be organized. Each Usonian citizen would be entitled to one acre (0.4 hectare) of land, and a new road system would allow for easy automobile access over a large and potentially almost infinitely extendable developed area, whose basic element would be the standard American six-square-mile (1,554-hectare) agricultural section first legislatively established in 1785. Services and cultural institutions would not be located near a "monarchical center," but would instead be spaced at half-mile (0.8-kilometer) intervals along the roadways. Huge, double-level "county highways" carrying ten lanes of auto traffic, with trucks on separate roadways below (with continuous warehousing running alongside), and with high-speed monorails in the medians, would link Broadacre City's dispersed industry, markets, cultural and sports facilities, and motels. Utilities would be provided in underground conduits, and factories would be sited near their sources of raw and/or manufactured materials. The new pattern would render existing cities obsolete (an idea already proposed by Clarence Stein in his article "Dinosaur Cities" in *The Survey* [1925]), and in 1940 Wright predicted that Pittsburgh would soon become a toxic "rusty ruin" as a result. Wright's Broadacre City had no official support, but he publicized it widely, and built a large model with his apprentices in his Taliesin Fellowship, which was exhibited at Rockefeller Center in 1935.

Less radical ideas of modern architecture and urbanism were present in the design of two major American world's fairs in the 1930s, including the 1933 "Century of Progress" exhibition in Chicago, which moved 48.5 million visitors through a series of streamlined modern pavilions on Northerly Island, an artificial island in Lake Michigan called for in Burnham's *Plan of Chicago*. This exhibition also included a version of the Dymaxion House by R. Buckminster Fuller (1895–1983), a prefabricated glass-enclosed modern house raised on a central mast for services, and Keck and Keck's House of Tomorrow, whose all-glass enclosure anticipated in some ways the American work of Mies van der Rohe, who was invited to teach at what became IIT (Illinois Institute of Technology) in Chicago in 1938. The initial site planning of the 1933 Fair was done by a team of Beaux-Arts architects, and the supervising architects Louis Skidmore (1897–1962) and Nathaniel Owings (1903–1984) laid out the final plan. In 1936 they opened their Chicago office, the start of what would become the international architecture firm SOM.

The Chicago "Century of Progress" exhibition was soon overshadowed by the better-known New York World's Fair in 1939, organized by City Parks Commissioner Robert Moses (1888–1981), which also offered an eclectic mix of modern- and traditional-style pavilions at Flushing Meadow in Queens. Though attendance was slightly less than the "Century of Progress" exhibition, it drew far more national and international attention. An especially memorable element was the General Motors pavilion, by industrial designer Norman Bel Geddes (1893–1958), who was assisted by the young Eero Saarinen (1910–1961). Its Futurama exhibit included a model of a future American city in 1960, loosely based on St. Louis, then the eighth-largest city in the country. It was shown as rebuilt with a sleek downtown of high-rise, glass-clad towers, linked by massive new freeways leading to and from idyllic suburban enclaves. Part of the exhibit included the "intersection of the future," a multilevel junction designed by Saarinen that took Hilberseimer's 1920s idea of separating vehicular from pedestrian circulation and adapted it to the American world of downtown department store shopping. SOM also worked extensively at the 1939 New York World's Fair, after Skidmore and Owings had opened their New York office in 1937. They hired Gordon Bunshaft (1909–1990) as a designer that year, and in 1939 officially founded Skidmore, Owings and Merrill with engineer John O. Merrill (1896–1975).

Though it was in the 1930s that many European avant-garde directions began to influence North American urban patterns, many earlier

American development patterns persisted. Outside of New York City, the detached single-family house, ideally sited in carefully controlled land-scaped surroundings, was still typically preferred over multifamily housing and urban densities, which were thought to undermine family life. As a result, as CIAM members noted at CIAM 4 in 1933, North American cities like Detroit and Los Angeles were unique in the world at this point for two reasons: their extensive areas of detached single-family dwellings, accessed in the 1920s by both streetcars and automobiles, and their large high-rise downtowns. The downtowns were strictly divided socially in several ways, between the office buildings for white male office workers, who made daily commutes from the suburbs, and the more female-oriented world of the department stores and some other commercial and social activities, reflecting the widely held belief that women should otherwise continue to remain at home with their children.

Though rarely mentioned at the time, these downtowns were also divided racially, as African Americans were by custom for the most part completely excluded from higher paid and more "respectable" work, and were also not welcome in many public settings, such as department-store lunch counters. In the American South, African Americans were also forced to ride in separate rail and street cars, and could sit only in the rear seats on buses. As a result, they, like recently arrived European immigrants, tended to live closer to industrial areas near downtown, often in substandard rental buildings in older central urban areas that were considered undesirable because of their lack of indoor plumbing and high densities. In the United States, urban planning efforts of the 1920s focused on decentralizing these dense urban centers into self-contained Garden Cities, using what Lewis Mumford had identified in 1925 as the new key region-building technologies of hydroelectric power and automobiles.

These patterns became significant as the Great Depression became more severe. President Franklin D. Roosevelt, who took office in March 1933, announced a "New Deal" for American workers to rebuild the shattered economy and put millions of unemployed people back to work. By 1934 the federal government had begun to sponsor the widely popular clearance and rebuilding of older working class areas in the central parts of cities, which often displaced poor African Americans. In 1930 Catherine Bauer (1905–1964, later Catherine Bauer Wurster), a Vassar College–educated associate of Lewis Mumford and a member of the Regional Planning Association of America (RPAA), had visited Frankfurt, where she took a three-day housing course for visitors offered by Ernst May and his design team. On her return, she wrote a prize-winning article about it for *Fortune* magazine (1931), which she then expanded into a book, *Modern Housing* (1934). Like many Europeans and the members of CIAM, she believed that the organized working class should demand that the government build subsidized low-cost housing, and do so in a way that did away with the overcrowding and bad sanitation of earlier slums. An admirer of Alfred Kastner and Oscar Stonorov's Carl Mackley Homes (1931–33) in northeast Philadelphia, a union-sponsored low-rise housing project based on Le Corbusier's housing ideas, Bauer in 1934 became a member of the Labor Housing Conference founded by John Edelman, an officer of the American Federation of Full-Fashioned Hosiery Workers, the developer of the Mackley project. She and Edelman joined forces with the Housing Study Guild, an offshoot of the RPAA that included Lewis Mumford, Henry Wright, and Albert Mayer (1897–1981), to press the Roosevelt administration to advocate that the newly established federal Public Works Administration (PWA) build public housing along similar lines.

Supported to an extent by labor unions like the American Federation of Labor (AFL) as well as by the newly formed National Association of Housing Officials (NAHO), these efforts led to the beginning of federal involvement in public housing in the United States. Modern architects like Clarence Stein and Henry Wright, who were part of these efforts, quickly lost control of the process of setting government design standards, which were put in place in 1935. Government bureaucrats instead took over and insisted on the use of reductive design standards to ensure that public housing would be easy to build and maintain and would not compete with privately developed housing. These bureaucratic standards were a reduced version of the housing strategies advocated by various architects in the previous decade, which called for "superblock" housing complexes that eliminated many cross streets. Traffic was to be limited to bordering streets so pedestrian circulation could take place in parklike open areas separated from traffic. Stein had designed one such project, Hillside Homes in the Bronx (1933), which provided 1,416 units of mostly two-bedroom apartments in five-story, plain brick courtyard buildings on five blocks of vacant land in the northern part of the borough. Tenants were mostly white salesmen and their families, and most came from the surrounding area. Various community facilities like a playground, nursery school, and assembly room and classrooms were provided, creating a greater sense of community than was typical in New York City apartment buildings. In line with the approaches that the Housing Study Guild had identified as the most economical and socially desirable, the apartment wings were surrounded by grassy lawns, and small numbers of light-filled units were grouped around common staircases, based on the entry system used in the recent dormitories built by Harvard and Yale Colleges.

Around the same time, federal funds also allowed for the creation of the nation's first public housing authority in New York City. After experimenting with modifications to an existing tenement Manhattan block on East Fifth Street between Avenue A and First Avenue by removing every third building and combining the rear yards into a common garden

72. Richmond H. Shreve, William Lescaze, Arthur Holden, et al., Williamsburg Houses, Brooklyn, New York, 1935–38 (Clarence Arthur Perry, *Housing for the Machine Age* [New York: Russell Sage Foundation, 1939], 239).

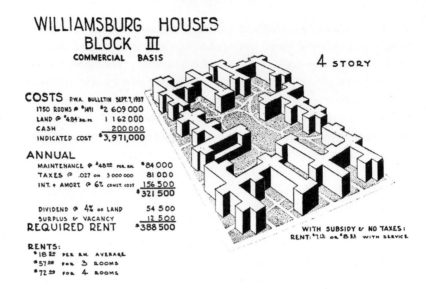

WILLIAMSBURG HOUSES
BLOCK III
COMMERCIAL BASIS

4 STORY

COSTS PWA. BULLETIN SEPT. 7, 1937
1750 ROOMS @ $1491 $2 609 000
LAND @ $4.84 sq. ft.   1 162 000
CASH   200 000
INDICATED COST $3,971,000

ANNUAL
MAINTENANCE @ $48°° PER RM. $84 000
TAXES @ .027 ON 3 000 000   81 000
INT. + AMORT @ 6% CONST. COST 156 500
                              $321 500

DIVIDEND @ 4% OF LAND   54 500
SURPLUS & VACANCY   12 500
REQUIRED RENT $388 500

RENTS:
$18°° PER RM. AVERAGE
$57°° FOR 3 ROOMS
$72°° FOR 4 ROOMS

WITH SUBSIDY & NO TAXES:
RENT: $71² OR $8²² WITH SERVICE

to create "First Houses," the New York City Housing Authority (NYCHA) undertook its first new construction with Harlem River Houses, approved in December 1933 and opened in 1935. It was a four-story walk-up perimeter block courtyard complex, sited on eight and a half acres (3.44 hectares) at West 151 Street and the Harlem River, just north of the Dunbar Apartments, and had 574 units. Unusual for reform housing, it was intended for African American tenants. Its architectural team, led by society architect Archibald Manning Brown, also included Horace Ginsbern, a self-taught expert in designing New York City garden apartment complexes, and John Lewis Wilson (1898–1989), one of the few African American graduates of the Beaux-Arts–oriented architecture program at Columbia University, who was added to the design team at the insistence of New Deal Secretary of the Interior Harold Ickes. Harlem River Houses' site plan combined classical axial formality with perimeter block apartment wings, that were a further development of earlier strategies, all centered on a paved courtyard with sculpture and planted with London plane trees. The complex also included a nursey school as its major social program element, managed by the private New York Kindergarten Association.

Harlem River Houses was paralleled by the other major early efforts of NYCHA, Williamsburg Houses in Brooklyn, planned for white tenants, which opened in 1938 (fig. 72). Its racial segregation was the result of the "neighborhood composition rule" established by Secretary Ickes, and then followed by the Federal New Deal Public Works Administration and U. S. Housing Authority (USHA). The rule required that the racial mix of tenants in a new public housing project had to match the racial composition of the residents who had previously lived on the site. The Williamsburg Houses design team was led Richmond H. Shreve (1877–1946), principal of the firm that had designed the Empire State Building, with

William Lescaze (1896–1969), a Swiss émigré modern architect who had worked with George Howe on the PSFS Building in Philadelphia (1931) as the chief designer. Williamsburg Houses was a complex of four-story walk-up buildings of reinforced concrete with brick infill and steel casement windows, which were later replaced with aluminum double-hung windows. Its grassy lawns and light-filled units were also grouped around common staircases. Its site planning also followed the PWA guide-lines and the CIAM-related ideas then being advocated by Henry Wright and the Housing Study Guild in his *Rehousing Urban America* (1936). Once again the architects found that it was more economical to organize the buildings as a series of cruciform plan clusters around common stair-cases, each serving only three or four units per stair, rather than using long single- or double-loaded corridors, as in many American hotels. In many ways Williamsburg Houses was similar to earlier reform housing efforts in New York City, but with two important differences that marked it as the first "modern" public housing project. One was the decision to orient the site plan such that it was 15 percent off alignment with the existing street grid. This made the street fronts appear to not follow the street line, suggesting a radical new form of urbanism that had noth-ing to do with existing urban patterns, inspired by Ernst May's Bruch-feldstrasse "zig-zag" housing in Frankfurt. The other was the use of long horizontal steel windows to give the facades the appearance of "Inter-national Style" horizontality. This was not in fact very "functional," and was rarely used again in American public housing.

NYCHA adopted the national public housing standards required by the PWA in 1935, which made both Harlem River Houses and Williamsburg Houses unusual in relation to later, more standardized slum-clearance public housing projects. The PWA standards did not allow for the exten-sive design involvement throughout the entire planning process advo-cated by modern planners and architects at the time, nor for any input by the prospective tenants. Instead of replicating the high architectural quality of Mackley Homes or Harlem River Houses, the standards usually resulted in the now-familiar government-sponsored "projects" that have since been either extensively renovated or enthusiastically demolished over the past forty years, which Bauer Wurster herself would begin to strongly condemn by the late 1950s.

The first public housing with elevators in the United States was NYCHA's Red Hook Houses in Brooklyn, which opened in 1939 and was extravagantly praised by Catherine Bauer (later Bauer Wurster) in *Fortune* in an article titled, "It's Heaven, It's Paradise." It was also initially a white-only project, in keeping with the "neighborhood composition rule." By 1941, some thirty-two black families had been admitted to it, along with 2,513 white families. Red Hook also combined cost-reduced conventional New York apartment design with some modernist site-planning ideas like the relatively wide spacing between the high-rises, though the overall site plan was still Beaux-Arts in its formality. Another project in Harlem that soon followed it, East River Houses (1941), began to use more asymmetrical site planning determined by cost calculations, and set the pattern for most of the later NYCHA projects. Its design architect was Perry Coke Smith, who clustered units around common elevator cores to produce towers of varying heights that were also cruciform in plan. This approach had been previously advocated by the Housing Study Guild and refined by NYCHA in-house architect Frederick Ackerman. The plan chosen for its 1,170 units used six-, ten-, and eleven-story buildings, the first full high-rises built for public housing in the United States. The design of these was then widely replicated throughout New York City by NYCHA over the next several decades. Built in East Harlem, when it opened in 1941, East River Houses admitted 1,044 white families but only 126 black families.

More significant for urbanism in the long term than these early urban public housing projects were the decentralist policies of the New Deal. The term "urbanism" was introduced to an American audience in the 1937 report of the Federal National Resources Committee, *Our Cities: Their Role in the National Economy*, but its recommendations that the New Deal should raise urban living standards and attempt to improve urban governance were largely ignored. A year later, one of the authors of the report, the Chicago sociologist Louis Wirth (1897–1952), published an influential article, "Urbanism as a Way of Life," which defined the term as primarily referring to the differences between urban and rural life. Cities were not only dense, but also included more social heterogeneity and allowed for greater individualism, tolerance, and freedom. This position would later inform much postwar American urbanism, but in the 1930s it was instead the convergence of earlier Garden City planning ideas and the anti-urbanism of Henry Ford that underlay the large federal physical planning efforts such as the Tennessee Valley Authority (TVA) and the Greenbelt towns. Continuing the single-family residential zoning and highway-building initiatives of the Hoover administration, the general trend of New Deal planning was toward urban decentralization, evident in the Federal Housing Administration's subdivision guidelines of 1935 and later, which would provide the design basis for much American metropolitan sprawl after 1950.

Regional plans like the first Regional Plan of New York and the RPAA's Radburn model of compact, mostly single-family-house neighborhood units, versus the total decentralization of cities as envisioned by Wright in Broadacre City, were all debated and applied in various ways during the 1930s. In marshaling support for continuing suburban development, the New Deal built upon many of the initiatives begun in the 1920s by President Hoover, including expanding efforts to offer long-term mortgages to promote home-ownership, with the buyer needing to provide only 10–20 percent of the purchase price in cash. To do this effectively

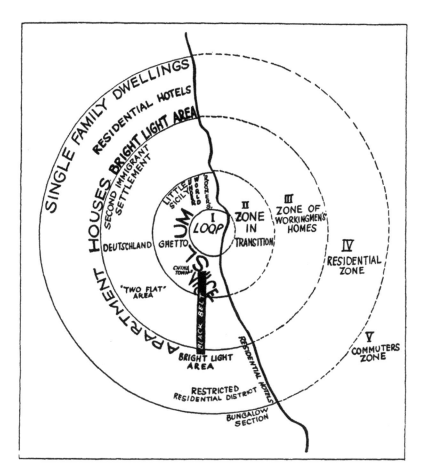

Within the diagram:
SINGLE FAMILY DWELLINGS
RESIDENTIAL HOTELS
BRIGHT LIGHT AREA
SECOND IMMIGRANT SETTLEMENT
APARTMENT HOUSES
LITTLE SICILY
WORLD
ROOMERS
I LOOP
II ZONE IN TRANSITION
III ZONE OF WORKINGMENS HOMES
IV RESIDENTIAL ZONE
V COMMUTERS ZONE
DEUTSCHLAND
GHETTO
CHINA TOWN
VICE
BLACK BELT
"TWO FLAT" AREA
BRIGHT LIGHT AREA
RESIDENTIAL HOTELS
RESTRICTED RESIDENTIAL DISTRICT
BUNGALOW SECTION

73. Robert E. Park and Ernest Burgess, theoretical diagram of urban growth as applied to Chicago, 1925 (Ernest Burgess, "The Growth of the City," in Robert E. Park and Ernest W. Burgess, *The City: Suggestions for Investigation of Human Behavior in the Urban Environment* [Chicago: University of Chicago Press, 1925], 55).

required new national standards of real estate appraisal to better assess possible future risks, so that the federal government could safely insure the mortgages. An approach to rating neighborhoods for such risk was developed by the Home Owners Loan Corporation (HOLC), founded early in Roosevelt's administration in 1933, and this approach was then taken up and widely used by the Federal Housing Administration (FHA), established in 1934. Its methods combined standard American real estate practices with the sociological studies of Robert Park and Ernest Burgess at the University of Chicago in the 1920s, which they had published as *The City: Suggestions for Investigation of Human Behavior in the Urban Environment* in 1925. The research of these "Chicago sociologists" focused on mapping the spatial patterns of residence of various ethnic groups in urban areas, ranging from what they identified as the inner-ring "zone of transition" adjacent to downtown, where many new arrivals first found low-cost housing, and then moving concentrically outward toward newer and more desirable middle-class areas at the urban periphery (fig. 73).

Under the New Deal, Homer Hoyt (1895–1984), a University of Chicago-trained sociologist, and others transposed this "concentric zone" metropolitan model into federal risk assessment research for HOLC. By 1939, in

74. "Coincidence of Factors Indicative of Poor Housing, Richmond," 1939 (Federal Housing Administration, *The Structure and Growth of Residential Neighborhoods in American Cities* [Washington, D.C., 1939], 47).

the FHA publication *The Structure and Growth of Residential Neighborhoods in American Cities,* Hoyt was confidently able to publically set out the FHA's "four factors" of neighborhood risk, which were defined as areas of low rents (under $15 [$253 in 2016] per month); condition of structures (25% or more needed major repairs or were "unfit for use"); the age of buildings (75% or more were built before 1904); and an area population that was 50 percent "other than white" (fig. 74). This terminology recalled that of the 1930 U.S. census category of "non-white," which in Los Angeles included Mexicans and Asians as well as African Americans, but in most cities usually referred to African Americans. Secret maps (now

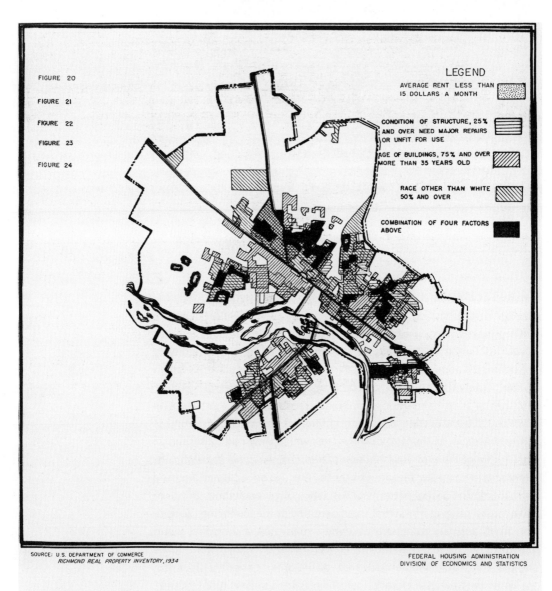

usually called HOLC maps) with risk categories indicated by both letter codes (from A=safest to D=highest risk) and colors (A=green; B=blue; C=yellow; D=red) were made available by the FHA only to private lenders, so they could determine which areas the federal government considered to be too risky to offer mortgage insurance. Those areas coded red, class D, nearly always included the older central areas, in what the Chicago sociologists had termed the residential "zones of transition" near downtown, along with any small pockets of African American residence in more outlying sections.

The decisions that followed these 1930s federal assessments of mortgage risk for the most part simply codified earlier American private real estate lending practices, which had typically seen the "invasion" of any "Negroes" into a residential area as a grave threat to future property values. Widely used deed restrictions on who could buy homes were intended to "protect" more affluent areas from this risk, and were generally enforced until they were ruled unconstitutional by the Supreme Court in 1948 in its *Shelley v. Kramer* decision. Standard real estate appraisal manuals produced in the 1930s suggested that the presence of "undesirable groups" in an area would lower land values. Hoyt's research identified that under these conditions, the effect of African Americans moving into an urban area would at first raise house prices, but then precipitate a drastic decline as white residents departed. To avoid such outcomes, the New Deal policy of denying mortgage insurance in central urban areas was meant to speed up what had been identified as a natural process of "ethnic succession" that led to urban decentralization. In postwar America, it instead "froze" the once-changing central urban patterns of the 1930s in a negative way, ensuring that central urban and African American areas would be denied Federal mortgage insurance. Without such mortgage insurance, most central urban areas became very risky in real estate terms, and were put on a path of almost unavoidable social and economic decline for decades thereafter.

Because these HOLC maps were supposed to be secret, their existence and long-term urban social effects were not widely discussed in print until the 1980s, when they were publicized by the historian Kenneth T. Jackson in his book *Crabgrass Frontier* (1985). Following Chicago School of Sociology theory, which saw the "zones of transition" with their mixtures of older urban housing and commercial and industrial uses as doomed in real estate terms, these redlined areas were where new slum-clearance projects for lower-income housing began to be built. An early example of this was Neighborhood Gardens in St. Louis (1934), a privately sponsored philanthropic, low-rise garden apartment complex of 252 units, designed by Hoener, Baum, and Froese. The architects' models were similar to perimeter-block projects in Amsterdam and Vienna, and this "for whites only" project was built to clear a very dense slum area, one of two that had been indicated as "blighted" by St. Louis planner Harland

75. Federal Housing
Administration (FHA)
subdivision guidelines
(Federal Housing
Administration, *Planning
Profitable Neighborhoods*
[Washington, D.C., 1939]).

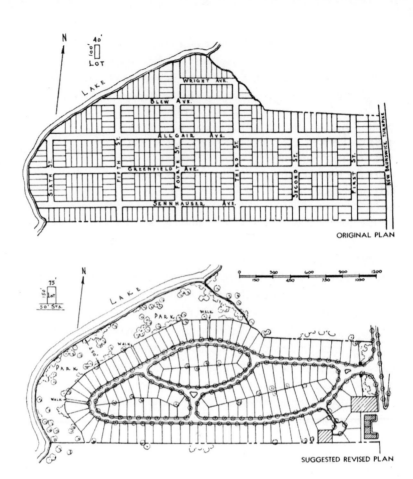

Bartholomew in 1917. Harlem River Houses, designed around the same time, followed a similar design pattern, but it was succeeded by many later public housing projects that avoided perimeter-block courtyard organizations in favor of variations of more row building–type site plans, with lawns and parking areas set between the low-rise buildings.

All such efforts to build federally supported public housing were fiercely resisted by the National Association of Real Estate Boards, which had the Republican Party's support in attempting to limit government's role in housing, beyond mortgage support for single-family home ownership for the white middle class. Yet in a sense both sides of the housing debate achieved their goals in the 1930s, as the FHA was able to stimulate the home building industry with federal mortgage guarantees, while the U.S. Housing Authority aided local public housing agencies in clearing and rebuilding inner-city slums. Following the recommendation of the President's Conference on Home Building and Home Ownership, the FHA also began to issue subdivision guidelines for new suburban residential areas (fig. 75). At the conference, Thomas Adams and Harland Bartholomew offered recommendations about the use of the single-family house neighborhood unit with cul-de-sacs and a centrally located elementary school, which then became the basis for the 1936 FHA bulletin *Planning Neighborhoods for Small Homes*. These guidelines firmly rejected the grid plan as the basis for new American residential neighborhoods, a position that the FHA has often upheld since. The FHA objections to the use of the grid were that it required more paved street area than was absolutely necessary, which increased traffic hazards, as well as less quantifiable objections that the grid created a "monotonous uninteresting architectural effect," which "fails to create a community aspect." By 1938, FHA subdivison plan reviewers were "suggesting" the use of its standard layouts of curving streets to developers as a necessary requirement for them to obtain FHA mortgage insurance, effectively turning these guidelines into a design code for American residential suburban site planning.

As it took these successful steps to revive the private real estate market, the New Deal also undertook immense regional modernization projects, beginning with the Tennessee Valley Authority (TVA) in 1933. This involved building over twenty new hydroelectric dams in the multistate Tennessee River watershed, which stretched from southwestern Virginia across Tennessee and northern Alabama up to the confluence of the Tennessee and Ohio rivers in western Kentucky (fig. 76). When the project began, 30 percent of the area's mostly rural population was infected with malaria, and earned very low average annual incomes, in part the result of depleted soil. The TVA's goal was to realize the RPAA's vision of decentralized industrial regions with a high standard of living that used energy from sources other than "paleotechnic" coal. Transportation would be provided not by rail, which was seen as an outmoded technology at the time, but by vehicles, which required extensive new highways. The Blue Ridge Parkway (1935) and the Natchez Trace Parkway (1938), some of the many new highways of the 1930s funded by the federal government, ran through the region, and new towns with dispersed layouts were constructed there as well. Notable among these was Norris, Tennessee (1934), named after the Nebraska Senator George W. Norris, who had first advocated the idea of regional development based on hydroelectric power there in 1925. The dispersed layout of single-family houses and a modest community center at Norris, adjusted to the topography of its hilly site, was created by Earle Draper (1893–1994), chief planner for the TVA, and Tracy Augur, an RPAA member. Draper, a former associate of John Nolen (1869–1937), a leading American Garden City planner, established his office in Charlotte, North Carolina, in 1917, designing hundreds of new company towns in the Carolinas and Georgia during the 1920s.

The Greenbelt Towns were a different form of New Deal regional development, one based directly on Garden City ideas about creating compact, self-contained communities with a range of employment, commercial, and cultural opportunities. The program began in April 1935

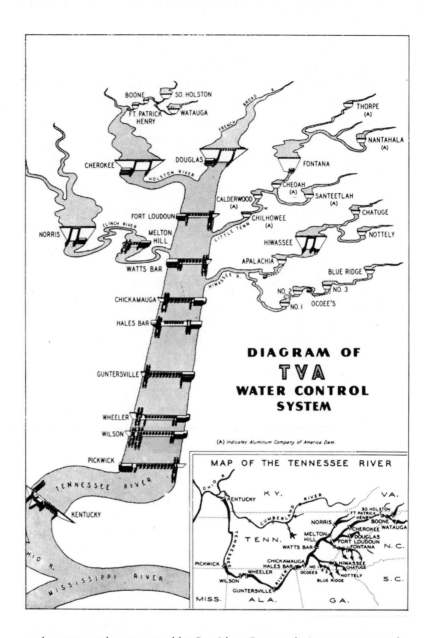

76. Diagram of the Tennessee Valley Water Control System, 1933.

and was strongly supported by President Roosevelt. It was overseen by a new Resettlement Administration within the Federal Emergency Relief Administration, headed by Rexford Guy Tugwell (1891–1979), an agricultural economist and, from 1938 to 1940, city planning director for Mayor Fiorello La Guardia in New York City. Along with regional redevelopment efforts like the TVA, Tugwell advocated moving unemployed rural agricultural workers into new towns at the edges of metropolitan areas, to bring them closer to potential industrial jobs. Frank Lloyd Wright presented his Broadacre City idea to the Resettlement Administration, with the impossible condition that he have complete control over the design of the project. Eventually, four Greenbelt towns were planned in detail: Greenbelt, Maryland, about thirteen miles (21 kilometers) northeast of

Washington, D.C.; Greenhills, Ohio, near Cincinnati; Greendale, Wisconsin, near Milwaukee; and Greenbrook, New Jersey, near New Brunswick.

Greenbelt, planned by Hale Walker and others, opened in 1937 and grew to 7,500 people by the 1940s. It is the best known of the three towns actually built, and its design is a hybrid of Garden City approaches and May's New Frankfurt. Like Radburn, the model for all the Greenbelt towns, Greenbelt, Maryland, was designed for vehicular access, but also included large areas of open green spaces, with pedestrian paths for children to walk to the central school-community building, sited such that it was within a half-mile (0.8-kilometer) walk of every house. Most of the housing took the form of two-story painted cinderblock row houses, or four-story walk-up apartments, all organized in an open layout to maximize sunlight in each unit. Initially some five hundred families grew food on 50 × 50 foot (15.24 × 15.24 meter) plots. Greenbelt also included a civic center, with ample parking, some stores, a co-op food store, and a movie theater. Greenbrook, New Jersey, northwest of New Brunswick, was planned by Albert Mayer, Henry S. Churchill, and Henry Wright, and was the most ambitious of the four towns. It was stopped because of objections by some large landowners in the area. In 1939, as charges began to be made that the entire Greenbelt town program was "socialistic," the U.S. Supreme Court ruled that the program was unconstitutional, as the Resettlement Administration, unlike the public housing authorities, had not been formally granted government powers to build housing.

Another aspect of the Resettlement Administration's work during the New Deal was construction of housing settlements of the Farm Security Administration (FSA) in western states. These settlements were intended as temporary housing for rural migrants, many of them farmers and farmhands from Oklahoma fleeing the Dust Bowl, a climate event that had destroyed thousands of acres of farmland. FSA design teams, led by architect Burton D. Cairns at the FSA's West Coast office in San Francisco from 1937 to 1941, included Vernon DeMars (1908–2005) and were organized to foster collaboration among architects, engineers, and landscape architects. These teams would design dozens of government-sponsored camps for migrant workers on the West Coast and in Arizona. Garrett Eckbo (1910–2000), an FSA landscape architect and later the founder of the corporate landscape architecture firm EDAW, pioneered the concept of "site planning" in these designs, which approached the design of the "total site space as one operation." Instead of more traditional definitions of architecture, Eckbo advocated that the design of what he called the "human environment" be based on the "four basic elements" of "people, space, materials, and specific conditions." Eckbo, DeMars, and the other FSA designers were among the first to apply this synthesis of architecture, landscape, and planning at a large scale. Their work paralleled and, in Eckbo's case, overlapped with Dean Joseph Hudnut's efforts to create a Graduate School of Design (GSD) at Harvard University by combining the formerly separate Schools of Architecture, Landscape Architecture, and Planning in 1936.

The directions set by planners and the federal government in the 1920s and 1930s were also evident in the defense programs begun by President Roosevelt in 1938, in response to the likelihood of a world war involving Nazi Germany, Japan, and the Soviet Union. Hundreds of new industrial plants for defense-related industries were commissioned throughout the country, many of them designed by Detroit-based Albert Kahn Associates. Their siting generally reflected the 1930s consensus that it was best "to get people out of the cities and into the country" by relocating industries into small towns, as the president had written to Henry Ford in 1934. At first the majority of these new defense plants were sited in outlying areas of existing industrial cities, in places known since the 1980s as the "Rustbelt," an area north of Appalachia extending from the western edges of the Northeast Corridor to the Great Lakes, and south to the St. Louis area. By April 1941, according to a member of the federal Plant-Site Committee, efforts were under way to encourage wider distribution of plants across the country. Many new plants were located in "the Southern and Southwestern States," where Depression-era unemployment had remained high. In all regions the plants were usually located at the urban periphery, producing the decentralizing effects strongly advocated by both Henry Ford and Roosevelt and by planners and architects at this time of both modernist and classicist inclinations.

This new pattern was the culmination of two decades of American vehicle-centered development, and it had little precedent in previous urbanized societies. It was also closely linked to new development practices encouraged by the FHA, and brought together the growing aerospace industry in Los Angeles and the large FHA-backed homebuilders there. Many of these big employers precipitated the construction of new single-family-house subdivisions near defense plants on then-open land in places such as Toluca Wood in North Hollywood; Westchester, just north of Los Angeles International Airport; and Westside Village. Technologically these developments pioneered the use of preassembled wood framing and plumbing components, along with the assembly-line construction methods often associated with the postwar Levittowns built near New York City and Philadelphia.

The prewar defense buildup took place during a period when the planning profession still had considerable prestige, but the physical outcomes of this massive metropolitan transformation were for the most part makeshift and not admired even at the time. The emphasis was on rapid production and crisis management in defense priority areas. What planning there was tended to be loosely based on Garden City precedents, as filtered through the experience of the Tennessee Valley Authority. In addition to standard small-house developments, TVA architects and technicians had developed various types of trailers as shelter options, which then set international standards. Trailers based on the TVA model and other kinds of prefabricated shelters were then used as temporary housing in war-devastated parts of Europe, notably in Britain, and Le Corbusier himself offered his services to the TVA to design some on his American visit in 1946. Trailer camps became an important part of the defense housing effort, and remained in place after the war as an essential element of the postwar American vernacular landscape. The whole regionalist conception of the TVA, based on creating a harmonious balance between human settlement, agriculture, and industry, became a key reference point for subsequent international planning in Latin America, India, Africa, and elsewhere in the postwar decades.

This wartime experience of mass government-organized suburban decentralization also coincided with the entry of large numbers of women into the industrial workforce. In a few cases, as at the Federal Public Housing Authority defense housing settlement for Kaiser Shipyard workers at Vanport, near Portland, Oregon, designed by planner J. M. Moscowitz with architects Wolff and Phillips, these directions also had some impact on the site plans. During the war, Vanport was briefly the second largest city in Oregon, and efforts were made there to provide extensive daycare provisions with a trained staff for the large number of women defense workers. Some three thousand other such daycare centers were constructed around the country during the war. As a planned community, Vanport's planners concerns about women workers' daily experience was the exception, and after the war the traditional gender divisions, where men were again seen as the primary wage earners and women as largely responsible for raising children at home, returned. This pattern then became characteristic of new American suburban developments for returning veterans and their families, until it began to be widely challenged by women in the 1970s.

URBANISM AND MODERNIZATION IN ITALY, GERMANY, AND THE JAPANESE EMPIRE IN THE 1930S

In Mussolini's Fascist Italy (1922–43), Hitler's Nazi Germany (1933–45), and imperial Japan (1895–1945), both neoclassical and modernist directions also had numerous applications in ambitious plans for new cities and urban districts. In the 1930s, varying kinds of architecture and urban design were infused with nationalistic and Fascist ideological content, resulting in many postwar debates about the political meaning of specific forms and projects. In Italy, a group of architects formed Gruppo 7 in 1927 to advance a version of modern architecture they called "rationalism." One of their members, Giuseppe Terragni (1904–1943), designed an apartment house in Como called the Novocomum, influenced by the Soviet avant-garde. Another key monument of Italian architecture at this time was the Fiat-Lingotto factory complex in Turin (1914–23), designed in part by company engineer Giacomo Matté-Trucco (1869–1934), whose models were the reinforced concrete factories of Albert Kahn in Detroit.

The Futurist fascination with technology then converged with Gruppo 7's architectural interests in the Casa Elettrica (Electric House), a show-case of modern domestic electrical appliances at the Monza Triennale in 1930 designed by Gino Figini (1903–1991) and Luigi Pollini (1903–1984), who then went on to be the chief architects of the Olivetti typewriter factory town (1934–1990s) on the outskirts of Ivrea, near Turin. Adalberto Libera (1903–63), another Gruppo 7 member, founded the MIAR (Italian Movement for Rational Architecture) in 1928, which garnered the sup-port of Rome gallery owner and patron Pier Maria Bardi (1900–1999) in 1931. Bardi married Lina Bo Bardi (1914–1992) in 1946, later an influential Brazilian architect, and both emigrated to São Paulo. MIAR then sought Mussolini's official support for modern architecture, which was not forthcoming. Instead, his regime increasingly looked to the more classi-cal work of Marcelo Piacentini (1881–1960), whose competition-winning town center of Brescia (1928–32) set a pattern for modernized classical urban center renovation in Fascist Italy and its colonies, which then in-cluded Libya, Eritrea, parts of Somalia, and, from 1935 to 1943, Ethiopia.

Piacentini also oversaw the new campus of the University of Rome (1932), designed in a similar stripped classical manner (later sometimes inaccurately called "Mussolini modern"). Mussolini also began to build new monumental boulevards in Rome after the Lateran Pact of 1929, which eased relations between the Papacy and the regime. The remains of ancient Roman ruins were restored, surrounding structures removed, and mass tourism encouraged. The new traffic arteries included the Via dell'impero (1932) next to the Roman forum, and the Via della Conciliazi-one (1936), which linked the Vatican and St. Peter's Basilica to the ancient and Renaissance parts of the city east of the Tiber River. The regime also supported the Instituto Casa Populare (ICP), which built and renovated existing buildings for low-rent housing, which by 1930 housed 7 percent of Rome's population, a percentage of urban residents in public housing second in Europe only to Rome's then political opposite, Red Vienna.

Mussolini's regime also built a series of new towns in the Pontine re-gion, an agricultural area of recently drained marshland south of Rome. The first city to be built was Littoria (1932, now Latina), originally planned for six thousand residents. Its plan was shown at CIAM 4, where it was criticized by Piero Bottoni (1903–1973) as being based on "outdated" Garden City principles. More well-known was the Pontine administrative center town of Sabaudia (1933), designed by former members of MIAR, including Luigi Piccinato (1899–1983). Its simplified classical architecture was preferred by Mussolini, more so than the Le Corbusier–influenced (and today more well-known) Casa del Fascio party headquarters build-ing in Como (1932–37) by Terragni.

77. Ernesto Bruno La Padula, Giovanni Guerrini, and Mario Romano, Palace of Italian Civilization, Esposizione Universale Roma (E42), 1938–43.

The culmination of this period in Italian architecture was the E42 world's fair, planned in 1938 for a site six miles (10 kilometers) south of Rome, for a planned 1942 World's Fair that was never held. A design team lead by Piacentini produced an imposing classical campus-like organization for the site, which was intended to become a satellite city linked to Rome by rail and the city's first expressway, the Viale Imperiale (1937, now the Via Cristoforo Colombo). This highway was also the main axis of E42, along which were sited permanent buildings, culminating in the Palace of Italian Civilization (1937–42), a reinforced concrete structure with six floors of simple, identical arches clad in travertine, the marble-like material widely used by the ancient Romans (fig. 77). Adalberto Libera (1903–1963) also planned an unbuilt aluminum parabolic arch to be built over the highway as a gateway to the fair, in a form resembling that of Eero Saarinen's later stainless steel and concrete Gateway Arch in St. Louis, designed in 1947–48. Accused in print of Fascist sympathies by Gilmore Clarke because of this similarity, Saarinen denied any inspiration from Libera's design, which instead was probably derived from the parabolic arch in Le Corbusier's unbuilt Palace of the Soviets competition entry of 1931 and its built predecessor, the prestressed reinforced concrete parabolic dirigible hangars by engineer Eugène Freyssinet (1879–1962) at Orly airport near Paris (1921–23), which were destroyed by Allied bombs in 1944.

Nazi Germany (1933–45) officially rejected CIAM and modern avant-garde movements in art and architecture, but it continued Weimar-era developments in transportation and military technologies that were then among the most advanced in the world. Europe's first expressway had been the AVUS expressway (1913–21), built through the Grunewald in Berlin. Privately funded proposals to build a national highway system were proposed in the 1920s, but only a small segment linking Cologne to Bonn was built before 1933. The Nazis were convinced that a national express highway network (Autobahn) would provide jobs for the unemployed and assist in national defense. The Reichsautobahnen Gesellschaft (National Autobahn Company) was established to build the system, which was designed by engineer Fritz Todt (1891–1942), a Nazi party member since 1922. The first section, between Frankfurt and Darmstadt, opened in 1935. By 1940, some 2,486 miles (4,000 kilometers) of express highways had been constructed, linking all the major German cities and including monumental iconic elements such as classical columns decorated with eagles and swastikas. Two types of Autobahn service stations were built, one in a traditional German vernacular style and the other more streamlined and modern, indicating the stylistic eclecticism of the regime, which did not officially favor any one style. Along with constructing the Autobahn system, Hitler also decided to offer the German masses a small, affordable "people's car," the Volkswagen, which went into production at the new Nazi planned city of Stadt des KdF-Wagens (later Wolfsburg) in 1940, after World War II had begun.

Hitler's regime also sought to remake Berlin as a more imposing imperial capital, and his favorite architect Albert Speer (1905–1981) was commissioned to redesign its circulation system, linking the new Tempelhof airport (fig. 78), the first large passenger airport, designed by Ernst Sagebiel, a former associate of Mendelsohn, to an immense new "Volkshalle" by Speer, sited next to the former German parliament building, the Reichstag. The Reichstag was deliberately left in ruins to remind

78. Ernst Sagebiel, Tempelhof Airport, Berlin, 1936.

Germans of the failures of democracy to create a stable social and economic order during the Weimar period in the 1920s. Speer's bombastic neoclassical plan (sometimes inaccurately called the "Germania" plan) was only partly carried out, though substantial demolitions of older areas along the routes of the new boulevards took place even before the massive Allied bombings of Berlin began after 1940.

Parallel to these directions, which led in 1936 to the declaration of the Rome-Berlin "Axis" against communism, imperial Japan established the puppet state of Manchukuo in northern China in 1932, signaling its intention to expand its influence in Asia and resist further Western encroachments. Japanese planners began to make theoretical proposals for fortified new Japanese agricultural settlements there, proposing a system of collectives of 150 households, each with 24.7 acres (10 hectares) of farmland, ten times the average held by a poor farmer in Japan. By this point the Dōjunkai, the Tokyo social housing agency, had also shifted its focus to rural life, issuing a five-hundred-page report on life in the Japanese countryside, indicating a new direction parallel to decentralist ideas elsewhere. Extensive intellectual exchanges began to take place between German and Japanese urbanists, with the "central place theory" of Walter Christaller (1893–1969) beginning to be applied by Uchida Yoshizō in his proposals for Japanese colonial agricultural settlements in Manchuria. In 1933 Christaller had published the results of his studies of agricultural market towns in southern Germany, postulating that since every town was linked to at least one or two others, a roughly hexagonal circulation network made each a "central place" in relation to each other, much like biological cells. This theory was a further extension of earlier efforts to understand human settlements as biological systems, and paralleled the early work of Austrian biologist Ludwig von Bertalanffy (1901–1972), one of the founders of systems theory. In his *Kritische theorie der Formbildung* (1928, translated as Modern Theories of Development), von Bertalanfly developed a theoretical biology, based on the study of recurring patterns and the effort to understand self-regulating systems, which he had begun to present in lectures at the University of Vienna in 1931.

After Japan invaded China in 1937, brutally occupying Beijing (known as Beiping until 1949), Shanghai, Nanjing, and other cities, imperial Japanese urbanists began to receive commissions for other projects in Japanese-occupied China. In 1938 Datong, a new capital for the occupied Northern Shanxi Autonomous Region, was established, and a team including Kenzo Tange's later thesis adviser, the planner Eika Takayama (1910–1999), developed a comprehensive plan. This called for the preservation of the ancient central city, a center of Buddhism under the Northern Wei dynasty (AD 386–534). Takayama proposed a surrounding new urban district for 180,000 people, organized along a gently curving axis, as well as two satellite towns of 30,000 people. The basic planning unit was the "neighborhood unit," each consisting of about 5,000 people, based on Radburn and Clarence Perry's work, but also reflecting the many German applications of the housing settlement concept, examples of which had been published by the Dōjunkai in 1936. The basic housing type at Datong was a hybrid of traditional Chinese courtyard houses, but using Japanese tatami mat proportions and including Garden City ideas about the need for front-yard setbacks. The plan also demonstrated an extensive knowledge of advanced planning ideas of the 1930s, some already then being applied by CIAM President Cor van Eesteren in Amsterdam, including a large central park, greenbelts, and public plazas. Planning legislation of the kind then being called for by CIAM was also proposed, modifying the 1919 Japanese laws.

CIAM itself continued to meet in Europe until 1939, but was illegal in both Germany and the Soviet Union. Nonetheless, related ideas about urban planning continued to evolve in both countries. In Germany, there was extensive planning for a large eastern region that was expected to open up for German settlement in the wake of Nazi conquests and genocide. In 1940 the Deutsche Akademie für Städtebau, Reichs-und Landesplanung (German Academy for Town, National, and Regional Planning, originally founded in 1922, during the Weimar years) was given a new charge "to scientifically investigate the ordering of German *Lebensraum* [national living space]." Its findings resulted in the writing of a publication in 1944, eventually published in 1957 (with some changed terminology) as *Die gegliederte und aufgelockerte Stadt* (The Ordered and Dispersed City). This set of concepts later became the basis for 1960 West German planning legislation, which also included elements from Christaller's central place theory. Its authors were Johannes Göderitz; Hubert Hoffmann (1904–1999), a leftwing graduate of the Bauhaus and CIAM member (who, like some other German modernists, also worked for the Nazi regime); and Roland Rainer (1910–1999), an Austrian architect who worked for the Nazis and after 1945 had a long postwar career as Vienna's city architect and as a designer of low-rise high-density housing in Austria. Though this 1957 publication changed the Nazi terminology of the original report (terms such as *Volkshygiene* were removed), its planning concepts remained close to those of prewar CIAM, and had many parallels to modern planning concepts that were also then being widely applied in Britain and elsewhere.

MODERNIZATION AND URBANISM IN THE 1930S IN BRAZIL

Outside of Europe, Asia, and the United States, architects and designers also attempted to shape modernization patterns in the 1930s, often along similar lines. In Brazil, a military coup in March 1930 by Getúlio Vargas (1882–1954) led to the centralization and modernization of the formerly fractious country, deeply divided regionally between its poor, plantation-oriented North, where a majority of the population was descended from

African slaves, and the areas south of Salvador, where there were more descendants of European immigrants, many arriving in the nineteenth century. Among the many reforms of the Vargas era, which eventually included the suppression of both communist and Fascist influences, was the construction of a new Brazilian national identity as both Portuguese-speaking and multiracial, following the ideas of the historian Gilberto Freyre (1900–1987), a student of the anthropologist Franz Boas (1858–1942). The regime also focused on architectural modernization. The previously Beaux-Arts oriented Escola Nacional de Belas Artes (ENBA) in Rio de Janeiro was put under the direction of the young recent graduate Lúcio Costa (1902–1998), who asserted the need for a "radical transformation" of architectural education, in line with student opinion at the time. Costa invited the São Paulo architect and CIAM member Gregori Warchavchik and others to teach there, and hosted Frank Lloyd Wright and Eliel Saarinen as lecturers at the school. Political pressures forced Costa's resignation in September 1931, but he remained active as an architect in Brazil. In 1936 he was hired by Vargas's minister of education, Gustavo Capanema, to lead a team of young architects that included Oscar Niemeyer (1907–2012) and others to design the new Brazilian Ministry of Education and Public Health (BMESP) building in Rio, the capital of Brazil until 1960. Costa successfully advocated that Le Corbusier be added to the design team, who then gave a popular series of lectures in 1936 on his "Radiant City" design concepts.

At sixteen stories, the Brazilian Ministry of Education and Public Health building was one of first modernist high-rise buildings in the world. It used Le Corbusier's "five points of a new architecture" as the basis for its design (fig. 79). These were the free facade; horizontal strip windows; and the free plan, all made possible by the flexibility of reinforced concrete construction based on free-standing columns, or *piloti;* and also the use of roof gardens, explained by Le Corbusier as returning the area beneath the building as a usable outdoor space on the roof. To accommodate the tropical climate, the south-facing facade (the equivalent of a north-facing facade north of the equator) was a transparent glass curtain wall with an oblique view of the ocean, while the north-facing facade was given horizontal concrete brise-soleil (sunscreens) that pivoted on fixed vertical concrete panels. This kind of fixed-element shading system, which by the 1960s had become a modern design cliché in many tropical climates, had already been used a few years earlier by Brazilian architects Luis Nunes in Recife and by the Roberto Brothers at the ABI Building (1936–38), a few blocks from BMESP, as well as having been proposed by Le Corbusier in some of his earlier unbuilt projects for Algeria.

Niemeyer was influential in convincing the design team that movable, rather than fixed, sun-shading devices were preferable, and also in raising the height of the piloti at the landscaped street-level plaza from the 9 feet, 10 inches (3 meters) proposed by Le Corbusier to the

79. Lúcio Costa, Affonso Eduardo Reidy, Carlos Leão, Ernani Vasconcellos, Jorge Moreira, Oscar Niemeyer, with Le Corbusier and Roberto Burle-Marx, Brazilian Ministry of Education and Public Health building (MESP), Rio de Janeiro, Brazil, 1936–43.

more effective 33 feet (10 meters) in the built version. The project's landscape architect was Roberto Burle-Marx (1909–1994), who designed the extensive street-level gardens as well as several roof gardens, which also included works of modern sculpture by Jacques Lipchitz and others. The gardens were in some cases visible from the offices above and used different flower species to create painterly curvilinear forms and patterns, establishing Burle-Marx as a key figure in modern landscape architecture internationally. This project and many other works of what came to be known as *carioca* (the term for residents of Rio) Brazilian modernism were then publicized internationally in the "Brazil Builds" exhibition held at the Museum of Modern Art in New York in 1943, organized by Philip Goodwin and American architect-photographer G. E. Kidder-Smith (1913–1997). Niemeyer emerged at this point as the primary architect of the carioca school, designing a set of buildings in 1939 for a resort

The Emergence of Avant-Garde Urbanism in the 1920s and 1930s

at Pampulha, near Belo Horizonte, that quickly became internationally influential. Brazil in the 1930s also saw a shift to middle-class high-rise residential buildings in the major cities, encouraged by government lending policies and the ideas of Le Corbusier. Cities such as Rio and São Paulo had been replanned with large boulevards in the Beaux-Arts tradition by Alfred Agache and others, but by the early 1940s, modernism in reinforced concrete began to supplant classicism as the preferred residential style, making Brazilian cities among the first places to take up modern architecture on an urban scale.

FURTHER READING

Richard Cartwright Austin, *Building Utopia: Erecting Russia's First Modern City, 1930* (Kent, Ohio: Kent State University Press, 2004).

Eve Blau, *The Architecture of Red Vienna* (Cambridge, Mass.: MIT Press, 1999).

Eve Blau and Ivan Rupnik, *Project Zagreb* (Barcelona: Actar, 2007).

Mardges Bacon, "Le Corbusier and Postwar America: The TVA and Béton Brut," *Journal of the Society of Architectural Historians* 74:1 (March 2015): 13–40.

Luis E. Carranza and Fernando Luiz Lara, eds., *Modern Architecture in Latin America* (Austin: University of Texas, 2014).

James Dahir, *The Neighborhood Unit: Its Spread and Acceptance* (New York: Russell Sage Foundation, 1947).

Kenneth Frampton, *Modern Architecture* (New York: Thames and Hudson, 1992).

Sigfried Giedion, *Walter Gropius: Work and Teamwork* (New York: Reinhold, 1954).

Paul L. Knox, *Palimpsests: Biographies of 50 City Districts* (Basel: Birkhäuser, 2012).

Le Corbusier, *The Radiant City* (New York: Orion, 1967).

Neil Levine, *The Urbanism of Frank Lloyd Wright* (Princeton: Princeton University Press, 2016).

Eric Mumford, *The CIAM Discourse on Urbanism* (Cambridge, Mass.: MIT Press, 2000).

Planning Amsterdam: Scenarios for Urban Development, 1928–2003 (Rotterdam: Netherlands Architecture Institute, 2003).

Maurice Frank Parkins, *City Planning in Soviet Russia* (Chicago: University of Chicago Press, 1953).

Gail Radford, *Modern Housing for America: Policy Struggles in the New Deal Era* (Chicago: University of Chicago Press, 1996).

Hugo Segawa, *Architecture of Brazil: 1900–1990* (New York: Springer, 2013).

Nasrine Seraji, *Housing, Substance of Our Cities: European Chronicle 1900–2007* (Paris: l'Arsenal, 2007).

Evelien van Es et al. eds., *Atlas of the Functional City: CIAM 4 and Comparative Analysis* (Zurich: gat Verlag/Thoth, 2014).

CHAPTER FIVE

Mid-Twentieth-Century Modern Urbanism

THE TRANSFORMATIONS OF WORLD WAR II

In the late 1930s, world powers divided between the Axis—initially an anti-communist alliance of Mussolini's Fascist Italy, Hitler's Nazi Germany, and imperial Japan—and the Allies, led by the British and French empires and the United States. In France, a rapid succession of mutually hostile elected governments focused on building a state-of-the-art fortification, called the Maginot Line, along the border with Germany, but the French government did not extend this complex multilevel defensive structure along the Belgian border. In August 1939, Germany and the Soviet Union signed a nonaggression pact, allowing Hitler to invade Poland, and beginning the conquest of eastern lands that the Nazis had slated for future German settlement. Hitler then sharply escalated the genocide of Jews and other groups in Eastern Europe. After Britain and France declared war on Germany, the Nazis stunned the world by using highly developed military techniques, including tank battalions linked by radio communication, airplanes, and strategic bombing, methods already theorized and applied in various ways after 1911, to quickly overrun Western Europe with these "Blitzkrieg" tactics in spring 1940.

Paris and northern France were then directly occupied, but the Nazis allowed the establishment of a nominally independent French state in the southern part of the country, with its capital in the small spa town of Vichy. The authoritarian new government there, headed by French World War I hero Marshal Phillippe Pétain, was technically independent, but applied many Nazi policies, eventually including the deportation of Jews and opponents of the Vichy regime to Nazi death camps. In other ways, Vichy France continued many of the modernizing French directions of the 1930s, including the use of technocratic experts to determine highly centralized national policies about the development of the built environment. Vichy engineers oversaw the continuation of such large projects as the infrastructural elements of Henri Prost's 1936 Paris regional plan, which called for ring roads and planned housing developments in the larger region.

Large public works firms specializing in prefabrication and construction management were established in the Vichy era to rebuild war damage from 1940, and planning laws were passed to give the new government agencies extensive control over reconstruction. Among the Vichy-appointed expert committees for national reconstruction was one that included Auguste Perret and the playwright and diplomat Jean Giraudoux (1882–1944). Like many of the French technocrats at the time, Giraudoux was an admirer of Marshal Hubert Lyautey, whose modernization of Moroccan cities in the 1910s had set a pattern for French modern urbanism. The Vichy Commissariat a la reconstruction immobilière (Commissariat for Property Reconstruction) in 1941 issued its *Charte de l'architecte reconstructeur* (Reconstruction Architect's Charter), a set of stylistically conservative official design principles for architects to use in reconstruction projects. This Vichy Commissariat also briefly employed Le Corbusier in 1941 as the director of a study commission on housing and reconstruction. He wrote at the time to CIAM Secretary-General Sigfried Giedion in Zurich that he found the Vichy atmosphere "very favorable" for CIAM on European reconstruction, but Le Corbusier and CIAM's focus on modern collective housing was rejected by the Vichy Commissariat, which preferred traditional, regionalized architectural styles. His presence on the commission was judged to be a "scandal," and he went into hiding until the Allied liberation of France in 1944.

In 1942, Le Corbusier founded a new French CIAM group, which he called ASCORAL (Assemblée de constructeurs pour la rénovation architecturale/Constructors' Association for the Renovation of Architecture). This new group had links to the French-Algerian resistance to the Vichy regime, and included Roger Aujame (1922–2010) and Eugène Claudius-Petit (1907–1989), the latter a member of the French Resistance. Its goal was to set out the architectural and urban direction for postwar reconstruction in France, building on the expert knowledge in urbanism developed for France's North African colonies. Le Corbusier and ASCORAL published *La Charte d'Athènes* (The Athens Charter) in Paris in 1943, a sort of counter-charter to Vichy urbanism based on the results of the CIAM 4 conference, which formulated the "four functions" of modern urbanism as dwelling, work, transportation, and recreation. After the Allied victory in 1945, the Athens Charter became a central point of reference for modernist urban reconstruction.

By summer 1940, Hitler had turned to the conquest of Britain, launching the Blitz, the Nazi aerial bombardment of London and other major English cities, including Coventry. The war then entered an even more destructive phase when Hitler broke his 1939 nonaggression pact with Stalin and invaded the Soviet Union in June 1941, seeking to eradicate Leningrad and Moscow and to turn European Russia into additional space for German ethnic colonization. Japan had joined the Axis military alliance in 1940, and in December 1941 it attacked without warning the American naval base at Pearl Harbor, Hawaii, bringing the United States fully into the war. With Japan now allied with Germany and Italy, at this point the United States joined Britain and the USSR in the war with the Axis in both Europe and the Pacific.

By 1942, Japan had conquered most of the European- and American-held colonial territories in East Asia. These included previously British-controlled Hong Kong, Singapore, Burma (now Myanmar), and what is now Malaysia; the former Dutch East Indies (Indonesia); French Indo-China (which then included Vietnam, Laos, and Cambodia); and the Philippines, a colony of the United States since 1898. To celebrate this new "Greater East Asian Co-Prosperity Sphere," which also included Japan's wartime ally, Thailand, a competition was held in 1941 to design a monumental complex to be sited at the base of Japan's sacred mountain, Mount Fuji. The entry by Kenzo Tange (1913–2005), then a student of Eika Takayama and a former employee of Japanese CIAM member Kunio Maekawa (1905–1986), combined elements of traditional Japanese architecture with references to Michelangelo's Campidoglio in Rome, anticipating Tange's extensive design of Japanese civic centers and his regional plans in the postwar era.

By 1943, when the German advance into Russia and Ukraine was finally stopped by the Soviet Red Army near Stalingrad, World War II began to turn in favor of the Allies. A popular revolt in Italy that year overturned Mussolini's government, after the Allied invasion had begun. In Germany itself, and in the parts of Europe still under Axis occupation, British and American bombers began to systematically destroy major industrial and urban centers. In addition to factories, rail depots, and military sites, large urban concentrations of working-class residents became de facto targets. By 1944, German historic cultural sites like Dresden were also largely destroyed in the Allied bombing campaign as revenge for the German aerial attacks on British cities. In Japan, American bombers firebombed all the major cities, killing millions of civilians and demolishing many urban areas, before finally using atomic bombs on two major industrial Japanese cities, Hiroshima and Nagasaki, in August 1945. The use of these atomic bombs was justified by the Allies as a way of avoiding the millions of casualties that almost certainly would have resulted from the planned American land invasion of Japan. After surrender, Japan, with some 115 of its cities in ruins and over two million housing units destroyed, was then under direct U.S. military occupation from 1945 to 1952.

Using techniques discovered by European scientists by 1940, the American atomic bomb had been rapidly developed by a team of academic scientists in a secret research effort called the Manhattan Project. It was first tested at the Trinity site in New Mexico in July 1945. Before then, aerial bombing targets typical of the housing and other buildings found in Japanese and German cities were constructed by the U.S. Army at the Dugway Proving Ground in Utah with the assistance of architects Antonin Raymond (1888–1976), a Czech émigré who had worked for Frank Lloyd Wright and in Japan and India; Eric Mendelsohn, who had moved from British Mandate Palestine to the United States in 1941; and Konrad Wachsmann, a German architect-engineer who was a partner with Walter Gropius in developing the General Panel prefabricated housing system.

The Allied war effort also resulted in the development of many technological advances, including radar and early forms of digital technology, which were initially used to break the German "enigma" code. New materials such as plastics, acrylics, fiberglass, spray foams, and Styrofoam began to be widely used, eventually becoming part of worldwide postwar consumer culture. The production of already developed building materials, like plywood, laminated timber, and gypsum interior wallboard, was also greatly increased. In 1941, U.S. Navy architects developed the corrugated steel Quonset hut, an easily moved metal structure that could be flexibly used for hospitals, airplane hangars, storage units, and housing. R. Buckminster Fuller was involved with related efforts with his Dymaxion deployment units (1941–42), round steel houses 20 feet (6 meters) in diameter inspired by metal midwestern grain bins and intended to be produced at a rate of a thousand per day. These were used as U.S. radar stations and at various strategic locations abroad, including in Iran and East Africa. Fuller also worked for the U.S. government Board of Economic Warfare, issuing his Dymaxion World Map in 1942, first published in *Life* magazine, which suggested new ways of conceptualizing world human occupation and its energy flows. László Moholy-Nagy, who had left Germany for London in 1934 and then opened his "New Bauhaus" in Chicago in 1938, developed camouflage strategies to conceal urban targets from the air. There were 20 million Americans who enlisted in the military during the war, and many modern architects, landscape architects, and planners, including Eero Saarinen, Dan Kiley, Paul Rudolph, I. M. Pei, Bruce Goff, Kevin Lynch, Willo von Moltke, and many others worked in a variety of American military service positions during and immediately after the war.

It was at this time that official patronage began to shift toward modernism in architecture and design. SOM's modernist team-based design approach had impressed American government and corporate leaders, and in 1943 SOM was commissioned to design the then-secret "Atom City" of Oak Ridge, Tennessee, a town of 75,000 designed with former Tennessee Valley Authority (TVA) town planner Tracy Augur. Augur, by then director of the Urban Targets Division of the federal Office of Defense Mobilization, became a strenuous advocate of urban decentralization for military reasons, arguing that dense existing industrial cities were vulnerable targets of enemy bombers. Yet SOM and Augur's winding

arterial road network for Oak Ridge and their efforts to preserve picturesque natural areas did not become a planning model for the postwar
urban transformation of the United States.

During the war, the first American long-distance express highways
began to be built, inspired by the German Autobahn. The first completed
was the Pennsylvania Turnpike, which opened in 1941. It initially linked
outlying areas east of Pittsburgh to near Harrisburg, reusing some railway
tunnels from the 1880s that passed through the Allegheny Mountains,
and linked the Northeast Corridor to the Midwest by express highway
for the first time. The Pennsylvania Turnpike was begun around the same
time that President Roosevelt appointed a National Interregional Highway Committee (NIHC) to propose a national system of such highways.
The NIHC included several state highway commissioners; the president's
uncle Frederic Delano (1863–1953), then chair of the National Resources
Planning Board who had been a patron of the Plan of Chicago and the
Regional Plan of New York; and two planners, Rexford Guy Tugwell of
New York and Harland Bartholomew of St. Louis.

The group's views split between the state highway officials and the
planners over the issue of "traffic first" planning—that is, whether routes
should be chosen to be the shortest route between major urban centers,
to be built on the cheapest and most easily acquired land, or chosen for
their relationship to topography, historic sites, and other planned development. The engineers' traffic first approach largely prevailed, while the
planners' preferred model, shown in the GM Futurama at the 1939 New
York World's Fair, with its highways designed as part of a larger modernist urban pattern, built at the edges of residential neighborhood units
and carefully related to airports, train stations, and other transit, was
implemented only in part. Although the planners argued against running
the new highways through parks or areas that required the demolition of
individual historic structures, this happened frequently in the construction of the interstate system. What would become most of the route
map of the American national interstate system in 1956 was published
in an NIHC report in January 1944 and was then approved by President
Roosevelt (fig. 80).

For selecting the routes within cities, St. Louis–based planner Bartholomew argued for the NIHC that new highways could revive central
areas by removing slums and making downtowns more easily accessed
by car from outlying suburbs, creating decentralized city-regions where
the downtown would remain the focal point of business and higher-
density residential uses. Downtowns could then be surrounded by parklike areas of new housing and social services. These ideas to some extent
informed the routing of interstate highways, which were often used as a
device of slum clearance, most infamously by New York City construction
coordinator Robert Moses in building the Cross-Bronx Expressway in New
York (1948–72). New highways were also a major part of Bartholomew's

Comprehensive City Plan for St. Louis (1947), which defined all the areas adjacent to downtown as "obsolete." He expected that, once cleared, these areas would be rebuilt with denser new housing, and the Pruitt-Igoe housing project was then built in one such area. This use of highway building to demolish dense residential neighborhoods considered to be slums was favored by planners at the time, who typically favored razing what today would often be considered valuable historic neighborhoods.

The new national defense highway system was approved as many new auto-based building types and settlement forms were also being built as part of the war effort. The Federal Public Housing Authority issued guidelines for shopping center design in 1942, and SOM designed what may be one of the first modern strip malls, for Aero Acres, adjacent to the Glenn L. Martin defense plant in Middle River, Maryland, built along with 600 new prefabricated dwellings for defense workers.

World War II transformed, often traumatically and with unparalleled suffering, prewar social and physical urban patterns. In Europe, the years of Nazi occupation and wartime destruction in many countries left conditions that led to major changes to urban areas that often broadly followed the lines demanded by CIAM and other modern planners. In the United States, the defense buildup unfortunately went along with an escalation of New Deal efforts to decentralize cities and to reorganize them for easier vehicular access, damaging in the process many valuable central areas and laying the groundwork for their massive postwar expansion along new highway routes.

80. National Interregional Highway Committee report map of proposed express highways, 1944 (NIHC, *Interregional Highways* [Washington, D.C., 1944]).

DECENTRALIZATION: POSTWAR URBANISM IN THE
UNITED STATES

After 1945, as the preponderance of world military power moved to the
United States and the former Soviet Union, the world's financial and cultural centers also shifted somewhat, from London and Paris to New York,
the largest city in the world between the 1920s and 1960. This partial
shift coincided with the growing worldwide popularity of the American
model of mass suburban consumption, often symbolized by Coca-Cola.
During this Cold War era (1949–91), several new directions in urbanism
emerged. They all took place against the backdrop of immense wartime
destruction, which had in many places created what were understood
then as tabula rasa (blank slate) conditions for new ways of physically
and socially organizing urban life.

In the United States from 1949 to the early 1970s, millions of dollars
of federal funds were disbursed to many cities to clear and rebuild central urban areas. The New Deal focus on slum clearance public housing
was expanded to include more business and institutionally oriented efforts, such as those in Chicago by the South Side Planning Board (SSPB),
founded in 1946 and centered on IIT and Michael Reese Hospital, and directed by the Harvard GSD–trained planner Reginald R. Isaacs (1911–1986).
Only a few such efforts were successful, and instead of the decentralized,
master-planned regions sought by architects and planners, the broad
outlines of the urban transformations of this era are now familiar in cities across the United States. The shift that had begun in the 1920s from
mixed-use streetcar cities to single-family-house, auto-based suburban
communities intensified, in response to the rapid relocation of industrial jobs to defense plants in new, sprawling metropolitan areas. In older
industrial centers such as Chicago, Philadelphia, Detroit, and St. Louis,
returning veterans briefly increased the urban population, which now
included many African Americans who were barred by then-standard
real estate practices from moving into the new suburban areas. When
such racially restrictive covenants were ruled unenforceable by the Supreme Court in 1948, the rapidly changing demographics of many urban
neighborhoods led to massive "white flight" to the suburbs. This was
occurring at the same time as the urban renewal efforts of the 1950s,
which displaced many African Americans, who then often moved into
formerly all-white areas. Yet until the mid-1960s, most professional and
office jobs remained in old rail-based downtowns, even though in many
cities, existing streetcar systems were removed.

These trends affected various central cities differently. New York remained the most important city in the United States, and in 1947, after a
site selection process that also considered Philadelphia and Westchester
County, the newly founded United Nations accepted John D. Rockefeller, Jr.'s offer of a prime waterfront site on the east side of Manhattan for

its headquarters (1947–52). A design team organized by Wallace K. Harrison (1895–1981), a New York architect who had married into the Rockefeller family and had worked on Rockefeller Center, was put in charge of the design of the new building, which was to include a tall office building, the Secretariat, and a complex of meeting spaces, the General Assembly. Harrison selected Le Corbusier (France), Oscar Niemeyer (Brazil), Sven Markelius (Sweden), Matthew Nowicki (Poland), Liang Sicheng (China), and others for the design team. Le Corbusier objected to Harrison's final design, which called for an immense east- and west-facing curtain wall of green-tinted thermopane glass instead of the concrete sunbreakers that he had advocated, a decision justified by Harrison as a better form of temperature control in a snowy climate. Nonetheless, the U.N. Headquarters building immediately set a pattern for new downtown high-rises. Its construction was paralleled by that of Pietro Belluschi's glass-clad Equitable Building in Portland, Oregon (1946), and Ludwig Mies van der Rohe's Lakeshore Drive Apartments in Chicago (1948–51). These were soon followed by Lever House (1950), New York's first all-glass commercial office building, designed by Gordon Bunshaft of SOM on a formerly residential stretch of Park Avenue, which then led to much further Midtown office development just north of Grand Central Station.

Soon, other architecturally ambitious commercial structures of all kinds were being built worldwide, including Sven Markelius's Hötorgscity mixed-use complex of five towers in central Stockholm (1952). The street-level urbanistic complexity of some of these buildings is now often overshadowed by their visually spectacular use of new technologies, canonically on display in SOM's Inland Steel in Chicago (1956) and Crown Zellerbach in San Francisco (1959). Mies's Seagram Building (1954–58) in New York, designed with Philip Johnson, became the most well-known example of this kind of downtown office building (fig. 81). The choice of Mies as the architect for Seagram was advocated by the client's daughter, Phyllis Lambert, who had been a student of Mies's at IIT.

Architects at this time did not see these modern office towers as isolated and egotistic monuments, as they would often be characterized by later generations. They were intended to be models for new forms of urban organization, and the Seagram Building was the reference point for the revised New York zoning code of 1961, which encouraged developers to set aside public spaces like Seagram Plaza in exchange for greater rentable height and bulk. These zoning factors were calculated through the concept of floor area ratio (FAR), defined as the ratio of the overall lot size to the number of building stories, so that a lot fully built out to one story would have an FAR of one. From the 1960s to the 1980s, many other cities, notably Houston and Toronto, began to build similar downtown office buildings sited in open plazas whose emptiness, minimal design, and modern "plop art" frequently elicited postmodernist criticism.

81. Ludwig Mies van der Rohe, Seagram Building, New York, 1954–58 (Ezra Stoller © ESTO).

At the same time, extensive efforts were made to create networks of pedestrian connectivity in what began to be called the downtown CBD (central business district). The City of London Corporation had approved a thirty-mile (48-kilometer) system of upper story pedestrian routes in 1947, and William Holford's reconstruction plans included some of these multilevel elevated walkways. By the 1950s, central London's "Comprehensive Development Areas," including such multilevel pedestrian routes, were being built at the Barbican, along the South Bank, and elsewhere. Related systems of "skywalks" began to be constructed in Minneapolis in 1962, and by the late 1960s many other such systems were being built. In Toronto, a system of underground pedestrian passageways, begun under the Royal York Hotel in the 1920s, was extended and eventually included Mies's Dominion Centre complex (1964–69). In Montreal, I. M. Pei's Place Ville Marie, developed by William Zeckendorf, eventually included Vincent Ponte's designs for the underground passages of La Ville Souterraine (1960). Related ideas were also used by the Detroit-based Japanese-American architect Minoru Yamasaki (1912–1986) at the former World Trade Center, New York (1962–75). The now-destroyed iconic twin towers were built over a complex that included pedestrian plazas, an underground shopping mall, and a subway station.

In other North American cities, the outcomes of such ambitious new projects were often very different than in New York or Chicago. In Atlanta, the architect-developer John Portman (born 1924) designed and built the Peachtree Center (1967), which popularized the idea of an enclosed, multistory, inward-facing "atrium" within a downtown commercial project. The successful Peachtree Center concept led to Portman's commissions for similar projects in Los Angeles (Place Bonaventure, 1974) and downtown Detroit (the massive Renaissance Center, 1977). These projects created architecturally elaborate interior worlds of shopping, offices, hotels, restaurants, and other public amenities, sometimes linked to downtown pedestrian passageways. Yet their success was understood at the time as depending on their being largely sealed off from the adjacent downtown streets. The public, defined as those able to arrive by private car and park in the large garages, could then move freely through interior multilevel spaces, which were often skylit and included plants, artworks, and other amenities. This separation from the everyday pedestrian world of the streets outside—which in many places was increasingly conflicted in the 1960s, first by the protests of the Civil Rights Movement and then by street crime—led many architects and critics to view these projects very negatively by the late 1970s.

Mass-transit systems were also a focus of North American planners in the 1950s. Hans Blumenfeld (1892–1988), a German-born architect who had worked in the Soviet Union between 1930 and 1937 and then under Edmund Bacon in Philadelphia from 1945 to 1953, planned the successful Toronto mass-transit system after his arrival on the Metropolitan Toronto Planning Board in 1955. His transit planning was part of his 1959 Toronto regional master plan. In Chicago, during the administration of Mayor Richard J. Daley, Sr. (1955–1976), SOM designed subway stations for the extended transit lines placed in the medians of the city's new interstate highways. During the same era many racially segregated high-rise public housing projects were also built there. These were mostly demolished in the 1990s, but for a time they set an image of Chicago as a city where business towers in the Loop sharply contrasted with the high-rise poverty on prominent display to visitors arriving on the new interstates. Other notable Chicago skyscrapers of the time included SOM's 100-story John Hancock Center on North Michigan Avenue (1965), which placed over 50 floors of luxury apartments above a 44-story office building, and their Sears Tower (1968–74). The Sears Tower (now Willis Tower), the tallest building in the world when completed, was constructed with a new structural tube system developed by an SOM team led by Bruce Graham (1925–2010) and engineer Fazlur Khan (1929–1982), who also taught at IIT.

Despite these globally influential, if often criticized, design achievements in North American downtowns in the postwar years, the decentralizing urban trends of the 1930s and 1940s intensified. They led to the emergence of corporate and other suburban campus environments that by the 1980s would greatly reduce the importance of older downtowns as office and shopping centers. Eliel and Eero Saarinen's firm Saarinen, Swanson & Saarinen had been commissioned by General Motors in 1944 to design one of the largest wartime projects in the country, a suburban research campus located in Warren, Michigan, twelve miles (19.3 kilometers) north of Detroit. Although GM executives had seen Eliel Saarinen's more traditional campus at Cranbrook Academy as a potential model for their GM Technical Center, the Saarinen firm eventually proposed something that they thought would better express the company's focus on modern precision manufacturing. By 1948, with Eero as the lead architect, the firm had produced a design for a series of three-story glass- and steel-enclosed rectangular buildings on a flat 320-acre (129.5-hectare) site. These new office buildings, inspired by Mies van der Rohe's IIT campus in Chicago, were set in landscaped parking lots that became a model for auto-scaled suburban corporate campuses in many other places. Each of the research center's functions was housed in a different building, 25 in total, set around a rectangular 22-acre (8.9-hectare) pond, with a forest of 13,000 trees at the perimeter. Artworks by Cranbrook sculptor Harry Bertoia (1915–1978), émigré Constructivist artist Antoine Pevsner (1886–1962), and others were displayed, some at the Styling Building, where Harley Earl (1893–1969) designed many classic American cars that were presented every year to the postwar mass media in the GM Styling Dome.

It was around this time that Eero Saarinen also won the St. Louis Jefferson National Expansion Memorial (JNEM) competition to design a large new monument and riverfront park to commemorate the Louisiana Purchase of 1803. Of the 171 entries received in the 1947–48 national competition, judged by a jury chaired by William Wurster and including Richard Neutra, George Howe, Roland Wank, and Herbert Hare, Saarinen's winning design, developed with his Cranbrook design team and the landscape architect Dan Kiley (1912–2004), was a proposal for a 630-foot (192-meter) tall stainless steel arch (fig. 82). It was to be located on the site of the old Mississippi riverfront commercial area that had been cleared in 1939 for a neoclassical monument to Jefferson, chosen in 1936, which had remained unbuilt. Along with its large Kiley-designed landscape park and proposed riverfront restaurant and museum, Saarinen's bold design indicated the postwar shift away from both traditional pedestrian urban monumentality and prewar modernist functionalism. Instead, it indicated a turn toward what Giedion, Sert, and the painter Fernand Léger had begun to call "the New Monumentality" in 1943.

In a 1944 essay on this topic, Giedion argued that all forms of Beaux-Arts classical "pseudo-monumentality" were inextricably linked to nineteenth-century ideals. He saw them as all basically equivalent, arguing that there was little difference between recent American classicism and the monumental structures favored by both the Nazis and Soviets in the 1930s. Giedion instead called for a modern collaboration between artists and architects like that between Costa, Niemeyer, Burle Marx, and Le Corbusier and team's prewar Brazilian Ministry of Education and Public Health in Rio. This direction would better express postwar cultural aspirations and would lead to a new architectural and design approach better related to contemporary human needs. These ideas had wide influence beyond the JNEM competition, including Harvard University's effort to hire Oscar Niemeyer as dean of the Graduate School of Design in 1952, and in the design of SOM's Air Force Academy (1954) in Colorado Springs, Colorado, a project led by SOM partner Walter Netsch (1920–2008).

Saarinen's mostly auto-accessed Gateway Arch and his GM Technical Center campus clearly indicated a new direction, one then often supported by American corporate and governmental elites. The Gateway Arch was to be built on the erased site of the earlier St. Louis waterfront, while the GM Technical Center moved well-paid service jobs out of downtown Detroit into a fast-growing new suburban area accessible only by car. Both indicated that existing downtowns would no longer be the site of traditional classical monuments, like the last large Beaux-Arts public buildings built in Washington, D.C., the Jefferson Memorial (1936–43) and the National Gallery (1936–43), both designed by John Russell Pope. In 1939, Eliel and Eero Saarinen's competition-winning Smithsonian Gallery of Modern Art (1939), to be sited near the Capitol and opposite the National Gallery, had been left unbuilt due to objections over its modern

82. Eero Saarinen, Jefferson National Expansion Memorial (JNEM), St. Louis, 1948–65.

design, but a different atmosphere had taken hold by 1945. Along with the classical Pentagon in suburban Arlington, the world's largest office building at the time of its completion in 1941, as the U.S. entered the war, these highly visible official Beaux-Arts projects marked the end of the City Beautiful movement's direct impact on American cities.

Frank Lloyd Wright's decentralized Broadacre City remained a popular alternative model for urbanism at this time, but it also did not triumph in the postwar era. Wright's public reputation had been compromised by his vehement prewar isolationism, though after the war he was frequently commissioned for individual buildings. These included some sixty Usonian houses, the compact modern suburban house prototype Wright had first built in Madison, Wisconsin, in 1936, with the idea that at least some of the construction could be done by the owner. With the Usonian house model Wright pioneered the one-story plan in which two or more bedrooms were accessed along a corridor leading from the living room, with compact "laboratory" kitchens and radiant slab heating instead of basements. In 1939 Wright was commissioned to design a group of such houses for a planned cooperative community, Usonia 1, in Lansing, Michigan, but it was not built due to opposition from the FHA, which stated that "the unusual design makes sales a hazard." Wright designed two other Usonian subdivisions near Kalamazoo, Michigan, in 1947, Parkwyn and Galesburg Villages, with the houses sited on circular one-acre house lots with collective common spaces between. These subdivisions, along with a community of fifty houses on a hilly ninety-seven-acre (39.3-hectare) tract near Pleasantville, New York, thirty miles (48 kilometers) north of New York City, were Wright's only built Usonian house communities, and they were not widely imitated.

In the Los Angeles area, which includes the auto-oriented city that eventually overtook Chicago and Philadelphia to become America's second-largest by 1990, John Entenza (1905–1984), the editor of *California Arts and Architecture,* sponsored a series of "Case Study" modern houses intended to demonstrate the advantages of efficient steel-framed modern design to the vast numbers of returning servicemen seeking new suburban homes there. Its most well-known outcomes were Charles and Ray Kaiser Eames's Case Study House #8 (1945, now the Eames Foundation in Pacific Palisades), a simple pair of steel-framed boxes sited on a hillside overlooking the Pacific Ocean. Conceptualized as part of the modernist planning agenda as it had developed by the 1940s, which typically called for neighborhood-unit-type suburban subdivisions related to topography and solar orientation, the Case Study program and related modernist directions like the Eichler home developments in both northern and southern California metropolitan areas did not become the mainstream form of postwar American residential development.

Instead of these critically acclaimed, but rarely imitated, modern suburban housing design models, it was Levittown (1949), on Long Island

83. House in Levittown, Pennsylvania, under construction, 1950 (*Rassegna* 14 52/4 [December 1992]: 13).

near New York, that indicated the form that postwar American suburbs would soon take. Levittown's developers, the brothers Abraham, Alfred, and William Levitt, applied their experience in building semi-prefabricated war housing in Norfolk, Virginia, to these developments, intended largely for returning white veterans and their families. The Veterans' Administration (VA) mortgage program (called the "G.I. Bill") of 1944 expanded federal assistance by offering generous mortgage insurance so that banks could lend to those who would not have been able to afford to buy a home. Both the FHA and the VA favored loans for new construction in the suburbs but did not typically view modern-looking houses like those of Wright or the Case Study program as very good investments. Instead, like most of postwar residential development, the Levittown houses' layout and designs followed FHA design guidelines of the 1930s and later. The FHA's suburban focus was justified by its continuing use of the Chicago School of Sociology's concentric ring model of metropolitan development, which predicted that "interior locations" in cities near downtown would continue to decline and become blighted.

In 1947 the Levitts purchased 4,000 acres (1,619 hectares) of former potato farms in Hempstead, Long Island, about a half hour from Manhattan. They began by building 2,000 rental houses, but the incredible demand for affordable housing soon led them to build inexpensive two-bedroom houses for sale instead (fig. 83). They obtained FHA-VA mortgage guarantees and aimed the houses at a market of prewar white urban tenants who had not previously been able to buy a home. Sales began in 1948 with extensive publicity, and by 1951, 17,500 new homes had been sold. Buyers who were veterans did not need to have a down payment, and since it was cheaper to buy a house with a mortgage in Levittown than to continue to rent an apartment in New York City, a mass white outmigration occurred. Until the mid-1960s, federal lending policies were openly discriminatory, refusing to lend to African Americans, female-headed households, and other applicants not seen as desirable suburban residents. Levittown's initial basic housing unit was a modified and modernized version of the compact story-and-a-half, two-bedroom Cape Cod cottage, the result of federal and local policies that favored traditional, pitched roof forms.

Architect Royal Barry Wills (1895–1962) had designed many such small houses that combined colonial detailing with modern utilities in the 1930s, a direction that Alfred Levitt then further adapted to the postwar market. In 1949, the Levitts introduced a ranch model that included a wood-burning fireplace, and their success with suburban house models set a pattern for much subsequent American suburban development, even as house and lot sizes grew in the decades that followed. The Levitts' Long Island development was soon followed by two more near Philadelphia: Levittown, Pennsylvania (1950), and Levittown, New Jersey, built across the Delaware River in Willingboro (1952). The latter was studied by the University of Pennsylvania trained sociologist Herbert Gans (born 1927), who presented his findings in *The Levittowners* (1967).

The FHA favored such single-family subdivisions with curvilinear streets, but in 1946 it also began the "608" program, insuring mortgage loans to developers to build garden apartments and sometimes other apartment complexes in urban areas. Massive corruption in the program caused the 608 program to be terminated in 1950, but some seven thousand apartment projects were built under it, including some of the postwar apartment buildings on Lake Shore Drive in Chicago. A parallel effort was undertaken around the same time by large New York insurance companies to build apartment housing for middle-class veterans, most notably at Stuyvesant Town, where 8,800 apartments went up on 75 acres (30.35 hectares) of urban land cleared by Robert Moses in his role as city construction coordinator between 1943 and 1948. The architect of Stuyvesant Town, Irwin Clavan (1900–1982), had designed the large Parkchester apartment complex in the Bronx in 1938 for the Metropolitan Life Insurance Company, where he had developed a simple repetitive approach to housing by using 12- to 13-story red-brick-faced blocks, with the apartment units efficiently clustered around elevator cores. Each apartment building was surrounded by parklike open spaces with parking and play areas for children. To address concerns about racial discrimination, a much smaller but similar project, Riverton, was built in Harlem at the same time.

The design approach used in both complexes was an awkward hybrid between conventional New York apartment house design and early CIAM site-planning ideas. It was also quite similar to the design direction taken by the architects of the New York City Housing Authority's Red Hook Houses in Brooklyn (1938). At Stuyvesant Town, Clavan was joined by Gilmore Clarke, who had been one of the landscape architects for the Westchester County parkways. Clarke's firm, Clarke and Rapuano, then worked extensively all over the New York region, with projects that included the landscape architecture of the 1939 and 1964 New York World's Fairs, Moses's proposal to locate the new United Nations headquarters in Flushing Meadow, Queens, and the landscaping of the Garden State Parkway in New Jersey. Clarke also served as dean at Cornell University from 1939 to 1950 and later set landscape design standards for the federal interstate highway system.

In all these North American projects, the designs emphasized visual simplicity and efficiency in design and construction and avoided much ornamentation, while seldom embracing the visual strategies of the International Style. Smooth white facades, open balconies, roof gardens, piloti, and the inclusion of modern artworks were rare. The landscaping also typically used standard park plantings, with large grassy lawns surrounded by iron fences, and usually included extensive asphalt parking areas and service drives, as well as occasional playground areas, often laid out in semiformal classical patterns rather than in the topographically related design approaches then beginning to be advocated by such modern landscape architects as Thomas D. Church (1902–1978), Garrett Eckbo (1910–2000), James Rose (1913–1991), and Dan Kiley.

Against these mainstream trends toward monotonous, efficient design in both cities and the new suburbs—the context in which eleven million Americans were able to buy their first homes with FHA-VA financing—architects and planners began to propose counter directions intended to produce more egalitarian and what today would be called sustainable outcomes. These differed from the racially and economically divided American metropolitan urban structure based on highways that was then beginning to emerge. Rather than remaining dynamic centers of culture, older central cities were becoming residential areas of last resort for those unwilling or not allowed to move to the suburbs. To address these problems, Congress, supported by President Harry S. Truman, passed the 1949 Housing Act. Truman's concern for both urban real estate values and "newly identified urban minorities" led to making federal funds available for cities to clear and redevelop large central areas with high-density housing.

Design professionals disagreed over how to approach this redevelopment. Many modern architects favored CIAM-type high-rise projects on cleared central urban slums, such as Yamasaki's Pruitt-Igoe Homes in St. Louis (Hellmuth, Yamasaki & Leinweber, 1950–55, demolished 1972–76). Others, such as Clarence Stein, Tracy Augur, and Catherine Bauer Wurster, continued to support the RPAA's decentralist position. They suggested Stein's Baldwin Hills Village (1941) apartment complex near Los Angeles as a model; it was designed with Reginald D. Johnson and Wilson, Merrill & Alexander Associates, with landscape architect Fred Barlow, Jr. Baldwin Hills Village had 627 units organized into quadrangles on 80 acres (32.4 hectares). The buildings only covered 15 percent of the site and were organized in 1,100 × 2,750 foot (335 × 838 meter) pedestrian superblocks of two-story attached units, sited around 100-foot-wide (30-meter) central green spaces. There were three types of units: 55 one-story bungalows; 216 two-story attached houses; and 356 apartments, 40 of which were three-bedroom units. Parking for every unit was accommodated in street-facing paved courts with rows of garages, similar to earlier Los Angeles apartment complexes but built on a more expansive scale, with extremely popular but rarely imitated results.

Still other designers, like Ludwig Hilberseimer at IIT, offered a modified CIAM approach in *The New City* (1947), which continued prewar modernist calls for the complete removal of existing cities and rebuilding with widely spaced housing, alternating glass-clad housing slabs with low-rise town houses for a range of incomes. This trend shaped planning education at IIT for many years and had relatively socially successful built outcomes at SOM's Lake Meadows (1949–63), a racially integrated, middle-income high-rise slab apartment complex built by the New York Life Insurance Company on the Near South Side of Chicago, and at Mies, Hilberseimer, and landscape architect Alfred Caldwell's Lafayette Park housing complex in Detroit (1958–65). Both projects remain successfully integrated, middle-income urban housing to the present.

By the early 1950s, another new suburban building type, the American suburban shopping mall, also began to appear. Pioneered by various architects, including Clarence Stein, the Saarinens, Morris Ketchum, and John Graham, it soon began to be strongly identified with the Viennese émigré architect Victor Gruen (1903–1980), who had practiced as a store designer under the name Victor Gruenbaum in Vienna before fleeing Austria for New York in 1938. He began designing postwar suburban department stores in Los Angeles, and in 1950 his firm was commissioned by the Hudson's department store chain in Detroit to build a shopping mall to be known as Northland (1950–54) in the nearby suburb of Southfield. Like many modern architects at the time, Gruen saw this mall as a new form of pedestrian community center, and he commissioned artists who included Loja Saarinen to provide artworks for it. He also established patterns of efficient parking and pedestrian movement, with the goal of using a full parking lot as a demonstration of the country's postwar prosperity and industrial prowess. Each mall was "anchored" by several major department stores, with smaller businesses facing outdoor pedestrian streets in between. The formula was immensely successful, making it unnecessary for shoppers, many of them women with small children, to travel downtown or to ride on streetcars or other forms of mass transit, which began to decline in popularity at the time. In 1956,

Gruen's firm then designed the world's first enclosed shopping mall, Southdale, in the Minneapolis suburb of Edina, and this form of the mall was then widely replicated down to the 1980s.

PLANNED DECENTRALIZATION: BRITISH PLANNING DURING AND AFTER WORLD WAR II

In postwar Britain, where a Labour government replaced wartime Prime Minister Winston Churchill's Conservative administration of 1940–45, a receptive but short-lived environment emerged for Le Corbusier's and CIAM ideas. Well before the war, in 1937, a Royal Commission on the Distribution of the Industrial Population, chaired by Sir Montague Barlow, had issued a report recommending the dispersal of industry from central cities and the creation of a central authority to redevelop urban areas. A greenbelt around London had been proposed by the Greater London Regional Planning Committee in 1935, and land for it immediately began to be acquired by private philanthropists. The effects of the Nazi Blitz, which by May 1941 had destroyed parts of some sixteen British cities, including London, raised urgent issues of reconstruction. This led to passage of the Town and Country Planning Act of 1943, which granted legal authority to localities for planned reconstruction. By this point a successful campaign to build popular support across the political spectrum for planning led to very different planning outcomes in Britain than in the United States. The British state, acting through elected local governing bodies, was granted extensive powers to control urban development for what was understood to be the general welfare.

In the United States at this time, on the other hand, multiple political divisions had developed around issues of land-use control. In existing large cities, slum clearance and racially segregated public housing supported by organized labor had acquired mainstream political support. In the then nearly all-white suburban areas, a consensus had emerged in favor of continuing development of mostly private, suburban single-family houses. There, land values were usually protected by restrictive covenants, zoning laws, and local custom rather than by direct federal involvement in housing. By the mid-1930s this private development pattern was nonetheless sustained by extensive federal support for new highway construction and by FHA standards and mortgage insurance, which was allocated in an openly racially discriminatory way until 1948.

In the British wartime context of mainstream political support for direct governmental planning, the British CIAM group, MARS, put forward a plan overseen by Arthur Korn (1891–1978), a German-Jewish CIAM architect from Breslau and later a professor at the Architectural Association in London (1945–66). The MARS Plan of London (1942) proposed rebuilding London as a linear city along lines similar to those proposed by Milutin and Ernst May in Soviet planning debates of the early 1930s (fig. 84).

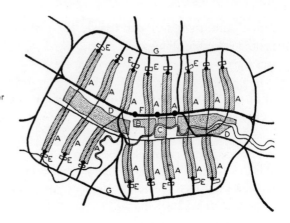

84. MARS (Modern Architecture Research Group) Plan of London, 1942 (Arthur B. Gallion, *The Urban Pattern* [New York: Van Nostrand, 1950], 387).

PLAN FOR LONDON
by the M.A.R.S. Group

A   Residential Units
B   Main Shopping Center
C   Administrative and
    Cultural Center
D   Heavy Industry
E   Local Industry
F   Main Railway and
    Passenger Stations
G   Belt Rail Line

Its main element was to be an east-west transit axis that paralleled the Thames River, grouping industry and metropolitan services. Branching off of it were sixteen proposed linear cities two miles wide (3.2 kilometers) and eight miles long (12.9 kilometers), each composed of neighborhood units, with a total proposed population per branch of 600,000 people. The detailed design of the neighborhood units followed the patterns developed by MARS member E. Maxwell Fry (1899–1987), which he then published in his book *Fine Building* (1944).

The MARS plan was immediately criticized as too radical, and it prompted efforts to develop a more realistic master plan for the London region. The British Ministry of Works and Buildings, established in September 1940, commissioned the County of London Plan (1943) by Sir Patrick Abercrombie, a leading British planner, with London County Council chief architect J. H. Forshaw (1895–1973), which was soon followed by their Greater London Plan 1944. The County of London Plan was the result of both the urgent need for rebuilding and the outcome of decades of activism on the part of the Garden Cities and Town Planning Association to reshape the British metropolitan environment. It also demonstrated an effort to respond to the planning challenges of what Le Corbusier would term a few years later the "three human establishments": "the radio-concentric city of exchange, the linear industrial city, and the modernized rural environment," all to be linked by new and existing forms of transportation (fig. 85). The County of London Plan was in many ways the model for planning the "radio-concentric city of exchange" set within a transportation-accessible region of decentralized industry. But instead of the "linear industrial city" called for by Le Corbusier and postulated in the MARS Plan of London, the County of London Plan's immediate successor, the Greater London Plan 1944, proposed a concentric set of ring roads and Garden City–like New Towns, each with industry, beyond the existing greenbelt.

The legislation necessary for implementing these plans during the war years, codified as the Town and Country Planning Act of 1944, was popular across most of the British political spectrum, and it extended

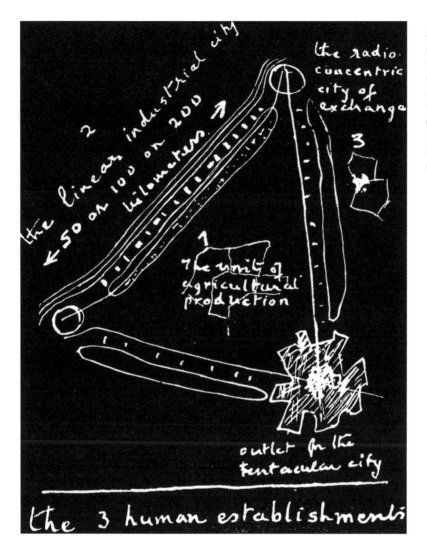

2 the linear industrial city
← 50 on 100 on 200 kilometers →

the radio-concentric city of exchange

3

1 The unit of agricultural production

outlet for the tentacular city

the 3 human establishments

85. Le Corbusier, diagram of the three human establishments (Le Corbusier, *The Three Human Establishments*, translated by Eulie Chowdhury [Chandigarh, 1976], 79). © F.L.C./ADAGP, Paris/Artists Rights Society (ARS), New York, 2016.

planning controls to all land in the United Kingdom. The Town and Country Planning Act allocated extensive powers to a new Ministry of Town and Country Planning, and to local authorities to use eminent domain to buy land determined to be either war damaged or simply "blighted," and then to redevelop it according to an approved master plan. The goal of granting such sweeping powers to reorganize urban conditions was to harmonize conflicting claims for various uses, such as housing, industry, agriculture, parks, roads, and airfields, into an unprecedented governmental effort to shape new development nationally.

Its key provisions were intended to reduce traffic congestion in central London, following the example of the Regional Plan of New York and Its Environs (1929–31), which had called for a system of express highways as part of a "metropolitan loop" of transit ringing Manhattan, most of it then built in the 1950s and 1960s. The County of London Plan, which covered the entire large area under the jurisdiction of the London County

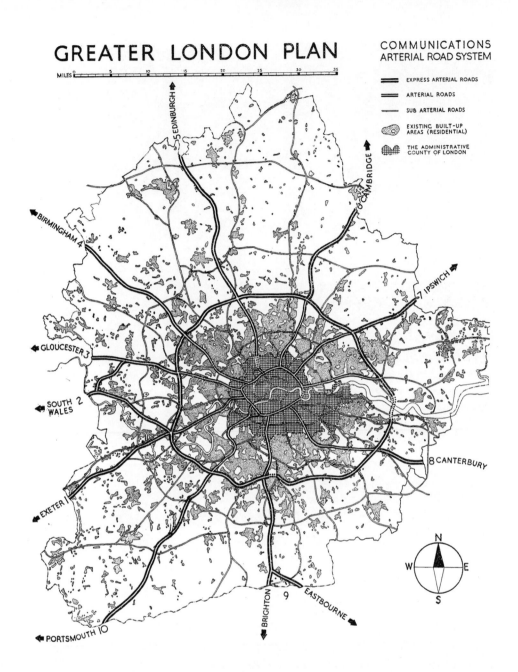

GREATER LONDON PLAN

COMMUNICATIONS
ARTERIAL ROAD SYSTEM

MILES

EXPRESS ARTERIAL ROADS

ARTERIAL ROADS

SUB ARTERIAL ROADS

EXISTING BUILT-UP
AREAS (RESIDENTIAL)

THE ADMINISTRATIVE
COUNTY OF LONDON

86. The London concentric express ring road system (Sir Patrick Abercrombie, *Greater London Plan 1944* [London, 1945], 78).

Council, proposed extending two already-begun outer ring roads, as well as constructing two new inner ring roads, with the innermost ring linking the numerous commuter train stations at the edges of the central area (fig. 86). For residential reconstruction, the plan advocated the use of the neighborhood unit concept to organize the metropolitan area into units of six thousand to ten thousand people, each with its own elementary school (fig. 87).

The Greater London Plan of 1944, also prepared by Abercrombie for the Ministry of Town and Country Planning, covered an expanded planning area. Following the Barlow report, it was based on the idea that

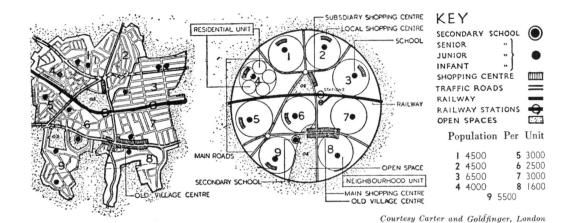

KEY

SECONDARY SCHOOL ◉
SENIOR   " ⎫
JUNIOR   " ⎬ ●
INFANT   " ⎭
SHOPPING CENTRE   ▥
TRAFFIC ROADS   ═
RAILWAY   ▤
RAILWAY STATIONS ⊖
OPEN SPACES   ▦

Population Per Unit

1	4500	5	3000
2	4500	6	2500
3	6500	7	3000
4	4000	8	1600
		9	5500

Courtesy Carter and Goldfinger, London

87. Neighborhood unit reorganization of a London district, from the *County of London Plan Explained* by E. J. Carter and Ernö Goldfinger [London, 1945], 26).

heavy industries and their workers should be "decanted" from what were then densely inhabited, mostly nineteenth-century neighborhoods into greener and healthier surroundings at the urban periphery. In this aspect, the Greater London Plan paralleled the general direction of North American planning in the interwar years, as both saw almost no value in the existing pedestrian density and mix of uses in old central residential areas. Yet unlike the situation for planning at the same time in the United States, where the massive New Deal interventions that had reshaped America in the 1930s were beginning to be privatized, in Britain a wide political consensus had instead formed around the idea that national "reconstruction" (a concept first put forward in British national politics in the 1930s, before wartime damage changed its meaning) would require the careful central planning of the entire environment to improve metropolitan life for the majority of the people. This effort, as well as many of the specific physical provisions of the Greater London Plan of 1944, set the general pattern for the many postwar regional master plans that were then being issued, if not always carried out, in many cities around the world.

Specific provisions of the plan, often echoed in later regional planning, included formalizing the greenbelt as an area from which development would be permanently prohibited. In London, it was a ring of agricultural and other land of varying widths that began about twelve miles (19.3 kilometers) from Charing Cross in central London. Beyond the greenbelt, the Greater London Plan called for eight new towns, whose industries and inhabitants would come from central working-class areas, fulfilling the Garden City dream in a modernized way. The concept had been discussed since the 1890s, but by the early 1940s only two new towns near London had actually been constructed: Letchworth and Welwyn Garden City (1920). Instead, most British metropolitan areas had been built up densely with a combination of semidetached villas (called double houses in the U.S.) and low-rise County Council housing estates for workers, designed along transit lines and generally following Garden City ideas.

The first eight postwar New Towns, called the Mark I New Towns, challenged this pattern by relocating 380,000 people from central London into them. A new transportation network to serve this new metropolitan pattern was also proposed, based on a series of concentric ring roads served by ten new radial highways. Unlike the New Towns themselves, the expressway parts of the plan, subsequently funded by the Special Roads Act of 1949, were built very slowly, and the first sections of the English express highway system, the M6 and M1 routes, did not enter construction until the late 1950s. At the same time, only some of the new towns had fast rail access to central London, limiting their appeal and constraining their commercial potential.

The New Towns themselves went into construction quickly, with the first to be built, Stevenage, designed by Gordon Stephenson (1908–1997) beginning in 1946; it was followed by Harlow, designed by Frederick Gibberd (1908–1984), beginning in 1947. Both were designed using neighborhood units separated by parkways as their main organizing principle. Another source for their design was the New Deal Greenbelt Towns, which were a modernized version of Radburn, and it is not surprising that in some ways their overall design, based on several neighborhood units sited along curving access roads and providing a commercial and institutional town center, was also paralleled in a few postwar American projects. These included Park Forest (1946), a rail-accessible planned suburb south of Chicago intended as an American New Town, which included a mix of low-rise suburban housing types and a now-demolished town center designed by Loebl, Schlossman & Bennett that was one of the first postwar suburban shopping centers.

In Britain, the provisions of the Greater London Plan, which included new roads, the rebuilding of slums with a mixture of high- and low-rise housing, and decentralized industrial development, as well as the New Towns, were largely carried out as proposed down to the mid-1960s. The unexpected appearance of the baby boom generation, and the unanticipated growth economy of southeast England, the wealthiest part of the country, led the government to propose still more New Towns, located at greater distances from London itself, in a proposal published as *The South East Study* (1964). These Mark II New Towns included Milton Keynes, fifty miles (80 kilometers) from London, whose design, by Richard Llewellyn-Davies (1912–1981) and Derek Walker, was intended to apply systems theory insights from the postwar United States to British new town design. Its plan was based on a curving grid of streets thought to replicate some of the "autopic" aspects of Los Angeles celebrated by English architectural historian Reyner Banham (1922–1988) in his *Los Angeles: The Architecture of Four Ecologies* (1970). Milton Keynes also reflected the postwar general systems theory interest in patterns, networks, and self-regulating systems. The Milton Keynes plan rejected the neighborhood unit as its organizational basis and instead attempted to apply the concepts of Berkeley sociologist Melvin Webber (1920–2006), who in 1964 had influentially argued in favor of an auto-based, metropolitan "non-place urban realm."

Another important aspect of the London plans of the 1940s was a focus on urban reconstruction and slum clearance. The County of London Plan (1943) had called for three residential density zones, ranging from 100 people per acre (0.4 hectare), lowered in practice to 70 people per acre, for the outer zone, which would be primarily single-family residences; 136 people per acre for a middle zone, where 45 percent of the residents would live in apartment complexes, mostly limited to three stories; and 200 people per acre in the inner zone, where all the residential buildings would be seven- to ten-story housing blocks. The provision for high-rise, high-density residential reconstruction was controversial even in the London area, and only three inner-London boroughs voted to allow ten-story housing blocks. The Garden City–oriented Town and Country Planning Association objected to apartment-building of any kind, but more Labour Party and left-wing political groups, including the London branch of the Communist Party, began to support the idea. High-rise housing was nonetheless legislatively forbidden in the 1940s in Manchester, Coventry, and some other English cities.

The first realization of this CIAM-inspired vision of high-rise urban reconstruction was Powell & Moya's Churchill Gardens (1946–62) in the central London district of Pimlico in the borough of Westminster, directly across the Thames River from the Battersea Power Station. It was a nine- to ten-story slab housing complex on thirty acres (12 hectares) of former working-class housing destroyed in the Blitz (fig. 88). It was arguably the first large high-rise modernist urban housing complex, other than the slightly earlier projects of the New York City Housing Authority and the Metropolitan Life Insurance Company's Stuyvesant Town. Unlike those projects, whose form was largely determined by bureaucratic decision-making with roots in earlier New York tenement housing reform efforts, Churchill Gardens was designed by the winners of a 1946 international design competition, Philip Powell (born 1921) and J. Hidalgo Moya (born 1920), both recent Architectural Association graduates. Powell had visited Van Tijen & Maaskant's Plaslaan apartments in Rotterdam (1937–38), and he then adapted and multiplied its Gropius-inspired housing slab design for Churchill Gardens. The initial phase consisted of four nine-story blocks with 370 units, which went into construction in 1948. The project, built with a reinforced concrete frame, ultimately contained 1,661 units, many with exterior balconies. It had the first district heating scheme in Britain, which linked all the buildings into a more efficient central heating system. A major design element was its 136-foot (41-meter) accumulator tower, which stored hot water discharged from the nearby power station. Churchill Gardens also included a series of street-oriented shops along Lupus Street,

housed under segmented concrete arches that soon became a postwar modern design cliché.

Critical response to Churchill Gardens was mixed: Henry-Russell Hitchcock, Colin St. John Wilson, and G. E. Kidder Smith all praised it highly, while Lewis Mumford, a lifelong Garden City advocate, denounced it as "grim." Reyner Banham worked there as a laborer and does not seem to have commented on its design. By the time it was completed, many other high-rise slab housing projects had been begun by the London County Council architects department, then headed by Sir J. Leslie Martin (1908–2000). Many of them are better known than Churchill Gardens today. These include the Finsbury estate by Berthold Lubetkin's firm Tecton, and Denys Lasdun's Paddington Estate reconstruction, both exhibited at CIAM 7 in Bergamo, Italy, in 1949. They also included modern housing slabs such as the LCC Bentham Road and Alton estates, Roehampton, the latter exhibited at CIAM 9 in Aix-en-Provence in 1953. These projects were applications of the urban concepts Le Corbusier had demonstrated in his Saint-Dié project (1945) and then built at the Unité d'Habitation in Marseille.

At Alton West, the new concrete slabs were sited so that much of an existing eighteenth-century landscape park was retained. In the LCC project, that part of the development was polemically countered by another version of modern housing, also by LCC architects, which was based on Swedish-inspired "point block" towers, which were faced with brick, rather than concrete. This part of the estate also included attached two-story brick town houses, designed to "soften" the harshness of modern architecture with "people's detailing" that used traditional materials like brick and wood and suggested aspects of traditional English architecture. This stylistic split between "Swedes" and Corbusians gave built form to the English architectural debates of the time, between the New Empiricists—the name given them by the editor of the *Architectural Review*, J. M. Richards (1907–1992), who favored what was seen as this Swedish-inspired direction—and their Corbusian architectural opponents, who included such later influential figures as Leslie Martin, Alan Colquhoun (1921–2012), Colin St. John Wilson (1922-2007), and others.

Both of these groups of London modern architects were largely socialist in their politics, and both saw their design work as part of a specifically architectural approach to rebuilding cities. The New Empiricists were aware that Socialist Realism was still the official style in Moscow, and they saw their efforts to accommodate popular tastes in postwar mass housing with traditional materials as part of the political transformation of Britain toward Swedish-type socialism in the immediate postwar years. The Corbusians objected to this direction architecturally, which they found sentimental, and they detested the popular interwar British suburban areas celebrated by J. M. Richards in his *The Castles on the Ground* (1946), where he attempted to offer an approach to modern architecture based on the Swedish example. Instead, in the Corbusians' view, the British public needed to be educated to appreciate what they saw as a more demanding, but ultimately more satisfactory, modern architecture, one based on real human needs. This often paralleled the kind of integrative thinking about the larger environment that would later be termed socially and ecologically "sustainable." Their uncompromisingly modernist stance was often institutionalized (with many local variations) in postwar architectural education in places like Cambridge University, where Leslie Martin led the architecture school beginning in 1955. By the 1980s, in the Prime Minister Margaret Thatcher era (1979–90) of neoliberalism, this modernist stance also became a target of postmodernist historicists, leading to a complete discrediting in some quarters of the modern architect's expertise in general.

The application of modernist models in postwar Britain extended to primary and secondary school design as well, after the passage of the Education Act in 1944. This raised the age when students could leave school to fifteen years, creating a need for many new schools. Between 1945 and 1955, some 2,500 schools were built in Britain, for 1.8 million pupils. Their design was typically overseen by County Council technical offices. The Hertfordshire County Council office, led by Charles H. Askin

(1893–1959), introduced a prefabricated steel structure construction system with reinforced concrete ceiling and wall panels, which became an international model for postwar school design. Of these schools, by far the most well known is Alison and Peter Smithson's Hunstanton Secondary Modern School in East Anglia (1949–54). This school combined the minimalism of Mies van der Rohe, then becoming the mainstream icon of modernism in the United States, with a tough, industrial-era sensibility about exposed materials that would develop into what they and their colleague in the London Independent Group, Reyner Banham, would term "the new Brutalism" by the mid-1950s.

CONTINENTAL EUROPEAN POSTWAR URBANISM: GERMANY, FRANCE, SWEDEN, AND FINLAND

After 1947, the Soviet Union extended its wartime victories over Nazi Germany to control the Eastern Bloc of European countries, which remained dominated by Moscow until 1991. In Berlin, Hans Scharoun (1893–1972), a socialist German CIAM member who had opposed the Nazis, and his CIAM associates put forward their Collective Plan for the reconstruction of Berlin in 1946. Exhibited at what Germans called the *Stunde Null* (zero hour) for their ruined capital, whose population had shrunk from 4.3 million in 1939 to 2.3 million in 1945, Scharoun's plan proposed removing most of its remaining built fabric and reorganizing the city as a series of highway corridors shaped according to the underlying natural landscape. These corridors would lead to peripheral modern housing neighborhoods, continuing the Weimar efforts advocated in the 1920s by Martin Wagner and others to decentralize the city and increase its green area.

Scharoun's plan was rejected as unrealistic, and instead a Berlin version of the concentric Greater London Plan by Karl Bonatz was approved in 1948, just before the city was divided between the Soviet and Allied sectors at the start of the Cold War. The division resulted in the damaged city center remaining in East Berlin, while West Berlin was kept in the Allied sphere through extensive efforts that began with the American Berlin airlift of food and supplies in 1948. At the same time, the U.S.-supported Marshall Plan funneled billions of dollars into the economic and social reconstruction of eighteen Western European countries from 1947 to 1952, leading to phenomenal economic growth in West Germany and elsewhere. To reduce the appeal of the Soviet system and ward off a return to Fascism, the United States sought to stimulate growth by reducing barriers between countries and regulations, while also encouraging union membership within an American-dominated capitalist framework.

The Cold War division of Berlin made it a key site for each side to present its urban design approaches. Beginning in 1951, the Soviet-backed government of East Berlin built five thousand units of housing along the new Stalinallee (now the Karl-Marx-Allee) in East Berlin. These neoclassical seven- to ten-story street-oriented apartment buildings were ostensibly to house the working class, but were in fact available only to favored supporters of the regime. In deliberate contrast, in West Berlin, the war-destroyed district of Hansaviertel was rebuilt in 1953–57 with the widely spaced housing towers and extensive green areas of the "Interbau '57" international building exhibition. A large group of German and international modern architects that included Gropius, Niemeyer, Aalto, Bakema, and others designed a range of innovative modern housing blocks near a rebuilt subway station. By the late 1950s, East Berlin had begun to follow a similar though less architect-focused path, and also built gigantic modern high-rise complexes using prefabricated concrete construction systems called Plattenbau, which were also used extensively in similar projects of Eastern Europe and the former Soviet Union.

Equally significant in the immediate postwar years were the political conflicts about the role of the state in shaping cities, often expressed in differing choices of architectural styles and planning strategies. In France, Perret's concrete classicism, a direction he had developed early in the twentieth century, was the preferred direction for postwar urban reconstruction, and it was visible on a large scale in his rebuilding of the port city of Le Havre (1947). It was countered by the CIAM modernism exemplified by the work of Le Corbusier, whose unbuilt 1945 project for rebuilding the French border town of Saint-Dié-des-Vosges as a series of high-rise concrete housing slabs set in open space was offered by CIAM in an exhibition at Rockefeller Center in 1945 as a world model for postwar urbanism. Yet with the exception of a few demonstration projects like his well-known seventeen-story Unité d'Habitation (Neighborhood Unit) in Marseille (1946–52), Le Corbusier's urbanism was not widely imitated in France itself until a decade or so later, and then mostly in outlying high-rise suburban housing projects known as *les grandes ensembles.*

Perret's Le Havre and Le Corbusier's Marseille Unité were commissioned by the French Ministry of Reconstruction (MRU) during the provisional government in 1944–46 of General Charles de Gaulle (1890–1970). De Gaulle had led the Free French Resistance forces that replaced the Vichy government after the Allied Normandy invasion in 1944, but it was only later, with the creation of the French Fifth Republic, that he served as the president of France, from 1958–69. In 1945, a new Ministry of Reconstruction and Urbanism was established under De Gaulle, led by Raoul Dautry (1880–1951), the former head of construction for the national railways and a member of the government committee that had overseen Henri Prost's 1936 plan for the Paris region. Dautry had been minister of armaments in 1939, just prior to the German invasion, and though he had himself avoided working for the Vichy government, many of his former employees had done so, and they continued in their planning-related positions after the war.

Much of the organizational structure and practice of the MRU continued the relatively authoritarian, highly centralized administrative planning apparatus of the prewar and Vichy eras, with Perret's street-oriented modern classicism remaining its preferred architectural approach. In 1945, Dautry commissioned Perret to oversee the reconstruction of Le Havre, a strategic port that been partly destroyed by Allied bombings in 1944. Perret designed the new town hall and the iconic, towering Church of St. Joseph (351 feet/107 meters), and supervised the rebuilding, which used a precast concrete structural system organized on a roughly twenty-foot (6.24-meter) modular frame to create a new version of a street-oriented European urban environment, which included pedestrian arcades and underground passages, as well as new highway, rail, and port infrastructure.

Dautry faced little political opposition to this reconstruction direction, often called "MRU style," as French socialists and communists, many of them involved with the Resistance during the war, also saw the need for the rapid postwar reconstruction of French cities along similar lines. Dautry, and the political coalitions that supported him, found Le Corbusier and ASCORAL's Athens Charter to be too radical, but Dautry attempted to accommodate some of these directions. He appointed Le Corbusier as the chief architect for the reconstruction of the port city of La Rochelle (1945–47), where he was assisted by a young Latvian-born Polish architect and former soldier then working in his atelier, Jerzy Soltan (1913–2005). Le Corbusier's proposal for a series of slab apartment buildings for La Rochelle was rejected, which also happened with his semi-official proposal for Saint-Dié, one of three proposals offered by rival groups in the town, which caused the MRU to appoint its own architect instead of any of the local teams.

Like most French decision makers at the time, Dautry was not very enthusiastic about Le Corbusier's work, and in 1945 the MRU issued its own *Charte d'urbanisme*, loosely based on the Athens Charter but emphasizing a more Garden City–oriented approach. Yet one of Dautry's successors as minister of reconstruction, serving from 1948–52, was Eugène Claudius-Petit (1907–1989). Claudius-Petit, a former member of the French Resistance and founder of a new postwar French social democratic party, was a strong supporter of Le Corbusier. By this point, Le Corbusier had created a team he called ATBAT (Atelier des Bâtisseurs/Builders' Workshop), which included André Wogenscky (1916–2004), Vladimir Bodiansky (1894–1966), Blanche Lemco (later Blanche van Ginkel, born 1923), and others. Bodiansky, an architect-engineer, had worked on the Cité de la Muette in 1933, one of the first large prefabricated high-rise housing projects in the world, and, like Le Corbusier, was inspired by the planning organization of the TVA. Its objective of modernizing a regional watershed through infrastructural and architectural interventions corresponded to the ambitious postwar goals of ATBAT.

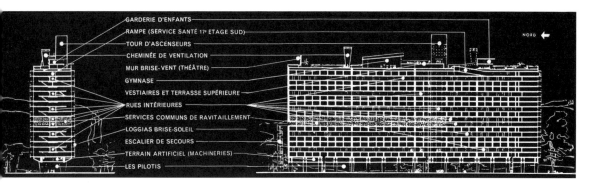

GARDERIE D'ENFANTS
RAMPE (SERVICE SANTÉ 17ᵉ ETAGE SUD)
TOUR D'ASCENSEURS
CHEMINÉE DE VENTILATION
MUR BRISE-VENT (THÉÂTRE)
GYMNASE
VESTIAIRES ET TERRASSE SUPÉRIEURE
RUES INTÉRIEURES
SERVICES COMMUNS DE RAVITAILLEMENT
LOGGIAS BRISE-SOLEIL
ESCALIER DE SECOURS
TERRAIN ARTIFICIEL (MACHINERIES)
LES PILOTIS

NORD ⬅

Le Corbusier, Claudius-Petit, Bodiansky, Andre Sivé, and Michel Eco-chard (1905–1985), a French urbanist then active in Morocco, had been sent to the United States on a French government "Mission on Architecture and Urbanism" in 1945–46. They visited Knoxville, Norris, and the Fontana TVA dam in Tennessee and were impressed by the TVA's interdisciplinary approach of "design by committee," which combined the development of new infrastructure such as highways, dams and canals, new residential neighborhoods, and government buildings. For ATBAT, the first demonstration of this "comprehensive approach" was the Unité d'Habitation. Planned to house 1,500 residents, with stores, a school, a daycare center, a medical clinic, recreational facilities, and a laundromat, the project had 337 units (fig. 89). These were organized into twenty-three types, which ranged from one-person units to one for a family with up to eight children. Each had a double-height living room with a 15-foot, 9-inch (4.8-meter) ceiling, and a large window measuring 12 feet × 15 feet, 9 inches (3.66 × 4.8 meters). These two-story units were inter-locked over a corridor that ran on every other floor, a system developed by Moisei Ginzburg in Russia in the 1920s. Claudius-Petit exempted the Marseille Unité from the usual construction permit process and arranged for the government to buy most of the units. This caused controversy, as war victims who had wanted to live there found themselves excluded.

The exterior of the Unité was left as rough, unfinished concrete, de-scribed by Le Corbusier as "béton brut" (raw concrete). This was in part a result of the difficulty of getting skilled construction workers on the site, but Le Corbusier's use of it at the Unité and then at Chandigarh made "Brutalism"(the term itself originated in Sweden and was taken up in England in the 1950s) one of the mainstream architectural design directions of the postwar years. The Unité also marked the point where Le Corbusier introduced a new proportional system, which he named the "Modulor." This was based on two Fibonacci series of numbers derived from the six-foot height (1.83 meters) of an ideal male figure with an upraised arm. The proportions chosen were determined by the Golden Section, a classical proportion of 1 to 1.618, which had since the Renaissance been thought to determine the sides of a particularly visually pleasing rectangle. The

89. Le Corbusier and Pierre Jeanneret, with ATBAT, Unité d'Habitation, Marseille, 1945–52. Section. (Le Corbusier, *Oeuvre complète, 1946–52* [Zurich: Éditions Girsberger, 1953], 194). © F.L.C./ADAGP, Paris/ Artists Rights Society (ARS), New York 2016.

Modulor was Le Corbusier's response to the 1936 *Bauentwurfslehre* (Architects' Data) of Ernst Neufert (1900–1986), a former associate of Gropius's who had been deeply involved with Nazi building standardization efforts between 1936 and 1945. These standards remained the building component and space standards in postwar Europe and are now used worldwide. Le Corbusier argued that the Modulor was less mechanistic, in that it was based on human proportions rather than ease of production and construction, but it did not find wide acceptance.

The 1930s had also seen the emergence of the national "welfare state," which provided universal health care, free college tuition, and other benefits to an entire population, regardless of income. Aspects of this direction had been anticipated in a variety of earlier situations, including in Dutch cities in the 1910s and Red Vienna between 1919 and 1934. They were continued in a variety of places in Europe and the USSR across the increasingly polarized political spectrum of the 1930s. In Sweden, this direction began in a major way with the election of the Social Democratic Party in 1932, which then began to reshape Swedish society. Its influence extended to Britain in the 1940s, and then to Italy, Israel, Japan, and many other places after the war. The Swedish approach to architecture and planning was first made evident at the Stockholm Exhibition in 1930, organized by the historian Gregor Paulsson (1889–1977) and designed by the Swedish modern classicist architect Gunnar Asplund (1885–1940).

The Stockholm Exhibition was a popular presentation of this new social and architectural direction strongly influenced by CIAM and the example of Weimar Germany, but one also accepting the centrality of commercial life in the modern city, where modern advertising was increasingly replacing traditional ornament. Swedish CIAM members Paulsson, Uno Åhrén (1897–1977), and others issued a CIAM manifesto at this time, *acceptera,* which urged Swedes to accept the new realities of industrial mass production, the arrival of women in the labor force, the suppressed needs of the working class, new methods of production, and new lifestyles.

In *acceptera* Swedish CIAM members argued that the city was a living organism that expressed movement and life, and they noted the French philosopher Henri Bergson's statement that "life in general is mobility itself." The manifesto also influentially distinguished between "A-Europe," an interdependent modern environment linked by infrastructure, and "B-Europe," isolated, agrarian, and economically stagnant. In most of the Nordic countries (Scandinavia and Finland), this idea was soon combined by architects like Aalto with a romantic view of northern Italy as a place where people lived in harmony with the natural environment and had developed a rich cultural life.

After the election in 1932 of Social Democratic Prime Minister Per Albin Hansson (1885–1946), the Swedish government began to extensively build social housing, which included a range of services for residents. Hansson himself moved to a modest new worker's row house, designed by Paul Hedquist, to demonstrate his commitment to the new social movement. The sociologist couple Gunnar Myrdal (1898–1987) and Alva Myrdal (1902–1986), strong supporters of the Social Democratic Party, began to work with Swedish CIAM architects Åhrén and Sven Markelius (1889–1972) in a Social Housing Committee to formulate a program for the new building effort, which then became the basis for mainstream Swedish housing construction by the 1940s. Unlike most of CIAM projects in 1930s, these "Swedish modern" housing projects were explicitly intended to express social equality by providing similar accommodations for all and to denote popular democracy by using more traditional materials like brick and wood. In addition, they often used less aggressively modern forms, such as gently pitched roofs.

The role of individual architects as design figures was downplayed, and Swedish CIAM members were not very admiring of the work of Le Corbusier or his CIAM disciples elsewhere. Instead, new government policies determined interior design and domestic equipment in the new social housing, based on directions that had developed in Swedish and Danish design by the late 1920s. These were then further extended by Alvar and Aino Aalto, particularly in their designs for wood furniture and housewares, which they sold through Artek, founded in 1935. Markelius and other Swedish architects also specifically designed collective housing for households in which both parents were working, as well as state-supported orphanages, elderly housing, and collective homes for single women. Efforts were also made in Stockholm by architects like Albin Stark (1885–1960), who had worked in Beijing in 1922–23, to retain some of the city's medieval center while clearing the interiors of overbuilt blocks to allow adequate light and air into housing units.

By the late 1930s, regional planning also started to be a focus in Sweden. The Garden City Movement was already well known there, and Lewis Mumford's *Culture of Cities*, published in 1938, became influential. In 1941, a new metropolitan subway line was approved for Stockholm, and it became a key element in Markelius's General Plan of Stockholm (1945–52). A new town planning law was then passed in 1948, which allowed the city of Stockholm to plan the more than seventy-three square miles (19,000 hectares) it had been acquiring at the urban periphery since 1904. Housing was to be built there to provide more options for those being disadvantaged by rising housing costs in the urban center. Much of this peripheral housing was already being organized by Markelius into New Towns along new transit lines that linked to the city center. The first of these was Årsta (1943–54) begun during the war, when Sweden was neutral. It was followed by Vällingby, a new town for 23,000 whose site had been bought by the city in 1930; Farsta; and others. Vällingby's town center (1945–57) was designed by Swedish CIAM members Bäckstrom & Reinius and was the most well known of the Swedish New Towns.

Many new Swedish social-housing units were also built, some in the New Towns themselves, as well as in parts of Stockholm and other cities. Notable examples include Bäckstrom & Reinius's Grondal (1944), 216 mid-rise low-rent apartments organized into hexagonal wings overlooking Stockholm harbor, and their triform wing-plan housing at Rosta-Örebro (1949). Urban commercial spaces were also a focus at this time, including Ralph Erskine's Luleå shopping center (1955). The Ikea chain was founded in Sweden around this time, bringing inexpensive versions of Scandinavian design to a wide consumer public.

In Finland, which passed a town planning law in 1931, Aalto began working in a related way for private companies interested in planning better industrial settlements. These projects included a settlement for the Sunila sulfate mill, some eighty-four miles (135 kilometers) east of Helsinki near Kotka (1936). It was one of the first large modern social housing projects in Finland, built in a rural setting by a forest products company. It set a pattern for Finnish urbanization, in that Aalto quickly saw parallels to the decentralist contemporary efforts of the TVA. The housing design was based on the Swiss CIAM Neubühl project (1930–32) in Zurich, but Aalto also designed the cellulose plant to relate to the picturesque coastal landscape, insisting that large rock formations be retained rather than blasted away. Its splayed site plan, responsive to topography and views, was designed to create the impression of housing sited in a forest rather than in an urban setting. Among the several housing types that Aalto designed for Sunila were stepped terrace houses without elevators, which Aalto would use again in the small industrial settlement of Kauttua (1938–39).

This concept of decentralized clusters of worker housing served by the latest technologies was an idea that Aalto had been advocating at least since 1932. Even more than other CIAM housing work of the 1930s, Aalto's plan rejected traditional urban patterns entirely, requiring more extensive use of vehicles, which was seen as desirable by most modern planners in the 1930s. Aalto was visited by California Bay Region architect William Wurster (1895–1973) and landscape architect Thomas D. Church in 1937, as well as by MIT assistant professor Lawrence B. Anderson (1906–1994) and Yale architecture student Harry Weese (1915–1998), the latter later a leading Chicago architect. Like other CIAM members such as Gropius, who had accepted the chair of architecture position at the Harvard Graduate School of Design that same year, Aalto was increasingly interested in the United States as a receptive environment for his work. In 1938 and 1939 he made his first visits there for the opening of his Museum of Modern Art exhibition, meeting with the curators and Nelson Rockefeller (1908–1979), lecturing on "the humanization of architecture," and visiting Eliel Saarinen at the Cranbrook Academy of Art.

On his second visit he supervised the construction of his widely admired Finland Pavilion at the 1939 New York World's Fair and then continued on to Los Angeles to meet Neutra. He visited San Francisco, where he met with Wurster and Lewis Mumford, and presented an initial version of his proposed Institute for Architectural Research to Wurster. This institute was to be a transnational "brain trust" of architects, sociologists, psychologists, physiologists, and economists who could collectively create a new architectural synthesis related to his ideas about prefabrication and regionalist urbanism inspired by the TVA. In Sweden Aalto also sought to start a journal titled *The Human Side* with the Swedish historian and CIAM member Gregor Paulsson. The first issue would have had articles by Lewis Mumford and the Swedish sociologist and CIAM member Gunnar Myrdal.

All these efforts were cut short by the beginning of World War II in September 1939. After briefly teaching at MIT, where he had developed concepts about semi-prefabricated wood construction for "An American Town in Finland," Aalto returned to serve in the army and was then invited in April 1941 to Switzerland by Madame Hélène de Mandrot, the founding patron of CIAM, to lecture on his ideas about Finnish reconstruction and "flexible standardization." Most of Europe at this point was under Nazi rule, and there was strong support for Finland's struggle against the USSR. Aalto articulated his ideas on reconstruction to Swiss CIAM members led by Alfred Roth (1903–1998), who organized his visit. His widely influential lecture, titled "The Reconstruction of Europe Is the Key Problem for the Architecture of Our Time" (later called his "Swiss Sermon on the Mount" by his biographer Göran Schildt), set out his idea of the "growing house" based on "core cells" of basic services and enclosure that could be gradually extended into larger houses as circumstances allowed. Aalto also sent a German-language version of his ideas to Ernst Neufert in Berlin, then in charge of German standardization efforts.

Later in 1941, Finland's alliance with Nazi Germany in its second war with the USSR (1941–44) put Aalto in a difficult situation with his American and other international contacts. However, he was able to have his flexible standardization suggestions taken up by the Finnish Reconstruction Office in 1942, where they later became the basis for much postwar reconstruction planning in Finland. Aalto demonstrated these ideas in a series of regional plans, including the influential, though unbuilt Kokemäenjoki River Valley Regional Plan (1940) for the town of Pori and its region, and the Säynätsalo town plan project, 1942–46, where only Aalto's well-known town hall was later built in 1949–52. These projects, begun while Finland was battling the USSR alongside Nazi Germany, and consequently largely cut off from the Allies, coincided with the publication in the United States of José Luis Sert's *Can Our Cities Survive?* (1942), which included some of Aalto's work in the context of the first major publication of CIAM concepts in English.

In 1942 Aalto also began to work in then-neutral Sweden for the owner of an international shipping company in partnership with the

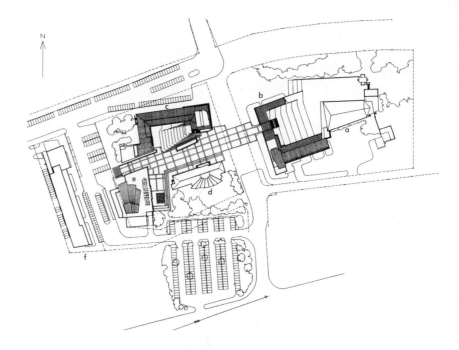

Swedish architect Albin Stark. This team produced numerous unbuilt projects at this time, including the Aalto and Stark proposal for a
new enclosed town center for Avesta, Sweden (1944). This was to be a
pedestrian-oriented community center, which anticipated both Aalto's
postwar Säynätsalo Town Center and the enclosed central pedestrian
spaces of Swedish and English New Towns. It is also contemporary with
Sert and Wiener's civic center in their influential unbuilt project for the
Brazilian Motor City, which marked a similar departure from earlier CIAM
functional city planning.

After the war Aalto found himself much in demand again in the
United States, despite (or perhaps because of) Finland's still-unresolved
strategic situation, again in the shadow of Soviet power after a 1944
peace treaty with the USSR. In the course of seven separate trips to the
United States between 1945 and 1948, Aalto was offered a partnership
with Eliel and Eero Saarinen in their suburban Detroit office, a senior
professorship at the Harvard GSD, and a visiting professorship by Dean
Wurster at MIT in conjunction with his also receiving the commission from
MIT for the Baker House dormitory on campus. He also lectured widely on
Finnish reconstruction, presenting his 1944 "reindeer horn" plan for the
reconstruction of Rovaniemi, the capital of Lapland destroyed in the Nazi
retreat. On his return to Finland, Aalto then went on over the course of
his career to apply these ideas in built master plans, including the Imatra
Master Plan (1947), the Seinajoki Civic Center (1960–68), and many others
that remain important points of reference for many architects and urban
designers today (fig. 90).

LATIN AMERICAN POSTWAR URBANISM: MEXICO, BRAZIL, AND BRASÍLIA

The war and immediate postwar era was also transformative in Latin America. Brazil entered the war on the Allied side in August 1942, after the United States had begun, in 1940, to make loans to encourage investment in heavy industry there. This step had been preceded by the Good Neighbor Policy, a set of economic and cultural initiatives in the 1930s that sought to expand American influence, rather than Axis influence, in the region. Nelson Rockefeller, a New York philanthropist and supporter of the Museum of Modern Art (MoMA) in New York, was appointed the State Department coordinator of Inter-American Affairs in 1940, and the Walt Disney studio (founded in Los Angeles in 1923) began to make animated films aimed at Brazilian and Mexican audiences. The Brazilian Pavilion at the 1939 New York World's Fair, by Costa & Niemeyer—with interiors by Paul Lester Wiener (1895–1967), a German émigré designer in New York—introduced millions of visitors to *carioca* modernism, which skillfully merged Le Corbusier's purist design approach of the 1920s with a sensuous use of materials and spatial effects inspired by Brazilian Baroque architecture. The MoMa exhibition "Brazil Builds" (1943) that followed, one of the first full-color architecture exhibitions, led to a brief vogue in the United States for Brazilian modernism.

At the same time, Wiener began to advocate modern urban planning in lectures in Rio de Janeiro under the auspices of the U.S. State Department, and he founded the firm Town Planning Associates (TPA) with Josep Lluís Sert in New York in 1941. Sert had emigrated there after the fall of the Spanish Republic in 1939, and he joined Wiener in TPA after a brief partnership in 1941 with Ernest Weissmann (1903–1985), a Zagreb architect that Sert knew from Le Corbusier's office. In 1943, TPA was commissioned to design a new "Motor City" near Rio around an airplane engine factory, whose construction was backed by large U.S. loan guarantees to bring previously neutral Brazil into the war on the Allied side (fig. 91). TPA's Motor City was a clear demonstration of the prewar CIAM emphasis on the four functions of dwelling, work, transportation, and recreation, but unlike Le Corbusier's Radiant City, Motor City included a pedestrian civic "core." This central and most innovative aspect of the project was an early expression of postwar CIAM's efforts to "bridge the gap between a socially functionalized city and the city as symbol of civic or national identity and power," as the English architect Alan Colquhoun would later put it.

In TPA's Motor City, the core was inspired both by the Brazilian Ministry of Education and Health building, which integrated modern architecture with landscape design and public art, as well as by Lewis Mumford's 1940 suggestion to Sert that CIAM focus more on the civic center and the

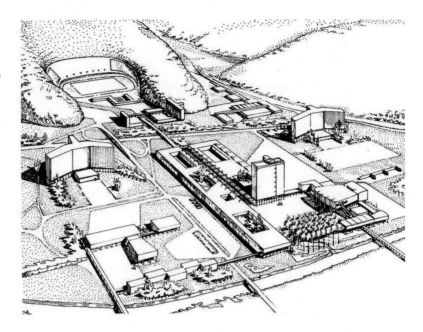

cultural aspects of urbanism for *Can Our Cities Survive?,* portions of which were published in Spanish in Argentina and Peru.

The Motor City project also demonstrated an increasingly precise focus in CIAM on organizing traffic by type and speed, including locating and designing parking areas. It also showed the CIAM acceptance of the concept of the mixed-use pedestrian-based residential neighborhood unit, widely influential in British and Nordic planning at the same time. But TPA did not obtain any other commissions in Brazil. Instead, Niemeyer and other carioca school architects like Affonso Reidy (1909–1964) built extensively throughout the country, developing related concepts in a distinctively Brazilian way.

In other parts of Latin America, modern architecture and urbanism had many complex national outcomes. In Puerto Rico, a former Spanish Caribbean colony acquired by the United States in 1898, Rexford Guy Tugwell was appointed governor by President Roosevelt, serving from 1941 to 1946. Tugwell's brief time as New York City Planning Commissioner (1938–40) had ended with Robert Moses, then New York Parks Commissioner and a key advisor to Mayor Fiorella La Guardia, leading the rejection of Tugwell's ambitious decentralist master planned vision for the city. In Puerto Rico, Tugwell sought to apply New Deal principles of strengthening both working-class and rural communities by building schools, low-cost housing, healthcare centers, and infrastructure. He appointed Neutra as a planning and architectural consultant there (1943–45); Neutra later described his approach to the tropical conditions in *An Architecture of Social Concern in Regions of Mild Climate* (1948). Neutra saw his designs for open-air schools, clinics, and hospitals as applicable in similar geographic regions.

Tugwell also supported the work of Henry Klumb (1905–1984) in Puerto Rico. Klumb was a German émigré architect influenced by Frank Lloyd Wright who had previously designed houses in Greenbelt, Maryland, and had worked in Philadelphia with Louis Kahn, and then designed rural schools and many government structures on the island. In 1946 he was commissioned to design many of the buildings on the Río Pedras and Mayagüez campuses of the University of Puerto Rico (1948–59). The unusually early receptivity to modern architecture in Puerto Rico, relative to most of Europe and the East Coast, may also have been a factor in the success of two young architects there: Osvaldo Toro (educated at Columbia University in 1937) and Miguel Ferrer (educated at Cornell University in 1938), who, with Luis Torregrosa, won a 1945 competition for the Caribe Hilton on the Golden Strip in San Juan. The Caribe Hilton was the first modern highrise slab Hilton hotel, and the first to be built outside the continental United States. Its construction was intended to promote tourism, and the Toro, Ferrer & Torregrosa ten-story building, with its open-plan ground-floor lobby, deep balconies for every room, and use of air-conditioning, set a pattern for resort hotels around the world for decades.

In Mexico, modern architecture and urbanism had a complex national history that was well under way by the 1930s. Juan O'Gorman (1905–1982), who had designed the Le Corbusier–inspired studio house for the Mexican artists Diego Rivera and Frida Kahlo in Mexico City in 1931, called for a rational and functional architecture to address the pressing needs of the Mexican masses. Mexico's relatively close relations with the Soviet Union in the 1930s made CIAM membership illegal for modern architects, but the work and activities of O'Gorman and other Mexican architects in the 1930s were quite parallel to those of CIAM members elsewhere. O'Gorman was commissioned to design fifty-three public schools in Mexico City in 1932, of which twenty-five were built. These used a simple concrete frame, organized on a nearly ten-foot (3-meter) grid, featured mass-produced fixtures and architectural elements, and were painted in what O'Gorman called "strident" colors. Parallel to the ideas of Clarence Perry in the United States, who advocated that schools be used as community centers outside of school hours, the schools were seen as important to social life. O'Gorman's work took place as debates occurred between Mexican architects over functionalism versus aesthetics similar to those in early CIAM, debates that became even more complex when Hannes Meyer arrived in Mexico in 1936 after leaving the Soviet Union. The architect-engineer Félix Candela (1910–1997) arrived in Mexico from Spain in 1939 and began to design innovative buildings using thin concrete shell construction, including the Cosmic Rays pavilion at the National University (UNAM) in Mexico City in 1951, as well as some stations for the Mexico City metro.

Beginning in 1938, Max Cetto (1903–1980), a Weimar German architect who had worked as part of May's Frankfurt design team, was a key figure in the design of houses in the celebrated Mexico City model subdivision of the Jardines del Pedregal de San Ángel, begun on 865 acres (350 hectares) of rocky land by Mexican architect-developer Luis Barragán (1902–1988) in 1945. Barragán had traveled extensively in Europe in the 1920s and had practiced as an architect in Mexico beginning in 1927. He was inspired by Diego Rivera's call to develop the Pedregal's volcanic landscape, with its strong pre-Columbian associations, and along with Cetto designed many of its modern houses, which as dramatically photographed and published by Armando Salas Portugal had a profound impact on postwar perceptions of the possibilities of Latin American architecture.

Directly adjacent to the Pedregal, a new Mexican public university campus was begun in 1946 under the presidency of Miguel Alemán, the Universidad Nacional Autónoma de México (Mexican National Autonomous University), or UNAM (fig. 92). This was an early example of a large modern campus devoted largely to science and technology as a means of attaining national modernization. It was to some extent inspired by the unbuilt City University project in Rio de Janeiro (1936) of Le Corbusier and a team of Brazilian architects that included Costa, Reidy, Niemeyer, and others. Never exhibited at a CIAM conference, the team-designed UNAM campus on the Insurgentes Avenue was nonetheless a clear demonstration of the postwar CIAM focus on the synthesis of the arts with modern urbanism. Its final design was developed by Mario Pani (1911–1993) from a 1946 competition-winning design by the architecture students Enrique Molinar, Armando Franco, and Teodoro González de León. Organized axially, and including a large new stadium and an administrative quad, with a fifteen-story Rectoría building by Pani and Enrique del Moral (1952), it was centered on an imposing high-rise library building with an immense pre-Columbian–inspired mosaic mural by O'Gorman. Pani and others then went on to long careers in Mexico, designing many large urban complexes and large *multifamilares* (housing projects) in a context of rapid urbanization, as the Mexico City population rose from three million in 1950 to almost nine million in 2016, within a metropolitan area of over twenty million.

In postwar Brazil, as in Mexico, the idea that the country needed to become a major industrial nation continued to be popular. Many Brazilian architects of the postwar years took up the carioca modernism that had emerged under the Vargas regime in Rio in the 1930s, and Oscar Niemeyer, nominally still a CIAM member down to 1956, was commissioned for many major works across the country (fig. 93). In 1941, his client at Pampulha, an elite resort around an artificial lake north of Belo Horizonte, had been Mayor Juscelino Kubitschek (1902–1976), who was then elected governor of Minas Gerais state in 1950. In 1956, as a presidential candidate, Kubitschek won the election with the promise to finally build Brasília, the long-anticipated new national capital to be sited in the central highlands in the distant interior of the country.

92. Juan O'Gorman, Gustavo
Saavedra, and Juan Martinez
de Velasco, Universidad
Nacional Autónoma de
México (UNAM), 1950
(Compania Méxicana
Aerofoto/ICA Foundation).

The concept of a central capital for a country whose main cities had
all developed along the Atlantic coast after Portuguese colonization
began in 1500 had been discussed since 1789. After Brazilian independence in 1822, building the new interior capital was made part of the
first constitution of the Empire of Brazil (1822–89). In 1891, after slavery
in Brazil had finally been abolished in 1888 under the first republic, a site
was selected for the new capital and a federal district laid out. In 1922
and 1946, initial surveys for it took place. For Kubitschek, the new capital
would be a "growth pole" for new economic development, as well as a
way of stabilizing his precarious centralist administration. A new government agency, Novacap, was founded to oversee its construction, and
Niemeyer was engaged as its design advisor. Le Corbusier wrote to President Kubitschek offering his design services at no fee, but it was decided
instead to hold a design competition only open to Brazilian architects,

93. Oscar Niemeyer, COPAN building, São Paulo, Brazil, 1951–57.

with proposals due in March 1957. Twenty-one proposals were received, most of them influenced by Chandigarh, except for São Paulo architect Rino Levi's innovative proposal for linear blocks of skyscrapers floating over unbuilt adjacent natural areas. An international jury that included Niemeyer awarded the commission to Lúcio Costa, who famously submitted his entry as a few sketches on notecards with a descriptive letter.

Costa's *Plano Piloto* (pilot plan) for Brasília is cruciform, intended to evoke both ancient Roman grid planning and the sign of the cross used by the Portuguese colonists to indicate their taking possession of a site, in what was understood by early European colonizers to be *terra nullius,* territory unclaimed by Christians. Costa's plan called for an east-west Monumental Axis, along which were sited the main governmental buildings, while the other, gently curving ten-mile (16-kilometer) Residential Axis is organized along a planted parkway, lined with 128 six-story housing blocks called *superquadras*, surrounded by rows of trees (fig. 94). At the east end of the Monumental Axis was Three Powers Square, facing the National Congress Building, the Brazilian Supreme Court, and the Presidential Palace, all designed by Niemeyer. Three Powers Square was a clear manifestation of the CIAM idea of the pedestrian heart of the city, intended as a place for democratic assembly, and indeed it functioned in that way in 1986, when Brazilians assembled there and successfully demanded direct elections, ending twenty-two years of military dictatorship.

Brasília's plan was a version of Le Corbusier's 1930s vision of a Radiant City of high-rise buildings set in greenery, with transportation primarily based on cars and buses. Yet by the 1950s its auto-centered urban structure was criticized by Giedion, who wrote to Niemeyer from the Harvard GSD, suggesting that he change the plan to make it more usable by pedestrians. But Kubitschek's government was committed to developing the Brazilian auto industry, and, like many clients in the 1950s, it did not see pedestrian infrastructure as a significant priority. Brasília's relatively empty open spaces and lack of pedestrian street life were never particularly appealing to most Brazilians, who preferred to remain in the major cities, yet Brasília nonetheless became a worldwide icon of modernist planning in the postwar years. Its tabula rasa design inspired the planners of new capitals elsewhere, including Greek planner Constantinos Doxiadis's Islamabad (1959), the new capital of Pakistan, and the Japanese CIAM member Kenzo Tange's plan for Abuja, the new capital of Nigeria, as well as the central plaza of Shenzhen, the new Chinese industrial center near Hong Kong planned in the 1980s.

Many other design aspects of Brasília were also immediately influential, including Niemeyer's efforts to create a synthesis of Baroque and Corbusian design at the Alvorada Presidential Palace (1957), the Itamaraty Palace of the Brazilian Foreign Relations Department, and the Ministry of Justice (1962). Philip Johnson's work in the late 1950s, including his New York State Theater at Lincoln Center and Amon Carter Museum in Fort Worth, was also strongly influenced by this direction. The organization of Brasília's superquadras on blocks of 984 square feet (300 square meters), much larger than the typical Brazilian residential blocks of about 328 square feet (100 square meters), were set in groups of four across the parkway of the Residential Axis, and became a widely imitated way of organizing modern urban housing projects. Within these sets of four blocks is a pedestrian communal street with shops, cinemas, and churches, all accessible both from the residential blocks and from the parkway. Though offered by Costa and Niemeyer as a fully egalitarian urban model, with all classes living with an appropriate amount of space according to family needs in the superquadras, demand for these well-designed, centrally located residences led to many poorer residents of Brasília moving to outlying satellite towns, some self-built favelas, with long bus commutes to jobs in the capital.

Kubitschek had also worked with Burle Marx at Pampulha, but they did not get along, and it was Kubitschek's political opponent, the

94. Lúcio Costa, Brasília, pilot plan for the new capital of Brazil, 1956–60.

conservative journalist Carlos Lacerda, who as mayor of Rio in 1952 commissioned Burle Marx to design a new waterfront for the city. This ultimately stretched from Santos Dumont airport (1937) to Copacabana, with the last sections completed in 1970. Burle Marx worked on landfill from the flattened hills that had stood just south of downtown, which had also been cleared of favelas for the new beach parkways. He skillfully deployed plantings and pathways over the three hundred acres (121 hectares) of parkland to create new public amenities around and beyond Reidy's Museum of Modern Art (1954). At Copacabana, a luxurious beach and high-rise hotel area, Burle Marx also designed concrete and stone patterned pathways along the beach, whose abstract designs recalled both traditional Portuguese mosaic paving and modern painting.

POSTWAR TRANSFORMATIONS IN EAST ASIA

Globally, World War II and its aftermath were also transformative in many places outside of Europe and the Americas. In China, the Nanking KMT government and the Communist Party of China (CPC) had agreed in the 1930s to jointly resist the Japanese occupation, putting aside differences that almost immediately resurfaced after the Allied victory over the Japanese Empire in 1945. After having briefly established a Communist republic in Kiangsi (now Jiangxi) province from 1931–34, the CPC had retreated from the KMT's forces in its Long March into remote northwestern China, where Mao Zedong (1893–1976) emerged as its leader. During its War of Resistance against Japan, which included World War II, the CPC gained the trust and support of much of the Chinese rural population, which made the return of the KMT government to power in 1945 fraught with conflict. Nonetheless, the KMT Republic of China government was seen as a key ally of the Western powers in 1945–49, and it was given a seat on the newly founded United Nations Security Council just as Liang Sicheng was invited to be the Chinese representative on the U.N. Headquarters design team. By this point, his studies of traditional Chinese architecture were becoming influential on new construction in China, a direction that continued after the victory of the CPC in 1949 and its founding of the People's Republic of China (PRC).

As vice-director of the Beijing City Planning Commission, Liang sought to preserve the old center of Beijing, which then still had many fine courtyard houses, sited along alleys called hutongs, as well as its Ming dynasty city walls. To best preserve it, Liang advocated for locating the new administrative center of the PRC in the western suburbs. This view was overridden by the Soviet experts whom Mao had brought in to help guide China's modernization after his trip there in 1950, when he had secured massive amounts of Soviet foreign aid from Stalin. Eleven thousand Soviet advisors were brought in by Mao to help modernize China, and many Chinese students attended Soviet universities between

1951 and the early 1960s, when the alliance ended. In China itself, architectural and urban design education programs were modified to become more technically oriented during this period.

The Soviet alliance also brought a more conservative architectural direction in urbanism into China in the 1950s, related to the Socialist Realist style of Western classicism favored by Stalin, which was then rejected in the USSR in the late 1950s. This was an approach that he had ordered in 1932, which was to be "socialist in content and national in form." In China it began to be hybridized with the traditional Chinese "big roof style" buildings with upturned eaves that Liang had helped to popularize earlier. In planning, though, the Soviet advisors countered Liang's views about Beijing, and insisted that the new administrative center be built right in the middle of the Old City of Beijing, with some limited preservation efforts for historic sites nearby. This was part of the Soviet doctrine, developed in the Moscow 1935 plan, of a "single center" urban administrative structure, a concept then strongly present in the Beijing plans of 1953–54 and 1957–58.

Beijing's old city walls were dismantled for a second ring road, with a subway line constructed beneath, and only two of its gates were preserved. The ring road's route roughly followed a master plan produced in 1938 during the Japanese occupation, which also called for new towns in the eastern and western suburbs, separated by a greenbelt between 0.62 and 1.86 miles (1 and 3 kilometers) wide. The western satellite town was to have been open only to Japanese residents, while the eastern town was to have been largely industrial. This plan, as modified by the KMT, had not been fully carried out by 1945, but the KMT government's Beiping Master Plan of 1947 was based on it. Much of the same general planning direction, quite similar in many ways to the Moscow 1935 Plan and the Greater London Plan of 1944, was then continued after Beijing returned to being the capital of China in 1949.

Some eight hundred new factories were also built in Beijing in the 1950s, mostly in suburban locations, many as part of "work-unit estates." These involved both state-owned enterprises and adjacent worker housing, which was usually laid out with very high-density mid-rise apartment buildings spaced in axial patterns similar to Stalin-era Soviet housing. Each work-unit estate was to house some 10,000–20,000 residents, and also included schools and other facilities. Around the same time, many of the old courtyard houses in central Beijing were demolished for the new buildings. Many other courtyard houses were confiscated by the government, which had followed Soviet precedent in abolishing private property and nationalizing all industry. These houses were then turned into low-rent public housing, with residents allowed to build into the courtyard spaces. Low-cost "dime houses" were allowed on vacant sites; these were typically small, three- to four-story unheated apartment buildings with common kitchens and toilets, with each household legally limited to 339 square feet (31.5 square meters) of floor area. In 1958 the central government established the *hukou* system of urban residency permits, which controlled the number of Chinese in-migrants from the countryside into certain cities. By 1960 living space per person in Beijing was estimated at about 35 square feet (3.24 square meters).

In Tiananmen Square, at the center of Beijing along the north-south axis of the Forbidden City, Liang Sicheng and his wife and collaborator Lin Huiyin (1904–1955) designed the Monument to the People's Heroes for the new government in 1951–58 (fig. 95). It took the form of a traditional Chinese stone memorial stele, a ten-story obelisk with eight bas-reliefs showing revolutionary episodes in the history of China, from the

95. Liang Sicheng and Lin Huiyin, Monument to the People's Heroes, Beijing, 1951–58.

　　　Mid-Twentieth-Century Modern Urbanism

destruction of opium at Humen in 1839 to the war of resistance (1931–45) and the final battles of the Chinese Civil War in 1949. In this era of Soviet influence, the PRC also launched "ten major constructions" in 1958, including the Great Hall of the People by Zhang Bo and the National Museum of History by Zhang Kaiji, as well as a new Beijing Central Railway station by Yang Tingbao and many other administrative and other official buildings. The east-west axis of Chang'an Avenue was also extended at this time. Despite their radically different political and cultural contexts, in many ways these buildings and urban spaces were a direct continuation of earlier American City Beautiful and Soviet Social Realist directions in twentieth-century Chinese urbanism.

CHANDIGARH, INDIA, 1950–60

The planning directions that appeared in mid-century Britain had extensive international influence. Numerous other planning agencies worldwide prepared similar master plans in the postwar years, including Tokyo in 1956, and many cities in India, Pakistan, Sri Lanka, and elsewhere. In British India before 1947, modern architectural ideas parallel to those in Britain had already begun to be widely influential in the 1930s, as figures like the engineer R. S. Despande published books of modern house plans and predicted the "inevitable evolution" of Indian architecture toward modernism after independence. Despande also argued against urban overcrowding, suggesting that it was particularly dangerous for women in traditional purdah households, which forbade them from leaving their houses and children. Mumbai, then known as Bombay, was a major site for modern housing, much of it built for elites along the coast in an Art Deco style parallel to areas from the same era in Rio de Janeiro and South Miami Beach. Bombay enclaves like Malabar Hill and Marine Drive became iconic symbols of the emerging global metropolis, somewhat like Copacabana in Rio.

In the postwar global political situation of the Cold War, modern urbanism then also began to be deployed by the British and French as a way of countering the social issues raised by the spread of Soviet Communism, as former colonies were prepared for what was often still an economically dependent independence. In West Africa, the British CIAM architects E. Maxwell Fry and Jane Drew (1911–1996) designed numerous university campuses and housing settlements that attempted to extend elements of the climatically sensitive South American modern architecture of the 1930s into new soon-to-be postcolonial regions in West Africa and South Asia. Like Neutra and the Brazilian architects, Fry and Drew based their approach on efforts to relate modern design to local climates and cultures, a direction they articulated in their *Tropical Architecture in the Humid Zone* (1956) and related to the teaching of Otto Koenigsberger (1908–1999), who had been involved with the design of the later phases of the Tata steel model town of Jamshedpur (1944). Koenigsberger followed Fry in 1953 as a professor at the Architectural Association School of Tropical Studies, later the Development Planning Unit of University College London.

Extending the ideas of Patrick Geddes and elements of early CIAM, Fry and Drew and Koenigsberger emphasized "biological necessity" as an element of planning, advocating climatically and topographically responsive strategies of site planning. They denounced the mindless application of two-dimensional street patterns of any kind. Fry and Drew's work, at University College Ibadan in Nigeria and at many other campuses in Nigeria and what in 1957 became Ghana (then called the Gold Coast), in the Gambia, as well as in Kuwait, demonstrated these ideas in practice. They also designed commercial complexes, such as the Fry, Drew, Drake & Lasdun Cooperative Bank of Western Nigeria buildings, constructed in Lagos and Ibadan in 1960, the year of Nigerian independence.

After India's independence in 1947 and the extreme violence of the partition between India and Pakistan (which also included Bangladesh from 1947–71), the English and American orientation of the South Asian (and in many cases English-speaking African) architectural professions continued for many decades. The Indian Institute of Architects was an affiliate of the Royal Institute of British Architects in London, and British models, notably the School of Civic Design at Liverpool University, set the patterns for new programs in town planning established at Bengal Engineering College in 1949, what became the Indian Institute of Technology at Kanpur, and the University of Delhi School of Planning and Architecture by the mid-1950s. The Institute of Town Planning of India was established in 1951, affiliated with the Town Planning Institute in London.

In Israel, founded in 1948 in part of what had been British Mandate Palestine, CIAM member Arieh Sharon (1900–1984) led a team of 180 planners, architects, and other experts in the creation of the National Outline Plan, which established planning regions for the new state and a national water plan. Sharon had studied at the Bauhaus and worked with Hannes Meyer before opening his office in Tel Aviv in 1931, and had designed many housing estates and kibbutzim, but many aspects of the national plan followed the British planning directions that were then becoming widely used internationally.

In 1950, Fry & Drew were commissioned by the new Congress Party Indian socialist government of Prime Minister Jawaharlal Nehru to design Chandigarh, a new capital for an Indian state that had been partitioned with the separation of India and Pakistan at independence in 1947. The creation of Pakistan as a Muslim state meant that both the Punjab, whose capital was Lahore, and Bengal, governed from Calcutta, required that both former British-controlled Indian regions be split into eastern and western halves along religious lines. Mass violence was prevalent as entire populations were required to move in this process, and by 1948 East Punjab was filled with refugees. Encouraged by Nehru, the state government decided to build a new capital as a way of compensating for the "psychological loss" of Lahore to Pakistan.

Chandigarh's site was selected in 1949, and its development required the relocation of 9,000 scattered villagers. The name was taken from one of these existing villages, which had a temple dedicated to the Hindu goddess Chandi, considered an auspicious manifestation of the female principle in Hinduism. Nevertheless, this religious aspect was not emphasized in Nehru's modernizing vision; instead, he called for a new city "unfettered by the traditions of the past, a symbol of the nation's faith in the future." Unlike Mahatma Gandhi (1869–1948), the spiritual and political leader of Indian independence who had advocated a Ruskinian-inspired rejection of industrialization and urbanization in favor of a return to the traditional economic and social life of South Asian villages, Nehru envisioned India as a modern welfare state based on an advanced industrial economy. Gandhi's assassination in 1948 ensured that Nehru's modernizing vision would prevail.

Chandigarh was part of Nehru's influential combining of Soviet-type state development of public sector mining and manufacturing institutions, whose activities were to be guided by five-year national development plans, with American New Deal–inspired efforts to advance democratic participation, extend educational opportunities, and create new scientific and cultural institutions. The TVA was also a model for new Indian hydroelectric dam projects, including the Bhakra Nagal Dam near Chandigarh, which Nehru saw as "temples of modern India." Chandigarh's first architectural team, commissioned in 1949 by the Punjab state government, was led by Albert Mayer (1897–1981), an American architect and planner who had served in the U.S. military in India during the war and had been involved with the New Deal Greenbelt towns program. Mayer had been working as a planning consultant in India since 1947, where he had advocated the influential idea that "village-level workers" should act as liaisons between their villages and the government. He also worked on master planning for Bombay intended to accommodate new north-south expressways and on early versions of plans for the new area across the bay that would later become Navi (New) Mumbai.

At Chandigarh, Mayer was given a program by the state that called for a low-density English-type Garden City with bungalows. Mayer's proposal for "East Punjab capital city" was instead a fan-shaped plan organized by a curving grid of highways following the terrain, composed of residential neighborhood "superblocks," each a rectangular area 4,429 × 2,953 feet (1,350 × 900 meters) bounded by planted boulevards. Each superblock was to contain schools, markets, health facilities, and recreation. Mayer hired the Polish émigré architect Mathew

(Maciej) Nowicki (1910–1950) to visualize the architecture, and he made some preliminary renderings that combined modern architecture with abstracted Indian traditional elements. Nowicki's death in a plane crash over Egypt in 1950 led to the hiring by the state government of Fry & Drew in London, who then added Le Corbusier and his cousin and partner Pierre Jeanneret to their design team. By this point, debates about the type of capital to be built had been resolved in favor the vision of chief engineer of the state public works department, P. L. Verma, who advocated a single new city of five hundred thousand, as opposed to earlier ideas about building three Garden Cities with separate administrative, university, and industrial uses.

The master plan by Le Corbusier, Fry & Drew, and Jeanneret then determined the outline of what was built at Chandigarh, based on a combination of Mayer's initial proposal with a superblock plan using principles similar to what Le Corbusier had established with Town Planning Associates (Wiener and Sert) in their joint planning for Bogotá in 1950. There they had divided the city into 35 "sectors" (a term they introduced at this point to replace "neighborhood unit"), each composed of 5 "conjuntos," or complexes, of 250 housing units, or 1,250 units total per sector. Each sector, which could contain housing of various heights, was bounded by high-speed-traffic roads that formed the new expressway system of the city, and each sector included a school, social services, and recreational facilities and open space, all within a short walk of the housing. This sectorial focus was a further development of the "precinct planning" of the County of London Plan (1943), which attempted to bring the pedestrian, place-based qualities of London—areas such as around Westminster Abbey and the Houses of Parliament, in Bloomsbury, and near the University of London and Bedford Square—as planning models into a rapidly growing city in the developing world.

At Chandigarh, as in the Bogotá plan, the highways were categorized according to Le Corbusier's "7V" system, which sorted routes by speed, from high-speed V1 or V2 superhighways through V4 commercial main streets to V7 pedestrian greenways. This kind of system also was anticipated in the County of London Plan, which similarly advocated the sorting of traffic by speed and the complete separation of pedestrian routes from vehicular ones. In Le Corbusier's application of the "sector" concept to the plan, each of the thirty-nine built-out sectors was to have a north-south green strip, bisected by a commercial road running east to west (fig. 96). He also reduced the plan area from 6,908 acres to 5,380 acres (2,117 hectares), reducing the area given over to roads and open space and increasing the density by 20 percent. But Le Corbusier's ability to alter the Indian state's still more or less Garden City program for the city was limited, and his efforts to build a series of high-rise residential unités were not successful. Instead, fourteen low-rise housing types were specified, nearly all designed by Pierre Jeanneret and Fry & Drew, as

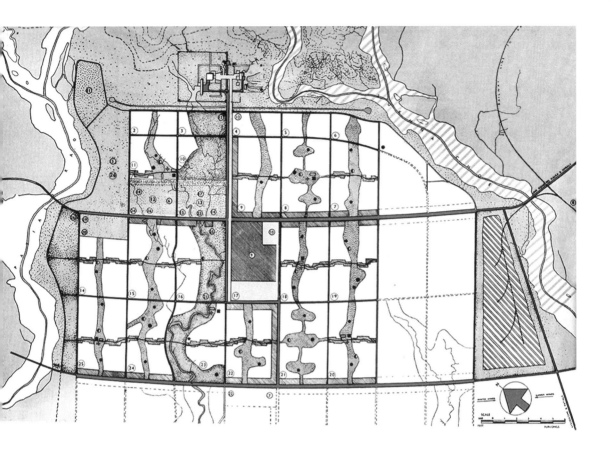

Le Corbusier then decided that his only real interest in the project was the Capitol, or Monumental Core.

This new city, built between 1950 and 1960, soon became an icon of modern urbanism. Chandigarh's planning and architecture indicated a new phase in the modern movement. Its most famous element, Le Corbusier's design for the Monumental Core of high court and other government buildings, had been exhibited at CIAM 8, sponsored by the MARS group and held near London in 1951 and dedicated to the theme "the heart of the city." This new direction for CIAM reflected the views of both Le Corbusier and his Barcelona disciple Sert, president of CIAM from 1947–56, who thought that the increasingly auto-based spread of modern cities required that architects begin to design new civic center elements that would synthesize architecture, landscape architecture, and city planning to create places for pedestrian gathering and democratic debate. At the same time, in Sert and Wiener's mostly unbuilt plans, such as those for the Brazilian Motor City, Chimbote (1947), and Medellín (1948), the civic cores were compact, pedestrian-oriented spaces, while at Chandigarh, Le Corbusier intentionally designed the Monumental Core as a vast space, requiring the use of vehicles to move around it. These differences would become increasingly significant in the decades that followed.

96. Le Corbusier, Fry & Drew, Pierre Jeanneret, Chandigarh, India, 1950–60 (Le Corbusier, *Oeuvre complète, 1946–52* [Zurich: Éditions Girsberger, 1953], 146). © F.L.C./ADAGP, Paris/ Artists Rights Society (ARS), New York 2016.

FURTHER READING

Luis E. Carranza and Fernando Luiz Lara, eds., *Modern Architecture in Latin America: Art, Technology, and Utopia* (Austin: University of Texas Press, 2014).

Peter Hall, *Cities of Tomorrow: An Intellectual History of Urban Planning and Design Since 1880* (London: Blackwell, 1988).

Seng Kuan, *Tange Kenzō's Architecture in Three Keys: As Building, as Art, and as the City* (Cambridge, Mass.: Harvard University dissertation, 2011).

Eldridge Lovelace, *Harland Bartholomew: His Contributions to American Planning* (Urbana: University of Illinois Press, 1993).

Pierre Merlin, *New Towns: Regional Planning and Development* (London: Methuen, 1969).

Eric Mumford, "Alvar Aalto's Urban Planning and CIAM Urbanism," in Mateo Kries and Jochen Eisenbrand, eds., *Alvar Aalto—Second Nature* (Weil-am-Rhein, Germany: Vitra Design Museum, 2014), 278-309.

W. Brian Newsome, *French Urban Planning, 1940–1968* (New York: Peter Lang, 2009).

Peter G. Rowe and Seng Kuan, *Architectural Encounters with Essence and Form in Modern China* (Cambridge, Mass.: MIT Press, 2002).

Mark Swenarton, Tom Avermaete, and Dirk van den Heuvel, eds., *Architecture and the Welfare State* (London: Routledge, 2015).

Hasan Uddin-Khan, Julian Beinart, and Charles Correa, *Le Corbusier: Chandigarh and the Modern City* (London: Mapin, 2010).

Lawrence Vale, *Architecture, Power, and National Identity* (London: Routledge, 2008).

Yi Wang, *A Century of Change: Beijing's Urban Structure in the 20th Century* (Hong Kong: Pace, 2013).

Jennifer Yoos, Vincent James, and Andrew Blauvelt, *Parallel Cities: The Multilevel Metropolis* (Minneapolis: Walker Art Center, 2016).

CHAPTER SIX

Urban Design, Team 10, and Metabolism After 1953

By the mid-1950s, it was clear that despite considerable central city building activity in a few cities like New York, Chicago, Philadelphia, and San Francisco, North American cities in general were beginning to decentralize, even as millions in federal urban renewal funds were being spent to raze and rebuild whole neighborhoods under the provisions of the 1949 Federal Housing Act. Josep Lluís Sert (1902–1983), president of CIAM from 1947–56, was appointed dean of the Harvard Graduate School of Design in 1953, and he responded to this situation by proposing that architects take up the new field of urban design. "Urban design" was a term that had occasionally been used by Eliel Saarinen in the 1930s and 1940s at the Cranbrook Academy of Art near Detroit, where Philadelphia planner Edmund N. Bacon (1910–2005) and HOK founding partner Gyo Obata (born 1923) had both studied. In his book *The City* (1943), Saarinen had proposed a new pattern of "organic decentralization" for American cities, one where dense clusters of business, educational, and institutional activities would be dispersed across the auto-scale metropolitan areas then emerging. Their central pedestrian plazas, inspired by the Piazza San Marco in Venice, would have a range of housing types within walking distance. Each of these dense, decentralized urban units would be surrounded by greenbelts and linked by transportation routes, as in Eliel Saarinen's Helsinki plan (1917–18).

Sert advocated related ideas in a 1944 essay, "The Human Scale in City Planning," combining them with elements of the MARS Plan of London. At the Harvard GSD he extended and developed this direction beyond what Saarinen had begun at Cranbrook, putting new emphasis on existing pedestrian cities as sites for new housing for all income levels, as well as places for new institutional facilities. With these ideas of urban design, Sert was attempting to retain the main values of CIAM. But rather than criticizing the super-density of older urban centers, as CIAM had done in the 1930s, Sert in 1953 echoed Lewis Mumford in identifying contemporary culture as "a culture of cities, a civic culture." Continuing the themes of both CIAM 8 and of Le Corbusier's postwar concept of "Ineffable Space" (1945)—the perceptual and emotional effects of architectural space, which cannot easily be put into words—Sert revived the City Beautiful focus on architecturally designed urban centers. But the main idea was not only a formal one; Sert also saw these complexes as sites of face-to-face pedestrian interaction, and he argued that such spaces were the only places where a civic culture could continue. In them he thought it might be possible to resist the centralizing and undemocratic forces of mass media–based politics, then just emerging. Despite this implicitly critical aspect of the heart of the city idea, Sert offered his vision of urban design to 1950s Americans in the same apolitical spirit as other kinds of postwar modernism, which also tried to distance themselves from the movement's highly politicized socialist beginnings in prewar Europe and the Soviet Union.

Sert's approach to urban design did not exclude the American public housing and highways then being built or planned, but it focused less on slum clearance and more on strengthening civic culture in physically transformed pedestrian-oriented central urban settings. Sert's views on the advantages of pedestrian urban life were the basis of the Harvard Urban Design program well before the publication of either Aldo Rossi's *L'architettura della città* (The Architecture of the City) in 1966 or of Bacon's *Design of Cities* (1967). At the same time, Sert continued to advocate many of the same architectural devices as Le Corbusier, not only in architectural design approach but also in the use of the "human scale as a module." Both had argued that the "natural frame of man" had been destroyed in large contemporary cities and that these cities fell short, as Sert put it, in "facilitating human contacts so as to raise the cultural level of their populations." In his new position as dean (1953–69), and until 1963 as also chair of architecture at the GSD at Harvard, Sert was able to make this view the focal point of the program. In doing so he both continued the legacy of CIAM and, in parallel with the postwar Italian CIAM group, added a new element of pedestrian-based "urban consciousness" to modern architecture.

A 1953 article in *Architectural Forum* by Paul Lester Wiener and Sert, "Can Patios Make Cities?" presented the central design concept behind this Latin American town-planning work, advocating it for North American cities as well. Wiener and Sert emphasized that the use of the enclosed courtyard (patio) form at various scale levels could give an "underlying coherence" to each city plan. These scales ranged from the house to the neighborhood to individual public buildings to the monumental city center; the last could be composed of a "series of gigantic piazzas (or big patios) that form places of outdoor assembly for all citizens." They contrasted the "typical American residential street of today"—a series of single-family houses on individual lots—with this approach, which used less space, provided more private outdoor areas, shortened utility lines, and created a more coherent urban design. Unlike suburban open space, these community patios, which Sert and Wiener illustrated with a model of their pedestrian core for Puerto Ordaz, Venezuela (1951), would be walled-in spaces, which they called "outdoor rooms." Continuing Sert's polemics from CIAM 8, they argued that in such spaces people would "associate with others more freely than they would in an 'unframed' park area," such as the central green spaces at Radburn. They also contrasted this patio approach with the less formal "village green" at Clarence Stein's Baldwin Hills Village. They illustrated their approach with model photos of their patio row houses and a "patiopark" they had designed for a proposed Havana subdivision, Quinta Palatino (fig. 97). Though economically feasible, the patio-house concept had almost no influence in the United States, then or later; but it was widely used as modern housing in numerous other countries in the 1950s, notably in Peru and the Middle East.

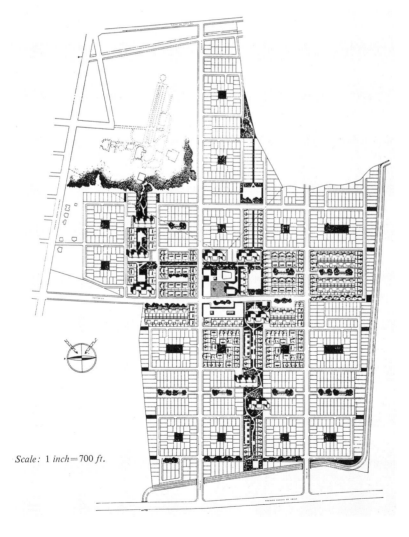

97. Town Planning Associates (Paul Lester Wiener and Josep Lluís Sert), Quinta Palatino subdivision, Havana, 1954 (Maxwell Fry and Jane Drew, *Tropical Architecture in the Humid Zone* [New York: Reinhold, 1956], Fig. 168, 149).

Scale: 1 inch=700 ft.

The modernist urban civic centers that Sert also advocated, on the other hand, were a well-established North American type by this time, even though his firm had not yet obtained any commissions to design them in North American cities. I. M. Pei (born 1917), a Chinese architect who came to the United States in 1935 and attended MIT and then the Harvard GSD, began designing mixed-use pedestrian central-city projects for New York developer William Zeckendorf (1905–1976) at the Mile High Center in Denver (1952–56). This was followed many other Pei-designed projects for Zeckendorf, including the Place Ville-Marie (1956–66, with Henry Cobb) mixed use development in downtown Montreal. Other prominent though usually less architecturally successful projects were begun soon after—including Lincoln Center in New York, a joint design by Philip Johnson, Harrison and Abramowitz, Pietro Belluschi, and Eero Saarinen (1955–69) on a cleared tenement area shown just before its demolition in the film version of *West Side Story* (1961).

At Harvard in 1955, Sert also hired one of the first women to teach full time at the GSD: Jaqueline Tyrwhitt (1905–1983), the English planner and CIAM organizer. A member of the first group of women to attend the Architectural Association in London in the 1920s, Tyrwhitt (pronounced to rhyme with "spirit") had been involved with planning in Britain since the early 1930s, initially from a Geddesian direction. In the 1930s Tyrwhitt had become part of the circle of George Pepler (1882–1959), then a British Ministry of Health official monitoring German planning, and she had studied in Berlin in spring 1937 with Gottfried Feder (1883–1941), a Geddesian Nazi planning theorist. Back in England, Tyrwhitt then enrolled at the short-lived Architectural Association School for Planning and Research for National Development, organized by E. A. A. Rowse (1896–1982), who was forced to separate the innovative new school from the still classically oriented Architectural Association (AA) in 1938.

After involvement in British government demographic surveys and mapping for the planning efforts, some of which would result in the Greater London Plan of 1944, Tyrwhitt became part of the MARS Town Planning Committee in 1942, chaired by the British CIAM member Maxwell Fry. In 1943 she was commissioned by the British War Office to organize a "Correspondence Course on the Background of Planning" for Allied soldiers during World War II. This course used a Geddesian regionalist approach, which centered on the geographical region as the key planning unit. After the war Tyrwhitt began to give lectures, on planning, in Canada and the United States under the auspices of the British Ministry of Information.

As a member of the MARS group Tyrwhitt became involved with the organization of CIAM 6, held at an aluminum prefabricated housing factory near Bristol, England, in 1947. She then organized the first CIAM Summer School in London in 1948. During this time Tyrwhitt continued to teach planning in London and supervised the work of John F. C.

Turner (born 1927), a British army veteran who wrote a paper for her on Geddes's notation of life diagram as an early precursor to Ludwig von Bertalanffly's general systems theory. This may have been related to unsuccessful efforts supported by Catherine Bauer Wurster to have Tyrwhitt direct an urban research center at Vassar College using data. Tyrwhitt remained involved with the International Federation for Housing and Town Planning (IFHTP), of which Pepler was then president, and she edited the influential British *Town and Country Planning Textbook* (1950), a codification of the Geddesian planning practices that were being legislatively institutionalized in Britain in the 1940s.

In 1947, Tyrwhitt published a selection of Geddes's Indian planning reports as *Patrick Geddes in India,* rekindling interest in his work and indicating its continuing relevance in the emergent era of European decolonization. Around the same time she began having a clandestine affair with the German-speaking CIAM secretary-general and historian Sigfried Giedion, whom she first met at CIAM 6. Following the massive success of his *Space, Time and Architecture* (1941), an influential modern architectural history textbook, Giedion published *Mechanization Takes Command* (1948), an innovative history of the technological changes that had dramatically altered human existence since 1850. Tyrwhitt took on the then-common role of female assistant to a major male literary figure, assisting Giedion with translations and substantially editing all of his books after 1949. Along with Sert and the Italian CIAM architect Ernesto Rogers (1909–1969), Tyrhwitt was one of the lead organizers of CIAM 8 in 1951, held at a conference center in Hoddesdon, north of London. She taught planning for four years at the University of Toronto, working with the pioneering sociologist of media, Marshall McLuhan (1911–1980), seeking to link his research to Giedion's. In 1952, she became involved with U.N. planning efforts through Ernest Weissmann (1903–1985), a former associate of Le Corbusier's and briefly a design partner of Sert's in New York in 1941. Weissmann joined the U.N. Bureau of Social Affairs' Housing and Town Planning section in the 1940s.

Tyrwhitt was approached by Weissmann at this time about U.N. efforts to focus on "habitat for the greater number," the growing populations of poor in-migrants to cities outside Europe and North America. This direction had been begun by Vladimir Bodiansky (1894–1966) and Jean-Jacques Honegger (1903–1985), French and Swiss CIAM members, respectively, working under Ecochard in Morocco in the ATBAT-Afrique group around 1950. It was in this postwar Moroccan context that French planners began to examine the planning and social issues around the massive growth of *bidonvilles*, tin-can shanty towns built by recently arrived in-migrants from the countryside searching for work in newly industrializing cities.

It was also at this time that the United Nations began to send missions of technical experts—such as the American planner Jacob Leslie

Crane (1892–1988) and the New York real estate lawyer, developer, and public housing advocate Charles Abrams (1901–1970)—to research housing conditions in "tropical areas" of many emerging nations. These included Ghana, Turkey, Pakistan, Thailand, Malaya, the Philippines, and Singapore. The Morocco-based U.N. project that was to involve Tyrwhitt was indefinitely postponed in 1953, and Weissmann instead suggested that she become a project director for the U.N. Technical Assistance Administration to advise the government of India on a planned international exhibition of low-cost housing in New Delhi. Tyrwhitt had published her *Patrick Geddes in India* to coincide with Indian independence, with the goal of emphasizing the importance of Geddes's "bio-realism," focused on human settlements in regional watersheds, for worldwide postwar reconstruction. She also emphasized his ideas of citizen participation in planning, the use of "conservative surgery" for dense urban areas rather than massive slum clearance, and the concept of an "ecological economics" grounded in biological planning principles, all in contrast to the main focuses of modernist urbanism at the time. She further expounded on these Geddesian principles in a 1951 article in the *Journal of the Town Planning Institute,* emphasizing his idea of the Valley Section and relating his planning ideas to those of CIAM.

Tyrwhitt accepted this U.N. position and, with Sert's enthusiastic approval, planned to use at the New Delhi seminar some of the project presentation grids from CIAM 9, held in 1953 in Aix-en-Provence, France, as models for future housing worldwide. She focused the event on a model village core, which she conceptualized within the context of the Indian modernization led by Prime Minister Nehru. The Indian Village Center core was inspired by Gandhi's idea of Basic Schools, itself a version of Rabindranath Tagore's Ruskin-inspired concept of teaching through craft skills that had also been admired by Geddes. A pilot example, designed by Albert Mayer, had already been built. At the U.N. seminar, Tyrwhitt met the Greek planner Constantinos Doxiadis (1914–1975), and in 1955 she began to assemble readings for him on housing and planning in the developing world, an activity that she continued at the Harvard GSD and that eventually led to the journal *Ekistics,* which she would edit for Doxiadis from 1957 to 1972.

Educated in town planning in Berlin in the 1930s, Doxiadis had been involved with the Greek resistance to the Nazi occupation during World War II. He served as minister of reconstruction during the Greek civil war (1946–49) and was the Marshall Plan coordinator for Greece. He began to argue in the postwar world that individual buildings could not be the primary focus of architects. Instead, he advocated for a new role, where architects produced built environments that met human needs, and thus created communities. He participated at the New Delhi seminar with Crane, Abrams, the Israeli planner Arieh Sharon, and Frederick Adams, then chair of planning at MIT.

Just prior to Tyrwhitt's appointment as an assistant professor at the Harvard GSD, Dean Sert invited her to speak on the "human problems of housing and planning in India," based on her recent experiences there. The position she held at the GSD (1955–66/69) was to coordinate the linkages between architecture, landscape architecture, and city and regional planning for Sert's Master of Urban Design program, which officially began in 1960. Unlike Sert and most other mid-century planners, Tyrwhitt questioned the validity of the neighborhood unit concept, a view she shared with Reginald R. Isaacs (1911–1986), then chair of the GSD planning program. Isaacs was a protégé of Gropius's who along with Martin Meyerson (1922–2007) had been extensively involved with efforts to rebuild the Near South Side of Chicago as a racially integrated urban area centered on local institutions such as IIT, Michael Reese hospital, and various new housing complexes. Isaacs worked on this effort with Gropius and Chicago Housing Authority director Elizabeth Wood (1899–1993) in the late 1940s, but the project ended in 1954 after much local political opposition.

Isaacs and Tyrwhitt both thought that the walkable neighborhood unit as it was being applied in American cities was almost inevitably a tool of racial and social segregation. In 1949, Tyrwhitt suggested that perhaps metropolitan areas be organized into larger mixed neighborhoods of 15,000 people, which could be paired and centered on a high school, rather than on the neighborhood unit ideal of an elementary school sited within a half mile (0.8 kilometer) of all its students. After a conversation with R. Buckminster Fuller at the Institute of Design in Chicago that year, Tyrwhitt also began to argue that Christaller's central place theory indicated that loosely hexagonal nets of circulation linking urban nodes surrounded by open space to a central metropolitan core would be preferable to the urban sprawl and tightly bounded segregated suburbs that were then being built across the country.

Sert's, Giedion's, and Tyrwhitt's efforts at Harvard (1953–66) involved synthesizing architectural design, art, and architectural and urban history into a new focus on the pedestrian city, with landscape architecture, a department then chaired by Hideo Sasaki (1919–2000), remaining in a relatively minor supporting role. Sert also invited Italian CIAM member Ernesto Rogers, a founding partner of the Milan firm BBPR, to teach at the GSD as a visitor in 1954–55, bringing the Italian CIAM emphasis on urban "ambience" and historic context into modern urban design education. For Rogers, new architectural interventions in the city should strive for continuity with the past, though this did not necessarily imply direct formal imitation, an approach evident in the Torre Velasca in Milan (1958), a skyscraper designed by his firm BBPR (fig. 98).

At the Harvard GSD around this time, Sert and Rogers began defining a position that was both modernist and culturally conservative in emphasizing the continuing value of the urban fabric of historic European cities,

98. BBPR, Torre Velasca, Milan, 1958 (Oscar Newman, ed., *CIAM '59 in Otterlo* [Stuttgart: Karl Krämer, 1961], 94).

one where a focus on walkable central cities could become a primary value for modern architecture. Giedion was a key influence on this direction. In 1956 Sert hired Eduard Sekler (1920–2017), a protégé of Tyrwhitt's and a Viennese art historian educated at the Courtauld Institute in London. Giedion and Sekler began to teach a four-semester architectural history survey, a new component of the GSD curriculum that reinforced Sert's approach to urban design. Students made detailed analytic drawings of historic urban spaces and structures, analyzing them alongside the latest urban design projects of Le Corbusier, Costa, Niemeyer, and Town Planning Associates.

Assisted by Tyrwhitt, Sert also undertook preparations for the First Harvard Urban Design Conference, a task he began while still president of CIAM, which voted to dissolve itself at CIAM 10 in Dubrovnik in 1956.

This conference, held in April 1956, was centered on Sert's concept that "after a period of rapid growth and suburban sprawl" the centralized city should remain a key element of American culture. The speakers at this conference in different ways challenged what had become conventional decentralist planning wisdom by 1956, and many of their ideas would have a profound influence on thinking about cities in the following years. The mayor of Pittsburgh, David Lawrence, insisted that cities were not technologically obsolete, but as New York housing expert, lawyer, and developer Charles Abrams (1901–1970) was among the first to point out publicly at this event, there was an emerging American city-suburb divide, as "darker skinned migrants" were moving into overcrowded central cities, and the white middle class was moving out. Lloyd Rodwin (1919–1999), a planner and protégé of Catherine Bauer Wurster's who a year later would cofound the MIT Harvard Joint Center for Urban Studies with Martin Meyerson, called for institutional action to save cities. A young associate editor of *Architectural Forum*, Jane (Butzner) Jacobs (1916–2006), a last-minute substitution for editor Douglas Haskell, first put forward her ideas at this event on the importance of small businesses, institutions, and local "eyes on the street" to neighborhood street life. MIT professor Gyorgy Kepes (1906–2001) discussed some of the findings of his Rockefeller Foundation–funded research on the "Perceptual Form of the City" that he and MIT planning professor Kevin Lynch (1918–1984) were doing, published as Lynch's *The Image of the City* (1960). Kepes emphasized how human value scales are "certainly defined by the images that we create about ourselves and about our relation to the world around us."

The case studies presented at the First Harvard Urban Design conference were the redevelopment of Pittsburgh's Golden Triangle; the planning of Philadelphia City Planning director Edmund N. Bacon, both for the Society Hill area and the public housing project of Louis I. Kahn (1901–1974) that he had commissioned for the Mill Creek area of West Philadelphia; as well as Victor Gruen's proposal for "A Greater Fort Worth Tomorrow." Pittsburgh was a national model for urban renewal at the time, building not only public housing but also partnering with the private sector to create Gateway Center, a twenty-three-acre (9.3-hectare) office complex developed by Equitable Life Assurance Society. The center—much of it designed between 1943 and 1949 by Irwin Clavan, the architect of Stuyvesant Town in New York—was adjacent to the newly created Point State Park at the meeting of the Monongahela and Allegheny Rivers, on the demolished site of the city's original settlement. Frank Lloyd Wright had also planned an unbuilt, architecturally ambitious civic center for this same site in 1947.

Bacon, executive director of the Philadelphia City Planning Commission from 1949–70, offered a somewhat different approach to urban renewal, one that emphasized the articulation of space "for its experiencing

by people." This went along with an effort to create a "continuity of space experience, the realization that we are dealing not with one single sensation but a series of sensations in sequence." Though by this point Bacon had stopped commissioning Louis Kahn for city planning work, he credited Kahn with providing the "directive for the principle of co-ordination of individual projects in redevelopment areas," and he used Kahn's Philadelphia Mill Creek project as an example of this approach. According to Bacon, Kahn had introduced the Greenway Principle, the use of linear pedestrian routes based on "significant existing symbols such as churches, schools, and clubs," which Bacon was then applying in his Philadelphia planning. Bacon proposed that the next several million dollars of federal urban renewal funds be used to create a "disbursed series of open-space nuclei and greenways evenly distributed throughout the blighted neighborhoods on the basis of a fair and uniform standard," though he admitted that this concept was "altogether contrary to the established procedures in the federal administration."

The most influential of the presentations at the 1956 Harvard conference was Gruen's proposal to pedestrianize downtown Fort Worth (fig. 99). His plan would have linked the central business district to the newly built interstate highways around it with six large parking garages, each holding six thousand cars, from which shoppers and office workers could use moving sidewalks to access the downtown. The plan would have required little demolition of existing business buildings, and downtown deliveries would have been made through a new underground vehicular tunnel system. Gruen noted that the resulting pedestrianized streets would "become a series of different kinds of spatial rooms." Though not carried out, the plan was a major influence on downtown pedestrianization efforts for decades, including the partially realized 1960 Plan for Downtown St. Louis and Gruen's own internationally influential built plans for Kalamazoo, Michigan (1958), and for Midtown Plaza in Rochester, New York (1958–62).

The social and political value of pedestrian encounters "at the core" had been put forward by Sert as a central element of the postwar agenda of CIAM. The approaches advocated by Bacon in Philadelphia and proposed by Gruen at the First Harvard Urban Design Conference instead emphasized the aesthetic value of pedestrian urban experiences rather than the shaping of spaces for democratic political action. Bacon's approach was related to an Eliel Saarinen–inspired organicist social vision, and it could in some way be related to the heart of the city idea, though Bacon never seems to have directly done so in print. Gruen's approach, however, was almost entirely commercially based. It was a further extension of his idea that shopping centers could become the modern equivalent of medieval town centers, an idea he had promoted in his 1953 national traveling exhibition, "Shopping Centers of Tomorrow."

When completed in 1954, Gruen's Northland Center in Southfield near Detroit was described as having a "tincture of the village common idea," but unlike some earlier suburban civic center proposals, such as Saarinen's for the unbuilt defense workers' town of Willow Run or Charles and Ray Eames's "City Hall for 194x" project, Gruen's Northland was focused on an anchor department store and contained few noncommercial uses. At the first Harvard Urban Design Conference, these presentations by Bacon and Gruen subtly modified Sert's CIAM focus on the heart of the city. Instead of providing spaces for political assembly, each in different ways offered an aesthetic basis for the new focus on pedestrian spaces in the central city, which they now saw as valuable primarily for its capacity to provide a series of sense experiences related to characteristics that were historical, symbolic, and perceptual, anticipating a direction that would later be described as "phenomenological."

Similar directions were also being articulated in Britain at the same time, notably Gordon Cullen's idea of "townscape," a response to what he had identified in 1953 as the bleak "prairie planning" of the British New Towns. "Townscape" as a concept was first put forward by Cullen in 1949, and was initially intended as a design method for making new housing environments more appealing, as well as a way to insert modern buildings into historic urban contexts (fig. 100). Cullen's intentions were parallel in some ways to the ideas of Sert and Rogers, as well as related to the English preservation efforts of Sir Nikolaus Pevsner (1902–1983), whose *Buildings of England* series (1951–74) documented the country's vast stock of historic buildings and landscapes. These directions were also related to the work of the Danish architect Steen Eiler Rasmussen (1898–1990), whose *Towns and Buildings* (1949) presented detailed architectural drawings of historic Beijing and various European urban sites and palace complexes, and whose *Experiencing Architecture* (1959) put a new emphasis on the individual experience of buildings.

Both Gruen's and Bacon's 1956 Harvard Urban Design Conference proposals were based on the idea that creating such pedestrian spatial experiences should be the primary concern of urban designers. In this they continued the approach begun by Sitte in 1889 that had been extended, in differing ways, by Eliel Saarinen and then Sert. Unlike these predecessors, Bacon, Kahn, and Gruen emphasized the value of the built patterns of existing cities, suitably modernized and modified for cars, as a framework for these new perceptual experiences, in a way that had close parallels to those proposed in Sert and Wiener's Latin American urban plans. This approach put a new value—one based mostly on perceptual

100. Gordon Cullen, *The Concise Townscape* [New York: Van Nostrand Reinhold, 1961], 166).

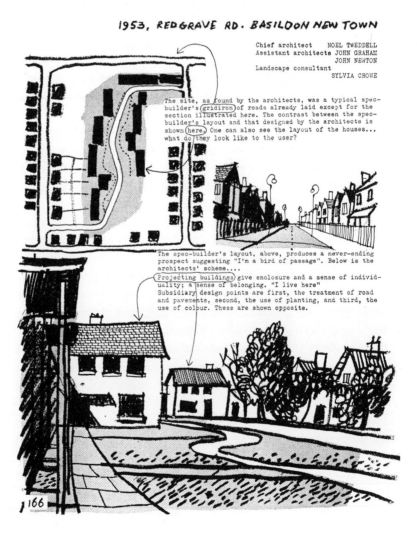

1953. REDGRAVE RD. BASILDON NEW TOWN

Chief architect   NOEL TWEDDELL
Assistant architects JOHN GRAHAM
                     JOHN NEWTON
Landscape consultant
                     SYLVIA CROWE

The site, as found by the architects, was a typical spec-builder's gridiron of roads already laid except for the section illustrated here. The contrast between the spec-builder's layout and that designed by the architects is shown here. One can also see the layout of the houses... what do they look like to the user?

The spec-builder's layout, above, produces a never-ending prospect suggesting "I'm a bird of passage". Below is the architects' scheme....
Projecting buildings give enclosure and a sense of individuality; a sense of belonging. "I live here"
Subsidiary design points are first, the treatment of road and pavements, second, the use of planting, and third, the use of colour. These are shown opposite.

experience and historic associations—on the "obsolete" downtowns and older urban neighborhoods that were then being cleared and rebuilt. Their efforts arguably laid the basis for much of the American urbanism that followed, and indeed defined a type of urban design based on re-using existing cities that is widely used today.

At the same time, many other figures were actively involved with urban renewal in a number of locations. From 1940, the French urbanist and Yale University professor Maurice Rotival (1892–1980) designed auto-parkway–based plans for New Haven, including a revised 1953 plan that included a freeway stub intended to clear the Oak Street neighborhood (1959), a project that would later become a reviled reminder of the urban renewal era. By then New Haven's urban renewal effort was being over-seen by Edward J. Logue (1921–2000), who served as city development administrator from 1954 to 1960. Logue then went on to a similar role at the Boston Redevelopment Authority from 1961 to 1967, where he over-saw the Government Center redevelopment, masterplanned by I.M. Pei. He was then recruited by Governor Nelson Rockefeller to head the New York State Urban Development Corporation from 1968 to 1975, where his major projects included the "new town in town" of Roosevelt Island (1970–75), which included new racially integrated, mixed-income high-density housing by Sert, Jackson and others.

Much urban design during this period was also concerned with urban decentralization, which remains the mainstream of American metropol-itan development even today. Sert noted in 1957 that designers should be aware that "dispersion and low densities have frequently resulted in suburban sprawl." He believed that planning authorities should "aim at reurbanization not suburbanism, which has resulted in the develop-ment of patterns that are neither country nor city." Probably referring to French sociologist Jean Gottmann's influential research, published in 1961 as *Megalopolis: The Urbanized Northeastern Seaboard of the United States,* Sert mentioned recent news reports on the emergence of the Northeast Corridor as a "vast metropolis 600 miles [966 kilometers] long, with a population of 27,000,000 people" from Washington to Boston, "probably the largest urban region in the world today." He urged urban designers to "try to devise new patterns and think in new terms."

This gap between urban design experiments in architectural educa-tion and actual American development patterns of the time can also be seen in the work of CIAM member Serge Chermayeff (1900–1996), who taught at the GSD from 1954 to 1962. With Christopher Alexander (born 1936), then a Harvard Arts and Sciences doctoral student, Chermayeff published a study of low-rise, high-density housing prototypes, *Com-munity and Privacy* (1963). Funded by the MIT-Harvard Joint Center for Urban Studies under Rodwin and Meyerson's directorship, and written before Chermayeff left Harvard for the Yale School of Architecture in 1962, this work had developed out of Chermayeff's students' studies of the "urban family house," a patio-type, higher-density alternative to the detached-house suburbia. Chermayeff had made several unsuccessful efforts to build complexes of such houses in Cambridge, and in 1959 he received a Joint Center grant to do further research on this topic, and he worked with Alexander to develop an early computer program to study its variables.

In their description of the project, Chermayeff and Alexander began with a continuation of the CIAM critique of single-family-house suburbia, which for them had neither "the natural order of a great estate nor the man-made order of the historic city." Suburbia was "too dense to be countryside," but it also "fails to be a city because it is not dense enough, or organized enough." They were also critical of "enemy number one," the car, as a creator of traffic congestion and accidents. Their goal was to identify thirty-three key pattern elements essential to desirable housing patterns, whose overlapping interactions they analyzed using an IBM 704 mainframe computer at MIT. From this they generated a set of design patterns that produced results that were arguably derived to some extent from the courtyard house patterns of Sert and Wiener's Chimbote project. These patterns were all mostly clusters of atrium houses sited close to controlled trafficways, with small shared parking areas, and linked with extensive networks of pedestrian circulation to larger natural "pedestrian domains." This book, still widely admired, produced almost no built outcomes in the United States.

As Sert introduced the discipline of urban design at Harvard in the 1950s, a massive amount of urban development was taking place globally. The world population rose from 2.52 billion in 1950 to 3.68 billion in 1970. By then, many former European colonies had become independent nations. Earlier concepts of white European racial superiority had begun to be questioned by some, and efforts began to address the challenges of housing and urbanism in many contexts that differed significantly from those that had been used previously in either Europe or the United States. For example, at the time the capital of a conservative kingdom dominated by the British Empire and Iraq Petroleum, the London firm of Minoprio and Spencely, with P. W. McFarlane, were commissioned by the Lord Mayor of Baghdad to design a new master plan for it in 1954. Many other cities around the world opted for similar approaches.

From his Athens office, Doxiadis also began to be commissioned for master plans for many cities in the Mideast, South Asia, and Africa, beginning with his planning for West Baghdad in 1955. These avoided high-rise schemes and focused on transportation infrastructure and platting for all or partially self-built urban areas. Doxiadis Associates began a plan for Beirut in 1958, and in 1959 the firm won a competition for the design of Islamabad, the new capital of Pakistan. His firm then went on to design many other new districts, town plans, and buildings in many countries between 1955 and 1975. These plans typically organized existing and future urbanized areas along highway corridors using neighborhood units of one- or two-story houses. Within each neighborhood unit, common spaces were provided in a walkable neighborhood center, which in many Islamic countries included one or several mosques. At the same time, Doxiadis recognized that modern cities tended to rapidly grow outward along transportation spines, and he suggested this condition could be addressed with his concept of "Dynapolis," cities whose downtowns were perpetually being rebuilt along a transportation spine that was continually moving farther from the original center of settlement. Aware of Jean Gottman's Megalopolis concept, based on his detailed study of the actual development patterns of the postwar U.S. Northeast corridor, in 1968 Doxiadis also put forward the influential idea of *Ecumenopolis* (1974), predicting that the world's major urban regions would all grow into each other along highway routes by 2100.

As Doxiadis was beginning to work globally, Town Planning Associates was working in pre-Castro Cuba, where the firm was commissioned in 1955 by the corrupt U.S.-backed military government of President Fulgencio Batista for the Plan Piloto de la Habana (Havana Master Plan) for a city of then about 800,000 residents. Sert and Wiener had begun formulating a national planning program for Cuba in 1953, similar to what they had previously proposed in Colombia. Batista seems to have commissioned these efforts as part of an effort to create a new architectural image for his government to attract North American investment. Sert worked on the Havana part of the plan with Cuban architect Mario Romañach (1917–1984), director of Havana's metropolitan planning department, during the summer of 1955, and with Wiener proposed a comprehensive restructuring of the transportation, recreation, and public space structure of the city. This included a proposal for the (later much criticized) remodeling of the Old City, which called for controlled development of pedestrian-oriented high-rises. A key, though ironic, feature of the plan was a network of civic cores for democratic public assembly, located adjacent to residential urban sectors with social services sited throughout the city.

After the Cuban revolution (1959), Town Planning Associates sought to continue the work under the early (pre-Soviet) Fidel Castro regime, but dissolved their firm after this request was denied. Sert, by then working with his new Boston-area firm, Sert, Jackson & Associates, went on to design numerous highly regarded urban infill projects at Harvard University, Boston University, University of Guelph (Canada), and other sites in the late 1950s and 1960s (fig. 101). At the same time, Wiener designed the large superblock slabs of the Washington Square Village project (1959) near New York University without Sert's involvement, and the innovative urban design work of TPA in Latin America between 1944 and 1958 quickly faded into historical obscurity, forever shadowed by its Cold War political circumstances.

101. Sert, Jackson & Associates, Peabody Terrace Married Student Housing, Harvard University, 1963–65.

TEAM 10 AND ITS CONTEXTS, 1954–81

By the late 1950s, CIAM-inspired modernist planning had become a world-wide phenomenon and included the design not only of new cities like Chandigarh and Brasília, but also of many high-rise urban mass housing and university campus projects in the 1950s and 1960s. As these projects were being designed, CIAM urbanism itself was undergoing significant revisions, resulting in the approaches offered by Sert at the Harvard Urban Design program and in the parallel work of Doxiadis Associates. It was at this time that modern urbanism also began to be criticized from a variety of directions. These critical directions ranged from the relatively subtle revisions of CIAM doctrine from within by Sert, Rogers, and Tyrwhitt in favor of more pedestrian street life and responsiveness to existing urban contexts, to the more radical rejections of modern urbanism by the Situationists, Jane Jacobs, and postmodern urbanism, discussed in Chapter Seven.

The first criticisms of modern urbanism established ways of thinking about CIAM modernism that are still widespread. These were voiced both by Team 10, a group of CIAM youth members that emerged in 1954, and by members of the Paris-based Lettrist International, a radical avant-garde group of artists founded in 1946. Team 10's founding members included the young British architects Alison (1928–1993) and Peter Smithson (1923–2003); the Dutch architects Jacob Bakema (1914–1981) and Aldo Van Eyck (1918–1999); Georges Candilis (1913–1995), a French architect of Greek ancestry born in Baku, Azerbaijan, and Shadrach Woods (1923–1973), an Irish-American, both of whom had worked for Le Corbusier on the Unité d'Habitation project as part of the ATBAT team in 1948 and then worked under the French planner Michel Ecochard

Urban Design, Team 10, and Metabolism After 1953

(1905–1985) in Morocco on the ATBAT-Afrique group until 1952. Some of these CIAM members (though not the Smithsons) had also attended the Sigtuna, Sweden, CIAM meeting of 1952 with Tyrwhitt, representing the MARS group, where they had begun discussing the future of CIAM in light of postwar concerns about the "human habitat" generally.

These younger CIAM members found that they shared some dissatis-factions with the organization as it then existed with the young British MARS group members William and Gillian Howell, John Voelcker, and the Smithsons, who were invited at the last minute to CIAM 9 by Bill How-ell, who had been Tyrwhitt's assistant on the CIAM 8: The Heart of the City publication. At CIAM 9 these CIAM "youth members" found common ground with Van Eyck, who was vehemently opposed to Walter Gropius's technocratic, corporate, American-based postwar architectural views centered on prefabrication. Instead, they began to call attention to the validity of "non-Western" architectural cultures for CIAM, as well as to the need to respond to the needs and values of actual urban working-class inhabitants of European cities.

The Moroccan housing work of Candilis and Woods exhibited at CIAM 9 had attempted to lay out what would later be called a "sites and services" approach to self-built housing. This involved the use of an 8 × 8-meter (26-foot, 3-inch) housing grid that could be provided with sewer lines and possibly other utility services, which could then be in-filled by residents building their own houses. This approach had some precedents in colonial and other planning, including earlier French ef-forts in Moroccan cities, and its use at CIAM by Candilis & Woods was an effort to raise the issue in CIAM of the design of mass housing in cities for what the ATBAT-Afrique member Vladimir Bodiansky began to call at this time "la plus grande nombre" (the greater number). Sert and Tyrwhitt were extremely interested in CIAM addressing these ideas, yet at CIAM 9 the group was unable to come to any general agreement about how to approach them, much less agree on the worldwide "Charter of Habitat" that Le Corbusier had called for postwar CIAM to produce.

It was at this point that the Team 10 group of "youth members," orig-inally intended by Sert and the CIAM council to reenergize the organiza-tion, began to challenge the control of the Harvard GSD-centered group of Gropius, Sert, Giedion, and Tyrwhitt. The youth members were given the task of organizing CIAM 10, which Sert and Tyrwhitt were then planning to hold in Algiers in 1955, but Team 10 characterized the CIAM leadership as out of touch with postwar European and North African cultural and urban realities. They linked this with what they saw as the group's reduc-tive earlier approach to urbanism, which focused on the "four functions" of dwelling, work, recreation, and transportation. Team 10 also mostly rejected Sert's advocacy of both the patio house and the concept of the heart of the city, though they retained Sert's emphasis on pedestrian urban experience. At CIAM 8, Dutch CIAM member Bakema had shown a project for a community core for Rotterdam by the Opbouw group and had asked, "At what moment can we really speak of core—the core that we can place in architecture and town planning?" He answered that perhaps the core was not a space but rather the "moment when we become aware of the fullness of life by means of cooperative action," meaning that the core should be understood not as a monumental civic plaza but rather as a moment of collective awareness that could be enhanced (but not produced) by architecture. Bakema then recalled a recent visit to Asplund's Stockholm crematorium, which he suggested might also be a core of sorts, and proposed that even a Finnish sauna might function as one as well.

Around the same time, in a 1951 letter to Van Eyck, Bakema inaccurately derided Le Corbusier's Bogotá, Colombia, core project, commissioned by an elected mayor, as a monument designed for a "dictator who recently took power in a military coup." Van Eyck would later suggest that the core might have validity as a place where people could express "spontaneous feelings," but he questioned Sert's efforts to fit this concept within the CIAM framework: "The inadequacy of the old analytical approach became very apparent during the next congress in Hoddesdon in 1951. It became clear that it was just the functions which elude classification within the rigid grid of the four functions that make the concept of 'core' so much richer than the concept 'civic center.' In other words, it became apparent that the things which endow a city with real urbanity—make it a city—fall through the coarse mesh of the four functions. It became clear that they lie beyond the narrow scope of rational and analytical thinking."

With their "Doorn Manifesto" in 1954, Team 10 members publicly rejected the four functions–based urbanism of CIAM and sought to distance themselves from the Harvard GSD-based "American professors," as the Smithsons described the CIAM Council members Gropius, Sert, Giedion, and Tyrwhitt in 1956. During and after CIAM 9, energized by their common sense of discontent with CIAM as a group, these younger members began to meet as "Team 10." Although Team 10 rejected Tyrwhitt's influence in CIAM, the Doorn Manifesto nonetheless continued her efforts to link CIAM's approaches with the regionalist and ecological planning ideals of Geddes. Unlike Tyrwhitt, though, Team 10 also rejected CIAM categories, and instead advocated that urban research and design be organized according to a version of Geddes's Valley Section. This was redrawn by Peter Smithson in a way that suggested that urban environments could be analyzed on a "transect," a term not used by Team 10 but which would later be used in the 1990s by the Congress for the New Urbanism. It would run from isolated houses in the countryside through suburban areas into dense environments in the central city.

Instead of the CIAM four functions, Team 10 proposed that "human association" be examined within this Geddesian "field" on a "scale of association," and that this approach should become the basis for analyzing the projects at CIAM 10. Team 10 suggested that the functional terminology of CIAM, based on a set of categories that had emerged out of the demands of prewar working-class political movements, be replaced with a "hierarchy of human associations" based on direct phenomenological experience of metropolitan environments, which they saw as more relevant. Instead of the CIAM four functions, the Smithsons proposed "house, street, district, and city" as the organizing categories for the comparative analysis of CIAM projects.

Team 10's polemics oversimplified the ideas of CIAM as it was then being reoriented by Sert, Rogers, and Tyrwhitt, but Team 10's views shaped perceptions of postwar CIAM for generations. Looked at less polemically, the ideas of Team 10 did not always break radically with those of postwar CIAM, though they generally used a different rhetorical and presentation style. CIAM and Team 10 shared the idea that urbanism was a global practice and that "no border line" could be drawn between architecture and city planning. They also both shared the belief that the built environment could be shaped by design with what Giedion called "spatial imagination," which he defined as an "imagination that can dispose volumes in space in such a way that new relations develop between differing structures, different edifices, so that they can merge into a new synthesis."

Team 10's focus on "habitat" was also a direct continuation of the efforts of postwar CIAM to write a "Charte d'Habitat" (Habitat Charter) to replace the Athens Charter. Producing this document was the official goal of both CIAM 9 and CIAM 10, but Team 10's challenge to the organization made this impossible. Related ideas, quite similar to those of Team 10, can be found in projects by other CIAM participants in the 1950s, as in the diverse works of Arne Korsmo and the PAGON group in Norway; Roland Simounet, Roger and Edith Schreiber-Aujame, and Atelier de Montrouge (Pierre Riboulet, Jean-Luis Véret, Gerard Thurnauer, and Jean Renaudie) in France and Algeria; and Georges Brera and Paul Waltenspühl of Geneva, among others. These were architects whose work and writings were for the most part written out of received modern architectural history in Van Eyck's and Alison Smithson's accounts of Team 10, and many of these architects remain obscure even today.

Most of the planning and urban design outcomes of such ideas were well in the future in 1954, and the more immediate result of the Team 10 responses to CIAM 9 was to offer a new sensibility about the potential for architecture to shape urban life. This was most clear in the Smithsons' CIAM 9 presentation, which showed their unplaced design in a competition for rebuilding a war-damaged area of the City of London known as Golden Lane. The drawings and photographs for this project, a series of linked sixteen-story slab buildings connected by "streets in the air," were influenced by the Smithsons' associations with artist members of the

London Independent Group (IG), which included the photographer Nigel Henderson and the artist Ed Paolozzi. This project anticipated the work of the Dutch artist Constant, the Situationist group, Metabolism, and Archigram, while at the same time continuing to explore then-mainstream CIAM ideas about housing patterns and urban mobility. The Smithsons' work and image, reflecting their working-class backgrounds in the North of England, was intentionally provocative. Inspired by their membership in the IG, they sought to create London-based conceptual projects in architecture, urbanism, and exhibition and graphic design that both continued the innovations of prewar modernists and challenged their postwar institutionalization. The Smithsons insisted that their work and activities could lead a younger generation of architects to recover the lost energy and social relevance of the avant-gardes of the 1920s by overturning the bland official acceptance of modernism after the war.

Their Golden Lane project reflects this moment clearly: the Smithsons' "urban re-identification" grid for CIAM 9 in 1953 was structured to subvert the grid's rationalistic intentions and provoke new ways of thinking about urbanism. Instead of following the systematic format developed by Le Corbusier and his French associates and based on the four functions, the Smithsons suggested reorganizing the CIAM grid with their new categories. They also implicitly questioned the uniform rationality of the grid presentation by using Henderson's photos of street children playing in the Bethnal Green district of London's East End, the kind of area that the MARS group, the sociologist Ruth Glass (1912–1990), and Tyrwhitt had been researching since the 1930s.

In contrast to the aspirations of the older generation of CIAM to systematically shape postwar urban development through legislation, pedagogy, and the exhibition of model projects, the new youth-oriented sensibility of the Smithsons and Team 10 was more elusive. It was disseminated in art exhibitions and events, publications, and in charismatic design studio teaching, much of it at the Architectural Association (AA), where Peter Smithson inspired students as diverse as Kenneth Frampton and Denise Scott Brown. The irrational, surrealist-inspired qualities of their work resonated widely in architecture in the late 1950s and early 1960s, an era of worldwide popularity for Hollywood films, rock and roll, Coca-Cola, cigarettes, and other products of American consumer capitalism. Alison Smithson praised American advertising in avant-garde London journals, particularly the 1954 Cadillac advertising campaign, and a photo cut-out of French movie star Gerard Philippe appears in the Golden Lane photomontage where a prewar worker might have been expected to stand. In another perspective, magazine cut-outs of movie stars like Marilyn Monroe interact along the Smithsons' proposed Corbusian pedestrian street deck.

Though they were unable to construct any such projects until 1966, the Smithsons made further elaborations of the idea in unbuilt

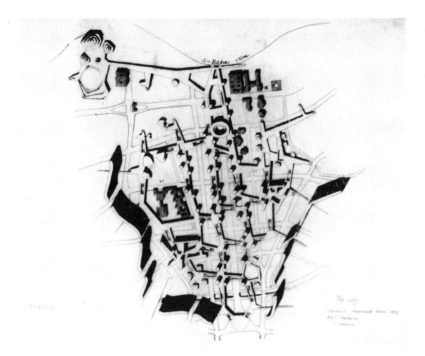

102. Alison and Peter
Smithson, with Peter
Sigmond, Berlin Hauptstadt
competition, third prize,
1957–58 (Alison Smithson,
Team 10 Primer [Cambridge,
Mass.: MIT Press, 1968], 56).

competition entries for Sheffield University (1953) and in their entry to the
Berlin Hauptstadt (Capital City) competition in 1957–58, designed with a
German associate, Peter Sigmond (fig. 102). Their team was awarded only
third place in the Berlin competition, but the Smithsons's well-publicized
project was intended to suggest a new urban structure that would "give
the motorist and the pedestrian equal rights to freedom of movement."
This perhaps echoed the demand in postwar West Berlin for a rebuilt city
that "does justice to the car." The Berlin Hauptstadt project elaborated
the Smithsons' concept of continuous pedestrian street decks, suggesting that these be built over what remained of the street grid in the heavily bomb-damaged central city. Their project indicated that these streets
should be the channels for auto traffic and casual parking, while various
new and existing cultural institutions would be accessed by continuously
running escalators to the second-level pedestrian decks, ninety-eight
feet (30 meters) above.

This project was soon followed by urban design works—by the
Smithsons, Candilis-Josic-Woods, Kenzo Tange, and others—that developed and extended the Team 10 challenge to the mid-century urbanistic certainties of CIAM, based on the siting of buildings with ample open
spaces between them and the separation of pedestrian and vehicular
traffic. Bakema's Lijnbaan project in the rebuilt center of Rotterdam
(1948–53), though not shown at CIAM meetings, was a widely influential
project that combined high-rise apartment and office buildings with a
pedestrian shopping street, offering a non-rhetorical way of rebuilding
cities to accommodate pedestrians and mass transit (fig. 103). It was

103. Van den Broek & Bakema, Lijnbaan mixed-use complex, Rotterdam, 1948–53 (Frits Monshouwer, from Hans Ibelings, ed., *Van den Broek and Bakema, 1948–1988* [Rotterdam: NAi Uitgevers, 2000], 105).

completed just after Dutch CIAM members Van Tijen and Maaskant's less well-known mixed-use commercial complex nearby, the Groothandelsgebouw (1947–52), whose complex, multifunctional interiors would inspire Rem Koolhaas. The Smithsons' former Economist building in London (1962) also put a new emphasis on pedestrian pathways on its urban site, as well as using a new, non-Miesian stone cladding system that also soon became widely used in downtowns worldwide.

At CIAM 8, Giedion had mentioned historical examples of the CIAM "core" concept, such as the agoras of Athens and Priene, the forum of Pompeii, the Roman forum, and Michelangelo's Campidoglio in Rome. All were projects laden with historical European political significance, and in some ways they may have seemed out of touch with the pragmatic atmosphere of the postwar era of decolonization. But Giedion had also noted Aldo Van Eyck's small Amsterdam playgrounds at CIAM 8, which his young Dutch protégé had begun to design by the hundreds on vacant sites for the Town Planning Section of the Amsterdam Public Works department. These typically included a sandpit, usually outlined as a simple geometric shape, with a low (1-foot/30-centimeter) wall of prefabricated concrete elements. Other elements included cylindrical concrete "stones" between 8 and 20 inches tall (20–50 centimeters), and 26 inches in diameter (65 centimeters), arranged in rings or rows, and evoking ancient sites and the Romanian artist Constantin Brancusi's park seats in Târgu Jiu, Romania (1935). More delicate constructions of metal tubing were sometimes used as well, to create climbing frames and arches, with the entire playground surrounded by hedges, shrubs, and sometimes trees. Van Eyck developed a multiplicity of arrangements for these simple elements, often inspired by such modern artists as Mondrian and Hans Arp. As more of the playgrounds were built, they were sited to create continuous networks of public places throughout the central residential areas of the city.

Their simple, durable, multi-use elements allowed children to use the playgrounds in a variety of creative ways, and they proved immensely popular, leading by the 1960s to the construction of many similar "adventure playgrounds" in America and elsewhere. Van Eyck wrote about the way the playgrounds made the city come alive through spontaneous activities in his 1956 essay, "When Snow Falls on Cities," and displayed some of them at CIAM 10 in Dubrovnik. By the 1960s they had become strongly identified with the Team 10 approach and had inspired many other urban designers, including Jan Gehl (born 1936) in Copenhagen, whose efforts to create informal pedestrian public space in the central city continue to generate many similar interventions worldwide.

A related design approach, though one that was in some ways less open ended, was used by Van Eyck for an institutional building, the Amsterdam Municipal Orphanage, commissioned in 1954 (fig. 104). To avoid the grim institutional forms usual in such buildings, typically organized as wings along double-loaded corridors, Van Eyck designed the project as a series of eight small "houses," each a living facility for children of the same age group, organized along a "meandering interior street with interior piazzas in such a way that they are invited to mix and go from one department to the other." At the entrance of the complex, on a busy traffic way in a nondescript area near a stadium just beyond the older central part of Amsterdam, Van Eyck designed an "entrance square," accessed under a two-story wing of staff offices. Each "house" had its own domed gathering space, inspired by North African vernacular mosques. The complex, interlocking organization of the Orphanage was described by Van Eyck as having "labyrinthine clarity," like the casbahs, or old Arab cities, of North Africa.

This interest in North African cities was not related to the many later waves of immigration to Europe from the Middle East, but was instead an extension of earlier elite European interest in the formal and exotic qualities of that region, which was shared by Van Eyck's fellow Team 10 members Candilis and Woods, who founded the Paris architecture firm Candilis-Josic-Woods in 1954. They and the Smithsons were all interested

at this time in new urban ordering systems for architecture that were flexible, open-ended, and potentially usable to address the needs of the masses of people then moving into cities. Unlike the CIAM effort to site structures for collective housing widely apart from each other, to preserve open ground and increase light, air circulation, and views, in Team 10's work there was an emphasis on "cluster," as the Smithsons would describe it, and a search for dense, pedestrian environments that would have some of the spatial and social qualities of premodern cities, rather than the dispersed suburban and public housing environments being built at the time.

This architectural interest in formal ordering systems had returned in the late 1940s through the influence of the German émigré art historian Rudolf Wittkower (1901–1971), who offered a new interpretation of the proportional and organizational systems of Renaissance architecture in his *Architectural Principles in the Age of Humanism* (1949). One of Wittkower's doctoral students at the Warburg Institute in London, Colin Rowe (1920–1999), began to use similar approaches to understand the ordering systems of modern architecture. Rowe's influential essay "The Mathematics of the Ideal Villa" (1947) suggested that the sixteenth-century classical villas of Andrea Palladio and the seemingly very different canonical modern houses of Le Corbusier in the 1920s in fact shared some basic planning and organizational patterns.

Rowe studied architecture at Liverpool University and served in the British military in World War II. After then briefly teaching at Liverpool he began teaching design and history at the University of Texas-Austin in 1953. While there, Rowe inspired a group of young faculty and students later called the "Texas Rangers." This group included the Swiss architect Bernard Hoesli (1923–1984) and the painter Robert Slutzky (1929–2005), who began to question the idea, which had taken hold in modern architecture, that architectural design was primarily a consequence of original individual talent. The Texas Rangers instead focused on architectural ideas, often expressed as visual metaphors, and introduced careful formal analytical studies of the plans, sections, and elevations of existing buildings, frequently those of Palladio, Le Corbusier, and Mies.

The Texas Rangers also reintroduced concepts from Gestalt psychology, already part of modern design in Germany in the 1920s, with a new focus on understanding visual hierarchies, dominant forms, figure-ground relationships, and notably, transparency. Rowe and Slutzky defined this quality in "Transparency: Literal and Phenomenal," an essay written in 1955 (though not published until 1963), as including both literal transparency, like that found at the Bauhaus building, or having instead what they described as "phenomenal transparency," the spatial experience of moving through built overlapping planes, as in the layered facades of Le Corbusier's Villa Stein in Garches.

There were many later outcomes of this kind of new "formalism" in modern architecture, among them an immediate shift in the direction of Louis Kahn's work in the mid-1950s, which had begun even before he had a prolonged conversation with Rowe in December 1955 on these topics. Kahn's Trenton Bath House (1955), designed with his Harvard GSD–educated associate Anne Tyng (1920–2011), departed from Miesian "universal space" and instead grouped a set of enclosed pool changing rooms with wood-shingled pyramidal roofs, built simply with concrete blocks, around a light-filled central open space. The resulting structure introduced abstract references to "timeless" ancient architectural spaces into an otherwise modern suburban project. This project, along with Kahn's drawings of unbuilt designs for Center City Philadelphia, also designed with Tyng, which called for pedestrianizing the center of the city several years prior to Victor Gruen's *Greater Fort Worth Tomorrow* project, led the Smithsons to invite Kahn to speak at the first Team 10 congress, CIAM '59 in Otterlo.

Kahn's "Talk at the Conclusion of the Otterlo Congress" introduced his influential idea that "architecture is the thoughtful making of spaces," with a new emphasis on the emotional effects of natural light. Kahn argued that since every architectural program has an existence-will (a concept Kahn took from the nineteenth-century philosopher Arthur Schopenhauer), the designer should always be asking, "What does the building or object want to be?" He suggested that in any large city, "the street in the middle of the town wants to be a building." Designed in this way, the street can have a place for both walking under the buildings and over them: "It is really a contour, it is really a level." Referring to the Smithsons' work, Kahn noted that streets can be a "kind of place." He also emphasized that "every city is made up of institutions," and therefore the making of cities involves their organization as well. These include not only auditoria, universities, schools, and houses, but even garages for cars arriving in the city, which Kahn in his Philadelphia projects proposed as sculptural monumental "gateways" to the pedestrian city. He emphasized that "a city has a framework based on movement."

The square is a place where pedestrians can stop, yet in a modern city it has lost the social centrality that European traditional squares once had. Unlike Sert and Tyrwhitt, Kahn doubted that American shopping centers had much potential to become true public spaces, as they were simply "devices for buying."

Instead, Kahn sought a new kind of modernist monumentality that in some ways continued the aspirations of the classical tradition with new forms (fig. 105). This was clearly evident in his commissions in South Asia, which included the Ahmedabad campus of the Indian Institute of Management (1962–74) and the new capital of what was then East Pakistan, Shar-e-Bangla-Nagar (1962–83), commissioned by the U.S.-supported Pakistani dictator Ayub Kahn. After its completion (with David Wisdom) it became the much-admired capital complex of Bangladesh, a new state founded after civil war in 1971.

At CIAM '59 in Otterlo, Team 10 decided to stop using the CIAM name, a decision regretted by many, including Kenzo Tange, the Japanese CIAM delegate. Yet it was Team 10, not CIAM, that became the main new direction in modern architecture around 1960. The "mat building" concept, a one- or several-level grid of enclosed and open spaces organized into an open-ended pattern, made its appearance in the Candilis-Josic-Woods competition entry for Frankfurt-Römerberg (1963), a proposal for rebuilding the bombed center of the city. Similar ideas were then used by the same firm in their built Berlin Free University project (1963–65) in West Berlin (fig. 106).

Candilis, Josic, and Woods had become major figures in the massive construction of peripheral new towns and social housing developments in France in the 1950s. Paralleling the Smithsons' interest in the effects of mobility and dense commercial development, they had designed two new town projects in 1961, Caen-Hérouville and Toulouse-le-Mirail, presenting the latter project at the Team 10 meeting at Abbaye Royaumont in 1962. These and other Candilis-Josic-Woods works called for the use of "stems" of circulation joined into "webs" to create a new urban structure. Large ten-story residential slab buildings were linked by low-rise linear pedestrian stems joining various public uses. Their goal was to provide a new form of continuous pedestrian-oriented urban development to counter the isolated towers set in open space of postwar mass housing,

which for Team 10 defined earlier CIAM urbanism. Woods believed that "the structure of cities lies not in their geometries but in the activities within them," which are "expressed or materialized by buildings and spaces, by ways and places, by the articulation of the public and private domains." In this articulation, as Shadrach Woods noted in 1962, a key issue was the "reconciliation of speeds" between cars and pedestrians. Candilis-Josic-Woods designed their projects so that private car journeys were "point to point," ending in cul-de-sacs linked to parking structures within the towers, while pedestrian movement in the stem elements could be more direct and open-ended. Woods saw their projects less as final master plans than as an expression of a "way of planning," which could change over time.

106. Candilis-Josic-Woods, Berlin Free University, 1963–65.

Several important Team 10 meetings were held in the early 1960s without reference to CIAM, including at Bagnols-sur-Cèze near Marseille in 1960, attended by Fumihiko Maki (born 1928). At the Royaumont meeting in 1962, about twenty mostly younger architects argued about the reciprocal relationship between building groups and infrastructure, a topic of great concern at the time as new housing projects and new expressway systems were transforming major industrial cities from London to Tokyo. Presentations included not only the work of Candilis-Josic-Woods but also megastructural projects by Bakema, by the Italian Team 10 member Giancarlo de Carlo (1919–2005), Josep Coderch (1913–1984) from Barcelona, and by the Polish Team 10 member Stefan Wewerka, as well as by the Japanese Metabolist Kisho Kurokawa (1934–2007), who presented his idea of a capsule tower, later built as the Nakagin Capsule Tower in Tokyo (1970). Royaumont also included James Stirling's presentation of his Leicester University Engineering Building (1959–63), which Alison Smithson later edited out of the published proceedings.

The Royaumont meeting also involved a dispute between core Team 10 members concerning the nature of urbanism itself. Van Eyck presented two student projects from his teaching at the Amsterdam Academy of Art, one of which, by his student Piet Blom (1934–1999) called "Noah's Ark," was a gigantic urban design scheme for housing a million people by linking sixty villages around Amsterdam into an "interurban entity" of seventy villages of ten thousand to fifteen thousand people. Each 148-acre (60-hectare) village was organized into interlocking built clusters that provided for a range of urban functions, all tied together by a four-level road network. By making the traffic infrastructure a basic part of the project, Blom proposed the total integration of infrastructure and building groups within it. Royaumont guests Guillermo Jullian de la Fuente (Le Corbusier's chief design associate at the time), Kurokawa, Wewerka, and then-Portuguese Mozambique–based Team 10 member Amancio Guedes (1925–2015) all admired the scheme, but the Smithsons and Voelcker were highly critical.

In his presentation Van Eyck had referred to Renaissance theorist Alberti's well-known analogy that a city should be like a large house, with each part characterized by both enclosure and openness. This idea was related to Van Eyck's efforts to develop a "configurative discipline" of urbanism, where he took issue with the then widely accepted view that architects should build for the anonymous ideal client of government housing corporations. Instead, architects should provide "urban interiors . . . built counterforms" to reinforce group identities, such as those found in vernacular villages and towns around the world, including those of the Dogon of Mali or the Zuñi Pueblo Native Americans of New Mexico. Van Eyck saw the Blom project as an excellent demonstration of these ideas, a city as "a hierarchy of superimposed configurative systems multilaterally conceived."

The Smithsons vehemently objected to the repetitiveness of Blom's project, and Alison saw it as a "completely Fascist" attempt to control all aspects of future urban growth, thus ending Van Eyck's efforts to develop his new urbanistic discipline within the framework of Team 10. Nonetheless, for Le Corbusier and Jullian de la Fuente, Blom's work was the inspiration for their unbuilt Venice Hospital project (1963–66). In the discussion of Blom's project, Van Eyck had added to the city/house metaphor by invoking the idea that a city should also have a tree/leaf structure, where the detailed organization of the leaf is then mirrored at a larger scale in the tree itself, or, as he put it in his famous leaf-tree diagram, "tree is leaf and leaf is tree—house is city and city is house."

In response, Christopher Alexander, then working in rural development in India, pointed out that "a tree is not a big leaf." This reflected his growing doubts about the hierarchical diagrams of 141 functional requirements that he had developed to guide the design of new villages in India that respected local Hindu customs and culture. He had prepared the diagrams for his Harvard University dissertation, which he published as *Notes on the Synthesis of Form* (1964). At the Royaumont meeting,

Alexander described how these efforts to quantify the various functional needs in turn produced a method to organize patterns of those needs into a series of linked categories, which were then used in early computer programs. He would then develop these into his influential concept of *A Pattern Language* (1968). By using this mathematically generated (though not statistically based) method, Alexander ultimately rejected Van Eyck's tree image in his article "A City Is Not a Tree" (1965), arguing that a city does not have a hierarchical treelike structure, but can instead be represented by a semi-lattice diagram of overlapping functional and cultural linkages that take account of overlaps, continuities, and accidents.

The Royaumont meeting in 1962 perhaps marked the high point of Team 10's efforts to continue CIAM-like deliberations on the future of architects' relation to urbanism, but the proceedings show that general agreement was no longer possible. Van Eyck and Blom would go on to be an influence on Dutch Structuralism and the work of Hermann Hertzberger (born 1932) and other architects, but this direction would have relatively little in common with Candilis-Josic-Woods's ultimately doomed efforts to restructure urban industrial societies in vast new megastructures, or with De Carlo's sensitive contextual interventions in historic Italian cities. Parallel to these efforts was McGill University architecture student Moshe Safdie's 1961 architectural design thesis, "A Three-Dimensional Modular Building System." Safdie used his system as the basis for Habitat—a demonstration mass-housing project built on an island in the Saint Lawrence River for Expo '67 in Montreal—which then became an influential housing model in many places for decades thereafter (fig. 107).

Despite its internal discord, Team 10 had extensive influence on built work in the 1960s, and many British urban and university projects were designed along Team 10 lines, some inspired by the Smithsons' unbuilt Sheffield University extension competition entry of 1953. These included

107. Moshe Safdie, Habitat, Expo '67, Montreal, 1965–67.

the large Park Hill public housing project in Sheffield (1957–61), a direct and successful application of the Golden Lane concept by the Sheffield City Architects Department (J. Lewis Womersley, Jack Lynn, and Ivor Smith). Denys Lasdun's University of East Anglia, Norwich (1963–66), was an example of the Smithsons' Brutalist megastructural campus idea that would also be widely imitated in North America in the 1960s, only to be vehemently rejected by many university administrations by the 1990s. Lasdun's work, a departure from his earlier CIAM-inspired slab housing with detached public facilities, was praised by the Smithsons, indicating the complete triumph of the ideas first put forward in their Golden Lane project over earlier CIAM planning concepts favored by the older generation of MARS group members.

JAPANESE METABOLISM, CIRCA 1960

After the massive destruction of World War II, Japan began to develop as a key link between the United States and East Asia. During the Korean conflict (1950–53), when United Nations forces led by the United States pushed back the Soviet- and Chinese-supported North Koreans from occupying the entire Korean peninsula, goods manufacturing for export in Japan greatly increased. Tokyo, Osaka, and other Japanese cities were quickly rebuilt and again began to grow rapidly. By 1960, Japan had begun to establish a new national identity as an international center of design and industry, a reputation that continues to the present. Kenzo Tange won a competition to design the Hiroshima Memorial Park in 1949, part of an overall master plan for the war-destroyed city. Tange's design, shown at CIAM 8 in 1951, was the first non-Western project to be shown at CIAM. He went on to design numerous civic projects in Japan in the 1950s, including an earlier version of Tokyo City Hall (demolished for Rafael Viñoly's Tokyo International Forum), and participated in the Team 10 meeting at CIAM '59 at Otterlo.

As part of the preparations for the World Design Conference in Tokyo planned for 1960, Tange also organized a group of younger Japanese architects who issued a bilingual pamphlet called *Metabolism/1960: The Proposals for New Urbanism.* These architects shared a view of cities as living organisms, able to adapt and evolve during periods of rapid growth or decline and always changing to fit the way that people live. At the same time, Tange designed and widely publicized a project for extending Tokyo over Tokyo Bay, a further development of an MIT studio project for mixed-use megastructures over water that he and his students had produced in 1959. The key principle in Tange's Tokyo Bay project was the distinction between fixed long-term infrastructural elements like highways and utility lines, and more changeable high-rise commercial and housing elements, which could be modified over time (fig. 108). The Metabolist group members around Tange, who included Kisho Kurokawa,

108. Kenzo Tange, Tokyo Bay project, 1960 (Kawasumi Kobayashi Kenji Photograph Office Co., Ltd).

Kiyonori Kikutake (1928–2011), and Fumihiko Maki, explored these related ideas, each in their own way, proposing urban projects that used new technologies to create new frameworks for urban life. Kikutake proposed a "Marine City" of floating structures—inspired both by contemporary off-shore oil platforms and by Bertrand Goldberg's Marina City in Chicago (1959)—that was included in the CIAM '59 publication, while Kurokawa developed frameworks for aggregated independent volumes of minimum living units, like his Nakagin Capsule Tower in Tokyo (fig. 109).

In the *Metabolism/1960* pamphlet, Maki and Masao Ōtaka (1923–2010) jointly wrote the essay "Toward Group Form," which they illustrated with their project to redevelop Tokyo's Shinjuku district. The project was part of a long series of large-scale urban revitalization projects in Japan that explored the issues of artificial land and civic centers in Japan in the 1950s. These issues were related to urban renewal projects elsewhere in the world, but were also part of efforts to overturn the Japanese building law that limited building heights to 100 feet (30.48 meters). By far the most important of Tokyo's commuter railway hubs, Shinjuku was identified as a candidate for the new law on "special urban zones" that would come into effect a year later, in 1961.

Maki, born in Tokyo, had studied with Sert at the Harvard GSD in 1953–54 before taking up an architectural design studio teaching position at Washington University in St. Louis in 1955, where he designed his first building, Steinberg Hall (1960). Ōtaka was one of the most important designers in the office of Kunio Maekawa (1905–1986), a Japanese CIAM member, in the 1950s. Ōtaka worked on urban-scale projects like the Momijigaoka civic center in Yokohama (1954), which used postwar-CIAM ideas of the urban core to compose the grouping of the Kanagawa Prefectural Library, Music Hall, Youth Center, and Women's Center. While in Maekawa's office Ōtaka also designed the Harumi Apartments (1958), intended to be a Japanese version of Le Corbusier's Unité. Maki and Ōtaka's

focus on "artificial land" led to studies by the Architectural Institute of
Japan in 1962–63 and to the construction of the Sakaide Artificial Land
development, a residential neighborhood in the rural town of Sakaide,
realized in over four phases between 1966 and 1986.

Maki's international influence increased with his cofounding of the
Washington University in St. Louis Master of Architecture and Urban Design program in 1962, supported by Dean Joe Passonneau (1921–2011),
a 1949 graduate of Gropius's and Dean Joseph Hudnut's Harvard GSD. In
1958, Maki won a traveling scholarship from the Graham Foundation in
Chicago; he went to Athens and across Asia before returning to Japan
to attend the World Design Conference. Not long after his return to St.
Louis, in 1962, Maki published his *Investigations in Collective Form* (1964)
with Jerry Goldberg, where he proposed Group Form as an urban design
method to allow for growth and change in urban environments. Since
these environments would inevitably be generated by many different
builders over time, Maki suggested that a consistent urban image could
be maintained through the use of repeating systems of generative built
elements. He cited historic examples that included Greek island towns

Urban Design, Team 10, and Metabolism After 1953

or the varied repeating traditional dwelling types of African villages. As in these examples, the overall urban image (cubic white stucco stone structures in the Greek islands, or round thatch in African village huts) remained constant, even as specific aspects of these built environments were continuously being modified.

Group Form proposed an evolving system of elements capable of proposing, through architecture, urban districts that could handle without visual disruption the new postwar scale of express highway systems, which could at the same time stimulate social vitality and interconnectivity in situations of permanent growth and change. It incorporated the ideas of urban legibility from Kevin Lynch and Gyorgy Kepes, with the goal of generating "master programs" to calibrate the dynamic equilibrium of forces in cities that Maki understood to be not only composed of static built elements but also to always be produced by systemic patterns of events. In this way, Group Form responded to the urban issues raised by the Situationists, but without sharing their explicitly disruptive and revolutionary political agenda. Maki also suggested that Group Form could avoid the problems of both static "Compositional Form" of monumental architecture (from Versailles to the Monumental Core of Chandigarh), as well as the excessive emphasis on technology in the new "megastructures" (a term that Maki coined in his *Investigations in Collective Form*), such as Tange's Tokyo Bay proposal.

At Sert's invitation, Maki joined the urban design faculty at the Harvard GSD, where he taught a series of urban design studios between 1962 and 1965 on "Movement Systems in the City." His students included the Argentine architect Mario Corea (born 1939), who would use related ideas in his many urban projects in Rosario, Argentina, and Barcelona. Maki's focus on Movement Systems at this time was conceptualized as part of a multimodal transportation plan for the "New Boston" being proposed by the Boston Redevelopment Authority (BRA) and its planning director, Ed Logue. Boston's aging transit system, which included the first subway system in the United States (1896), was renamed the "T" in 1964, and new color-coded lines inspired by the London Underground were designated, with graphics and station designs by Cambridge Seven Associates and others. Within this redesigned transit system, Maki and his students examined the potential of new kinds of pedestrian urban spaces, which they called the "City Room" and the "City Corridor." These concepts soon had considerable worldwide influence and were realized in part at Maki's Risshō University's campus near Tokyo (1967; demolished) and his Senri Central District Center (1970; demolished), a community center for a rail-accessible new town outside of Osaka with a planned population of 150,000. Design ideas related to both Group Form and Sert's urbanism were also present to some extent in one of Maki's most well-known early projects, the Hillside Terrace mixed-use housing complex in Tokyo (1968–92) (fig. 110).

Metabolist influences then expanded through East Asia. William Lim (born 1932), a Harvard GSD student in 1956–57, designed the Golden Mile complex in his native Singapore (1974), a stepped megastructure along the new downtown Beach Road, and many similar projects soon followed. These included mixed-use projects by Paul Rudolph (1918–1997) such as The Concourse in Singapore (1979–94), a mixed-use tower with four-story office sections, each with its own three-story atrium, and Rudolph's Wisma Dharmala Tower in Jakarta (1983–88), both prefiguring Ken Yeang's Menara Mesiniaga "tropical skyscraper" in Selangor, Malaysia (1990–92), and many other similar works in the now fast-growing cities of Southeast Asia.

FURTHER READING

Nicolas Adams, *Skidmore, Owings and Merrill: SOM Since 1936* (Milan: Electa, 2006).

Tom Avermaete, Serhat Karakayali, and Marion von Osten, *Colonial Modern* (London: Black Dog, 2010).

Edmund N. Bacon, *Design of Cities* (New York: Viking, 1967).

Paul L. Knox, *Palimpsests: Biographies of 50 City Districts* (Basel: Birkhäuser, 2012).

Seng Kuan, *Kenzō Tange: Architecture for the World* (Zurich: Lars Müller, 2012).

Alexandros-Andreas Kyrtsis, *Constantinos A. Doxiadis* (Athens: Ikaros, 2006).

Phyllis Lambert, *Building Seagram* (New Haven: Yale University Press, 2009).

Mori Art Museum, *Metabolism: The City of the Future* (Tokyo, 2011).

Eric Mumford, *Defining Urban Design: CIAM Architects and the Formation of a Discipline, 1937–69* (New Haven: Yale University Press, 2009).

Max Risselada and Dirk van den Heuvel, *Team 10: In Search of a Utopia of the Present, 1953–1981* (Rotterdam: NAi, 2005).

Timothy M. Rohan, *The Architecture of Paul Rudolph* (New Haven: Yale University Press, 2014).

Peter G. Rowe and Hashim Sarkis, *Projecting Beirut* (Munich: Prestel, 1998).

Josep Lluís Sert, "The Human Scale," in Eric Mumford, ed., *The Writings of Josep Lluís Sert* (New Haven: Yale University Press, 2015), 79–90.

Arieh Sharon, *Kibbutz + Bauhaus* (Stuttgart: Karl Krämer, 1976).

Ellen Shoshkes, *Jaqueline Tyrwhitt* (Burlington, Vt.: Ashgate, 2013).

Frances Strauven, *Aldo Van Eyck* (Amsterdam: Architectura and Natura, 1998).

Jennifer Taylor, *The Architecture of Fumihiko Maki* (Basel: Birkhäuser, 1999).

Alex Wall, *Victor Gruen* (Barcelona: Actar, 2005).

CHAPTER SEVEN

Crisis of Utopia

Rejections and Revisions of Modern Planning

**EUROPEAN URBAN CRITIQUES OF CIAM AND TEAM 10:
THE SITUATIONISTS, CONSTANT, YONA FRIEDMAN,
AND ARCHIGRAM**

At about the same time as Team 10's rejection of CIAM in 1959, other new critical directions in urbanism were emerging. These included the publication, in the Lettrist International journal *Potlatch* (1952–57), of the first appearance of what would become a standard criticism of Le Corbusier's urbanism, by the French Situationist artist Guy Debord (1931–1994). In an article later translated as "Skyscraper by the Roots" (1954, issue 5), Debord declared that modern urban planning had "always found inspiration by the directives of the police." It was fundamentally an architecture and urbanism of "closed, isolated units" in "societies under perpetual surveillance," with "no more opportunities for uprisings or meaningful encounters." This observation was related to the tense atmosphere in France at this time, a moment of considerable national political instability. Police troops were widely present in the streets, and popular discontent was high. France was losing its colonies in French Indochina (which included Vietnam and Cambodia) and the Algerian revolt was about to begin. The French Ministry of Reconstruction, under the Fourth Republic government, at the same time launched "Operation Million," an effort to halve the cost of a standard apartment through prefabricated construction. It held a competition for the design of four mass-housing projects on the outskirts of Paris, totaling four thousand units. These ambitious efforts soon led to the construction of many similar "grands ensembles" of CIAM-type housing around major French cities, many of them designed by Candilis-Josic-Woods.

At this same time, Asger Jorn (1914–1973), a Danish artist who had worked in Le Corbusier's atelier in 1937–38, painting the murals in his Temps Nouveau pavilion at the time of CIAM 5, had begun to argue that the Bauhaus had not been about advancing a "well-defined doctrine" of modern design, as the Swiss educator Max Bill (1908–1994) was advocating at his postwar Hochschle für Gestaltung Ulm, where Jorn had taught briefly. Instead, for Jorn, the Bauhaus was really about unconstrained artistic inspiration. He founded an "Imaginist Bauhaus" of artists and joined forces with Debord, jointly publishing a "psychogeographic guide" to Paris in *Potlatch,* an article then republished in more well-known form as *The Naked City* (1957). Its title appropriated that of a popular American detective movie of 1950, one of the first Hollywood films to film extensively on location, in gritty Manhattan neighborhoods.

Debord and Jorn suggested that the "unitary urbanism" that the Lettrist International had been calling for could be realized through a series of "operations within culture" that would overcome urban alienation and its tendency to cause people to mediate social relations through objects, instead of through lived communal experience. These included the construction of temporary urban "situations" intended to project countervisions to the "spectacle" of capitalist accumulation, whose clearest embodiment was the tightly controlled network television programming then becoming widespread in the 1950s. Other tactics of "unitary urbanism" advocated by Debord and Jorn in *Potlatch* in 1956 included the idea of understanding contemporary urban life through "dérives," long, possibly drunken, group random explorations of the "psychogeography" of different parts of the city; "détournement," the "hijacking" of dominant narratives and representation techniques for revolutionary ends; and resistance to the "recuperating" of subversive works by the mainstream culture. The Situationist goal was a Marxist revolution that would resist the authoritarianism of the Soviet-type regimes and at the same time liberate capitalist societies from their alienated focus on consumer commodities and media spectacles.

In 1957, Debord and the Lettrist International merged with Jorn's Imaginist Bauhaus group and became the Situationist International (SI), which lasted until 1972 and which had an immense influence on thinking about urbanism in the 1960s and beyond. Until 1961, the SI also included the artist Constant Nieuwenhuys (1920–2005), a sometime associate of Aldo Van Eyck in the CoBrA (Copenhagen-Brussels-Amsterdam) artists' group from 1948–51. Van Eyck and Constant had collaborated on an exhibition called "Man and Home" in Amsterdam in 1953, where they put forward the idea of using color to articulate urban spaces. Beginning in 1956, and continuing until 1974, Constant created visionary models and drawings for "New Babylon," an ever-changing, continuous megastructure that drew from the Smithsons' Golden Lane and Berlin Hauptstadt projects. Like those, it remained unbuilt. Constant, along with most of the other early SI members, was ejected from the group by Debord on the grounds that Constant's concrete urban visions were insufficiently radical for the SI's agenda. The SI then went on to have extensive involvement in the huge public protests and demonstrations in Paris and in American cities and campuses in the late 1960s.

A parallel figure at this time was the sometime CIAM member Yona Friedman (born 1923), a Hungarian-born Israeli architect. He had attended CIAM 10 as part of the Israeli CIAM group led by the planner Arieh Sharon but was critical of the vagueness of the Smithsons' and Team 10 urban themes of "mobility" and "growth and change." In response, Friedman founded the international (Israel-Paris-Holland-Poland) group GEAM (Groupe études d'architecture mobile/Mobile Architecture Study Group), which organized a conference in Rotterdam in 1958. GEAM argued that all institutions should be subject to periodic renewal. Inspired by Frei Otto (1925–2015), the German architect-engineer of lightweight frame tent structures, Friedman called for a "mobile architecture" (also the title of Friedman's book of 1959) and a "spatial urbanism" that would be built on a potentially infinitely extendable, multideck inhabitable space-frame. This would leave the ground level free for motorized transport, agriculture, wild nature, and historical monuments (fig. 111).

Another less politically driven extension of Team 10 and related ideas was put forward by a group of young London-based architects, who published a comic book series of visionary architectural projects called *Amazing Archigram* from 1961–70. The group eventually included Peter Cook (born 1936), Michael Webb (born 1937), Dennis Crompton (born

111. Yona Friedman, *L'urbanisme spatiale*, 1960–62. © 2016 Artists Rights Society (ARS), New York/ADAGP, Paris.

Crisis of Utopia

1935), Warren Chalk (1927–1988), David Greene (born 1937), and Ron Herron (1930–1974). The Team 10 members Alison and Peter Smithson were the mentors of some of Archigram's members, including Crompton, later an important architectural educator at the Architectural Association and globally. But Archigram was as critical of Team 10 as the latter had been of the English CIAM MARS group. Like the Metabolists, Archigram's members proposed a flexible, antimonumental use of modern technologies to generate continuously stimulating pedestrian urban environments, where chance encounters and readily available services would allow for an ever-changing flow of experiences. They saw this direction as opposed to the rigidly organized urban environments advocated by CIAM. Archigram's members also strongly identified with the postwar urban British working class, then at its high point of political power, and they valorized liberating environments like seaside amusement parks, rather than seeking what to them seemed like a false choice between the absurdly regimented and class-conscious spaces of traditional European urban plazas and what they saw as the ever-expanding boredom of American suburbia.

At the same time, Archigram also admired American visionaries like R. Buckminster Fuller and what came to be called "high-tech" environments, such as Cape Canaveral (renamed Cape Kennedy in 1964) on the Atlantic coast of Florida, the site of U.S. space missions that culminated in the moon landing of Apollo 11 in 1969. Fuller's fascination with the properties of energy flows, which he saw as the source of real wealth, had led him to propose logical structural systems that used the minimum of material to enclose the maximum of space, using triangular and tetrahedral figures, and these ideas were then taken up and extended by Archigram. Fuller had also developed the idea of the geodesic dome, originally also intended as a prefabricated housing solution, which used a spherical triangular space frame to quickly enclose the largest amount of area with the smallest amount of structure. The idea was not feasible as a mass-housing solution, but it became a very popular form for greenhouses, concert halls, and exhibition structures. The concept was also used by the U.S. military for transportable domes ("radomes") sited in northern Canada along the Arctic Circle to warn of a Soviet attack. With Shoji Sadao (born 1927), Fuller also designed the United States pavilion (1965) at Expo '67 in Montreal as a large geodesic dome exhibition structure, linked to a futuristic monorail, as a possible model for future urbanism.

Archigram's members saw that these technologically oriented futuristic directions that attempted to respond to popular desires were becoming more important in the 1960s than Team 10's or Josep Lluís Sert's more architecturally driven ideas about urban design. Crompton, Chalk, and Herron had all worked at the London County Council Architects' Special Works Division on the South Bank Arts Centre (1960–67), a highly visible Brutalist concrete landscape-building on a prominent site along the Thames River, with layers of pedestrian and vehicular circulation. Other Archigram members had worked as in-house architects designing large mixed-use commercial complexes at Taylor Woodrow Construction under the supervision of Theo Crosby (1925–1994), the architect who had also curated the "This Is Tomorrow" exhibition in London in 1956. Peter Cook had studied with Peter Smithson and James Stirling (1926–1992) at the Architectural Association, graduating in 1960, where he had become familiar with their work. He was also aware of the Independent Group's efforts to incorporate aspects of the emerging postwar commercial advertising culture, which would soon lead to Pop Art.

The Independent Group's sponsor, the Institute of Contemporary Art (ICA), held the Archigram "Living City" exhibition in 1963. This followed projects like Michael Webb's "Sin Centre" project for Leicester Square in London (1959–62) and the "Fun Palace," of Cambridge University–educated non-Archigram member Cedric Price (1934–2003), an unbuilt entertainment center sited on the River Lea in East London (1961–64) and commissioned by theater entrepreneur Joan Littlewood. These projects suggested that high-tech, multi-functional environments focused on mass leisure would be a welcome break from the solemn, anti-commercial, cultural, community, and health center projects of the postwar New Monumentality. Price was also working on his acclaimed "Potteries Thinkbelt" project for his native Staffordshire in 1963–66, where he suggested using an abandoned railway line as the basis for a roving higher education facility with mobile classrooms, labs, and residential modules to help drive economic redevelopment in a depressed region.

In 1962, Archigram members Cook and Greene proposed a "plug-in urbanism" for the Nottingham Shopping Centre, using U-shaped prefabricated concrete elements that could be put in place and possibly later moved by tall cranes. This project appropriated the logic of docks for container shipping, which had begun to expand in the mid-1950s using now standard-sized shipping containers (typically 8 ½ × 20 × 40 feet / 2.6 × 6 × 12 meters). These ideas soon led to Cook's well-known Archigram drawings of "Plug-in City" of 1964, and to many other visionary Archigram urban concepts, such as Crompton's "Computer City" collage of 1964 and Herron's "Walking City" of 1965. These drawn proposals were produced and publicized just as the Beatles and other British rock bands were acquiring international renown. The "swinging London" of the British invasion, initially centered on Carnaby Street in Soho, was just then emerging as a worldwide center of fashion and new lifestyles, and in 1964 the sociologist Ruth Glass coined the term "gentrification" to describe the social transformation of Islington.

Archigram's members had considerable technical knowledge, and they intended that their visionary projects could actually be built. All the necessary elements of structure, transit, wiring, ductwork, and networked connections were shown in great detail in the many intricate drawings made by its members. Politically, Archigram was less radical than the Situationists (or CIAM or Team 10 in some ways), designing projects for a new generation of relatively affluent urban workers using a systems approach to guide networks of pedestrian, transit, and vehicular flows. These directions were related to much official planning and intervention in Britain then favored by the technology-oriented Labour Party government of Prime Minister Harold Wilson (1964–70, 1974–76), particularly after the completion of the first sections of the British national express highway system and the publication of the influential book by Colin Buchanan, *Traffic in Towns* (1963).

Archigram had a wide impact on architectural thinking worldwide, some of it through the writings of the historian and critic Reyner Banham. In Florence, the 1966 "Superarchitecture" exhibition was inspired by Archigram, and from that event the group Superstudio, led by Adolfo Natalini (born 1941) and Cristiano Toraldo di Francia (born 1941), began to make widely admired drawings that suggested the possibility of a conceptual architecture unrelated to actual building, using "the irrational as a method" as a starting point. Particularly notable was the Superstudio's "Continuous Monument" project of 1969, a comment on the way the world was becoming standardized by technology and media, which the group also identified as "inevitable forms of imperialism."

Within architectural practice, Archigram's influence was more diffuse, and interest in its work dropped off sharply by the late 1970s, at a point when it was criticized for being naïve and overly focused on technology and theme-park-inspired visions. Yet two of its most enthusiastic student followers, Richard Rogers (born 1933), now Baron Rogers of Riverside, and Norman Foster (born 1935), now Baron Foster of the Thames Bank, both went on to be among the world's most successful architects by the 1990s, bringing design concepts inspired by Fuller and Archigram to cities and environments globally. Foster and Rogers founded the firm Team 4 in London with their spouses Su Brumwell and Wendy Cheesman, practicing jointly from 1963 to 1967. In 1968, Foster founded Foster & Partners and worked with Buckminster Fuller from 1968 to 1983. With the Genoa-based architect Renzo Piano (born 1937), Rogers won the Pompidou Centre (1971–76) competition in Paris. Built by the French government as a response to the massive student and worker urban unrest of May 1968, the Pompidou instantly created a colorful, high-tech intervention into the classical, stone-faced urban fabric of the city. Its twenty-four-hour cultural activities in some ways realized earlier post-CIAM urban visions (fig. 112).

KEVIN LYNCH, JANE JACOBS, PAUL RUDOLPH, AND THE AMERICAN CITY IN THE 1960S AND 1970S

In the United States, Sert's and Jaqueline Tyrwhitt's Harvard GSD–based concept of urban design (1953–69) was soon supplanted by the user-based urban theories of Kevin Lynch at MIT. This direction had emerged at the second Harvard Urban Design Conference in 1957, where Gyorgy Kepes and Lynch jointly presented their MIT-based research on "The Perceptual Form of the City," which had begun in 1954. In a report prepared in June 1955, Lynch had asserted that their working premises "affirm that a good urban environment has at least two basic qualities: it is coherent or connected; it is growth-facilitating." They defined coherence as a "physical patterning" that is "perceived as a perceptual, emotional, and conceptual continuity," with the "material environment." Their goal was to help create a "world which encourages human growth and development." In their Rockefeller Foundation–funded studies, Kepes and Lynch determined that the basic aspect of a city is the "flow of persons and goods," and they therefore proposed the study of the "perceptual consequences of circulation systems." Kepes had commented to Lynch that the basic issue was one of "maintaining continuity in a changing flow," principles that Kepes sought to develop from the "scattered early ideas" of Weimar avant-garde filmmakers Viking Eggeling and Hans Richter in 1919–23. Kepes and Lynch's research went beyond earlier efforts to identify what would later be called "user needs" by seeking what MIT professor Norbert Wiener (1894–1964) termed "user feedback" to better understand how ordinary people found their way in their urban environments.

In the mid-1950s, teams of Kepes/Lynch research assistants interviewed small groups of residents of Boston, Jersey City, and downtown

Los Angeles, and they then analyzed the results. They found that people generally understood their urban environments in terms of five categories of abstract, spatially orienting elements: paths, edges, nodes, districts, landmarks. From this, Lynch concluded that the best urban environments were where these elements were perceived as coherently connected. Central Boston was a prime example, with defined "paths" such as Commonwealth Avenue, clear "edges" like the banks of the Charles River, "nodes" like Harvard or Kendall Squares, compact, walkable "districts" like Beacon Hill, and "landmarks" visible from a distance, like the State House dome. Jersey City, though dense and containing extensive transit infrastructure, lacked many of these spatially orienting elements, and residents found it confusing to navigate, while downtown Los Angeles had some of these elements but was still not completely coherent to those interviewed as a pedestrian urban environment.

Lynch's work, inexplicably published without Kepes as *The Image of the City* (1960), then led to a new era in urban design after 1960, where the architect-directed, design-driven, and formally oriented approach that Sert had developed in the Harvard Urban Design program began to be seen as a sort of permanent negative alternative to what were then put forward as other, better planning directions. These approaches were typically understood as more socially engaged, data driven, and less formalistic, and eventually would often be linked to various projects of social and economic empowerment. In the 1960s, many urban designers began to see Lynch's work as a more relevant approach than Sert's architecturally centered focus on pedestrian-oriented civic spaces and mass-housing solutions. Lynch's approach was not intended to be a design method in itself; rather, it was about organizing user feedback on how people understood their urban environments in ways that Lynch thought would be useful for planners. His findings that urban inhabitants "cognitively map" (terms introduced by Lynch) their environments using this set of five physical elements suggested that planners could use these categories to give "imageability" to the urban environment, such as designing paths with "some singular quality" to make them memorable, like the line of trees in the middle of Commonwealth Avenue in Boston. The "kinesthetic quality" of a path was also important, the way that a sense of motion, "running, rising, falling," like traversing a great descending curve when approaching a city, contributes to its imageability.

Around the same time, a more radical critique of architect-driven urbanism appeared with Jane Jacobs, *The Death and Life of Great American Cities* (1961). Jacobs had studied at Columbia University and worked in journalism and for American government agencies during and after World War II. She was married to the New York architect Robert Hyde Jacobs. In the early Cold War years she had edited a popular magazine to be distributed in the USSR for the U.S. State Department, but she resigned in 1952 during the McCarthy period of anti-Communist hysteria. Jacobs then wrote extensively on American urban renewal efforts in the 1950s for *Architectural Forum,* often praising the urban renewal work of architects like I. M. Pei, Victor Gruen, and Harry Weese, and she spoke briefly at the first Harvard Urban Design conference in 1956.

Her *Death and Life* was written in 1959–60, with extensive financial support from the Humanities Division of the Rockefeller Foundation, and it quickly became a huge popular success. Jacobs influentially rejected the entire modern planning tradition from the City Beautiful and Garden City movements to CIAM and urban renewal. Her critical response was twofold, suggesting on one hand that planners sought to simply freeze the existing social order in physical form, and on the other arguing that the specific planning practices of modern urbanism were destroying pedestrian-oriented city life. For Jacobs, Ebenezer Howard's ideas were "monopolistic-corporate" and "almost feudal" in their expectation that the working classes would stay in their class positions when rehoused in peripheral settlements surrounded by farms and recreational greenery. In her view, Howard's goal had been to "freeze power, people, and their uses" into an "easily manageable and static pattern." Jacobs was also critical of Geddes and the Regional Planning Association of America (RPAA) members, including Lewis Mumford, Stein & Wright, and Catherine Bauer Wurster, indicating that they were primarily "decentrists" whose effective influence was only on suburban housing in the model schemes of Stein & Wright, such as Radburn. She also blamed them for advancing the idea that "the street is bad as an environment for humans, [and that] houses should be turned away from it and faced inward, toward sheltered greens." The RPAA's basic unit of design was the bounded superblock, not the street, and she thought that for them "the presence of many other people is, at best, a necessary evil."

Jacobs's main target was Le Corbusier, whom she saw as the key figure in getting such "anti-city" planning into cities themselves. Her attack was wide ranging and not always completely accurate; she slightly mischaracterized his 1922 Ville Contemporaine project as a city of towers with a density of twelve hundred people per acre (0.4 hectare) covering only 5 percent of the ground; it was in fact a proposal for a city of widely spaced office towers surrounded by parklike open space, with eight-story housing blocks sited within walking distance of the office towers. Oddly paralleling Guy Debord's 1954 critique of Le Corbusier as favoring a police state, Jacobs suggested that Corbu's utopian vision was one of "liberty from ordinary responsibility," where no one was "going to have to struggle with plans of his own." She acknowledged that the RPAA decentrists "were aghast at Le Corbusier's city of towers in a park," but she accurately emphasized that Le Corbusier's "Radiant City comes directly out of the Garden City." She saw him as making possible the mid-century planning consensus that the superblock, the "project neighborhood," and "grass, grass, grass" should be the planners' main goals. Yet without mentioning any by name, she also acknowledged that "virtually all sophisticated city designers today" tried to see "how many old buildings can be left standing and the area still converted into a passable version of the Radiant Garden City." Her wide-ranging critique of urban planning concluded with her subsequently extremely influential assertion on urban land-use master plans: "From Howard and Burnham to the latest amendment on urban renewal law, the entire concoction is irrelevant to the workings of cities." Instead, Jacobs argued, existing cities have "served as sacrificial victims" to these misguided planning ideas.

Jacobs then set out a detailed manifesto of better urban planning, grounded in her own observations of cities and particularly in her every-day life in a nineteenth-century townhouse on Hudson Street in Green-wich Village. Her main planning value was urban "diversity," by which she did not mean racial diversity per se, but rather dense concentrations of many different kinds of people walking on urban sidewalks in safety. To be safe, these sidewalks must have the "eyes on the street" of local residents on them. She extended this principle to parks and playgrounds as well. Jacobs also argued in favor of small blocks, to ease pedestrian movement, and argued against separating cars from pedestrians. Instead of the bleak uniformity of high-rise towers like those that Robert Moses had wanted to build to clear part of the West Village, which she successfully opposed, Jacobs argued for a varied mix of buildings of different ages and uses, organized along dense streets with many pedestrians. Jacobs found suburban areas "dull," and she doubted that the "semi-suburbs" that had been produced by Garden City planners, with densities of ten to twenty units per acre (0.4 hectare), could ever generate "city liveliness or public life." Jacobs was also sharply critical of the urban "discrimination against Negroes" which "operates most drastically today," noting that "a ghetto is where people, especially young people, will not stay willingly." This would change, Jacobs argued, only when "remaining in the inner city for a colored person must no longer mean acceptance of ghetto citizenship and status."

Despite some flaws as an accurate historical account of the intentions of modern architects, Jacobs's *The Death and Life of Great American Cities* had a transformative influence on American urbanism. Book reviews were generally favorable, and Willo von Moltke (1911–1987), the new director of the Harvard Urban Design program in the 1960s and a former associate of Edmund Bacon in Philadelphia planning in the 1950s, thought its publication was one of the most significant events in urbanism in 1961. Across the country, protest movements against the demolitions of urban renewal and proposed new highways greatly intensified. By 1959, San Franciscans had already rejected seven of the ten freeways proposed in the 1955 *Trafficways* plan, leaving only a few built stubs like the Embarcadero and Central Freeways, later themselves demolished. In New York, "advocacy planners" like Paul Davidoff and C. Richard Hatch emerged as leaders for groups directly affected by highway plans like Moses's 1963 proposal for a cross-Harlem freeway, influentially paralleling Jacobs's questioning of the premises of master planning.

By 1967, Jacobs had become widely known for her efforts to stop Moses's proposed expressway across lower Manhattan, from the Holland Tunnel to the Manhattan Bridge. This was one of the turning points in the rejection of modern urbanism in North American cities. Such a highway had been proposed since the 1920s, and a route for it along Broome Street was one of four cross-Manhattan expressways that Moses had advocated after the federal interstate program began in 1956. New York reform mayor John V. Lindsay, who was in office 1966–73, sought to implement an optimistic Great Society agenda and enthusiastically supported the expressway, which was then called LOMEX. In 1967 the Ford Foundation commissioned architect Paul Rudolph (1918–1997) to develop what he called a "city corridor" for it, an immense multilevel linear city with separate levels for different speeds of traffic linking to parking and a variety of housing and multiuse structures dramatically organized into a large continuous megastructure. Rudolph's scheme would have adjusted the height of the highway to the varied building contexts that it passed through, and it was designed so that it would run between Broome and Spring Streets such that it would not demolish the historic cast-iron facades of the empty industrial area that was just then beginning to be called SoHo ("South of Houston Street") (fig. 113).

Jane Jacobs and some two hundred New York community groups, including CORE (Congress on Racial Equality) and several organizations of new Soho artist-loft residents, vehemently opposed the Rudolph scheme, which was then canceled. It was one of the incidents, along with earlier charges of corruption in the Title I urban renewal process, that led to the discrediting of Robert Moses's many achievements. Jacobs's influence grew in the 1960s during the era of President Lyndon B. Johnson's "Great Society" effort (1964–68), when massive federal, state, and local resources were directed toward simultaneously addressing racism and inequality in American cities and, by 1965, escalating military intervention in Vietnam in a failed attempt to stop the Viet Cong's Communist revolution there.

Since the Watts riots in South Central Los Angeles in 1965, which occurred shortly after President Johnson signed the Civil Rights Act, American cities had been convulsed by racial conflict, much of it touched off by perceptions of racist policing. In Detroit in 1967, U.S. Army units as well as the Michigan National Guard were deployed. In 1968, the assassination of African-American civil rights leader Dr. Martin Luther King, Jr., touched off more riots in hundreds of American cities, turning urban "gray areas" into ghettoes. In many cases these areas had been the focus of the Ford Foundation's Gray Areas program in 1961, using a term taken from *Anatomy of a Metropolis,* a collection of essays jointly published in 1959 by the Regional Plan Association of New York and the Harvard

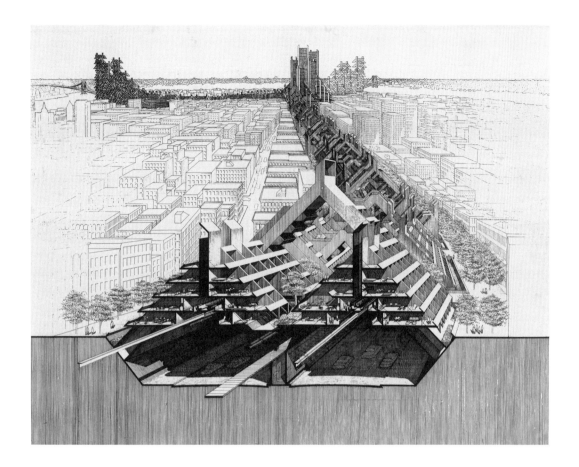

113. Paul Rudolph, Lower Manhattan Expressway (LOMEX) proposal, Broome Street extension, 1967 (Library of Congress).

Graduate School of Public Administration that provided detailed data about the postwar suburbanization and industrial decline of the New York area. One of its editors, Raymond Vernon, had suggested the term "gray areas" to describe declining inner-ring urban areas between downtown and the suburbs, an application of the Chicago School of Sociology's urban spatial model.

In response to this intense outpouring of anger and violence in American cities, New York Governor Nelson Rockefeller, like Mayor Lindsay a liberal Republican, announced the establishment of the New York State Urban Development Corporation (UDC), a $2 billion effort to "save" these problematic urban areas with extensive new housing and social service interventions. Edward J. Logue was hired as the UDC's director, and he commissioned many well-known architects, including Rudolph, Sert Jackson, Bond-Ryder, Richard Meier, Pasanella + Klein, Hoberman & Wasserman, Werner Seligmann, and others for large experimental housing complexes in cities across the state. The centerpiece of the UDC's efforts was the construction of new mixed-use housing on Roosevelt Island, a highly visible "new town in town" on the former Welfare Island opposite the elite Upper East Side of Manhattan with a master plan by Philip Johnson (1906–2005). These UDC efforts took place as Governor Rockefeller also oversaw the completion of the large new Empire State Plaza capital complex in Albany (1965–78), designed by Harrison & Abramowitz. After the Middle East oil crisis of 1973, the American economy went into a deep recession, and these ambitious urban projects of previous decades quickly began to seem like dinosauric relics of a distant past.

LEARNING FROM LAS VEGAS: VENTURI AND SCOTT BROWN, CHARLES MOORE, AND THE CULTURAL LOGIC OF "LATE CAPITALISM"

Despite continuing racial segregation, by the early 1960s the United States had emerged as the most affluent mass-consumer society in history. Millions of white returning veterans were able to buy homes, and the new suburban ways of living soon began to call into question the modernist architectural aspirations to construct a new society in dense mass-housing settlements served by mass transit. This popular questioning was different from the critiques of Jane Jacobs and the Situationists, in that existing urban environments were seen less as valuable pockets of social and cultural resistance to the designs of planners and more as potential places for leisure and entertainment, valued as much for their quirky historical forms as for any particular set of social ideas that these might embody. The new sensibility was apparent in the rediscovery and preservation of old neighborhoods in cities like San Francisco, the Old Town area of Chicago, and the brownstone districts of Brooklyn, as well as in new shopping and entertainment complexes like Ghiradelli Square in San Francisco (1964), where Wurster, Bernardi & Emmons repurposed an old chocolate factory with shops and parking (fig. 114). Its success was soon followed by Joseph Esherick's Cannery (1968), a similar complex adjacent across Larkin Street, and eventually by Fanueil Hall Marketplace in Boston (1974), a renovation by Benjamin Thompson Associates of a pair of early nineteenth-century waterfront market buildings called Quincy Market into an extremely profitable "festival marketplace." Many other projects like Ghiradelli Square soon followed, including the renovation of a 1930s refrigerator factory in São Paulo by Lina Bo Bardi (1914–1992) as a center for social services and cultural activities, SESC Pompeia (1977–86).

In the context of such efforts, modern architecture itself, often seen as exemplified by the work of Mies van der Rohe, began to draw criticism. Modern architects' disapproval of decoration and their focus on creating egalitarian and efficient environments began to seem disappointingly reductive. In 1966, Robert Venturi (born 1925), a Philadelphia architect and Princeton graduate who had worked for both Eero Saarinen and Louis Kahn, published his *Complexity and Contradiction in Architecture.* His work was part of, though ultimately peripheral to, that of the CASE group of mostly Ivy League architects and historians that Peter Eisenman (born 1932) had convened in 1964. Venturi argued against the Miesian

modernism then dominant in American architectural practice, which demanded a clear and minimal synthesis of space, structure, and social
purpose. Venturi instead called attention to a variety of formally complex and contradictory architectures of the past, and in his modest built
works, such as the house for his mother, Vanna Venturi, in the Chestnut
Hill section of Philadelphia (1962). Venturi sought to comment ironically
on various architectural ideas and their often imperfect junction of formal logics, social demands, and technical means. He was also among the
first modern architects to declare that "main street is nearly all right,"
reinforcing the significance of Jacobs's observations. At the same time,
his ideas about urbanism extended the growing concerns about manag-
ing urban complexity that can also be found at this time in the writings
of Fumihiko Maki and Christopher Alexander, as well as of Jane Jacobs.

Venturi's approach was soon extended by Charles W. Moore (1925–
1993), also a Princeton graduate, who had studied there in the 1950s with
Enrico Peressutti (1908–1976), one of the partners of BBPR. Moore sought
to introduce a sense of context into his work, and founded the Berkeley
firm of MLTW (Moore-Lyndon-Turnbull-Whitaker) in 1962. Sea Ranch, a
vacation condominium complex developed by a subsidiary of a Hawaii
property developer in 1963 some 122 miles (196 kilometers) north of San
Francisco, was designed by MLTW, Joseph Esherick, and other designers as

115. MLTW, with Lawrence Halprin, Sea Ranch, California, 1963.

series of residential clusters intended to preserve the natural landscape, whose intensive development along the California coast was then just becoming a serious concern. The site plan was by landscape architect Lawrence Halprin (1916–2009), who envisioned the community as a version of a kibbutz he had worked on in Israel. He saw Sea Ranch as a place where human habitation intersected harmoniously with natural ecosystems. He worked closely with MLTW and a range of other specialists to produce a new synthesis of modern planning concepts as well as an evocative reuse of the weathered wood forms of the local barns, some built by Russian settlers in the nineteenth century (fig. 115).

This sensitivity to the varieties of West Coast regionalism was then ironically used in a different way by MLTW at the University of California–Santa Barbara Faculty Club (1968), where they made abstract references to the widely popular Spanish Colonial revival style of the 1920s, as well as including Pop culture elements like neon "banners." These were combined with the abstract, thin white planes of early modernism, along with the double-height spaces of English medieval manors then thought to be necessary for such an institution. At the same time, Moore began to call attention to the vitality of contrived pedestrian commercial environments like Disneyland, which opened in Anaheim, California, in 1955 adjacent to the new I-5 freeway, suggesting that perhaps these were the only places where pedestrian activity would take place in the future decentered, auto-based metropolitan areas then emerging.

In 1962, Moore, along with Donlyn Lyndon (born 1936), Sim van der Ryn (born 1935), and Patrick J. Quinn, had been one of the authors of an article that criticized modernist urbanism and radically suggested that the American automobile commercial strip could inform design practice. The article appeared in *Landscape* (vol. 12, no. 1), a journal founded and edited from 1951 to 1968 by John Brinkerhoff Jackson (1909–1996). Jackson, an eccentric European- and Harvard College–educated scholar and advocate of American vernacular landscapes, had himself been questioning modernist planning since at least the early 1950s. He had celebrated the social utility, vitality, and nighttime beauty of such American commercial strips in an essay, "Other Directed Houses," published in *Landscape* (vol. 6, no. 2). After he began teaching as a visiting professor at the University of California at Berkeley in 1962, Jackson acquired a huge national academic following. He criticized what he postulated was an excessively European-influenced design focus by American modern architects, and instead celebrated the everyday vernacular environments and landscapes of the American West in his many essays and lectures.

A new focus on what Jackson called "cultural landscapes" emerged from his work, overturning earlier design approaches that had been more focused on monumental and residential environments. Among the many outcomes of his ideas was the founding of *Places* journal in 1983 by Lyndon and former MIT dean of architecture William Porter. Some of these directions then began to overlap with Team 10 in the ILAUD (International Laboratory of Architecture and Urban Design) summer seminars of Giancarlo de Carlo (1919-2005), founded in 1974, which were held in Urbino and other historic Italian cities and included architects such as Lyndon, the Smithsons, Sverre Fehn, Renzo Piano, Balkrishna Doshi, and others.

Denise [Lakofski] Scott Brown (born 1931), a British-educated planner born in what is now Zambia, was also strongly influenced by the Smithsons. She also became a J. B. Jackson enthusiast after she taught as a visitor at Berkeley in 1965, and visited him at his adobe-style ranch near Santa Fe, New Mexico, in 1966. She and Venturi, with whom she had been working since 1960 and married in 1967, then taught a design studio in 1968 at the Yale School of Architecture where they analyzed the Las Vegas strip with the same seriousness and graphic techniques as those normally used by architects to document and record historic cities like Rome. With their associate Steven Izenour they published the results as *Learning from Las Vegas: The Forgotten Symbolism of Architectural Form* (1972), a kind of manifesto about the role of architecture and urbanism in the new environments of postwar America.

They emphasized that as more commercial vitality was moving to such auto-based commercial "strips," earlier planning efforts to limit and control signage and "beautify" such areas with landscaping were deeply misguided. Instead, they suggested that the signage was an important kind of "heraldry," marking and indicating the status aspirations of the various businesses, and carrying most of the architectural meanings traditionally assigned to the facades of buildings. The visual appearance of the "information" part of the signage was relatively unimportant, as were the specifics of the exterior design of the casino buildings themselves, which they identified as "decorated sheds." From Venturi's earlier critiques of modern architecture in his *Complexity and Contradiction in Architecture* (1966) as boring, simplistic, and out of touch with contemporary American tastes, Venturi and Scott Brown began to develop what would by the 1980s become a wildly influential theory of architecture in which signification—what the building meant to various publics—was far more important than the social and material concerns of modern architects.

Learning from Las Vegas (1972) overturned the then-standard condemnation of American auto-based commercial strip environments, which had been presented as eyesores by modernist critics like Peter Blake (1920–2006). His book *God's Own Junkyard* (1964) was a searing critique of postwar American metropolitan sprawl. Appearing just as suburban and Sunbelt-type strip environments were replacing Main Streets across America as the interstate highway system reached completion, Venturi and Scott Brown's work made a strong case for architectural engagement with this pervasive form of commercial urbanism. Their work also seemed to many in the field to parallel the emerging architectural interest in semiology, the "science of signs" popularized by the French critic Roland Barthes (1915–1980). Like other French literary structuralists, Barthes was interested in analyzing the interplay between relatively arbitrary linguistic signs and the meanings that these signified. His work was important in extending such analysis beyond written and spoken language to signification in many areas of culture, including the built environment. In his 1967 essay "Semiology and Urbanism," Barthes argued that the signifying elements of urban environments were metaphorical, and in fact resistant to fixed relations of meaning, but were nonetheless a concrete spatial inscription of the collective unconscious. These could be precisely analyzed without necessarily passing judgment on them.

Umberto Eco (1932–2016) an Italian writer and public radio editor and, after 1966, a professor in the architecture department at the University of Florence, took up Barthes's ideas about the semiology of architecture and combined them with his concept, first put forward in 1962, of the "open work." Eco suggested that literary texts actively link between individual minds, society, and life. Eco's ideas were then extended to urban analysis, allowing cities to be documented as ongoing, open-ended projects made by many actors, which nonetheless may have an internal formal and social coherence.

As these ideas began to circulate by the time *Learning from Las Vegas* was published in 1972, modern architecture had entered a crisis from which it has arguably never recovered. The many failures of President Johnson's Federal initiatives in using modern architecture and planning to rebuild American cities led to an atmosphere of intense criticism of modern urbanism, along with many other aspects of mainstream American life and culture. By the mid-1970s, Jane Jacobs's urbanistic ideas had become influential for some architects, but she had little to say about the specific design of buildings, other than that they be oriented toward pedestrian street life and not out-of-scale with their neighbors. This uncertainty provided an opening for a new generation of mostly European architects, whose varied ideas about urbanism began to circulate, even though it would be a decade before these would begin to strongly affect American urban design.

A key figure was Aldo Rossi (1931–1997), whose *The Architecture of the City*, published in Italian in Milan in 1966 and in English in 1982, also rejected modernist urbanism. Rossi proposed an alternative approach, one centered on the abstract replication of the historic forms of premodern cities. Much of his approach was based on earlier ideas of urban context advocated in a general way by the Italian CIAM member Ernesto Rogers, with whom he had worked as an editor at the magazine *Casabella-Continuità* from 1955 to 1964. This general approach was employed and then further developed by Saverio Muratori (1910–1973), after 1954 a professor of architectural composition at the University of Rome. Muratori's built architectural work paralleled that of BBPR and Ludovico Quaroni in seeking to develop an Italian kind of Swedish and British "New Empiricism," such as that used at large urban public housing projects like Quaroni, Ridolfi & Aymonino's Tiburtino IV quarter in Rome (1949–54). His highly influential research and teaching focused on documenting the historic urban structure of cities such as Rome and Venice. Muratori took the postwar Italian motto of historic restoration, "com'era, dov'era" (as it was and where it was), and extended it into an effort to understand "that which, in history, seemed to resist change." This led him to examine with particular interest forms and materials with "internal coherence," such as masonry domes and arches, as well as building types that evolved slowly, if at all, over long stretches of historical time. In place of the modernist skepticism that saw historical building types as rigid codifications of outmoded ways of living and building, Muratori saw them as an "a priori syntheses" of use and form that allowed such types to logically connect urban fabric, streets, and topography.

Rossi's ideas developed in a related way, allowing him in 1966 to define architecture itself as the sum total of the buildings in historic cities built before modernism. Radically different from J. B. Jackson's or Venturi and Scott Brown's valorization of American vernacular environments, Rossi's interest in the abstractly reduced forms of historical urban typologies such as arcades, arches, towers, and small, square windows all also contributed to the new, anti-modernist movement that was named "postmodernism" by the critic Charles Jencks in 1977. Drawing from the work of French sociologist Maurice Halbwachs (1877–1945), who was killed in the Holocaust, Rossi emphasized that historic cities were also sites of collective memory. He also revived some of the ideas of the prewar French urbanists, ideas that had been institutionalized in Paris in the teaching of Marcel Poëte (1866–1950). Rossi interpreted the history of cities in light of how they grew from originating institutions such as fortresses, palaces, colleges, and religious establishments, instead of seeing them in modern architecture terms as a set of abstracted, repetitive residential units and functional neighborhood sectors, which could be multiplied without regard for collective memory or traditional ways of living. Rossi also stressed the importance of place, alluding to the "locus" of ancient city planning, the key sites where urban artifacts were placed which then communicated religious and cultural meanings, and lending their names to entire districts. These artifacts had formal properties that were often unrelated to their functions, as these changed over time, even as their typological formal qualities as architecture remain constant.

Working in conjunction with other Italian architects, notably Carlo Aymonino (1926–2010), within the Monte Amiata social housing project in an outlying district of Milan, Rossi designed the Gallaratese block (1967–73). Though he used a severe, abstract architectural vocabulary, his four-story building both evoked traditional Milanese tenements and created a variety of outdoor public spaces, including its much-illustrated first-floor loggias defined by narrow two-story concrete slabs. Rossi also continued to develop his theory of urbanism based on the study of traditional urban building forms, analyzing their interrelationships, which he found were usually distinctive to each city. These investigations would have a major impact on urban design by the mid-1970s. Aside from Rossi's own well-known work at the Modena cemetery (1972) and elsewhere, this direction also shaped the work and ideas of architects Giorgio Grassi (born 1935) and Vittorio Gregotti (born 1927). The latter's ZEN housing quarter in Palermo, Sicily (1969), where four parallel low-rise housing blocks based on ancient Roman *insulae* (apartment blocks) created interior courts and porticos, with slightly higher towers at the corners, was followed by his University of Calabria campus (1972), a streetlike arrangement of twenty-one university departments facing a long suspension bridge on an undulating site for a university that ultimately had thirty thousand students.

These Italian projects were highly influential in the 1970s, but some failed as social housing, much like many of the contemporary social housing projects built by the New York State Urban Development Corporation around the same time, designed by distinguished architects such as Sert, Jackson (Riverview, Yonkers); Richard Meier (Twin Parks Northeast, Bronx); Theodore Liebman and Kenneth Frampton (Marcus Garvey Village, Brooklyn); and others. This suggested to many architects at the time that different urban design decisions alone were not very effective in creating better social outcomes. It was at this same point that the Italian Marxist architectural historian and critic Manfredo Tafuri (1935–1994), a professor of architectural history at the University of Venice, began to develop a radical critique of what he called "architectural ideology." In his seminal book *Architecture and Utopia: Design and Capitalist Development* (1973), an expanded version of an article published in Italian in 1969, Tafuri traced "reason's adventures," the history of efforts by architects to improve the form of cities since the eighteenth century.

Using methods of social, psychoanalytic, and literary analysis drawn from the "critical theory" of the Frankfurt School and from French structuralist figures like Barthes and Michel Foucault, Tafuri concluded that despite the good intentions of designers from L'Enfant and Ledoux to Louis Kahn, architecture was unable to reform society, regardless of the design direction taken. Instead, he despairingly concluded that all that was possible for architecture was to create "form without utopia," and he devoted his later career as a historian to the social and formal history of Venice in the Renaissance. Despite the sometimes poor quality of the translations of his books, the extensive archival research of Tafuri and his associates at the IAUV transformed the field of architectural history, shifting its paradigm from being primarily about drawing attention to design precedents or valorizing the work of specific modern architects, as in the work of Giedion or Banham. Instead, the social, political, administrative, and technical factors that characterized entire historical periods were given new importance, radically altering the ways architectural history was taught and written and informing the work of several generations of architects and historians thereafter.

Tafuri's ideas were extended by the American literary critic Frederic Jameson, who in his 1982 essay "Architecture and the Critique of Ideology" raised the issue of how space can be considered "ideological." Continuing the emerging sense at this time that the main importance of cities and buildings was related to their ability to communicate social meanings, Jameson noted Henri Lefebvre's emphasis on "space as a category of politics." He rejected, however, the idea that Lefebvre's politics of space had any real potential to alter class relationships under what he identified as the new cultural logic of "late capitalism." Jameson saw this as a totalizing system, different from both earlier market capitalism and the quasi-imperialist postwar system dominated by the Cold War superpowers. This new phase, just then emerging in the 1980s, included not only conventional commodity-trade relationships but also media, agribusiness, and other aspects of contemporary life that transcended previous national and cultural boundaries. Instead of the modern aspiration for architects to design new and better urban environments, Jameson reiterated Tafuri's position that architects as designers are unable to devise a revolutionary architecture. As a result, architecture critics could not be "visionary proponents" of architectural styles of the future. Jameson advocated that they instead take a negative role and denounce existent and historical ideologies of architecture.

POSTWAR BERLIN, THE PROBLEM OF THE HISTORIC CITY, AND THE NEW URBANISM, 1964–80

By 1964 a new Berlin Kulturforum (Cultural Center) by Hans Scharoun, Mies van der Rohe, and others was under way (fig. 116), sited just west of the Berlin Wall, the "anti-fascist protective barrier" constructed by the Soviet-backed East German regime in 1961 to prevent its citizens from

116. Ludwig Mies van der Rohe, New National Gallery, Berlin, 1967.

leaving. In 1963, Scharoun had hired the young Cologne architect Oswald Mathias Ungers (born 1926) to teach architectural design at the Technical University in Berlin. Ungers had studied with the modern German architect Egon Eiermann (1904–1970) at the TU Karlsruhe and had attended CIAM 9 in 1953, where he met some of the future Team 10 members. He had nonetheless sided with Ernesto Rogers against Team 10 at CIAM '59. Ungers's early work in Cologne, which included houses and small urban apartment and commercial buildings, had attracted favorable interest from both Nikolaus Pevsner and Aldo Rossi by 1960. In projects such as the Neue Stadt project for Cologne (1963) and the Student Housing for Enschede, Holland (1964), Ungers explored "intrinsic" building morphologies independent of their functions, in ways that paralleled some of the urban concepts of Rossi, Muratori, and their Italian colleagues. Ungers also participated in the Berlin Team 10 meeting held at Candilis-Josic-Woods's Free University in 1965, along with the Smithsons, Van Eyck, De Carlo, Herman Hertzberger, Hans Hollein, and others. He published the results, noting the differences between the rectangular geometric order of the "Dutch structuralism" of Hertzberger (as he would term it in 1966) and the more "aformal" projects of the Smithsons and Candilis-Josic-Woods.

Ungers was at the time one of the architects of the Berlin Märkisches quarter (1962–74), along with several of Scharoun's students and others. This was a peripheral complex of seventeen thousand units of public housing in four- to sixteen-story buildings on 914 acres (370 hectares). Typical of the often ill-conceived modern urban renewal projects in both West and East Berlin at the time, the Märkisches quarter was harshly criticized by the public, leading Ungers to begin seeking new urban approaches. He began to invite architects and historians such as Kahn, Stirling, Peter Cook, Giedion, Banham, Colin Rowe, and others to his seminars at the TU Berlin. Rowe, by then teaching at Cornell University, in 1967 invited Ungers to teach full time there, which he did from 1967 to 1974. In 1971–72, Ungers organized a "Cornell chain teach" with twelve members of Team 10 that included Jaap Bakema from the Netherlands, Karoly Polónyi from Hungary, and Reima Pietilä (1923–1993) from Finland teaching for the longest periods. Peter Smithson, De Carlo, Van Eyck, Shad Woods, and other members also gave lectures. At this point the Smithsons had just completed their Kuwait City mat-building proposal, the result of a 1968 competition that had also included entries from Candilis-Josic-Woods, Pietilä, and BBPR. The Smithsons' project was based on a 66 × 66 foot (20 × 20 meter) grid of piloti, leaving the ground floor free for pedestrian traffic in a deliberately unmonumental way that they saw as related to traditional Arab urban spaces, with mosques as points of visual organization.

Major intellectual and academic-political conflicts soon developed at Cornell between Rowe and Ungers. Since about 1963, initially at the suggestion of the urban historian John Reps, Rowe had been exploring urban design ideas with his students that often questioned then-mainstream modernist approaches. His student design team was one of four invited by Arthur Drexler and Eisenman, his former Cambridge University student, to the Museum of Modern Art in 1967 to present a project for rebuilding Harlem. Paralleling recent Italian ideas, they suggested that central Harlem be rebuilt with improved versions of the standard New York urban block, but surrounded by parks and modern towers. With this approach, which then became widely influential in American architectural education after Rowe's publication (with Fred Koetter) of *Collage City* in 1978, Rowe combined his longstanding interests in the formal properties of both modern and traditional architecture (one of the sources for Eisenman's formal investigations at this time) with Karl Popper's idea of the "open society," which rejected what Rowe saw as the inevitably totalitarian aspects of any utopian urban scheme. Rowe and Koetter sought to reconcile Le Corbusier's urban visions with elements of traditional classical monuments and spaces like Hadrian's villa at Tivoli or the Piazza Navona in Rome. Their resulting urban "collage" intentionally produced not a total city plan, but a series of urban fragments, each with its own internal design logic.

In 1972, Ungers also invited the Dutch architect Rem Koolhaas (born 1949), another pivotal figure in later urbanism, to work with him on a design competition at Cornell. Koolhaas had worked as a journalist for the *Haagse Post,* the relatively conservative newspaper of the Dutch capital, and as a filmmaker before taking up art and architecture. He studied at the AA in London from 1968 to 1972, where he came into conflict with Peter Cook of Archigram, and was fascinated by the Russian avant-garde and the "critical utopias" of Superstudio. He had met Ungers in Berlin the previous year, where he had taken AA students on a 1971 field trip to see the Berlin Wall. Koolhaas was struck by the Wall's strong urban presence—not as an object "but as an erasure"—and concluded that such an absence could read more powerfully in the city than any built presence. With his associates back in London, Koolhaas developed his "Exodus" project in 1972, a megastructural "strip of metropolitan desirability" across London composed of twelve squares between high parallel walls that were to draw all urban activity within it. It evoked both the "social condensers" of the Soviet avant-garde as well as Superstudio's "Continuous Monument" project and Ungers's many 1960s seminar publications on Berlin.

At Cornell, Koolhaas then worked on a competition with Ungers for an architectural and infrastructural project for the Landwehrkanal in Berlin. Inspired by AA director Alvin Boyarsky (1928–1999), Koolhaas also began to collect postcards, and he read *Learning from Las Vegas.* This led him to the insight that even if the era of modernist manifestos seemed to be over, perhaps it was possible to write about cities "as if they themselves were a manifesto." It was around this time that he was invited by Eisenman to be a fellow of the Institute for Architecture and Urbanism (IAUS), a kind of free-form think tank that Eisenman and Philip Johnson had founded at the Museum of Modern Art in New York in 1967, which also published the journal *Oppositions* from 1973–84, with the editorial assistance of Joan Ockman. While in New York, Koolhaas began to write *Delirious New York* (1978), a "retrospective manifesto" for the chaotically dense, super-speculative, and inequitable capitalist city that had prompted modern architects like Le Corbusier to suggest that similar building and infrastructural technologies could be organized to produce better living conditions for all.

By the mid-1970s, Koolhaas, like many architects, was critical of modern urbanism, but unlike Rossi or the postmodernists, he did not seek to reenergize the social aspects of modern cities by returning to the urban forms of the past. Instead, in Manhattan he detected a "culture of congestion" that needed a "retrospective manifesto." This required a new appreciation of elements of the city that modern architects had rejected or found uninteresting, including the way each block in the grid could be designed according to its own formal logic, often with complete disregard for urban designers' efforts to produce harmonious environments through codes and legislation. He also identified a set of key twentieth-century architects in New York's actual development who included

Raymond Hood (1881–1934), Wallace K. Harrison, Harvey Wiley Corbett (1873–1954), and the renderer Hugh Ferriss (1889–1962).

In 1975, Koolhaas, with Madelon Vriesendorp and associates Elia and Zoe Zenghelis, founded the Office for Metropolitan Architecture (OMA), which described itself as being based in New York, London, and Berlin. This was at the same point that large American and British architecture firms like SOM, HOK, and Llewellyn-Davies were beginning to work internationally. The Middle East was a particularly active site, as oil in Saudi Arabia, first discovered by Standard Oil of California in 1932, had provided the financial means for the conservative Sunni Islamic desert kingdom to rapidly develop. Iran also, then under the autocratic rule of the Western-oriented Shah, invited many well-known designers, including Sert, Alvar Aalto, and Ian McHarg, to design urban projects there before its Shiite Islamic revolution of 1979.

Koolhaas/OMA and Ungers also both entered the 1975 Roosevelt Island competition in New York, which was initially intended to obtain ideas for the further extension of the mixed-use housing then just being completed by Sert, Jackson and others. The competition was held as New York City went bankrupt, leading to the complete reorganization of the UDC that year. The competition's entries by Robert A. M. Stern (born 1939), Ungers, and OMA marked the emergence of new approaches to urban design, a direction broadly identified with Rossi at the time and known as La Tendenza. In 1973, Rossi had organized the Milan Trienale exhibition on the ironically titled theme of "Rational Architecture," alluding both to the sometimes Fascist-leaning modernism of the 1930s and to the social dilemmas for modern architecture that had been identified by Tafuri. It brought together the work of Rossi, Grassi, Massimo Scolari, and Superstudio with Léon and Rob Krier, Mario Botta, Ricardo Bofill, and the New York Five (Eisenman, Meier, John Hejduk, Charles Gwathmey, and Michael Graves). These loosely associated members of La Tendenza shared the view that, contrary to modernist doctrine, architecture was not primarily about functional problem solving. Instead, Rossi and others insisted that the forms of architecture are significant in themselves and therefore relatively autonomous from other considerations, including issues of use and materials.

These ideas quickly caught on in the mid-1970s, as European architects like Ricardo Bofill (born 1939) designed several huge public housing projects in France using an overscaled, abstracted classical vocabulary like the one at Marne-la-Vallée near Paris (1978–83). Rossi, Botta, and the Kriers all became international architecture celebrities, with their work widely circulating in architectural journals. In Berlin, Ungers issued a "manifesto for the city in the city" in 1977, and Rob Krier, already active there, published his influential book *Urban Space* in 1978. All these directions argued in varying ways for the rejection of modern Zeilenbau strategies of site organization (often illustrated by Pruitt-Igoe, which had begun to be demolished with considerable television news publicity in 1972) and their replacement by a "reconstruction" of the city with traditional blocks, streets, and urban squares.

Ungers's efforts led to the decision by the West Berlin city government in 1978 to hold another International Building Exhibition (IBA) under the mottos "Repair the damaged city" and the then-new concept of "The inner city as a place to live." About 85 million German marks (about U.S. $152 million today) were appropriated by the city government, and twelve new "principles of careful urban renewal" were officially approved by the Berlin Senate in 1983. These ended earlier modernist clearance and high-rise housing strategies there, and instead put the main emphasis on planning with local residents and on reusing the existing building fabric. The urban mix of living, working, and commercial spaces was to be preserved, and public discussions of planning decisions and the accommodation of new public facilities without evicting the existing residents were established as legally enforceable priorities. Several districts, including the Kreuzberg area near the Berlin Wall, were the first focus of these efforts, led by the architect Josef Paul Kleihues (1933–2004). By 1987 the first results were substantially in place. Many German and international architects designed specific buildings and blocks for the IBA, including Ungers, Rossi, Grassi, Aymonino, the Kriers, Botta, Stern, Hejduk, OMA, Eisenman, Cook and Christine Hawley, Stirling & Wilford, Kurokawa, and Charles Moore's later firm, Moore, Ruble, Yudell.

NEW URBANISM IN AMERICA

These nascent new urban design directions came together again at the Venice Biennale exhibition in 1980, organized on the theme "The Presence of the Past." A central element was *La Strada Novissima* (The New Street), which included a series of storefronts by architects such as Rossi and Venturi, Rauch and Scott Brown. In the United States, the urban ideas of Rossi, the Kriers, and La Tendenza inspired the Congress for the New Urbanism (CNU), formally founded in 1992 as a kind of reverse CIAM by the architects Andres Duany (born 1949), Elizabeth Plater-Zyberk (born 1950), Peter Calthorpe (born 1949), and others. The CNU advocated using form-based, three-dimensional codes to counter American suburban sprawl (itself mostly the product of earlier zoning and real-estate appraisal standards) to create compact, walkable residential districts of architecture based on earlier architectural and planning models of various kinds.

A particularly influential concept that the CNU has put forward, Calthorpe's idea of the "pedestrian pocket," was first postulated by him in 1989. It was intended to create pedestrian-oriented, transit-linked, mixed-use developments covering up to a hundred acres (40 hectares). New Urbanists were also among the first urban designers to offer a coherent critical position on what had actually been built in mid-twentieth-century

American metropolitan areas, as opposed to the many previous efforts that proposed often flawed or unbuildable modernist countervisions. Their analysis identified "five components of sprawl": residential-only housing subdivisions; shopping centers surrounded by large surface parking areas; suburban office parks; suburban civic institutions such as schools, religious buildings, and town halls; and highways as typically the only available transportation routes. In response to these now-standard patterns of postwar American metropolitan development, New Urbanists proposed a series of dense, walkable, and partly mixed-use districts that initially put a strong emphasis on the reuse of historical architectural typologies and formal codes. This approach was first evident in the resort town of Seaside, Florida (1982), whose code-determined traditional forms were presented in ways inspired by the work and ideas of Rossi and the Krier brothers and drawn from the historic building types found in towns like Charleston and Savannah.

Despite its sometimes widely admired built designs for new towns, campuses, and urban districts, New Urbanism has not achieved its goals of reshaping North American metropolitan regions (fig. 117). It nonetheless has had an immense influence on American urban development over the past three decades. New Urbanists have encouraged the revaluing of central city environments, a direction already taken by most European cities after wartime destruction but until the 1980s not widely used elsewhere, as the otherwise dissimilar postwar cases of Los Angeles, São Paulo, and Tokyo have all demonstrated. Related ideas also quickly became mainstream by then, with the construction of large urban projects like Battery Park City in New York by Cooper Eckstut, begun in 1979, which attempted to replicate the setback tower forms of the 1920s in a new lower Manhattan district organized along a grid of streets, with

117. Duany and Plater-Zyberk, New Town, St. Charles, Missouri, 2003.

a new waterfront promenade and several squares. For a time, this approach proved to be a formally popular model worldwide, notably at Canary Wharf (1991), on the rebuilt London Docklands, though it was also an early signal of the gradual displacement of all but the wealthy from successful urban cores in what Saskia Sassen would define as the "global city" in 1991.

By the mid-1980s, many European cities, even some in the still Soviet-dominated East Bloc, had enthusiastically taken up this new focus on re-inhabiting central urban areas. After the end of the Franco dictatorship in Spain in 1975, Barcelona, the capital of Catalonia, a separatist region of around 4 million people, also began to use the idea of a "city of cities" as a planning strategy. Each self-governing district of 100,000 to 150,000 residents would work with public companies to address specific problems identified by their inhabitants. In the mid-1980s preparations also began there for the 1992 Olympics, where extensive public expenditure was used to modernize and extend the former industrial city. New ring roads carefully related to existing neighborhoods were built, new sports and other facilities constructed, and new housing districts and waterfront improvements carried out. The result was a particularly successful and influential example of the reconstruction of a dense, pedestrian European city, in this case by using mostly modern rather than neotraditional architecture, in a rather unusual political situation where great attention was paid to the social as well as physical aspects of the rebuilding (fig. 118). Pasqual Maragall, mayor from 1982 to 1997, and the architect Oriol Bohigas (born 1925) were particularly important figures in this effort, but many local architects and other professionals were involved as well. Unfortunately, this revaluing of traditional forms of urban life often also led to what came to be called gentrification, a term first used in working-class parts of north London in the 1960s that had become popular with prosperous house renovators. It has come to be associated with high housing costs in successful pedestrian cities, places where often the existing residents can no longer afford to live.

In the United States, by the 1980s, Portland, Oregon, had also become a widely admired model for retaining a transit and pedestrian-oriented downtown, while at the same time preserving open land at the edges of the metropolitan area. Once a major regional center in the Pacific Northwest, by the 1960s Portland had largely missed out on the postwar North American suburban boom, though a riverfront freeway recommended by Robert Moses had been built in the 1940s. In 1972, Mayor Neil Goldschmidt appointed a planning committee to address the central city's continuing loss of population. An SOM master plan to preserve the downtown as a walkable area extended the pedestrian-oriented modern urban renewal efforts of Lawrence Halprin in the 1960s, who had designed a pedestrian promenade in the Auditorium South renewal area that linked his three dramatic, multilevel concrete fountains with greenways.

118. Model of the new Olympic quarter of Barcelona, 1986–92.

By the late 1970s, Portland planners and residents had rejected Halprin's modernist approach and taken up New Urbanist ideas, approving the removal of the waterfront highway and shifting highway expenditures to the extensive new Tri-Met light-rail system. A transit mall based on the one completed in Minneapolis in 1977 was built, and by 2000, 43 percent of downtown Portland commuters arrived by public transit. In his *The Willamette Valley: Choices for the Future* (1972) report, Halprin had also predicted that the region was in danger of losing both farmland and scenic areas to uncontrolled sprawl. This led to an unusual North American coalition of farmers and conservationists in the Portland region, which supported the creation of the 1973 Oregon Land Conservation and Development Commission. This effort then produced a legally binding statewide requirement that every city and county define its goals for preserving farmland, access to affordable housing, and the orderly development of public services. In this context, in 1979 the Portland region agreed to set an urban growth boundary, within which transit-oriented development was encouraged, and which has remained in place to the present.

In *The Death and Life of Great American Cities* (1961), Jane Jacobs had argued that the massive slum clearance then taking place in many American cities, displacing hundreds of thousands of mostly poor, often

African-American residents, was resulting in an oppressive urban environment of regimented high-rise towers producing urban conditions far worse than those it had sought to replace. The urban history of the next thirty years would prove this judgment to have been substantially accurate, and ultimately most of these projects (except in New York City) were demolished by 2000, using federal funds from the Hope VI program. This Clinton era (1992–2000) program, strongly influenced by New Urbanism, funded the demolition and rebuilding of high-rise urban public housing sites with low-rise townhouse complexes that were intended to provide housing to a range of income levels. These were often successful in market terms, even if their bland, typically red-brick architectural design and ample secure parking areas rarely approached the architectural or urbanistic quality of housing infill projects in European cities. In many cases, the lack of stores and public amenities in Hope VI projects also replicated some of the problems of postwar suburbia that had led to the rejection of modernist urbanism in the first place.

Since the mid-1950s, the critiques of modernism that had first appeared in the European writings of Team 10 and the Situationists, which were then powerfully reinforced by Jacobs and architects like Venturi and Scott Brown, have become mainstream. Against these positions, numerous architects since the 1960s have offered their own urbanistic remedies, ranging from the still-modernist 1960s urban concepts of Sert, Lynch, Halprin, Rudolph, Yona Friedman, Paolo Soleri, and (as they see it) Venturi and Scott Brown, to the more overtly anti–Modern Movement directions of Charles Moore, Rossi, and the Krier brothers, as well as members of the Congress for the New Urbanism.

FURTHER READING

Robert Bruegmann, *Sprawl* (Chicago: University of Chicago Press, 2005).
Joan Busquets, *Barcelona: The Urban Evolution of a Compact City* (Rovereto, Italy: Nicolodi, 2005).
John Dutton, *New American Urbanism: Re-forming the Suburban Metropolis* (Milan: Skira, 2000).
Diane Ghirardo, *Italy: Modern Architectures in History* (London: Reaktion, 2013).
Florian Hertwecht and Sébastien Marot, *The City in the City* (Cologne: Lars Muller, 2013).
Paul L. Knox, *Palimpsests: Biographies of 50 City Districts* (Basel: Birkhäuser, 2012).
Igor Marjanović and Jan Howard, *Drawing Ambience: Alvin Boyarsky and the Architectural Association* (St. Louis, 2014).
Joan Ockman, with Edward Eigen, *Architecture Culture, 1943–1968* (New York: Rizzoli, 1993).
Michelangelo Sabatino, *Pride in Modesty: Modernist Architecture and the Vernacular Tradition in Italy* (Toronto: University of Toronto Press, 2010).
Josep Lluís Sert, "The Human Scale," in Eric Mumford, ed., *The Writings of Josep Lluís Sert* (New Haven: Yale University Press, 2015), 79–90.
Chris Wilson and Paul Groth, *Everyday America: Cultural Landscape Studies After J. B. Jackson* (Berkeley: University of California Press, 2003).

CHAPTER EIGHT

Globalization and Urbanism from the 1950s to the Present

"SITES AND SERVICES": THE CHALLENGE OF ORGANIZED SELF-BUILT SETTLEMENTS, 1950–80S

The world's population continued to rise in the 1980s and 1990s, reaching 6 billion by 2000 and now estimated at 7.4 billion and still rapidly increasing. During those same decades, the environmental outcomes of industrialization and the massive growth of human populations since the nineteenth century began to be a source of concern for some Western urbanists and development experts. Much of that urban growth was not the relatively technology-intensive development involving highways, mass transit, and utility networks that had come to be expected in Western metropolitan areas, but instead usually took the form of informal settlements sited on unbuilt land, often at the edges of less prosperous urban centers outside of Western Europe and North America. By the 1970s a consensus had emerged that a "sites and services" approach to organizing such mass urbanization should be used under these conditions.

This approach had a few precedents in European cities, where poor in-migrants were sometimes allowed to build temporary settlements in outlying areas. In Vienna in the 1920s, the collapse of the Austro-Hungarian Empire made it necessary to suddenly house many German-speaking refugees fleeing from former imperial territories. In the early 1920s, Adolf Loos and his associates, who included Margarete Schütte-Lihotzky, gave considerable thought to the design challenges of "wild settlements" of these in-migrants, whom the city government organized into cooperative housing associations. Related directions were also sometimes used in the British Empire, particularly after the late 1930s, when there were efforts to extend some of the provisions of English planning legislation to other parts of the Empire, notably in Trinidad in 1938. These efforts were intended to address long-neglected issues of bad sanitation, overcrowding, lack of infrastructure, and lack of schools and health facilities. This approach then began to be transferred to the then-British colonies of West Africa by Maxwell Fry and Jane Drew and others in the mid-1940s, and from there to South Asia after 1947.

In the postwar era, such approaches, which encouraged governments to set aside and sometimes plat tracts of land with streets and open spaces and to provide urban in-migrants with basic services, like fresh water, began to be further developed from several directions. Advocates of this sites and services approach included Doxiadis; the ATBAT-Afrique architects and planners in Morocco; and Jacob Leslie Crane (1892–1988), an American planner who worked at the International Housing office of the U.S. Housing and Home Finance Agency (HHFA) and became a housing consultant to the United Nations. Crane presented a paper at the 1951 International Housing and Town Planning Federation (IFHTP) conference where he called for a new kind of "planner-doer" to help people plan for themselves. Around the same time, Crane founded the CINVA center for housing research in Bogotá in 1951. Along with Puerto Rico, where New Deal governor Rexford Tugwell had supported similar efforts beginning in 1939, CINVA became a center for developing models of self-build housing, management, and construction in Latin America. These techniques then began to be advocated worldwide by the CIAM member Ernest Weissmann, assistant director of the housing section of the United Nations Department of Social and Economic Affairs, and by Charles Abrams, who along with Otto Koenigsberger and others, was a member of various U.N. technical assistance missions.

Such approaches favoring "sites and services" for all or partially self-built housing areas were initially conceptualized as part of more conventional mid-century planning agendas. These housing areas would be situated within modern regional master plans that typically included plans for a highway network, new towns, and industrial estates, with the expectation of possible future development more or less parallel to those then being applied in northern Europe. Such planning efforts ranged from the socially and climatically informed work of Fry & Drew in Ghana to various planning experiments in South Asia and Latin America to the racially segregated new towns built under the apartheid regime (1948–94) in the republic of South Africa. In 1956, Fry, Drew, Drake & Lasdun designed a new fishing village, Tema Manhean, in what is now Ghana, which they published as a model design in 1966. Their publication was introduced by Koenigsberger, then head of the department of Development at the School of Tropical Studies at the AA. At Tema there was extensive consultation with residents, and it was found that many would have preferred to remain in their ancestral villages and not change their agricultural practices, as was being demanded by the central government. In 1961, Doxiadis Associates was brought in to develop a master plan. DA took a radically different approach, designing a regional plan for the entire Accra-Tema area, which they envisioned as a dynamic and growing urban region along a new Pan-African highway linking the newly independent countries of West Africa. For Tema itself, Doxiadis planned a highway network that was to be a modified version of Le Corbusier's 7V system, with eight categories of circulation by traffic speed with a plan that incorporated the previous planning efforts, some of which were by then becoming defined as slums.

Despite numerous conflicts, many of them still unresolved today, urbanistic approaches related to these 1960s planning efforts continued to be applied, often on a large scale, as in Doxiadis's plan for Riyadh in 1972. The plan for the new capital of Nigeria, Abuja, begun in the 1970s, was partially based on Brasília and designed by a team that included the British firm Archisystems, Kenzo Tange, and WMRT, the Philadelphia firm founded by planner David Wallace and landscape architect Ian McHarg.

Related ideas were used in planning for the United Arab Emirates, which became independent of Britain in 1971. The Arab ports of the region had been partially dominated by the Portuguese Empire from the 1500s to 1750. After a period of unrest, which included mass enthusiasm for the radical Sunni Islam advocated by Muhammad bin Abdul Wahab (1703–1792), which was seen as a threat by both the British and Ottoman empires, the British invaded and began to put these "Trucial States" under imperial protection by 1819. In 1833, Dubai was established as an offshoot of Abu Dhabi, and eventually the al-Maktoum family became its sheikhs, though Sharjah remained the seat of the British political agent. By 1900, Dubai, with a population of ten thousand, had become an important British steamer port on the route to India, as well as a regional distribution center. In 1911, the British Navy under Winston Churchill's direction as First Lord of the Admiralty decided to use oil instead of coal as its main fuel source, leading to a greatly increased British demand for new oil sources. After the defeat of the Ottoman Empire in 1918 and the division of its former provinces and neighboring countries into European-dominated nation-states, the British development of the oil resources of the Persian Gulf region accelerated at Abadan (1910) in Iran, followed by Kuwait.

In 1932, the Kingdom of the Hejaz and Nejd was renamed Saudi Arabia, which then began to develop, with American and British investment, as a center of oil production. The discovery of oil in the Trucial States in 1966 gave the region an enhanced strategic importance during the Cold War. British companies began to bring in workers from South Asia, Iran, the Middle East, and Europe, who eventually outnumbered the citizens. A 1960 master plan for Dubai by British planner John R. Harris structured an expansive road system and also called for a new town center, residential quarters, two bridges, and a highway tunnel under the creek that divided the two sections of the city. The Jumeirah area was designated for residential development, and new industrial, health, education, and leisure areas were established.

By the early 2000s Dubai's population had grown to 2.5 million, with a seven-to-one ratio of immigrants to natives. A strategy of attracting tourism and international investment was aggressively pursued, in part by expanding the airport as an international passenger hub. Yet during these same decades the questioning of Western society that had begun in the 1960s, much of it initially related to the Algerian war against French colonial rule (1955–63) and the American civil rights movement, also led to growing doubts about urban planning in what was then called the "Third World." This term had been coined by French anthropologist Alfred Sauvy in 1952 to describe the world outside the Cold War's Western and Soviet blocs, and he saw it as paralleling the Third Estate, the common people, during the French Revolution.

The Third World's emergence as a focus of Western thinking coincided with new critical attitudes about modern urbanism. It also overlapped with the sociological critiques of it that grew out of French efforts to better understand the needs and expectations of residents in the new modern housing projects. French sociologist Paul-Henry Chombart de Lauwe's postwar work had been intended to guide better design for such projects, and the French Marxist sociologist Henri Lefebvre (1901–1991) had since the late 1940s focused on the observed "everyday life" of the working classes, as opposed to the abstract metrics and typological models favored by CIAM and French government planners. Lefebvre had become critical of the dull and overly controlled public spaces of the new French housing projects and began to focus on what he called the "social production of space." In his *The Right to the City* (1968), Lefebvre influentially argued for "spatial justice" and a focus on everyday practices and representations of urban space. Lefebvre defined space as a social construction based on values and socially produced meanings, and he advocated that research in urbanism should shift from abstract studies of space as something with unchanging and universal properties to the social and political processes of its production. In his *The Production of Space* (1974), Lefebvre began to distinguish between the terms "perceived space," as seen by the general public; space "conceived" by designers; and the "lived space" of urban residents.

These changing attitudes in the 1960s, the same decade that the critical ideas of the Situationists, Jane Jacobs, and others had begun to find a wide audience, also spurred interest in the advocacy of squatter settlements by the English architect John Francis Charlewood Turner (born 1927). Beginning in 1957, Turner had worked with the architect Eduardo Neira Alva (born 1924), a former member of the Peruvian CIAM group Agrupacion Espacio, on organized self-build projects sponsored by the Peruvian Ministry of Public Works, initially in Arequipa, then the second-largest city in Peru. After the Arequipa earthquake of 1958, Ernest Weissmann visited Arequipa and began U.N.-sponsored pilot projects for organized self-build in seven Peruvian cities, resulting in thirty thousand self-built houses being constructed there by 1962.

The design of the projects in these *barriadas* (the Peruvian term used for them prior to 1970) sometimes followed pre-Columbian and Spanish colonial precedents in using a regular grid plan with some open public plazas, with the houses often based on the same courtyard house precedents as those in the Town Planning Associates plan for Chimbote (1948). The governmental authorities typically offered prospective residents, usually recent migrants from the countryside, free land divided into plots, often on a 26-foot, 3-inch (8-meter) square module, to organized groups of self-builders so they could construct their own low-rise housing. This was typically then built using conventional masonry-block bearing walls with temporary wood joists, later replaced with concrete if possible. Plumbing and electrical services, sometimes including street lights, for a self-built area might be installed later, often provided by the government just prior to elections. Everything else would be organized and built informally, but in a highly standardized way. Many world cities began to grow in related ways, with forms specific to different cities, such as the *favelas* of Rio, the *colonias* of Caracas, or the *gecekondular* of Istanbul.

In the late 1950s, Weissmann also commissioned a U.N. study of residents' responses to public housing in seven places around the world (Gorki, USSR; Indonesia; the Belgian Congo; Morocco; Madrid; Santiago, Chile; and Guatemala City). This study found "widespread disillusionment" with public housing, leading Weissmann to begin to advocate for "aided self-help" as a less costly and unpopular alternative. This was the context of the strong reception to the series of articles Turner began to publish in 1963 in *Architectural Design* and other journals, where he suggested that squatters knew better than modern architects how to organize their own environments. His critiques of high-rise modernist mass housing, brought together in his *Freedom to Build* (1972), resonated widely among many architects, and the idea that self-build, rather than top-down master-planning, could provide a framework for organizing urban development was fully accepted by the United Nations, the World Bank, and other international organizations by the 1970s. This became clear at the U.N. Conference on Human Settlements (Habitat I), held in Vancouver in 1976, where earlier settlement design approaches developed by Fry & Drew for "the tropics," many of them then extended by Koenigsberger in the 1960s as "action planning," became the basis of a new world development planning agenda, one in which Sert was also involved. Koenigberger's and Turner's ideas about self-help and participatory planning led to the establishment of new ways of thinking at the U.N. and the World Bank about how to address massive and ongoing world urbanization processes through design.

Though these planners rejected the concept of the architect as the sole designer of the urban environment, their ideas grew directly from

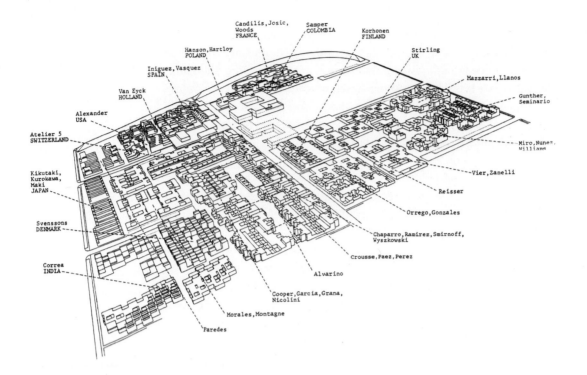

Candilis,Josic,
Woods
FRANCE

Samper
COLOMBIA

Korhonen
FINLAND

Hanson,Hartloy
POLAND

Stirling
UK

Iniguez,Vasquez
SPAIN

Mazzarri,Llanos

Van Eyck
HOLLAND

Gunther,
Seminario

Alexander
USA

Atelier 5
SWITZERLAND

Miro,Nunez,
Williams

Kikutaki,
Kurokawa,
Maki
JAPAN

Vier,Zanelli

Reisser

Svenssons
DENMARK

Orrego,Gonzales

Chaparro,Ramirez,Smirnoff,
Wyszkowski

Correa
INDIA

Crousse,Paez,Perez

Alvarino

Cooper,Garcia,Grana,
Nicolini

Morales,Montagne

Paredes

119. Peter Land, coordinator, PREVI complex, Lima, Peru, 1968–75, showing the architects selected for the various designated self-build sites.

late CIAM and Team 10 approaches, and all were similarly premised on the idea that cities should be designed for the health and well-being of their residents, using appropriate technologies to design in relation to available natural resources and natural systems. PREVI (1968–75), a demonstration project in a fast-growing part of north Lima organized by the Yale-educated English architect Peter Land, illustrated some of the difficulties of this direction (fig. 119). Commissioned near the end of elected President Belaunde's first presidency (1963–68) but continued under the left-wing military dictatorship of General Juan Velasco (1968–75), PREVI was an effort to combine architectural design with self-build methods. Land established the site plan, and the competition then resulted in the choice of 26 low-rise residential projects, which offered 468 housing prototypes, in a complex that also included educational, shopping, and leisure facilities, to be built by the state-funded PREVI office and then expanded by the residents. The architects chosen were divided into two groups: international figures like James Stirling, Fumihiko Maki, Aldo Van Eyck, Charles Correa (1930–2015), and others, and several Peruvian architects, including some well-established Lima architects such as Luis Miró Quesada (1914–1994), Jacques Crousse, and others. PREVI's pedestrian-oriented site plan still works well and provides a series of safe, landscaped pedestrian open spaces, some now filled with traditional Peruvian Catholic shrines, but the architect-designed aspects of most of the projects have been extensively modified over time by their residents, and now resemble most other self-built areas of northern Lima.

Velasco's short-lived radical Peruvian government also oversaw the development of another very large Lima experiment in organized self-build in the 1970s, the Villa El Salvador district. In May 1971 illegal residents in older central areas of city were relocated by the new governmental organization SINAMOS (Sistema Nacional de Apoyo a la Movilización Social/National Support System for Social Mobilization) to 2,400 platted acres (971 hectares) at the far southern edge of the metropolitan area. Hospitals were built and water was trucked in, and informal businesses providing basic services such as food and fuel supplies were encouraged. The gridded master plan by Miguel Romero Sotelo called for 120 residential clusters of sixteen blocks, each with its own public plaza. Each block had twenty-four lots measuring 66 × 23 feet /1,518 square feet (20 × 7 meters /140 square meters). The plan was correlated to a new political structure, where each resident could vote for and elect a council for his or her cluster. The council would then allocate the lots. Velasco's government soon fell, leading to decades of national instability, but Villa El Salvador developed very successfully, and by 2006 it included 185 clusters self-built on the same physical and social pattern, adjacent to many light-industrial and warehouse facilities. Though its grid plan is relatively rigid, and scarce resources severely limit landscaping in the designated public park and parkway areas, Villa El Salvador is a successful example of urban design for a largely self-built and self-governing urban area. (fig. 120).

In Western Europe, related ideas also began to have an impact by the 1970s. The Malagueira quarter in Évora, Portugal (1977), designed by Àlvaro Siza Vieira (born 1933), was a new development of some 1,200 stuccoed masonry row houses sited amid existing informal settlements on a historically layered 67-acre (27-hectare) site. Sponsored under the Portuguese socialist government that came to power after the overthrow of the Fascist dictatorship (1926–74), the Malagueira quarter both reflected earlier low-rise modern housing models and took a more contextual and open-ended approach. A newly built two-story concrete water channel echoed the Renaissance aqueduct that served the old walled city nearby, which Siza used as an organizing spine for the new housing. The new district was laid out on a grid of streets 19 feet, 8 inches (6 meters) wide, housing plots of 39 feet, 5 inches × 26 feet, 2 inches (12 × 8 meters). Each house had either street-facing or rear-facing courtyards and included a street-oriented room for possible business or storage use. Spaces were also set aside for vegetable plots, giving the development an overall density of thirty units per acre (0.4 hectare). Residents, many of them residents of former Portuguese colonial cities such as Luanda and Lourenço Marques (renamed Maputo in 1976), were extensively consulted throughout the design process, and the project was at one time seen as a model for future low-cost housing in Europe.

By the 1980s there were many other examples of successful low-rise, all or partially self-built housing districts worldwide, such as Aranya, an organized self-built settlement for forty thousand Hindu, Muslim, and Jain residents near Indore, India (1983–86). This Aga Kahn Award–winning project was designed by Balkrishna Doshi (born 1927), who laid out its sixty-five hundred building lots and designed several possible housing prototypes based on a plumbing core for one toilet and sink.

In Nairobi, Kenya, the Dandora Community Development project (1975–83), sponsored by the Nairobi City Council in cooperation with the World Bank, was begun as part of an effort to extend a northeastern metropolitan corridor proposed by the Nairobi Metropolitan Growth Strategy of 1973. This was an attempt to modify and extend the 1948 British colonial master plan for the city, which had formalized the division between the more elite, green suburban western areas and flat, higher-density and formerly South Asian areas of east Nairobi. The 1948 plan had been produced in a typical British colonial social situation when native Africans were denied residence in the city proper, and consequently forced to live in outlying squatter settlements. After independence from Britain in 1964, the new Kenyan government declared the city open to all residents and vastly extended the urban territory. Dandora allocated 6,000 lots to house over 72,000 residents, and it included a full range of services, including water and sewerage, electricity, and garbage collection. It was also to include schools, health centers, community centers, a sports complex, and several markets. It was organized along a central transportation spine linking five neighborhoods, much like the "stem" concept of Candilis-Josic-Woods. Bands of designated open space bounded the neighborhoods, which could be reached at multiple points by footpaths through them. The project was so successful that it led to some over-densification as new rooms for rent were constructed, but its design principles combining walkable urban densities with a clear transportation strategy have continued to be used in many other similar settlements.

In 1969, landscape architect Ian McHarg's book *Design with Nature* systematically presented a new approach to the design of North American metropolitan areas. McHarg, who had taught at the University of Pennsylvania since 1954, recognized that industrialization had disrupted architecture's premodern concerns with site, climate, and lighting conditions, all discussed in detail by Roman architect Vitruvius over two thousand years ago. By the 1950s and 1960s a range of new technologies, which by then included heavy construction equipment, air conditioning (a mass phenomenon in the United States by the 1950s), and fluorescent lighting (in use in factories by 1940), had made such concerns seem antiquated. Any site, it was thought, could be made suitable for building, and any climate or lighting condition could be designed for, if sufficient financial resources were available. These ideas were pervasive in architecture and urbanism at least until the 1990s, and they had the effect of devaluing any great attention to the specifics of place that did not have direct impact on cost or market appeal. In his teaching and practice in the Philadelphia firm WMRT, McHarg set out an influential new approach. His *Plan for the Valleys* (1962) for suburban Baltimore, designed with planner David A. Wallace (1917–2004), preserved the aquifer northwest of the city that provided the city's water supply by concentrating new residential development on higher ground, retaining the ecologically important stream channels as landscape corridors. McHarg also popularized the use of spreadsheet-like matrices of various elements of natural systems, which facilitated decision making and underlay the development of digital GIS (geographical information systems). Many of the basic elements of this Geddesian, data- and map-centered approach had been developed in British planning by the geographer Eve Germaine Rimington Taylor (1879–1966), whose largely forgotten work also provided some of the basis for Jaqueline Tyrwhitt's work and that of the British Association for Planning and Regional Reconstruction.

By the early 1970s, several large American suburban developments had begun to apply these methods, including the WMRT master plan for The Woodlands, a planned subdivision of 16,939 acres (6,855 hectares) located twenty-eight miles (45 kilometers) north of Houston. The Woodlands was planned for 47,375 housing units, of which 15 percent were set aside for low- and moderate-income households. These were organized into nineteen neighborhoods, six villages, and a metropolitan center, all connected and bounded by a network of open spaces. Related ideas were used by the Irvine Company under Ray Watson's planning leadership to form the Irvine Ranch in the 1970s, where the Orange County Back Bay estuary was protected from development and an extensive and very successful network of bike and hiking trails was put in place in this fast-growing, affluent, moderate-density suburban area south of Los Angeles.

New residential areas there were sited in conjunction with the massive redevelopment of new shopping-office "edge cities" at South Coast Plaza and Fashion Island at Newport Center, the latter redesigned by Jon Jerde (1940–2015) in 1989 as a series of walkable outdoor rooms (fig. 121).

These efforts at more compact, ecologically aware development by mainstream commercial developers, stimulated in some cases by the Middle East "oil crisis" of 1973, were paralleled by more socially alternative directions as well. Frank Lloyd Wright's architecture and urbanism had always been strongly related to particulars of climate, light, and site. One of his former Taliesin apprentices, the Italian architect Paolo Soleri (1919–2013), in 1951 founded the Cosanti Foundation near Taliesin West in the Phoenix area. Soleri wanted to construct a five-acre (2-hectare) utopian communal environment of "earth cast" concrete buildings. These used desert sand and soil as formwork for what Soleri envisioned would become huge concrete megastructures for future urban environments for the world's rapidly growing population. In 1970, Soleri began Cosanti II, also known as Arcosanti, near Cordes Junction, Arizona, planned as a settlement for five thousand. Its half-domes, reminiscent of ancient ruins, soon became icons of alternative architecture.

It was also in the 1970s that extensive and successful efforts were begun in Curitiba, then a city of some six hundred thousand in southern Brazil, to turn it into a model of ecological development. These efforts were based on a 1965 competition-winning master plan by São Paulo architect Jorge Wilheim (1928–2014), which called for new "axes of development" along large transit boulevards extending from the center, replacing the earlier, more conventional radio-concentric Beaux-Arts plan for the city from the 1940s by Alfred Agache. The new plan was supported by the Brazilian military government that had come to power with U.S. support in 1964, and which wanted the city to continue to develop as an industrial center. In 1966, the Institute of Urban Research and Planning (IPPUC) was established to carry out the plan. Five structural

121. Jerde Partnership, Fashion Island/Newport Center, Irvine Ranch, California, 1989.

122. Jorge Wilhelm (master plan) and others, part of the Curitiba master plan as built.

axes of public transit were established and in operation by 1974. Jaime Lerner (born 1937) was appointed mayor in 1971 and popularly reelected three times. He then successfully ran for governor of the Brazilian state of Paraná.

New Curitiba zoning allowing significant densities along the "Priority Avenues" was put in place, and new residential growth, much of it high-rise, was encouraged near public transit stops (fig. 122). Traffic was directed away from downtown on these newly built multilane streets, which separated slow-moving local traffic from both bus lanes and central higher-speed vehicular lanes. These changes resulted in a 30 percent lower consumption of gasoline than in other Brazilian cities by 2004. At the same time, Mayor Lerner created a twenty-four-hour pedestrian mall on a downtown shopping street, and historic preservation units were established to restore significant buildings across the city. Riverside preservation areas were also established, with twenty-six new parks designed to address flooding and sanitation issues in place by the 2000s. In 1976, informal settlers were moved from areas of environmental risk, and COHAB, the Curitiba public housing agency, took up a strategy of building a diversity of housing types within existing neighborhoods, some with daycare and public health facilities, as well as the Bairro Novo (1989), a self-built project with twenty-six thousand units. In 1980, with Curitiba's population still growing at over 5 percent per year, Lerner's administration established a bus rapid-transit system (RIT), which has since become an influential model for many other cities, including Bogotá and Cleveland. By the 1990s, with Curitiba's population having grown to 1.3 million, the city administration shifted its focus to job creation, public education, solid waste management, and the founding of the UNILVRE, the Open University of the Environment. Food stamps and transit tickets were offered to favela dwellers in exchange for collecting and sorting trash, and recovered materials were sold to local industries.

Curitiba's success as a fast-growing, ecologically oriented industrial center was not well-known internationally until the 1990s, and even today many of its specific aspects remain unfamiliar, even to planners. Urban-ecological concerns were often not taken very seriously in North American urban design in the 1980s and 1990s, as architectural and urbanistic debate frequently centered on the validity of New Urbanism versus the "neo-avant-garde," a direction crystallized at the 1988 Museum of Modern Art exhibition "Deconstructivist Architecture." The show presented the work of a set of somewhat divergent architects that included established practitioners such as Frank Gehry (born 1929), more theoretically inclined architects such as Peter Eisenman (born 1932), Daniel Libeskind (born 1946), and the Vienna firm Co-op Himmelb(l)au, as well as emerging young European architects such as Bernard Tschumi (born 1944), Rem Koolhaas, and the latter's Iraqi-born former Architectural Association student, Zaha Hadid (1950–2016).

In the following decades these architects, and many others trained and influenced by them, would receive numerous commissions worldwide, many at an urban scale. Their work appeared as digital technologies were transforming the design professions' understanding of the relationship between architectural form, technical systems, and social use away from both modernist and postmodernist certainties. Though intellectually productive, particularly through the popularity of these designers and their theoretical concerns in schools of architecture, Deconstructivism's impact on urbanism was felt mainly in some specific urban projects, like Tschumi's early Parc de la Villette in Paris (1982), which played with Bauhaus concepts of "point, line, and plane" to deploy a series of Russian Constructivist-inspired red pavilions sited on a grid over a ground plane that was skillfully layered with paths and canals to create a new kind of urban park (fig. 123). By the 2000s, many other projects that drew from land and conceptual art, as well as urban design, were being built worldwide, as figures like Gehry, Koolhaas, Eisenman, and Hadid became internationally known "star-architects," with numerous widely publicized competition entries and completed urban projects around the world.

Yet by the early twenty-first century, scientifically well-founded— though in 2017 still politically controversial—concerns about climate change and the effects of human activities like heating and cooling buildings and driving gasoline-powered vehicles were causing many architects and others concerned with the design of the built environment to shift their focus to urbanisms often described as landscape-centered, sustainable, or ecological. Many designers now seek to combine something like McHarg's ecologically driven design approach with various

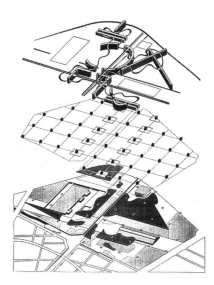

123. Bernard Tschumi, Parc de la Villette completion, Paris, winning entry, 1982.

forms of pedestrian urbanism, often merging multiple design models by using digital design techniques in new ways. These experiments, ranging from Norman Foster's ecological skyscrapers, like the Commerzbank in Frankfurt (1997), and his firm's low-rise, high-density Masdar City in Abu Dhabi (2015) to numerous ecologically designed new urban districts in Scandinavia, have yet to alter global patterns of urbanization.

Instead, most of the urban interventions of recent decades have either involved architecturally complex (and often very expensive) individual buildings that seek to improve the urban experience, such as Gehry's Disney Concert Hall (1991–2003) in downtown Los Angeles, Rafael Moneo's Los Angeles Cathedral (2002), and Toyo Ito's Sendai Mediathèque (2001), on one hand, or large mixed-use complexes and urban districts of various kinds on the other, often designed by global corporate design firms such as AECOM, SOM, HOK, KPF, Sasaki Associates, and others. It is entirely possible that in the economically successful global cities in western Europe, in the United States, and in parts of Asia that new synergies will continue to be achieved between the urbanist goals of increasing pedestrian connectivity with both architectural sophistication and ecological concerns. The lakefront Millennium Park in Chicago, by SOM and others (2000–15); Cheonggyecheon (2005), a historic river in central Seoul restored as a public greenway after a highway viaduct was removed (fig. 124); Olympic Sculpture Park in Seattle (2007) by Weiss/Manfredi, designed to span a freeway; and the High Line in New York (2008–), an influential reuse of an abandoned elevated freight line from the 1930s by landscape architect James Corner (born 1961) and the architects Diller Scofidio + Renfro, all indicate the potential of such directions to improve the pedestrian experience in existing central cities.

Yet the cities that can afford such projects now include only a very small percentage of the world's population, even when tourists and

124. Seoul Metropolitan Government, Cheong-gyecheon Restoration Project, a 7-mile (11-kilometer) restored historic river in central Seoul, South Korea, 2003–5.

occasional residents are included among their users. In much of the rest of the world, patterns similar to earlier phases of urban and metropolitan growth can be observed, but in an extremely accelerated way. China, the world's most populous country, with over 1.38 billion people, has gone from being a poor and largely rural country in 1978 to the world's second-largest economy, with over 50 percent of its population now living in urban areas, many of them constructed since 1992. As in nineteenth-century European cities, these immense changes have resulted in tremendous disparities in income and individual opportunity, as well as in severe ecological problems.

China's authoritarian government is now moving swiftly to further shift the country's population from rural to urban areas. The urban areas that have been constructed are not for the most part new versions of dense, historic cities but are instead composed of high-rise residential districts of widely spaced towers surrounded by open space and bounded by wide traffic streets. Much of the basic tower-and-park form of this urbanization derives from the same Weimar and later sources as modernist urbanism, but the typically two-bedroom apartments are now often individually owned. Units in these system-built high-rises are highly sought after, and the towers are usually preferred to more traditional, low-rise urban patterns, which tend to be associated with tourism, poverty, or both.

The definitive history of Chinese urbanism after 1978 has yet to be written, but it is clear that many of the norms and practices of this kind of development have antecedents elsewhere, notably in the 1950s and 1960s London County Council–inspired high-rise estates of Singapore and Hong Kong, both former British colonies, which then became models for Chinese urban development from the 1970s onward. This kind of urbanism is now ubiquitous and is being exported with some success to

the Middle East and to cities in sub-Saharan Africa, such as Addis Ababa, Ethiopia, and Luanda, Angola. It sometimes goes along with ambitious new infrastructure projects such as highways, airports, rail lines, shopping centers, business districts, and university and corporate campuses. This new global urban pattern is occasionally enlivened with a relatively small number of parks, greenways, and playgrounds. While it is unquestionably "urban" in its image and densities by Western standards, this high-rise, resource intensive urbanism does not currently seem to be sustainable, given the vast amount of natural resources required to build, maintain, and service it. This problem seems to have been acknowledged, rhetorically at least, in the Chinese Five Year Plan of 2005, the eleventh, which called for sustainable urban development, but may continue to be a major way of building new cities around the world for some time (fig. 125).

The global Chinese-type high-rise commercial city has been economically very successful and has spread elsewhere, but much of the world's burgeoning urban population still finds its housing in a less formalized way. Often fleeing violence, residents of informal settlements sometimes lack basic services—access to clean water, safe transportation, basic health care, and education. At the same time, they increasingly have access to cellphones and other modern consumer items. It is unclear how far current urban models can be extended with the world's available

125. Shanghai Urban Planning and Design Institute (master plan) and various architects, Pudong business district, Lujiazui, Shanghai, 1994.

resources under these conditions. In many places, varieties of the informal city, planned and unplanned, are now the main form of urban settlement. How political systems, and the designers who work within them, will respond to these realities as they become increasingly visible, remains to be seen. What is evident is that the urban forms of the future, like those of the past, will continue to be the product of deliberate decisions, and not the random outcomes of impersonal forces.

FURTHER READING

Joan Busquets, ed., *Deconstruction/Construction: The Cheonggyecheon Restoration Project in Seoul* (Cambridge, Mass.: Harvard Graduate School of Design, 2010).

Viviana D'Auria et al., *Human Settlements: Formulations and (Re)Calibrations* (Amsterdam: SUN Architecture, 2010).

Richard Harris, "A Double Irony: The Originality and Influence of John F. C. Turner," *Habitat International* 27, no. 2 (June 2003): 245–69.

Felipe Hernandez, Peter Kellett, and Lea K. Allen, eds., *Rethinking the Informal City: Critical Perspectives from Latin America* (New York: Berghahn, 2010).

Robert Home, *Of Planting and Planning: The Making of British Colonial Cities* (London: Spon, 1997).

Clara Irazábal, "Urban Design, Planning, and the Politics of Development in Curitiba," in Vicente de Rio and William Siembieda, eds., *Contemporary Urbanism in Brazil* (Gainesville: University Press of Florida, 2009), 202–23.

Sharif Kahatt, *Utopias construídas: Las unidades vecinales de Lima* (Lima: Fondo Editorial de la Pontificia Unversidad Catolica del Peru, 2015). In Spanish only.

Paul L. Knox, *Palimpsests: Biographies of 50 City Districts* (Basel: Birkhäuser, 2012).

Mary McLeod, "Henri Lefebvre's Critique of Everyday Life," in Steven Harris and Deborah Berke, *Architecture of the Everyday* (New York: Princeton Architectural Press, 1997), 9–29.

Paniyota Pyla, ed., *Landscapes of Development* (Cambridge, Mass.: Aga Khan Program, Harvard Graduate School of Design, 2013).

John F. C. Turner and Robert Fichter, *Freedom to Build: Dweller Control of the Housing Process* (New York: Macmillan, 1972).

Conclusion

Urbanism today is a field whose parameters, goals, and methods are unclear and often contested. While many designers now share an enthusiasm for dense, walkable urban environments of exuberant diversity, many metropolitan environments being built worldwide today still tend to be auto-based and highly stratified, both economically and in other ways. At the same time, the philanthropic efforts that emerged in the mid-nineteenth century to improve urban slums, which developed by 1909 into "town planning" and then by the 1930s into the mass-housing efforts of mid-twentieth-century welfare states, are now often seen as repressive and unfortunate efforts to suppress the social and cultural vitality of traditional cultures. To this we can add what seem to be realistic concerns about the future ecological impacts of continued world urbanization. These directions all appear to have brought many efforts at urbanism to a kind of impasse, with urban designers only rarely able to build their versions of better cities, even as massive physical and social problems continue to multiply in fast-growing urban environments, most of them now in Asia and Africa.

Many of the challenges that urban dwellers and designers still face—engineering better sanitation, designing dense affordable housing with good light and air circulation, remedying traffic congestion, finding ways to allocate space for parks and other safe and appealing public environments—now have a substantial history, whose outcomes do not end only in the well-known failures of mid-century modern planning in the West. At the same time, it is also clear that many of the motivations behind previous urbanisms, notably efforts to represent state authority through imposing monumental buildings of any kind, now often seem obsolete, if not actively objectionable. With these issues in mind, the need for a better understanding of the history of modern urbanism after the 1950s becomes clear, to assess what has been proposed and to identify those aspects of it that still seem important.

A key idea that has informed this book is that it is necessary to go beyond simply criticizing the past failures of Western urbanism, with its obvious and regrettably close linkages to colonialism, racial discrimination, and various other forms of social domination, to try to understand the larger picture of human life in modern cities as they have developed since around 1850. To not do so risks an implicit rejection of the possibility that humans can successfully design their own urban environments, with the resulting conviction that all successful design efforts are always about the self-aggrandizement of certain groups over others. The widespread cynicism that such an outlook produces about the desirability of urban planning and design occurs at the same time as unprecedented global urban growth continues to follow its own predictable sprawling patterns, ones that almost inevitably lead to traffic congestion, social segregation, housing shortages, and severe environmental problems.

Close attention to the proposals and outcomes of the past, many of which were motivated by efforts to address at least some of these same problems, must then include not only a record of failures but also an attentiveness to what kinds of urban environments have been successful over time, regardless of the original conditions of their production. Such an effort has of course informed the writings and design work of many postmodern urbanists, but I would argue in too narrow and instrumental a way, rejecting the possibility that various master-planned more or less modernist environments such as Curitiba might also be considered successful, and not only by architects. At the same time, it is also critically important to begin to consider the design issues around infrastructure, public health, and housing and neighborhood form in the vast informal settlements that now characterize many world cities, even if the paths forward for designers in doing so are by no means always clear.

Illustration Credits

The photographers and the sources of visual material other than the owners indicated in the captions are as follows. Every effort has been made to supply complete and correct credits; if there are errors or omissions, please contact Yale University Press so that corrections can be made in any subsequent edition.

A. C. Bosselman & Co.: 20

Missouri History Museum, St. Louis: 48

Eric Mumford: 50, 82, 101, 109, 110, 114, 116, 117, 118, 124, 125

Michelle Hauk: 69

Peter Land: 119

Wikimedia Commons: 1, 5, 7, 11–13, 15, 17, 22, 23, 28, 30, 32, 33, 36, 41, 51 (Charles F. Doherty, 1929), 53–55, 60–62, 70 (David Shankbone), 76–78, 79 (Maurice Gautherot), 94, 95, 104–7, 112, 115 (John Lambert Pearson), 120, 121 (D. Ramey Logan), 122, 123

Index

Numbers in *italics* indicate figures.

AA. *See* Architectural Association
Aalto, Aino, 171, 172, 233
Aalto, Alvar, 164, 167, 171, 172, 229, 232–36, 311
Abercrombie, Patrick, 76–78, 220–23
ABI Building (Rio; Roberto Brothers), 199
Abrams, Charles, 258, 261, 318
Abuja (Nigeria), plan for (Tange), 243, 319
acceptera, 232
Ackerman, Frederick J., 126, 129, 130, 131, 136, 184, 258
Adams, Thomas, 81, 89, 102, 132, 134, 189
Adams Brothers Adelphi Terrace (London), 27
Adshead, Stanley, 76–77, 102
Africa, regional planning in, 318–19. *See also individual nations;* West Africa
Agache, Alfred, 69–70, 75, 149, 201, 326
agricultural land, urbanization of, 102
Agrupacion Espacio, 320
Air Force Academy (Colorado Springs; SOM), 213
Alberti, Leon Battista, 9, 280
Albert Kahn Associates, 192
Alexander, Christopher, 265–66, 280–81, 301
Algiers, 27; plan for (Le Corbusier and Jeanneret), 170, *171*
Allgemeine Baugesetz (General Building Act; Saxon; 1900), 36
allotment gardens, 158
Alphand, Jean-Charles Adolphe, 23, 58
Alte Heide Siedlung (Munich; Fischer), 151
Altneuland (Old-New Land; Herzl), 108
Alton Estate (LCC), 226
Alton West (LCC), 226–27
Alvorada Presidential Palace (Brazil; Niemeyer), 243
Amazing Archigram, 290–91
American Association of State Highway Officials (AASHO), 115–16
American City Beautiful Civic Centers, *63*
American City magazine. 131–32

American City Planning Institute, 116, 119
American Institute of Architects, 129
American Institute of Planners, 119
American urbanism, 184, 265, 297. *See also* New Urbanism; urbanism; United States; *U.S. city listings*
American Vitruvius, The: An Architect's Handbook of Civic Art (Hegemann and Peets), 112
Americas, colonization in, 41–46
Amon Carter Center (Fort Worth, TX; Johnson), 243
Amsterdam, 139–41, 156, 166, 274–75, 280
Amsterdam Municipal Orphanage (Van Eyck), 275, *276*
Amsterdam School, 140–41, 143, 166
Amsterdam South (Berlage), 140
Anatomy of a Metropolis (Regional Plan Association of NY and Harvard School of Public Administration), 298–99
apartment buildings, 23, 81, 94. *See also* high-rises; public housing
Aranya (Indore, India; Doshi), 324
Archigram, 272, 290–94
Archisystems, 319
architects: ecological concerns of, 328–29; military service for, 205; new role for, 258; purpose of, 280
Architectural Association (London), 227, 256, 292, 310
Architecture of Country Houses (Downing), 55
architectural education, Beaux-Arts model of, 68
architectural ideology, 306–7
Architectural Institute of Japan, 284
Architectural Principles in the Age of Humanism (Wittkower), 276
architecture, 49, 67; ad culture and, 292; city planning and, 271; distinct from engineering, 35; enhancing the core, 270; existence-will and, 277; new applications for, 38; postmodernism in, 305; serving business, 152; signification in, 304; social meaning and, 307; social order and, 139, 152; surrealism and, 272; urbanism and, 141
Architecture of the City, The (Rossi), 305

Architecture since 1400 (James-Chakraborty), 3
Architecture of Social Concern in Regions of Mild Climate, An (Neutra), 238
Architecture and Utopia: Design and Capitalist Development (Tafuri), 306–7
Artek, 233
ASCORAL (Assemblée de constructeurs pour la rénovation architectural / Constructors' Association for the Renovation of Architecture), 203, 230
ASNOVA, 144–45
ATBAT (Atelier des Bâtisseurs / Builders' Workshop), 230, 231, 268
ATBAT-Afrique, 257, 269, 318
Atelier de Montrouge, 271
Athens Charter, 203, 230
Atlanta (GA), 53, 211
Augur, Tracy, 130, 189, 205–6, 217
Australia,75, 76–78, 103
Austro-Hungarian Empire, 13, 30
automobiles, 115–17, 122. *See also* commercial strips; highways; parkways; shopping centers; strip malls; suburbs
avant-garde, 139; Soviet, 145–46, 153, 154–55; Soviet rejection of, 168
Avesta town center proposal (Sweden; Aalto and Stark), 236
Aymonino, Carlo, 306, 312

Bäckstrom & Reinius, 233, 234
Bacon, Edmund N., 253, 254, 261–64
Bakema, Jacob (Jaap), 229, 268, 269–70, 273–74, 279, 309
Baker, Herbert, 73–75
Baldwin Hills Village (Los Angeles; Stein), 217–18, 255
Baltimore (MD), 47, 118, 325
Bangladesh, 248, 278
Banham, Reyner, 224, 226, 228, 293, 309
Barcelona, 28–30, 149; CIAM and, 169; city of cities strategy in, 314; housing in, *169;* plans for, 68, 173; reconstruction of, 314, *315*
Bardi, Lina Bo, 194, 300
Bartholomew, Harland, 118, 120, 132, 134–35, 187–89, 206–7

strip malls, 207

Structuralism, 281, 308

Structure and Growth of Residential Neighborhoods in American Cities (Federal Housing Administration), 186

Stübben, Josef, 36, 37, 38

Student Housing for Enschede (Holland; Ungers), 308

Stuyvesant Town (New York; Clavan), 135, 216–17, 225

Style and Epoch (Ginzburg), 153

subdivisions, 135, 137, 184, 188–89, 192

suburban campuses, 212

suburbs, 30, 52; apartment housing in, 82; civic center proposals for, 263; density of, 266; design code for, 189, 215, 216; development of, 54–55; gender and, 193; planning of, Olmsted's influence on, 59; postwar, form of, 215–16; questioning of, 300; racial discrimination in, 119; shopping malls in, 218–19; single-family housing and, 266; zoning laws for, 58

subways, 19, 148

Suez Canal, 122

Sullivan, Louis, 60, 127, 175, 176

Sunila sulfite mill, housing for (Finland; Aalto), 234

Sunnyside Gardens (Queens, NY), 129, 136

Sunset Hills (Kansas City, MO), 117

"Superarchitecture" exhibition (Florence, 1966), 293

superblocks, 91, 108, 130–31, 164, 181, 218, 249, 267, 296

superquadras, 242, 243

Superstudio, 293, 310, 311

Suresnes (France), 93–94

surveying, patterns of, 46–47

survey before plan, 101, 105

sustainability, 217, 227, 331

Sweden, 227, 232–34

Sydney (Australia), 9, 122

Sykes-Picot treaty (1916), 107

Syrkus, Syzmon, 170

systems approach, 293

systems theory, 224–25

Tableau de Paris (Texier), 24

Tafuri, Manfredo, 3, 306–7

Taiwan, 109, 110

Takayama, Eika, 197–98, 204

Tange, Kenzo, 197, 204, 243, 273, 278, 282, 319

Taut, Bruno, 95, 107, 139, 150–51, 158

Taylor Woodrow Construction, 292

Team 4, 294

Team 10 group, 141, 268–73, 275–81, 290, 291, 303, 308, 309, 316

Technical University (Munich), 107

Technische Hochschule, 35

Tema Manhean (Ghana; Fry, Drew, Drake & Lasdun), 318

Tempelhof airport (Berlin; Sagebiel), 196

Ten Books on Architecture (Vitruvius), 9

tenements: defined, 32–33; design of, 83–84; disease spreading in, 83; as investments, 79, 81; model, 79, 81, 87, 103, 106, 128, 135, 140–41, 151; reform and, 83–85

ten major constructions (PRC), 247

Tennessee Valley Authority, 184, 189, *190,* 192–93, 230–31, 235, 249

terrace houses, 79, 80

Terragni, Giuseppe, 193, 194

Texas Rangers, 276–77

textile industry, 16–17, 28, 85

The Cannery (San Francisco; Esherick), 300

Theory of the Leisure Class (Veblen), 136

Third World, urban planning in, 320

30 Rockefeller Center (NYC; Reinhard and Hofmeister; Corbett, Harrison, and MacMurray; and Hood, Godley, and Fouilhoux), 176, 177

Thomas, Andrew J., 130, 131, 135

Tiananmen Square (Beijing), 246–47

Tiburtino IV quarter (Rome), public housing in (Quaroni, Ridol & Aymonino), 305

Tokyo (Edo; Japan), 6, 109–11, 247, 282, 283, 313

To-morrow: A Peaceful Path to Real Reform (Howard), 87, *88*

Toronto (Canada), 209, 210, 211

Torre Velasca (Milan; BBPR), 259, *260*

Town and Country Planning Act of 1943 (Britain), 219

Town and Country Planning Act of 1944 (Britain), 220–21

Town and Country Planning Association, 225

Town and Country Planning Textbook (ed. Tyrwhitt), 257

townless highways, 124

town planning, 2, 33–34, 73, 78; concept of, 29; Germanic approach to, 96, 101, 114; profession of, 88, 101–2

Town Planning Act (Australia; 1920), 103

Town Planning Act (England; 1909), 101–3

Town Planning Associates, 237–38, 250, 267, 321

Town Planning in Balrampur (Geddes), 106

Town Planning Institute (London), 102, 248

Town Planning in Practice (Unwin), 101, 102, 108, 129

Towns and Buildings (Rasmussen), 264

townscape, 263–64

town squares, 37

Toynbee Hall (London), 99

TPA. *See* Town Planning Associates

traffic: categorization of, 250; circles for, 26, 69; circulation patterns, 26, 93; grids for subdivisions, opposition to, 189; organization of, 130–31, 238; as planning priority, 206

Traffic in Towns (Buchanan), 293

trailers, as housing, 192–93

transects, 100, 270

transparency, 276–77

transportation, regional planning and, 132

Trenton Bath House (L. Kahn), 277

Tropical Architecture in the Humid Zone (Fry and Drew), 247

tropical areas, housing conditions in, 258

Trustees of Public Reservations (US), 59

Tugwell, Rexford Guy, 190, 206, 238–39, 318

Turner, John Francis Charlewood, 256–57, 320, 321

TVA. *See* Tennessee Valley Authority

Tyrwhitt, Jaqueline, 256–60, 268–72, 294, 325

UDC. *See* New York State Urban Development Corporation

UNAM. *See* Universidad Nacional Autónoma de México (Mexican National Autonomous University)

Ungers, Oswald Mathias, 308–12

Union of Soviet Socialist Republics (USSR). *See* Soviet Union

unitary urbanism, 289

Unité d'Habitation (Neighborhood Unit; Marseilles; Le Corbusier and Jeanneret), 226, 229, 231, 268

United Kingdom. *See* Britain

United Arab Emirates, planning for, 319

United Nations, 257–58, 321; headquarters (NYC; Harrison), 154, 208–9; Security Council, 244; studying tropical housing conditions, 258; technical experts from, 257–58; U.N. Conference on Human Settlements (Habitat I), 321